Gender, China and the World Trade Organization

China's joining the World Trade Organization at the end of 2001 signified a milestone in the country's global integration after two decades of economic reforms that have fundamentally transformed the economic organization of China. This collection seeks to identify the gendered implications within China of the country's transition from socialism to a market economy and its opening up to international trade and investment. The changes have created greater wealth for some, while at the same time, serious gender, class, ethnic, and regional disparities have also emerged. Drawing from historical, analytical, and policy-oriented work, the chapters in this collection explore women's well-being relative to men's in rural and urban China by looking at land rights, labor-market status and labor rights, household decision-making, health, the representation of women in advertising, and beauty pageants.

This book was previously published as a special issue of the journal, *Feminist Economics*, the official journal of the International Association for Feminist Economics (IAFFE).

Günseli Berik is Professor of Economics at the University of Utah in the United States. Her recent research focuses on international trade, gender wage inequality and working conditions in Asia with a particular focus on Bangladesh, China, Korea, and Taiwan. Dr. Berik is a co-editor for the journal *Feminist Economics*, and a guest editor most recently of the journal's *Inequality, Development, and Growth* special issue (2009).

Xiao-yuan Dong is Professor in the Department of Economics at the University of Winnipeg, Canada, and an adjunct Professor of the China Center of Economic Research, Peking University, China. She received her doctorate from the University of Alberta, Canada. Her research focuses on China's economic transition and development.

Gale Summerfield is Director of the Women and Gender in Global Perspectives Program and Associate Professor of Human and Community Development at the University of Illinois at Urbana-Champaign. Her current research interests address gender and economic reform in China, human security (income, property rights, and health), and transnational migration.

This book and its previous publication as a special issue of *Feminist Economics* have been made possible by the generous support of Rice University, the Ford Foundation–Beijing, and Anne and Albert Chao. All contributions have been subjected to the journal's rigorous peer review process and comply with the journal's editorial policies, as overseen by the editor, Diana Strassmann, and the journal's editorial team.

Gender, China and the World Trade Organization

Essays from *Feminist Economics*

Edited by Günseli Berik, Xiao-yuan Dong and Gale Summerfield

Routledge
Taylor & Francis Group

LONDON AND NEW YORK

First published 2010 by Routledge
2 Park Square, Milton Park, Abingdon, Oxon, OX14 4RN

Simultaneously published in the USA and Canada
by Routledge
270 Madison Avenue, New York, NY 10016

Routledge is an imprint of the Taylor & Francis Group, an informa business

© 2010 IAFFE

Typeset in Baskerville Book by Value Chain, India

British Library Cataloguing in Publication Data
A catalogue record for this book is available from the British Library

ISBN10: 0-415-49904-6
ISBN13: 978-0-415-49904-0

CONTENTS

ABSTRACTS

CHINA'S TRANSITION AND FEMINIST ECONOMICS

Günseli Berik, Xiao-yuan Dong, and Gale Summerfield

Since 1978 China has been undergoing transition from a socialist to a capitalist economy and the opening up to international trade and investment. This process has been accelerated by WTO membership. This article presents an overview of the gendered processes and outcomes associated with China's reforms, mainly focusing on the post-1992 period when the pace of reforms accelerated. The imperative for accumulation and efficiency has resulted not only in impressive growth but also in the weakening of land rights for women, disproportionate layoffs for women workers in state enterprises, rising gender disparities in urban and rural wage employment, growing income insecurity, declining access to healthcare, and the adoption of Western/global commodified beauty standards. While jobs are expanding in new sectors and foreigninvested enterprises, these jobs are often associated with poor working conditions. This volume argues for reprioritizing equity and welfare on the policy agenda.

LAND MANAGEMENT IN RURAL CHINA AND ITS GENDER IMPLICATIONS

Denise Hare, Li Yang, and Daniel Englander

Women are an important mainstay of agricultural production in China, though their access to land is characterized by even greater ambiguity than that of their male counterparts. As part of its path toward liberalization, China undertook agricultural land management policy reforms that were aimed at increasing the security of land tenure rights, but these reforms have paradoxically exacerbated the uncertainty surrounding women's claims to land. Utilizing sample survey data collected from 412 rural households in Shaanxi and Hunan provinces in 2002, this paper documents and analyzes gender differences in land allocations. The findings of this study shed light on the degree to which community characteristics coupled with current local practices (such as frequency of reallocation) influence gender disparities. Results suggest that a growing number of women experience loss of contract land coincident with marrying, and this trend may be expected to increase given the current direction of land policy.

GENDER AND RURAL REFORMS IN CHINA: A CASE STUDY OF POPULATION CONTROL AND LAND RIGHTS POLICIES IN NORTHERN LIAONING

Junjie Chen and Gale Summerfield

Based on ethnographic fieldwork, this paper explores the gender dimensions of population control and land tenure policies in a rural village in Northeast China.

Gender bias was explicit in the implementation of both policies in the village between 1980 and the mid-1990s. Since that time, explicit gender bias has been reduced and both policies have stressed market incentives more, reflecting China's modernization goals and accession to the WTO. Yet the policies are not gender neutral in their implementation, effects, and interactions. Women remain the target of the eased population policy, and they are more likely to become "landless" at marriage. The policies work together to reinforce traditional and emerging forms of gender bias, though at times they offset each other. They impact women's bargaining power within the home, status in the community, and social security. Together they provide a richer view of the gendered experience of living in the village.

WOMEN' S MARKET WORK AND HOUSEHOLD STATUS IN RURAL CHINA: EVIDENCE FROM JIANGSU AND SHANDONG IN THE LATE 1990s

Fiona MacPhail and Xiao-yuan Dong

This paper addresses the question, "does market work improve women's household status in rural China?" using survey data of men and women working in Township and Village Enterprises in rural Jiangsu and Shandong. This paper measures household status by domestic labor time, responsibility for domestic tasks, and household decision-making control. It finds that women have lower household status than men, using these three indicators. Based upon regression results, this paper concludes that for women market wages reduce domestic work time and responsibility for domestic tasks but market hours do not. The nature of bargaining warrants further research since the evidence that financial resources contribute to increased household decision-making control is mixed. Should employment opportunities for women increase with China's membership in the WTO, improvements in women's household status will depend upon their wages and the gender wage gap.

GENDER DYNAMICS AND REDUNDANCY IN URBAN CHINA

Jieyu Liu

This paper focuses on employment narratives recounted in life history interviews with women workers in Nanjing, China. Drawing on feminist perspectives on gender and global economic changes, it examines the microprocesses that underpinned China's economic restructuring and, through a gender-based analysis, shows how working women lost out in this process. After an overview of the institutional context in which China's economic restructuring occurred, this paper examines women's experiences in the workplace and identifies factors that contributed to their disadvantageous position in the work unit and that increased their vulnerability in the changing labor market. The evidence of gender inequality, assumptions about women's labor capacities, and the gendered consequences of economic restructuring suggest that older, less educated women workers, mostly from the Cultural Revolution generation, are unlikely to gain any benefit from whatever advantages accrue from China's economic integration into the global economy.

AN OCEAN FORMED FROM ONE HUNDRED RIVERS: THE EFFECTS OF ETHNICITY, GENDER, MARRIAGE, AND LOCATION ON LABOR FORCE PARTICIPATION IN URBAN CHINA

Margaret Maurer-Fazio, James Hughes, and Dandan Zhang

This paper analyzes changes in labor force participation rates over time for gender- and ethnicity-differentiated groups in urban China. From 1990 to 2000, urban labor force participation rates fell substantially with women's rates declining more rapidly than men's and minority women's declining more rapidly than Han women's. Women's labor force participation is determined by a complex interaction of often gendered economic, demographic, and cultural factors that vary considerably by ethnic group. This analysis employs probit regression techniques to census data to explore possible explanations for the observed changes. This paper focuses on five of China's larger ethnic groups: the Han, Hui, Korean, Uygur, and Zhuang. Although many of the findings differ by ethnic group, for married women there is evidence of a return to more traditional expectations about gendered household roles that is consistent across groups. The research techniques also uncover evidence of discrimination against men of certain ethnic groups.

GENDER EQUITY IN TRANSITIONAL CHINA'S HEALTHCARE POLICY REFORMS

Lanyan Chen and Hilary Standing

This paper explores the gendered impact of Chinese healthcare reforms, drawing attention to the complex and changing nature of gender inequities in China's current economic and social transformations. Using official and academic sources, it examines the reforms' impact on access to reproductive healthcare, the gendered effects of changes in health sector financing – particularly the collapse of insurance systems and rising costs of healthcare, and the implications of China's demographic transition on women's informal healthcare roles. This paper suggests areas that policy-makers, researchers, and activists should prioritize to address inequity, including developing public health policy based on the systematic monitoring of health impacts and trends from a gender perspective, strengthening rural medical facilities to meet the basic healthcare needs of rural populations (including sexual and reproductive health needs), and reforming the healthcare system together with social security systems to equitably cover the poor and the elderly.

FOREIGN DIRECT INVESTMENT AND GENDERED WAGES IN URBAN CHINA

Elissa Braunstein and Mark Brenner

This paper documents the changing impact of foreign direct investment (FDI) on gendered wages in urban China. Combining household survey data from 1995 and 2002 with province-level macro-data, the paper finds that FDI as a proportion of investment has a sizable and statistically significant positive effect on both female and male wages in both years. In 1995, women experienced larger gains from FDI than men, but those gender-based advantages had reversed by 2002, with men experiencing larger wage gains from FDI than women. The paper argues that these results reflect the shift of foreign-invested enterprises to higher productivity and more domestically oriented production, a shift that interacts with gender-based employment segregation to more greatly advantage workers in male-dominated than female-dominated industries. These findings indicate that FDI can have considerable structural effects on economies that reach beyond the particular workers and firms linked to foreign investors.

GENDERING THE DORMITORY LABOR SYSTEM: PRODUCTION, REPRODUCTION, AND MIGRANT LABOR IN SOUTH CHINA

Pun Ngai

This article discusses the dormitory labor system, a specific Chinese labor system through which the lives of Chinese women migrant workers are shaped by the international division of labor. This dormitory labor system is a gendered form of labor use that underlies the boom of export-oriented industrial production in China, which has been further boosted by China's accession to the World Trade Organization. Combining work and residence under the dormitory labor system, production and daily reproduction of labor are reconfigured for the sake of global production, with foreign-invested or privately owned companies controlling almost all daily reproduction of labor. Drawing upon the findings of a 2003 – 4 case study of an electronics factory in South China, this paper analyzes the operation of the dormitory labor system, detailing both its role in increasing output and profits and its role in supporting workers' resistance to their employers.

CHINESE WOMEN AFTER THE ACCESSION TO THE WORLD TRADE ORGANIZATION: A LEGAL PERSPECTIVE ON WOMEN'S LABOR RIGHTS

Julien Burda

The World Trade Organization's law is a potentially powerful instrument for improving the labor rights of Chinese working women, if it is complemented by a broad global and multilateral approach. In contrast to much of the writing on core labor standards, this contribution is based on legal analyses, exploring what is possible, practical, and desirable in terms of WTO law. This paper seeks to assess whether the WTO could be used to pressure the Chinese government to improve women's labor rights. Trade sanctions, even if they fulfill the stringent conditions to be justified under WTO law, do not appear to be the best strategy. The incentive approach, based on both the Generalized System of Preferences (GSP) unilateral scheme and bilateral agreements, appears to be the best solution for improving women's labor rights. Any use of this tool must complement a global and multilateral approach, including better vertical and horizontal cooperation, among other international organizations and civil society.

WESTERN COSMETICS IN THE GENDERED DEVELOPMENT OF CONSUMER CULTURE IN CHINA

Barbara E. Hopkins

This paper examines the changes in China's gender regime during the reform period, especially during China's accession to the WTO. The analysis provides a framework to relate these changes to the consumption behavior of women, especially the increased consumption of cosmetics, to interpret the impact of accession on the gender regime in China. Institutionalist theories that model consumption decisions as a personal display of group identity are extended to the special case of gender identity. According to this framework, the desire to display identity, such as social status or lifestyles, shapes the decision to consume commodities that also display gender such as cosmetics. Thus, the new gender regime is an unintended consequence of a complex pursuit of identity. When consumption is understood as a performance of identity, we can see how the expansion of aggressive marketing tactics affects consumption by influencing the associations of goods with social status.

MEINÜ JINGJI/ CHINA' S BEAUTY ECONOMY: BUYING LOOKS, SHIFTING VALUE, AND CHANGING PLACE

Gary Xu and Susan Feiner

Along with the new products, modes of behavior, and economic relations that followed China's 2001 accession to the World Trade Organization (WTO) came the introduction of new words to everyday language. The term *meinü jing ji*, "beauty economy," is increasingly ubiquitous, describing everything from beauty pageants, modeling competitions, advertisement, cosmetics, and cosmetic surgery to tourism, TV, and cinema, and even extending to China's success in the Athens Olympics. One of the unexpected by-products of this new cultural focus on beauty as a significant source of individual economic success is the full bloom of beauty pageants endorsed by the state. This article focuses on these pageants: their history in China, their promotion of Anglo-European beauty norms, and their relationship with Chinese national identity and economic reform. The paper argues that the beauty pageants are a prerequisite of China's neoliberal policies as they promote consumerism, reinforce and symbolize commodification, divert attention to the personal, and undermine political protest of the ravages of economic reforms.

Notes on Contributors

Günseli Berik is Professor of Economics at the University of Utah in the United States. Her recent research focuses on international trade, gender wage inequality and working conditions in Asia with a particular focus on Bangladesh, China, Korea, and Taiwan. Dr. Berik is a co-editor for the journal *Feminist Economics*, and a guest editor most recently of the journal's *Inequality, Development, and Growth* special issue (2009).

Elissa Braunstein is Assistant Professor of Economics at Colorado State University in Fort Collins. Braunstein earned her PhD in economics from the University of Massachusetts Amherst and a Master's of Pacific International Affairs from the University of California San Diego. Her most recent work is the co-edited book (with Caren Grown and Anju Malhotra) *Trading Women's Health and Rights? Trade Liberalization and Reproductive Health in Developing Economies* (Zed Books, 2006).

Mark Brenner is a New York City-based journalist and labor activist who writes on labor and workplace issues. Brenner works as co-director of Labor Notes, the largest circulation cross-union national publication remaining in the US. He received his PhD in economics from the University of California Riverside.

Julien Burda is a PhD candidate at both the Graduate Institute of International Studies (IUHEI, Geneva, Switzerland) and the University of Paris II (Paris, France). A former teaching assistant at the Graduate Institute of International Studies and at the University of Lyon III (Lyons, France), he is currently working for an international law firm in Geneva.

Junjie Chen is a doctoral student in Anthropology at the University of Illinois at Urbana-Champaign. He has degrees in Sociology from Beijing University and is the author of a book and over twenty publications on China's demography and population issues. He received the Goodman Fellowship at UI and awards for Best Thesis and Outstanding Graduate Student. His current research is on the effects of China's population control policy at the village level, and he did fieldwork in northeast China in 2004 and 2005.

Lanyan Chen was the Gender Advisor for Northeast Asia appointed by the United Nations Development Fund for Women (UNIFEM) from 1998 to

2003. She has a PhD in sociology, with a strong emphasis on political economy. She taught gender and international development studies and gender in family and organizations at the University of Victoria in British Columbia, Canada for many years before joining UNIFEM. She has published research on poverty alleviation and women's cooperatives in China. She is now Professor/Foreign Expert in the Institute of Gender and Social Development Studies at the Tianjin Normal University of China.

Xiao-yuan Dong is Professor in the Department of Economics at the University of Winnipeg, Canada, and an adjunct Professor of the China Center of Economic Research, Peking University, China. She received her doctorate from the University of Alberta, Canada. Her research focuses on China's economic transition and development.

Daniel Englander graduated from Reed College in 2005 with a degree in International and Comparative Policy Studies. He now works as a paralegal at Mayer, Brown, Rowe, and Maw LLP in Washington, DC. He continues to have an interest in China's ongoing reform and plans a career in international law.

Susan Feiner, PhD, is Professor of Economics and Professor of Women and Gender Studies at the University of Southern Maine. She is the author (with Drucilla Barker), of *Liberating Economics: Feminist Perspectives on Families, Work and Globalization* (University of Michigan Press, 2004).

Denise Hare is Associate Professor of Economics at Reed College. Her research primarily considers markets and their influence on rural households in developing countries, with an emphasis on China and Vietnam. Her recent work has examined issues of property rights in agricultural land. Her newest project explores the impact of collective enterprise privatization on local government capacity to provide public goods and services.

Barbara E. Hopkins is Associate Professor of Economics at Wright State University. She has been a member of IAFFE since its formation. She has studied in Shanghai, China. Currently, she teaches courses in comparative economic systems and global economics. She has written about gender issues in transition economies and, specifically, in China.

James Hughes is the Thomas Sowell Professor of Economics and Chair of the Department of Economics at Bates College. His recent research has focused on labor market discrimination and related topics in both China and the US. Current research includes topics on discrimination in US academic labor markets and the social welfare implications of pharmaceutical patents.

Li Yang is Associate Researcher at the Research Center for Rural Economy of the Ministry of Agriculture in Beijing, China. Her research focuses on land policy and gender inequality in rural China.

Jieyu Liu is an Academic Fellow of the White Rose East Asia Centre based at the University of Leeds, having previously been a lecturer in Sociology at the University of Glasgow, UK. She is the author of *Gender and Work in Urban China: Women Workers of the Unlucky Generation* (Routledge 2007) and of journal articles on women in China.

Fiona MacPhail is Associate Professor of Economics, at the University of Northern British Columbia. Her research focuses upon gender and work and specifically, on the impacts of market reforms and migration in China, and the casualization of work in Canada.

Margaret Maurer-Fazio is Associate Dean of Faculty and Professor of Economics at Bates College and a Research Fellow in the William Davidson Institute at the University of Michigan. She serves on the editorial board of the Journal of Contemporary China. Her current research focuses on the economic status of China's ethnic minorities and men's and women's patterns of labor force participation in urban and rural China. She also writes on regional wage inequality, gender wage differentials, and the integration of China's urban labor markets. She is co-editor (with Sarah Cook) of *The Workers' State Meets the Market: Labour in China's Transition* (Routledge, 1999).

Pun Ngai is Associate Professor at the Division of Social Science, Hong Kong University of Science and Technology. She is the author of *Made in China: Women Factory Workers in a Global Workplace* (Duke University Press and Hong Kong University Press, 2005) and with Agnes Ku, *Remaking Citizenship in Hong Kong: Community, Nation and the Global City* (RoutledgeCurzon, 2004). Her current interests include global production, gender, and labor in China. She is also the President of the Chinese Working Women Network.

Hilary Standing is a social scientist working on health and development. Her areas of specialization include gender and health equity, qualitative methodologies for applied and intervention research, health systems change, reproductive health, and health impacts of economic transformation. She is the Director of a Research Programme Consortium on Realising Rights: Improving Sexual and Reproductive Health for Poor and Vulnerable Populations (2005–10), involving six partners in five countries.

Gale Summerfield is Director of the Women and Gender in Global Perspectives Program and Associate Professor of Human and Community Development at the University of Illinois at Urbana-Champaign. Since receiving her doctorate in economics from the University of Michigan in Ann Arbor, she has written extensively on gender aspects of reforms in China and other developing countries. Her articles appear in journals such as *International Journal of Politics, Culture, and Society; Feminist Economics; World Development;* and *Review of Social Economy.* She is co-editor of *Women and Gender Equity in Development Theory and Practice* and *Women's Rights to House and Land: China, Laos, Vietnam.* Her current research interests address gender and economic reform in China, human security (income, property rights, and health), and transnational migration.

Gary Xu, PhD, is Associate Professor of Chinese Literature, Comparative Literature, and Cinema Studies at the University of Illinois at Urbana-Champaign. He is the author of *Sinascape: Contemporary Chinese Cinema* (Rowman and Littlefield, 2007) and co-editor (with Vinay Dharwadker) of *Greenwood Encyclopedia of World Popular Culture, vol. 6, Asia and Pacific Oceania* (Greenwood, 2007).

Dandan Zhang is a researcher at the Institute of Population and Labor Economics at the Chinese Academy of Social Science and is currently a PhD candidate in economics at the Research School of Pacific and Asia Studies, the Australian National University. Her research interests focus on inequality, wage differentials, poverty, and gender issues.

CHINA'S TRANSITION AND FEMINIST ECONOMICS

Günseli Berik, Xiao-yuan Dong, and Gale Summerfield

INTRODUCTION

Since 1978, China has been undergoing major transformations that represent the dismantling of the socialist economy and the movement from an economy closed to foreign investment and most international trade to an open one. In an effort to increase efficiency and improve standards of living, China has undertaken far-reaching reforms: decollectivization and land tenure reforms in the agricultural sector, promotion (and later privatization) of township and village enterprises (TVEs), state sector reforms, and policies to encourage foreign direct investment (FDI) and trade liberalization. China's desire for membership in the World Trade Organization (WTO) contributed to trade liberalization over the course of the 1986–2006 period, first in preparation for membership and then to meet China's accession commitments. This paper evaluates the main features of the emerging picture of China's transformation from the vantage point of feminist economics.

Among transition and developing economies, China's reforms are seen as highly successful in producing impressive economic growth and reducing income poverty (Yingyi Qian 2003; Dani Rodrik 2003; Barry Naughton 2007). The emerging consensus is that this success owes to a divergence from the neoliberal blueprint for successful reform in transition economies and the neoliberal insistence on subjecting every aspect of the economy to market regulation as soon as possible. China pursued openness but limited its reliance on private economic initiatives and made few attempts at democratization. Also, in contrast to the shock therapy approach that caused crippling recessions in other transition economies, China's transition is characterized by gradualism in pursuing the goal of economic efficiency and experimentation with institutions, cognizant of the country's socialist past and local institutions. As a result, while China initiated its transition reforms earlier than other socialist economies, its reform process is still unfolding; and China is able to benefit from its socialist legacy of broad-based education and health, while many other former socialist economies were unable to do so.

Although China's transition policies are unique in many ways and have been successful in macroeconomic terms, negative trends associated with massive labor market restructuring have also emerged, and trade and investment liberalization associated with its WTO membership has exacerbated these trends. Given the size and diversity of China, the impacts of reforms and WTO commitments can be expected to vary by region and between urban and rural areas. Nonetheless, the dismantling of state-owned enterprises caused large-scale layoffs and urban unemployment, the rural–urban income gap and the gap between southern coastal areas and the inland widened, and overall income inequality increased (Martin Ravallion and Shaohua Chen 2004; Azizur Khan and Carl Riskin 2005).

As in other former socialist economies, China's transformation has far-reaching social, political, and economic gender-differentiated implications, which carry particular weight since the transformation takes place in a society where the state has a historic commitment to promoting gender equality (Susan Gal and Gail Kligman 2000). Gender analyses of China's reforms reveal disparities similar to those observed in developing countries and the Soviet Union and Eastern Europe as they underwent restructuring. If the success of reforms is evaluated in terms of improvements in the abilities of women and men to lead better lives, the outcomes are uneven. With the opening of the Chinese economy and the shift in the economic structure toward labor-intensive industry and commercial services, women's employment opportunities have expanded. Rural industries have emerged as a prominent source of employment for women and men.

Another growing source of jobs has been export-oriented, foreign-invested enterprises concentrated in the southern coastal provinces of China, which have drawn predominantly young women migrant workers by the millions. Yet, gender disparities in entitlements and capabilities have also appeared with decollectivization, privatization of rural and urban industries, and population policy. Some authors are more positive about the gender implications of the changes than others, but many points remain controversial because of the lack of gender-differentiated data.

This volume adopts a long-term perspective to examine the gendered effects of the reform process associated with the WTO accession, situating it within the context of the transformation after 1978. Given that China only joined the WTO in 2001, this short timeline presents a challenge for research on the impacts of the reforms associated with the accession itself, in view of the time lags in the production and analysis of both primary and secondary data. Moreover, the accession process has been unfolding since 1986 and accelerating since the mid-1990s, making it difficult to disentangle the effects of WTO reforms from those associated with China's post-1978 transformation. Thus, the articles in this volume focus on the period after 1992, which is considered a watershed year in the reform process. While in the 1980s the Chinese leadership sought reform within the socialist system and "a reform with no losers," the central government formally endorsed the full-fledged march towards capitalism after Deng Xiaoping's famous southern tour in 1992, and it accelerated steps toward integration with the global economy.

Our examination of the gendered processes and outcomes associated with China's reforms begins with an overview of insights from feminist research on structural adjustment programs in developing economies since the early 1980s and the economic reforms in transition economies in the 1990s. Following this discussion we focus on four main reforms to frame our review of the gendered impacts of China's transformation. We seek to identify what can be gleaned from gender-aware scholarship, the content of debates surrounding the transition process, and the research gaps. We situate the articles in this volume within the existing body of scholarship and highlight certain trends, without any claim to making generalizations for China as a whole.

FEMINIST ANALYSIS OF ECONOMIC RESTRUCTURING AND TRANSITION

China is not the only country undergoing economic restructuring in response to trade and FDI liberalization and the dismantling of the planned economy. Feminist researchers have examined similar reforms in developing countries as well as in economies transitioning from socialism to capitalism. Critique of these policies is recognized as one of the research areas that exemplifies the methodological distinctiveness of feminist economics (Marilyn Power 2004). Accordingly, when feminists evaluate transition reforms and structural adjustment – in contrast to conventional approaches in economics that focus on consumers, workers, and households – they differentiate outcomes and processes by class, ethnicity, age, as well as gender. Secondly, since feminist economists are concerned with the totality of activities necessary for the provisioning of human beings, they pay attention to unpaid caring activities, in particular how labor power is reproduced, and the interconnections between unpaid caring work and paid activities that conventional economists consider "economic" (Nilüfer Çağatay, Diane Elson, and Caren Grown 1995; Julie A. Nelson 1995; Lourdes Benería 2003). Feminist economists view economic activities as gendered, socially embedded, and imbued with meaning, and consider economic processes as much as economic outcomes (Diane Elson 1999). Third, feminists evaluate the success of economic policies in terms of changes in individual entitlements, capabilities, and agency, with agency being central to changing inequitable outcomes (Amartya Sen 1999; Martha Nussbaum 2003; Power 2004). Thus, growth in output and employment opportunities or increasing the availability of lower-priced consumer goods do not constitute the exclusive or the best indicators of well-being. To what extent these improvements affect individuals and enhance their abilities to lead better lives as they define them and whether the economic outcomes are fair are crucial, and explicitly ethical, concerns of feminist economists (Benería 2003; Drucilla Barker and Susan Feiner 2004).[1] Fourth, this broadening of the focus of economic research beyond the preoccupations of conventional economic theory necessitates the pluralism of methodology and research methods used by feminist economists (Günseli Berik 1997).[2]

Based on these methodological entry points, feminist economics scholarship has identified certain tendencies during transition and episodes of economic crisis and adjustment as the outcome of either gender-blind or male-biased policies.[3] The reforms themselves have a deflationary bias and a commodification bias, and they unfold in an institutional context that is biased toward the male breadwinner (Diane Elson and Nilüfer Çağatay 2000). As a result, gender biases in society tend to sharpen, new biases emerge, and women face greater burdens of adjustment compared to men. For example, women disproportionately bear the brunt of job losses and layoffs associated with the dismantling of the old economy as public enterprises are restructured and privatized and government jobs shrink. The burdens of adapting to the new trade regime tend to shift to households and, within households, to women. In response to the cuts or elimination of public services, women tend to pick up new unpaid caring tasks in the household, while scrambling to find paid employment. Privatization of healthcare and education disproportionately impedes women's and girls' access to these services. Women's increased care burden causes them to seek their children's help in household tasks, often cutting short their daughters' education. Immediate stresses on well-being and intergenerational decline in capabilities emerge as a result of the introduction of user fees for schools and healthcare institutions, which cause the rationing of use within families. Due to cuts in public spending, women may also lose benefits they were entitled to through their husbands. Rising work burdens also limit women's political representation and hence their participation in social decisions. Disparities in women's control of household resources and assets and access to credit limit their ability to participate in the opportunities that arise, such as opening export businesses. While the rapidly expanding export sectors generate new employment opportunities for women, these are low-paying jobs with poor working conditions, though they may pay higher wages than most alternatives locally available for women. These disadvantages in access to jobs and income affect women's intrahousehold bargaining power, often weakening women's say in household decisions (Carmen Diana Deere and Cheryl R. Doss 2006; Beneria 2003; Nahid Aslanbeigui, Steven Pressman, and Gale Summerfield 1994).

ENGENDERING CHINA'S ECONOMIC TRANSFORMATION

Given this record of gender disparities in economic restructuring, it is not unreasonable to expect similar gendered patterns in the course of China's reforms and WTO accession. However, China also presents a unique case in the panoply of transitions, in that it has pursued gradualism in reform, and, in general, diverged considerably from the neoliberal principles applied in past reform programs. Unlike most other countries that were unable to recover and get on a growth track after restructuring, China is experiencing tremendous growth. The country was essentially unscathed in the Asian Crisis in the late 1990s and does not suffer from a debt burden. Major shifts in policy, such as those in China, require adequate safety nets and funds to cushion the disadvantaged, and in the case of China, growth generates resources for safety nets and presents the opportunity to manage the de-equalizing tendencies and adjustment costs of transition. In a transition that is as carefully managed as China's has been, there is also opportunity to take proactive measures to prevent or at least limit the emergence of disadvantage. Indeed, as we highlight below, in many ways the Chinese government has done precisely that.[4] Yet, the sharp increase in inequality indicates that contradictions within the reform process have constrained the management of inequality. Concerns about fairness and equity have become secondary to the imperative for accumulation and efficiency, and the weakness of the rule of law has prevented the implementation of China's own labor laws (Ching Kwan Lee 2005). Nonetheless, China's unique reform path and the state's long-standing commitment to gender equity are causes for optimism in addressing the gender, class, ethnic, and regional inequities that have sharpened during reforms.

We frame our discussion of the gendered implications of China's transformation in terms of four main reforms pursued in the post-1978 period: decollectivization of agriculture and land reforms, expansion and privatization of TVEs, state-owned enterprise (SOE) reforms, and increased openness to FDI and trade. In view of China's gradualism and experimentation, each reform has evolved considerably since the early 1980s. We review the debates as well as points of agreement in the body of feminist scholarship on each of these reforms.

Decollectivization of agriculture and land tenure reforms

The household responsibility system (HRS) was introduced in 1978 to replace the team farming practiced under the commune system and increase agricultural productivity (Nicholas R. Lardy 1983). Almost overnight, this reform converted collectively cultivated land into small family farms, creating over 200 million farms, with typically no more than half a hectare per household. Land-use rights were allocated (contracted) on an egalitarian basis in both per capita and land quality terms; each individual was granted use rights to tiny plots of land. The initiation of the HRS and egalitarian land ownership have been credited with maintaining/ increasing living standards and providing insurance against shocks as well as raising agricultural output (Justin Lin 1987; John McMillan, John Whalley, and Lijing Zhu 1989; Xiao-yuan Dong 1996).

Initially leases lasted only for a few years in order to correct in a timely manner any inequalities that would emerge. Shorter contracts allowed for adjustments of land holdings size to accommodate marriages, births, and deaths. Specifically, through these adjustments, women who moved into a village through marriage (following the patrilocal/virilocal marriage customs) gained access to land in their own names. In order to encourage land improvement and output growth, however, land tenure policy quickly evolved to increase the security of use rights. By the mid-1980s, fifteen-year leases with frequent and minor redistributions became the policy. In 1998 the contracts were extended to thirty years with infrequent redistributions; the 2003 policy prohibited reallocations altogether (*People's Daily* 2003; Gale Summerfield 2006).

Until the late 1990s, there was limited scholarly attention to gender aspects of evolving land tenure rights. Feminist research on agrarian reforms mainly focused on the HRS, the harsh one-child policy, and rural – urban migration. When the HRS was introduced throughout China in the early 1980s, feminist researchers quickly questioned whether this change from collective to family farming would be a return to traditional

6

patriarchal relations in production and intrafamily decision-making, since women's contributions would become less visible (Judith Stacey 1983; Jean C. Robinson 1985; Margery Wolf 1985).[5] An early application of Sen's capability approach to China showed that the household responsibility system posed a threat to rural women's entitlements and capabilities by reinforcing traditional home-based production that could reduce women's control of income even if family income is growing (Nahid Aslanbeigui and Gale Summerfield 1989). The concern was that women would lose bargaining power in the household with their retreat from work outside the home (where labor was individually remunerated), which is considered to be key in influencing perceptions of contribution to the family (Amartya Sen 1990).

Feminist research problematized the implementation and outcomes of the one-child policy in rural areas, pointing out its contradiction with the HRS from the beginning (Stacey 1983; Ann Anagnost 1988). While the one-child policy was seemingly consistent with the goals of HRS in raising per capita output, the HRS provided implicit incentives for having children, which heightened rural resistance to the policy. The one-child policy was often harshly implemented and is associated with illegal sex-selective abortions, abandonment, and rare cases of infanticide of infant girls, as well as the neglect and hiding of some female babies. These practices have resulted in imbalances in the male/female sex ratio, which at birth is now typically at least 118/100 (compared to the global average of 106/100) (Elisabeth Croll 2000; Summerfield 2006). The one-child policy has also resulted in an increase in old age dependency, with gendered implications for work burden and well-being (Therese Hesketh, Li Lu, and Zhu Wei Xing 2005). The emergence of the "4:2:1" phenomenon – that increasing numbers of couples bear the responsibility of caring for one child and four parents – is likely to put women in charge of this caring work.

Another strand of gender-aware research on China's rural reforms focused on the implications of rising rural–urban migration that has become a tremendous force of change throughout the reform period. For the rural population, job searches and relocation to cities are difficult because of China's residence registration (hukou) system, which was designed precisely to prevent a surge of population and stress on resources in urban areas. Under central planning, the hukou system made access to jobs and government services contingent on a residency permit, which required an individual to live in the area designated on his/her permit (Tiejun Cheng and Mark Selden 1994). Unique among developing countries, the hukou system maintained long-term segregation between rural and urban areas. Under the pressures of transition, however, several attempts to reduce the restrictions of the hukou registration system have occurred since 2000 (China Daily 2003). Nonetheless, China's current land tenure policy and labor migration policies, both initially designed to ensure

7

equitable economic security for China's population, discourage whole families from relocating to the cities. In the absence of private property in land and land access being contingent on farmers using the land, rural populations fear the loss of their contract land if they move away (Deepak Bhattasali, Shantong Li, and Will Martin 2004a). Thus, the migration pattern during the reform period has most often been for individual family members to migrate (Yaohui Zhao 2002).

Women constitute an increasing proportion of the migrants, which by some estimates is up to 40 percent (Delia Davin 1998). Female migrants are typically young and unmarried, while male migrants include a wider range of age and marriage status (Shen Tan 1998; Linxiu Zhang, Alan de Brauw, and Scott Rozelle 2004). This massive movement of rural people has left many middle-aged, married women to run the farm and household businesses, providing income security for crises in the event of urban job losses, and to care for the husband's aging parents. The phenomenon, often referred to as the "feminization of agriculture," has negative implications for women's relative income-earning capabilities, since women are concentrated in the lower-income agricultural sector (Nahid Aslanbeigui and Gale Summerfield 1992; Xiaoyun Liu, Terry Sicular, and Xian Xin 2006). Other authors claim that agriculture has not become any more feminized than it traditionally was, and that the implications of the change are exaggerated (Alan de Brauw 2002).

In the late 1990s, research on land tenure reforms first highlighted that women's rights were becoming less secure and that women were the first ones to experience "landlessness," albeit in a land tenure system where all rural residents had land-use rights (Laurel Bossen 2000; Ford Foundation 2001; Ling Zhu and Zhong-yu Jiang 2001). Thus, middle-aged women are most likely to to stay on the farm to maintain the human security aspect of land for family support when others migrate, at the same time as younger women are experiencing substantial threats to their economic security because of the instability of their land rights.

Two articles in this volume examine the gendered impacts of changes in land tenure policies. Denise Hare, Li Yang, and Daniel Englander (2007) use 2002 survey data from Hunan and Shanxi provinces, and Junjie Chen and Gale Summerfield (2007) use ethnographic data from Northern Liaoning between 2002 and 2005. They show that policies providing greater tenure security, in fact, undermine women's access to and control of land, which in turn affects decision-making power in the household. New regulations guarantee women rights to retain their land allocation in their parental homes until they are allocated new land, but these rights are often not enforced or cannot be implemented because land is no longer available for redistribution when women marry.

Hare, Li, and Englander show that the year of marriage (which is a proxy for extension of land tenure to thirty years since the early 2000s) is the single most important predictor of landlessness among married women. Similar qualitative results are found in the case study of Northern Liaoning. After the land redistribution in 2001, women who marry into the village no longer receive land upon marriage. Even when they marry within the village, women typically lose control of their land allocation in their parents' household.

Chen and Summerfield examine how changes in land policies interacted with population policies to shape the long-term, gendered experience of rural life since the beginning of the reforms in the early 1980s. In the first period of reforms, not only was the population policy enforced harshly, but the local land allocation method also resulted in smaller allocations for girls and their families based on the idea that the girls would move out of the village upon marriage. In the second stage of reforms, while land policy has not been gender-biased by design and population policy has eased, these reforms continue to target women's bodies in population control and allow marriage to become a de facto source of landlessness for new wives.

Decollectivization of agriculture also meant the collapse of China's commune-based rural health system. As the government sought to increase the efficiency of the educational and healthcare systems, especially through charging higher fees for these services, gender disparities in access to healthcare and education emerged, mainly in rural areas (World Bank 1992). Lack of gender-disaggregated survey data presents challenges for gender analysis, but through a variety of methods, researchers were able to point out disparities such as the higher proportion of girls among the drop-outs (Xiaoxian Gao 1994). Some researchers argued that growing income would resolve the problems, but even the most optimistic among them have been concerned with the lack of health insurance coverage in rural areas (World Bank 1992).

In this volume, Lanyan Chen and Hilary Standing (2007) provide an assessment of the actual and likely gender-differentiated health impacts of China's reform process. China's process of privatizing its healthcare system interacts with the effects of its broader reform process, particularly the labor market restructuring and demographic transition, resulting in gendered inequalities in access to healthcare. Chen and Standing use a broad concept of gender equality that encompasses not only the equal treatment of men and women but also the equality of health outcomes, which requires taking into account gender differences in healthcare needs. They show that, similar to the privatization experiences elsewhere, healthcare reforms have made access to healthcare more costly; resulted in a decline in public healthcare institutions, virtually eliminating access to preventative services in rural areas (especially reproductive care); and contributed to a rise in the uninsured. Poor, older, and rural women are especially disadvantaged due to these changes. The lack of health insurance coverage for over 80 percent of the rural population is the most pressing healthcare problem in China.

Promotion and later privatization of township and village enterprises

The growth of rural industries has been one of the most distinctive features of the Chinese transition (Martin Weitzman and Chenggang Xu 1994). Enterprises owned by township and village governments (TVEs) were the successors of people's communes and production brigades. In the post-reform period, TVEs dominated the rural industrial sector, albeit with regional variations in their importance.[6] TVEs and private household businesses provided off-farm opportunities for women and men, became the main sources of rural income growth, and helped temper the rural–urban income gap. When output and employment growth in the TVE sector slowed in the early 1990s, the Chinese government launched a radical reform program to privatize the TVEs in order to reverse these trends. In the late 1990s, local governments transferred ownership rights of TVEs to private individuals – mostly enterprise managers – through subsidized sales or free transfers (Samuel P. S. Ho, Paul Bowles, and Xiao-yuan Dong 2003).

In 1996 TVEs provided wage employment for 54.4 million women, who accounted for 41 percent of all TVE workers (United Nations Development Programme [UNDP] 1999: 48). Thus, in light of women's prominent role in TVEs, earlier fears about women's loss of wage earnings under the HRS were unfounded. However, the study by Xin Meng (1998) shows that gender discrimination is more severe in China's rural industrial sector than in industrialized economies. Further, Scott Rozelle, Xiao-yuan Dong, Linxiu Zhang, and Andrew Mason (2002) show that while the unadjusted wage gap in the rural industrial sector increased from 31.5 percent in 1988 to 34.0 percent in 1995 the degree of wage discrimination remained unchanged. Xiao-yuan Dong, Fiona MacPhail, Paul Bowles, and Samuel P. S. Ho (2004) find that women in TVEs were segregated into shop-floor production type jobs, had less control over their work, did not receive returns for their work experience, and were subject to wage discrimination. Moreover, after the TVEs were privatized in the late 1990s, gender segregation and wage discrimination against women increased.

Women's self-employment prospects in the rapidly expanding, rural non-agricultural activities were also weaker compared to men's during the reform period (Sandeep Mahopatra, Scott Rozelle, and Rachael Goodhue 2007). Research indicates that self-employment in rural China is an attractive employment option, rather than a coping mechanism in response to the absence of formal wage jobs. However, between 1981 and 2000, the probability of women's participation in the relatively lucrative, highly productive self-employed activities was significantly lower compared to men. Other rural informal employment offers poor conditions for men as well as women (Lee 2005).

In this volume, Fiona MacPhail and Xiao-yuan Dong (2007) examine the impact of TVE employment on intrahousehold gender relations in Shandong and Jiangsu provinces in the late 1990s. Consistent with the capabilities literature (see, for example, Sen [1999]; Nussbaum [2003]; and Ingrid Robeyns [2003]), MacPhail and Dong go beyond income- or goods-based measures to focus on domestic labor time, the gender division of domestic tasks, and household decision-making power. They find that married women face greater overall work hours, domestic work burden, and responsibility for domestic tasks but have less influence in household decisions compared to married men. Multivariate regression analysis indicates that it is the level of wages rather than their hours of employment that matters for women's household status. Namely, women who earn higher wages are able to reduce their domestic labor hours and responsibilities. Evidence on the impact of TVE employment on women's decision-making is mixed, which is consistent with feminist conceptualizations and expectations of the contradictory effects that engaging in paid work has on women's lives (see, for example, Diane Elson and Ruth Pearson [1981] and Christine Koggel [2003]). MacPhail and Dong's study also supports the feminist argument that improving relative wages, rather than expanding women's employment, is the key policy variable in strengthening women's well-being.

State-owned enterprise (SOE) reforms

In urban areas, China's SOEs symbolized socialist commitment to employment and income security. They provided lifetime employment, subsidized housing, education, healthcare, retirement pensions, and some childcare. The enterprise-based provision of social welfare, the nature of state – citizen relations, and the egalitarian gender ideology all dictated the high levels of labor-force participation for men and women. Under central planning, SOEs and rural communes underpinned China's well-known high level of female labor force participation and small gender-wage gap. While research indicates gender-segregated employment patterns prior to SOE reforms (Gale Summerfield 1994; Hang-Yue Ngo 2002), in the 1980s, most working-age women in cities were employed on a full-time basis and earned more than 80 percent of the pay men received (Bjorn Gustafsson and Shi Li 2000).[7]

Efforts to improve the efficiency of SOEs in the 1980s focused on restructuring the incentives of workers and managers and enhancing the role of markets. For example, the wage-setting policies of SOEs became more decentralized; enterprise managers were granted autonomy to hire workers on short-term contracts instead of providing permanent employment (Barry Naughton 1996; Nicholas R. Lardy 1998). In China's gradual approach to reform, however, SOE managers were generally not allowed to lay off workers until the early 1990s.

After 1992, the central government initiated ownership reforms for SOEs. In consequence, a large number of SOEs were transformed into joint-stock companies, declared bankrupt, merged with other enterprises, or sold to private individuals. Accompanying the radical changes in property rights was the deepening of labor market reforms. In 1994, a new labor law was passed that sanctioned the right of employers to dismiss workers and put an end to the state as the source of employment security. In 1997, newly elected Premier Zhu Rongji announced a large-scale labor retrenchment program in an attempt to revitalize the SOE sector. As a result, nearly thirty million workers were laid off between 1998 and 2002 (John Giles, Albert Park, and Fang Cai 2006; Jieyu Liu 2007).

The SOE reforms were accompanied by reforms in the pension system, healthcare, housing, and social assistance, which sought to transfer the responsibility of social services and protection from the enterprise to the state, community, and individual workers (Gang Fan, Maria Rosa Lunati, and David O'Connor 1998). Despite these reforms, efforts to disconnect the social security system from individual enterprises achieved limited success until the late 1990s (Barry L. Friedman 1996). Because employers still played a prominent role in providing protection to workers, the SOE layoffs during the restructuring of the late 1990s took the form of "xiagang," which allowed laid-off SOE workers to retain their entitlements to pensions, healthcare, housing, and other benefits provided by the former employer (Hong Yung Lee 2000).[8]

Studies on the gendered implications of SOE reforms concentrate primarily on labor market consequences, indicating that in the late 1980s and early 1990s, women were disproportionately affected by being subjected to extended maternity leave, internal transfers, or other strategies that affected their working lives. Aggregate statistics suggest, however, that any layoffs that may have taken place have not been widespread. During the 1980s and early 1990s, women's employment prospects continued to improve, as is evident by the steady increase in women's share of the formal employment in urban China, from 32.9 percent in 1978 to 39.4 percent in 1995 (Xiao-yuan Dong, Jianchun Yang, Fenglian Du, and Sai Ding 2006). Opportunities in non-state enterprises and self-employment increased rapidly, especially for young, attractive, educated women (Summerfield 1994). Evidence on the gendered impacts of the SOE downsizing in the late 1990s is less controversial. Studies document consistently that women have borne a disproportionate share of the costs of public sector reforms. They have been laid off at rates much higher than men, have more difficulty finding re-employment in the private sector, and swell the ranks of precarious informal employment (Simon Appleton, John Knight, Lina

12

Song, and Qingjie Xia 2002; Lee 2005; Giles, Park, and Cai 2006; Fenglian Du and Xiao-yuan Dong 2007).[9]

The dismantling of the SOEs has had critical implications for gender inequalities in paid work. The state's weakening commitment to gender equality and workplace protections for women made paid work more onerous,[10] less fair, and less secure for women (Lee 2005). The decentralization of decision-making in state enterprises not only provided greater leeway for managers to reward productivity but also increased the scope for discrimination against women workers. Along with a disproportionate number of laid-off women and the resurgence of patriarchal values that call for women to return to the home and leave the labor market (Summerfield 1994; Janet Yee 2001), the workplace emphasis on efficiency over equity has led to the more dramatic decline in the labor force participation rates of women as compared to men following the SOE restructuring.[11] Nonetheless, in 2004, women's labor force participation rate in China was still the highest rate in the world (UNDP 2006).

Margaret Maurer-Fazio, James Hughes, and Dandan Zhang's study in this volume (2007) is the first to examine the differences and changes in labor force participation by gender and ethnicity. About 9 percent of China's population is comprised of ethnic minorities, some of whom are concentrated in the poorer, western provinces. There is evidence that the gaps between the Han majority and ethnic minorities widened in terms of occupational attainment (Emily Hannum and Yu Xie 1998) and per capita income during the reform period (Bjorn Gustafsson and Shi Li 2003). Maurer-Fazio, Hughes, and Zhang focus on four important minority groups (Korean, Zhuang, Hui, and Uygur) and find that between 1990 and 2000, controlling for human capital characteristics, urban labor force participation rates fell substantially, with women's rates declining more rapidly than men's, and minority women's rates declining more rapidly than Han women's. They find evidence for a return to more traditional gender roles in the household, in that married women reduced their participation in the labor force nationally and in each region where each of the four ethnic groups constitutes a sizable minority. They also isolate the effect of ethnicity from that of regional economic conditions (that is, the fact that ethnic minorities tend to live in poorer regions) and find that Korean and Zhuang women's participation rates converged to Han women's participation rates, while Hui and Uygur women's participation diverged from that of Han women.

While gender disparities in layoffs and reemployment are widely recognized, empirical studies of their underlying causes have just begun to emerge. In this volume, Liu (2007) explores the life histories of laid-off women workers to show that segregation in low-skilled industrial work prior to reforms not only made women more susceptible to layoffs than men but also made for poorer social connections that weakened their chances of finding jobs commensurate with SOE working conditions. Liu's research, conducted in Nanjing in 2003, offers a glimpse of the experiences that underlie the massive downsizing of the late 1990s and engenders the analysis of the role of social connections in post-redundancy job searches in China. In particular, she highlights the hardships experienced by older, less-educated women workers who belong to the "unlucky generation," as the Cultural Revolution cohort is commonly called. Ultimately, she calls for greater protections of laid-off workers and restitution for these women who have borne the costs of successive policy shifts and political upheavals in China's recent history.

Similar insights on reemployment prospects emerge from the econometric analysis of Du and Dong (2007). Rejecting the view that women are less serious about reemployment than men, their results show that women's lack of access to social networks, employers' prejudice against married women, unequal access to social reemployment services, and wage discrimination in the post-restructuring labor market hinder women's job search efforts.

As the relative importance of SOE employment declined and market regulation became the rule, gender segregation in employment and the gender earnings gap in urban China also increased.[12] However, there are mixed findings regarding the impact of reforms on wage discrimination. Gustafsson and Li (2000) find that while earnings for both men and women in the cities rose markedly, the extent of wage discrimination also increased from 1988 to 1995. Margaret Maurer-Fazio and James Hughes (2002) find that the degree of wage discrimination is largest in the most liberalized sector (foreign-invested enterprises) and smallest in the least liberalized sector (SOEs), whereas the opposite pattern of gender discrimination is reported by Pak-Wai Liu, Xin Meng, and Junsen Zhang (2000). All the aforementioned studies focus on the early years of reforms. As with the trends in employment, evidence on wage dynamics for the post-1992 stage of urban reforms is more consistent, indicating that both the gender earnings gap and wage discrimination have increased markedly in the post-restructuring urban labor market (Appleton et al. 2002; Dong et al. 2006). Overall, the reforms reinforced old patterns of urban labor market gender disparities, such as gender-segregated employment in SOEs, and produced new gendered employment practices: prolonged maternity leave against women workers' wishes, dismissals of women first, and preference in the recruitment of young, attractive women.

The loss of SOE jobs with healthcare benefits has left women with greater difficulties in access to healthcare. Chen and Standing (2007) in this volume indicate that the increasing elderly care burden in an aging economy is creating new vulnerabilities for women, as they are unable to keep jobs with healthcare benefits. Care for the millions of rural–urban migrants in cities is also inadequate. In particular, access to reproductive healthcare for rural–urban migrant women is poor (Lin Tan, Zhenzhen Zheng, and Yueping Song 2006). These young women work and live under conditions that create health problems; as non-residents they do not have access to urban social healthcare and have to pay for healthcare, and the urban healthcare services are inadequate.[13]

Foreign direct investment and trade liberalization

The formation of special economic zones (SEZs) in 1978–9 marked the beginning of China's "opening to the world" (Nicholas R. Lardy 1994). In the SEZs, as the export processing zones (EPZs) are known in China, the familiar set of concessionary policies – tax breaks, exemption from tariffs on inputs, and avoidance of some labor regulations – were granted to foreign companies to attract investment and promote exports. As in EPZs in other countries, the Chinese SEZs relied on light industry, especially textiles and electronics, and hired more women than men. From its inception, feminist research problematized the conditions of women's employment in the SEZs, highlighting the low wages, poor working conditions, lack of opportunity for advancement, and job insecurity (Phyllis Andors 1988). The special policies in SEZs were extended to the fourteen coastal cities in 1984, and new efforts were made in the 1990s to broaden the geographic coverage of these initiatives from the coastal areas to other regions (World Bank 1997).

Other reforms to promote trade liberalization were more gradual and national in scope. In the early 1980s, quota and licensing systems were adopted to replace the state mandatory plans for imports and exports, and the number of firms with rights to trade directly increased dramatically. China embarked on the process of greater integration with the global economy by applying for membership to the WTO in 1986, which accelerated the process of trade liberalization. In the 1990s China began to reduce tariffs; eliminate quotas, licensing, and other non-tariff barriers; and permit foreign companies to sell products in the domestic market. Along with the reform of foreign exchange markets and the consistently undervalued exchange rate, these policies contributed to China's phenomenal growth in trade.[14]

China became a member of the WTO in late 2001, after fifteen years of negotiations and reforms. By joining, China agreed to the basic principles of the GATT and the WTO that require it to treat its trading partners equally and to treat foreign companies doing business within its borders no differently from its local firms (Deepak Bhattasali, Shantong Li, and Will Martin 2004b; Jeffrey L. Gertler 2004). China also agreed to open up its markets by reducing import restrictions, get rid of export subsidies, create a business climate that operates according to rules of transparency and predictability, and to accept any trade protections (safeguards) that other countries may put in place in the event that China's exports cause or threaten disruptions in their domestic markets (for a period of up to twelve years).

Trade liberalization has integrated China more closely into the global economy and accelerated structural change. WTO accession was widely predicted to disrupt rural livelihoods and unleash an even larger-scale migration than that experienced in the 1990s and early 2000s (Bhattasali, Li, and Martin 2004a). As of 2004, about 70 percent of China's population, an estimated 757 million people, lived in rural areas, and agriculture provided the livelihood of 47 percent of the labor force (National Bureau of Statistics [NBS] 2005: Tables 4-1 and 5-2). The principal cause of disruption in rural areas is import liberalization that is expected to undermine grain and land-intensive crop agriculture through falling prices. While some farming communities are switching to cultivating labor-intensive crops that can successfully compete in the world market, this option is not feasible in all parts of China. Most farm households face increasing pressure to either diversify income sources or leave agriculture. In prosperous provinces such as Zhejiang, however, the opportunity cost of remaining in the low-income agricultural sector propels the transfer to urban industrial and service work.

Increased access to world markets for Chinese manufactured goods has fueled the expansion of export-oriented industries and growth of employment in services and industry, while the elimination or reduction of subsidies has brought about the decline in previously protected industrial sectors.[15] The opening of China's domestic market to foreign investment has multiplied FDI inflow and made China the largest recipient of FDI inflows.[16] Beginning in the early 1990s, FDI has moved beyond its conventional enclave of the SEZs and into diverse sectors such as utilities, transportation, wholesale and retail commerce, financial services, and advertising as restrictions on FDI were removed.

The reforms associated with WTO membership intensified the trends already under way, contributing to large-scale dislocations in the urban labor market, increased pressures for rural – urban migration, the widening of the rural – urban income gap, and overall income inequality (Ravallion and Chen 2004; Khan and Riskin 2005). Regional divergence sharpened as southern and coastal regions of China witnessed the rapid growth of jobs in export manufacturing and the proliferation of diverse industries, while inland provinces that were home to protected industries or producers of food staples stagnated.

The impacts of WTO reforms are far-reaching, felt in rural as well as urban areas, in agriculture as well as industry and services, and in consumption as well as production activities. They are intertwined with the effects of ongoing reform and difficult to disentangle. Commentators, however, have expressed concern that due to gender inequality in household responsibilities, educational levels, and access to social networks, women are likely to experience more difficulty moving into higher paying jobs and coping with labor market turbulence than men in post-WTO China. They predict that China's entry to the WTO will enhance the trends of feminization of agriculture, low-paying manufacturing jobs, and informal employment (UNDP in China 2003).

Three papers in this volume focus on themes that especially pertain to the WTO accession: wages and conditions of employment in firms that are the recipient of FDI, the spill-over effects of FDI on workers in other sectors, and the rise of consumerism. Elissa Braunstein and Mark Brenner (2007) examine the effects of FDI on the wages of urban women and men workers between 1995 and 2002, when FDI flows to capital-intensive sectors increased. They find that working in both foreign-invested enterprises and provinces with a higher level of FDI resulted in higher wages for women and men compared to other enterprises and regions. This result is consistent with other studies in China (see, for example, Minquan Liu, Luodan Xu, and Liu Liu [2004]) and holds for both 1995 and 2002. However, they find that in 2002 FDI was associated with smaller wage gains for women compared to men, which could be attributed to either the greater demand for male workers or men's greater bargaining power vis-à-vis employers as capital-intensity of manufacturing increases. Despite the slight widening of the gender-wage gap, urban women's earnings were 82 percent of men's earnings in 2002, which is a comparatively high gender-earnings ratio.

Pun Ngai's and Julien Burda's contributions to this volume add to the growing literature that problematizes labor conditions and the industrial labor process in China's export-oriented enterprises, particularly in the SEZs (Anita Chan 2001; Arianne M. Gaetano and Tamara Jacka 2004; Pun Ngai 2005). Under trade liberalization, employment in SEZs expanded substantially. By 2004, employment in Chinese SEZs reached over thirty million workers and dwarfed EPZ employment elsewhere, which totaled about twenty-three million workers (International Labour Organization [ILO] 2007). While the conditions of women's employment are often poorer outside of SEZs, as has been argued for EPZ employment in other countries,[17] both articles highlight the exploitative working conditions that accompany the rapid expansion of job opportunities for young rural women in export manufacturing and the discrepancy between stipulation and implementation of China's labor legislation.

Based on a 2003–4 case study of a foreign-owned electronics factory in South China, Pun (2007) provides a detailed analysis of the operation of the dormitory labor system that underlies the boom of export-oriented industrial production in China. The state's residency controls and the employer's integration of working space with living space are the twin forces that keep wage increases in check and maximize labor productivity and profits by labor practices that may be considered forced labor (see also Burda's contribution [2007]), such as work days in excess of legal limits, mandatory overtime work, continuous work without days off. In the tradition of feminist shop-floor research (see, for example, Karen Hossfeld [1990]), Pun also shows that the dormitory labor system supports workers' resistance to conditions of exploitation. Workers' victories are small, however, as they are inevitably limited by the short-term tenure of women's employment. While these jobs pay higher wages than available alternatives and there are benefits of employer-provided dormitories for workers, many of these jobs are associated with serious violations of China's own labor legislation.

With an emphasis on what is legally feasible in the post-WTO world, Burda reviews the range of options for improving women's working conditions in export-oriented industrial enterprises. The framework of WTO law all but rules out the possibility of a WTO member (or group of members) imposing trade sanctions against imports from another member country that has poor labor standards. While three of the exceptions in the GATT would permit trade sanctions, given the adverse effects of the trade sanctions route on developing countries, Burda favors using other trade rules (such as the Generalized System of Preferences [GSP] and bilateral trade agreements) that provide trade incentives to reward China for improving its working conditions. Burda concludes that improving labor conditions in China will require multiple strategies that would involve international organizations, nongovernmental organizations, and activism at the local and international levels.

Both of these papers touch on important concerns for feminist assessment. Pun Ngai's paper, in particular, underscores that a feminist assessment of the relative earnings of migrant women workers has to include the conditions that produce these jobs as desirable, the adequacy of these earnings for the reproduction of workers' labor power, and non-wage conditions of industrial employment. According to All-China Women Federation studies from the late 1990s, rural per capita income is one-seventh of what migrant women workers earn in foreign-invested enterprises, but migrant women workers' annual earnings are half the annual income of urban resident women (Tan, Zheng, and Song 2006). Further, while firms bear the costs of the daily reproduction of labor power through dormitory accommodation and wages (which yield firms sustained high labor productivity) most of the cost of intergenerational reproduction is borne by workers' families, as discussed by Pun (2007). Family responsibility for reproducing labor power has risen particularly as the state has reduced considerably universal welfare services, emphasized personal responsibility for benefits, and moved to a highly selective form of social assistance provision in the 1990s (Xinping Guan 2005). Also, the higher pay offered by these jobs is associated with stressful, unhealthy, abusive, unfair, and discriminatory working conditions. Women generate higher monthly or annual earnings based on the long hours they work, at the expense of their well-being, and when earnings are expressed in hourly terms these jobs may not look as favorable (Robert J. S. Ross and Anita Chan 2002).

While the papers in this volume do not differentiate among the labor conditions by the origin of foreign-invested enterprises, other studies show that enterprises from Hong Kong, Taiwan, and Korea have poorer working conditions compared to those from the European Union and US in terms of wages and compliance with laws on minimum wage and overtime wages (Ross and Chan 2002; Liu, Xu, and Liu 2004; Tan, Zheng, and Song 2006). Moreover, a higher export ratio of foreign-invested enterprise is associated with lower hourly wages and more overtime wage violations (Liu, Xu, and Liu 2004), reinforcing Pun's and Burda's message that China's export competitiveness is partly based on violations of labor rights, and these violations are a serious cause for concern for feminist economists.

And, as demonstrated by Burda, in addition to violations of China's labor laws, there are also problems with China's legal framework in terms of labor rights. China has not ratified the forced labor and union rights conventions of the ILO.[18] The only union organization allowed in China is the All-China Federation of Trade Unions (ACFTU), which sets up chapters in workplaces, manages a workers' welfare fund, but does not engage in collective bargaining or make demands on employers. Thus, workers in China do not have access to arguably the most effective means for improving wages and working conditions, and addressing discrimination and employer abuses.

Burda's paper touches on an essential concern for feminist economists, that of improving working conditions without the loss of jobs for women, by pointing to alternatives outside of trade sanctions. Among feminist economists, many have argued against trade sanctions on the grounds that it is not possible to both increase women's employment in export-oriented industries and improve working conditions at the same time in the short-run (Shahra Razavi 1999; Naila Kabeer 2004). Given China's role as the dominant supplier of a wide range of manufactured goods to the world economy, it may be difficult to pursue trade-linked strategies (of either the sanctions or incentives type) with China. Nonetheless, some international framework (including a trade-linked strategy) to put greater pressure on China is necessary, in addition to political pressure from various local and international NGOs, to ensure compliance with basic worker protections. The problem has a bearing on wages and working conditions in China's competitors as well as being a pressing concern for Chinese workers (Ross and Chan 2002).[19] Recent developments in union rights in China suggest that the fear of social instability associated with rising inequality may make the central government more receptive to grassroots pressure for the exercise of union rights (Jeremy Kahn 2006). Greater external scrutiny of China under conditions of greater international integration may also put pressure on the government toward broadening labor rights (Elliott and Freeman 2004).

Also in this volume, Barbara E. Hopkins (2007) and Gary Xu and Susan Feiner (2007) address two distinct ways in which global integration – specifically China's accession to the WTO – influenced the changes in the gender regime. Since the early 1980s, China has been moving away from a socialist culture that rejected displays of gender difference by a staunch insistence on women's equality with men in every way, including in appearance, to one that encourages and celebrates gender difference. The category of gender has become more complex, along with the restructuring of Chinese society in the post-Mao era, and sexuality is acquiring a greater role in the Chinese definition of gender (Susan Brownell and Jeffrey N. Wasserstrom 2002). The emphasis on femininity and beauty as an essential feature of women's gender identity has increased.

Hopkins focuses on the changing notions of femininity and masculinity as reflected in the cosmetics consumer culture. As China opened up its market to foreign companies, increasing competition and proliferation of marketing strategies in cosmetics have given further momentum to changes in the gender regime. Hopkins argues that this resurgence of femininity (and return to pre-revolution gender notions) has multiple meanings for women who consume cosmetics. Drawing upon institutionalist economic theories and feminist theories of gender as performance, Hopkins constructs a framework for interpreting the dynamics underlying aggregate changes in consumption.

Xu and Feiner explore the explosion of beauty pageants and the associated beauty economy since China's accession to the WTO. While China is not the only developing country that is experiencing a growing fascination with and staging of beauty pageants (Colleen B. Cohen, Richard Wilk, and Beverly Stoeltje 1996), China's adoption of the beauty pageant culture is remarkable in its speed, daring, and scale. Xu and Feiner discuss the relationship of the surge of pageants to the increasing (and accelerating) commodification that touches every aspect of Chinese society, including intimate relations and women's bodies. At the symbolic level, they point out, the epidemic of pageants is emblematic of China's rising economic power, its modernity, the increasing social value of whiteness, the rejection of Asian beauty, the rise in value placed on feminine beauty and all things Western, and the freedom to consume. The authors contend that beauty pageants facilitate the acceptance of neoliberal economic policies and quell political dissent. They end with a call to reflect on the older, Taoist notion of beauty in constructing alternative identities.

THIS VOLUME: GENDER, CHINA, AND THE WTO

The articles in this volume examine the gendered consequences of China's transition from socialism to capitalism and opening up to trade and FDI flows. They examine a wide range of questions from a number of disciplinary perspectives, representing growing interdisciplinarity under the rubric of feminist economics. Above all, the main contribution of the volume is new empirical evidence to the scholarship on transition, economic development, international trade, labor markets, and theories of consumption.

On the whole, the gender lens used by contributors to this volume highlights the adverse consequences of China's post-1992 transformation. As such, the articles reinforce the findings of recent feminist economic research on China. Compared to men, women's land rights are becoming less secure; their access to healthcare is more limited and has become more precarious. Women's employment opportunities in export-oriented manufacturing are expanding and jobs in foreign-invested firms and provinces with higher FDI are associated with higher wages. Yet, the conditions of employment are poor relative to China's own labor laws, and China's international commitments to the core labor standards of the ILO continue to be incomplete. Among married women who work in the rural TVEs, only those with higher earnings are able to exercise decision-making power and reduce labor hours in housework. In stark contrast to pre-reform ideals of beauty and gender, Chinese women are increasingly and intensely preoccupied with looks as their consumption choices expand and access to good jobs becomes contingent upon looks. The country as a whole is increasingly preoccupied with beauty contests that signify and reinforce the commodification of women's bodies. These developments signal China's convergence to commoditized, globalized, Anglo-European notions of femininity and beauty.

Thus, the uniqueness of China's transition does not appear to have prevented the emergence of greater disadvantage for women compared to men. In contrast to the 1980s, when reforms sought to minimize adverse gender consequences, once the transition unfolded, market regulation became the rule, and China became fully exposed to global competition, the gender outcomes in China became qualitatively similar to the gender patterns in other developing and transition economies. Thus, the overriding emphasis on the goal of efficiency and accumulation has contributed to the rise in labor market discrimination against women, particularly older women, in addition to the unintended disadvantages that resulted from gender-blind policies. However, in spite of this international convergence of gender outcomes, in comparative terms, China still represents the most egalitarian land distribution by gender, the highest female labor force participation, the smallest urban gender-wage gap, and the smallest gender disparities in adult and youth literacy rates among developing countries.

Each article in this volume exemplifies one or more of the characteristics of feminist economics scholarship outlined earlier. While a gender-aware perspective informs all of the articles, partly due to the constraints of research design, several of the papers focus primarily on a particular group of women (and not men): young, rural migrant women workers (Burda; Pun); older women production workers (Liu); or younger married rural women (Hare, Li, and Englander).

Consistent with feminist economists' broadening topical focus, this volume builds upon diverse research methods and methodologies. Several articles examine the labor market process (Liu; Pun), policy implementation (Chen and Summerfield), and intrahousehold dynamics (MacPhail and Dong) that generate gender inequality in outcomes or disadvantage for women. In order to examine the individual-level dynamics that underlie various policies and macro-structural changes, these studies rely on evidence generated by ethnographic research that includes in-depth interviews and participant observation (Chen and Summerfield; Liu; Pun) or they complement survey data with interviews (Hare, Li, and Englander; MacPhail and Dong). Several articles rely on regression analysis of survey-generated data, as called for by the particular research question (Braunstein and Brenner; Hare, Li, and Englander; MacPhail and Dong; Maurer-Fazio, Hughes, and Zhang). Others use various interpretive methods (Chen and Summerfield; Liu; Pun), including discourse analysis (Xu and Feiner); construct an argument based on legal scholarship (Burda); construct a conceptual framework (Hopkins); or provide a synthesis of the literature and the latest data (Chen and Standing).

While several articles highlight the likely intrahousehold gender disparities in well-being, capability, and decision-making, only MacPhail and Dong and Hare, Li, and Englander directly examine these issues. Many of the articles address questions of agency, by either focusing on women's agency (Liu; Pun; Hopkins) or ways of overcoming the male bias in policy (Burda; Liu; MacPhail and Dong). By emphasizing attention to discrimination in employment, poor wages and working conditions, and considerations of fairness in access to services, access to land, and in rectifying past injustices the studies in this volume provide the basis for gender-aware policies and political strategies.

CONCLUSIONS AND FUTURE DIRECTIONS

China's economic growth since the reforms began in 1978 has been impressive, and women as well as men have gained much from the new opportunities. Gender-aware scholarship on China, including several articles in this volume, shows that as China's economic policies converged toward the neoliberal recipe after 1992, gender inequalities have grown along with other forms of inequality.

Rising gender inequality and the decline in well-being for large segments of the population present a sharp contrast to and a repudiation of China's pre-reform socialist commitment to gender equality, even if socialist practice diverged from the rhetoric in many ways. If the reforms are gender-blind in conception and implementation, the costs can be expected to follow traditional biases of the pre-reform era whether or not that outcome is intentional. In order to tackle gender and class inequalities, equity and well-being must be put back on the forefront of China's agenda for change. We hold hope that the distinctive policy-reform tradition of China's central government will produce a strategy that speaks to the aspirations of Chinese people for fairness. There have been grassroots activities, emerging organizations, and spontaneous demonstrations that have increasingly drawn attention to grievances associated with reforms and such grassroots movements are essential to bring equity back on the policy agenda. There are hopeful signs that the Chinese government is becoming more responsive and moving in the direction of addressing inequalities and social injustices. Implementation of the agenda of growth with equity announced at the Sixteenth Chinese Communist Party Congress in 2002 would support the rural sector, the less developed regions, and provide social safety nets with broad coverage. Implementation of social security reform would increase income security, and the enforcement of the ILO's anti-discrimination Convention No. 111 that China ratified in 2006 would reduce discrimination against women. Ratification and enforcement of ILO conventions on union rights and forced labor would be a major step toward improving working conditions.

This volume opens up many topics for future feminist economics research. Research should examine changes in caring work; intrahousehold gender relations; the gender implications of various forms of income generation; rural–urban migration; trade, FDI, and industrial upgrading; and the nature and extent of gender disparities in human development and human poverty. Scholars also need to address systems of labor protection, healthcare reforms and health outcomes, urban welfare reforms, and village democratization. The entitlements and capabilities of men as well as women, with consistent attention to class and ethnic differences, have to be brought under systematic scrutiny in all of these studies. This research also has to push the boundaries of conventional empirical research methodologies and bring in the perceptions and voices of women and men.

Gender-aware economic research has already taken off in China among the young generation of economists with the Chinese Women Economists Network as attested by two contributors to this volume (Li Yang and Dandan Zhang). As researchers, we see our role as contributing to scholarship that could guide policies sensitive to gender, class, and ethnicity. As feminists, we are concerned about making change/action-oriented research, promoting equitable improvement in the lives of women and men, and reducing economic inequalities and discrimination. We hope that this volume will be a catalyst for change as well as a contribution to feminist economic scholarship on China's transition.

Günseli Berik, Department Economics and Gender Studies Program, University of Utah, 1645 E. Campus Center Dr., Rm. 308, Salt Lake City, UT 84112, USA
e-mail: berik@economics.utah.edu

Xiao-yuan Dong, Department of Economics, University of Winnipeg, 515 Portage Avenue, Winnipeg, Manitoba Canada R3B 2E9
e-mail: x.dong@uwinnipeg.ca

Gale Summerfield, University of Illinois at Urbana-Champaign, Human and Community Development and Women and Gender in Global Perspectives Program, 320 International Studies Building, 910 S. Fifth St, Champaign, IL 61820, USA
e-mail: summrfld@uiuc.edu

ACKNOWLEDGMENTS

This volume would not have been possible without the support, dedication, and enthusiastic participation of many people. We would like to express our gratitude to Diana Strassmann, the editor of *Feminist Economics*, for her tireless, capable, and creative efforts in envisioning this volume, bringing us together as the editorial team, securing funding, and overseeing the special issue process, and to the journal's editorial staff, particularly Raj Mankad, Mónica Parle, and Anne Dayton, for their dedication, support, and patience in all stages of the journal editorial process and the Rice workshop preparation. We thank Rice University and the Ford Foundation - Beijing for their generous financial support of this volume and for making possible the opportunities for intellectual exchange among guest editors. We are also especially grateful to Anne and Albert Chao for sponsoring a workshop at Rice University in March 2006 that permitted the contributors to the volume to present their papers in advance of publication. The workshop provided a wonderful opportunity for wide-ranging and in-depth inter-actions among authors, editors, and discussants, who traveled to Houston from five countries spread across three continents, and greatly enhanced all aspects of the publication of this volume. The articles were also presented at the 2006 annual conference of the International Association for Feminist Economics and at sessions in the 2006 and 2007 Allied Social Science Association meetings. In addition to the authors of articles in this volume, discussants at the workshop and conference sessions were: Nancy Folbre, Malcolm Gillis, Joyce Jacobsen, Marion Jones, Betty Joseph, Chinhui Juhn,

Janet Kohlhase, Steven W. Lewis, and Sarah Westpahl. We thank the discussants at these sessions for their useful comments. We owe special thanks to Joyce Jacobsen, who generously served as a discussant for almost all of the articles. We also thank Ebru Kongar and Minqi Li for comments on this paper. And finally, we are indebted to a large number of colleagues and scholars who served as anonymous reviewers of papers submitted for the Special Issue of *Feminist Economics* on Gender, China, and the WTO.

ABOUT THE REFERENCE FORMAT

The formatting of Chinese names in scholarship published in an international forum is a contentious issue. Because the Chinese convention of listing the family name first conflicts with the more prevalent Western tradition of putting the given name first, we were faced with making a decision of how to treat the names of Chinese scholars in this volume. Scholars working in the West, those working in China, or those that bridge these two cultures, may each determine a different method of dealing with this convention in their own work. Given the wide range of interpretations, we ultimately decided to allow the authors to decide whether to use the Chinese naming convention or the Western convention. For this reason, there may be some variation from article to article in the presentation of source material and in the naming of scholars in reference lists. We hope that this reflects the variety of approaches to conducting scholarship between cultures.

NOTES

[1] When international financial institutions or the reforms' academic proponents evaluate these reforms, they tend to focus on growth as the sole criterion for success, and they often overlook or minimize the costs of adjustment and the exploitative conditions of labor. At best, these assessments acknowledge the pain in store, without addressing the difficulties faced by those who bear the costs of adjustment. Jeffrey L. Gertler (2004: 28) reflects this approach, in saying: "we can do little more than wish China and its people '*bon courage*' as they venture down the extremely challenging path that stretches before them."

[2] Each of these methodological features contrasts with conventional economists' concerns with and approach to China's WTO accession as exemplified by Deepak Bhattasali, Shantong Li, and Will Martin (2004a).

[3] The key features of these structural transition reforms are the reduction in the state's role in the economy (through privatization and deregulation), liberalization of trade, financial flows, and the FDI regime, and export-orientation. Policy-makers in developing countries implement these reforms, called structural adjustment programs (SAPs), following a stabilization program that involves a devaluation of the currency, fiscal austerity, tight monetary policy, and restraint on income policy. For feminist analyses see, for example, Lourdes Benería and Shelley Feldman (1992); Nahid Aslanbeigui, Steven Pressman, and Gale Summerfield (1994); Isabella Bakker (1994); Diane Elson (1995); Ulla Grapard (1997); Susana Lastarria-Cornhiel (1997);

Elizabeth Brainerd (1998); Irene Tinker and Gale Summerfield (1999); and Marnia Lazreg (2000). See Lawrence Haddad, Lynn Brown, Andrea Richter, and Lisa Smith (1995) for the difficulties in making generalizations.

4 For example, Qian (2003) argues that by pursuing the dual track in prices in the phase-out of planned prices, the central government sought to both protect the weak from immediate exposure to market prices and maintain the legitimacy of reforms. Land policies and SOE reforms provide other examples.

5 As in other socialist societies, in pre-reform China, there was a gap between the rhetoric and the reality of gender equality, partly due to the limitations in addressing domestic labor. As a result, despite commitment to the equal pay for equal work principle, in rural communes there was a gender-wage differential (because wage scales rewarded better the labor qualities associated with men, and women could not put in as much labor as men due to their household responsibilities). While programs sought to reduce women's individual household responsibilities, their availability and quality were uneven (Elisabeth Croll 1981).

6 Between 1978 and 1993, the industrial output from and employment by TVEs grew at an average annual rate of 20.8 and 10.6 percent, respectively (National Bureau of Statistics [NBS] 1994: 362–3). By the mid-1990s, TVEs employed nearly 30 percent of the rural labor force and produced about half the exports of manufactured goods.

7 Because of the lack of systematic statistics for the Chinese economy prior to 1978, the literature uses the gender-wage gap in the 1980s as an indicator for the situation prior to the reform.

8 See Liu's contribution to this volume (2007) for the multiple categories of laid-off workers during the course of the SOE reforms, indicative of the experimental gradualism in policy and the concern for protecting the disadvantaged.

9 During the SOE restructuring of the late 1990s, many firms used mandatory early retirement to downsize their workforce, requiring workers to retire up to five years earlier than the official retirement age. Thus, the gender-differentiated retirement age under central planning, which retired blue-collar women workers at 50 and men at 55, resulted in women being retired much earlier than men.

10 China's Urban Labor Surveys show that the number of weekly work hours rose for both men and women between 1997 and 2002 but more sharply for women than for men – up by 1.7 hours for men and 2.0 hours for women – and the share of female workers who work overtime also increased from 26.9 to 39.9 percent (Dong et al. 2006).

11 Based on China's Urban Labor Surveys, Dong et al. (2006) find that urban labor force participation rates declined dramatically between 1997 and 2002 from 78.6 to 71.6 percent for men and 64.6 to 54.1 percent for women. These estimates are consistent with figures obtained by Margaret Maurer-Fazio, James Hughes, and Dandan Zhang (2007) from China's population census showing that 68.9 percent of women were in the labor force in 1990 and the rate fell to 57.7 percent in 2000, while the labor force participation rate for men decreased from 82 percent to 72 percent.

12 The Duncan index of occupational segregation for China was estimated to be 0.47 in 1982 and increased to 0.50 by 1990 (Ngo 2002). According to the second survey on the status of women taken jointly by the All-China Women Federation (ACWF) and the NBS in 2001, women earned 77.5 percent of men's pay in the urban sector and 79 percent in the rural sector in 1990, but by 1999, the ratio had dropped to 70.1 percent and 59.6 percent, respectively (ACWF and NBS 2001: 21).

13 Crowded and unsanitary dormitories, limited bathroom breaks during long shifts, and excessive work hours and obligatory overtime along with risky sexual behavior create health problems. These women tend to give up on healthcare because they have to

pay out of pocket, and their work hours constrain access to health services (Tan, Zheng, and Song 2006).

[14] Between 1978 and 2001 China's exports and imports grew at an annual average rate of 14.4 and 13.5 percent, respectively, and FDI increased by an average of 14.9 percent per year (NBS 2005: Tables 18-3 and 18-13).

[15] Since its accession to the WTO China's exports and imports have increased sharply, from US$266.1 billion and $243.6 billion in 2001 to $593.3 billion and $561.2 billion in 2004, respectively, and FDI to China went up from $69.2 billion to $153.5 billion (NBS 2005: Tables 18-3 and 18-13).

[16] Attracting more than forty billion US dollars of FDI each year since 1996, China has accounted for about one-third of total FDI inflows to developing countries (Naughton 2007: 401).

[17] For example, Linda Lim (1990) and Naila Kabeer (2004) argue that jobs in MNCs or in EPZs are worth protecting, as they offer better employment conditions for women compared to their alternatives in the local economy and a modicum of autonomy for women workers. See Elizabeth Fussell (2000) for evidence that supports the opposite conclusion.

[18] China has not ratified the ILO's Freedom of Association and Collective Bargaining Conventions (No. 87 and 98) and Forced Labor Conventions (No. 29 and No. 105), which are considered among the core labor standards.

[19] China's competitiveness in labor-intensive export manufacturing is based not only on low labor costs but also on non-labor aspects of competitiveness, such as superior transportation, communications, and customs facilities. However, violations of labor laws do contribute to low unit labor costs and likely exert downward pressure on wages and working conditions of mostly women workers in China's low-income competitors such as Bangladesh, Cambodia, Indonesia, and Vietnam (Yana van der Meulen Rodgers and Günseli Berik 2006).

REFERENCES

All-China Women's Federation and National Bureau of Statistics. 2001. *Main Result of the Second Survey of Women's Social Status in China.* Memo.

Anagnost, Ann. 1988. "Family Violence and Magical Violence: The Woman as Victim in China's One-Child Policy." *Women and Language* 11(2): 16–21.

Andors, Phyllis. 1988. "Women and Work in Shenzhen." *Bulletin of Concerned Asian Scholars* 30(3): 22–41.

Appleton, Simon, John Knight, Lina Song, and Qingjie Xia. 2002. "Labor Retrenchment in China: Determinants and Consequences." *China Economic Review* 13(2/3): 252–75.

Aslanbeigui, Nahid and Gale Summerfield. 1989. "Impact of the Responsibility System on Women in Rural China: An Application of Sen's Theory of Entitlements." *World Development* 17(3): 343–50.

——. 1992. "Feminization of Poverty in China?" *Development* 4: 57–61.

Aslanbeigui, Nahid, Steven Pressman, and Gale Summerfield. 1994. *Women in the Age of Economic Transformation: Gender Impact of Reforms in Post-Socialist and Developing Countries.* London: Routledge.

Bakker, Isabella. 1994. *The Strategic Silence: Gender and Economic Policy.* London: Zed Books.

Barker, Drucilla and Susan Feiner. 2004. *Liberating Economics: Feminist Perspectives on Families, Work, and Globalization.* Ann Arbor: University of Michigan Press.

Benería, Lourdes. 2003. *Gender, Development, and Globalization: Economics as if All People Mattered.* New York and London: Routledge.

—— and Shelley Feldman. 1992. *Unequal Burden: Economic Crises, Persistent Poverty and Women's Works.* Boulder, CO: Westview.

Berik, Günseli. 1997. "The Need for Crossing the Method Boundaries in Economics Research." *Feminist Economics* 3(2): 121–5.

Bhattasali, Deepak, Shantong Li, and Will Martin. 2004a. *China and the WTO: Accession, Policy Reform, and Poverty Reduction Strategies.* Washington, DC: The World Bank.

——. 2004b. "Impacts and Policy Implications of WTO Accession for China," in Deepak Bhattasali, Shantong Li, and Will Martin, eds. *China and the WTO: Accession, Policy Reform, and Poverty Reduction Strategies*, pp. 1–17. Washington, DC: The World Bank.

Bossen, Laurel. 2000. "Women Farmers, Small Plots, and Changing Markets in China," in Anita Spring, ed. *Women Farmers and Commercial Ventures: Increasing Food Security in Developing Countries*, pp. 171–89. Boulder, CO: Lynne Reinner Publishers.

Brainerd, Elizabeth. 1998. "Winners and Losers in Russia's Economic Transition." *American Economic Review* 88(5): 1094–116.

Braunstein, Elissa and Mark Brenner. 2007. "Foreign Direct Investment and Gender Wages in Urban China." *Feminist Economics* 13(3/4): 213–37.

de Brauw, Alan. 2002. Are Women Taking over the Farm in China? Working Paper 199, Department of Economics, Williams College.

Brownell, Susan and Jeffrey N. Wasserstrom. 2002. *Chinese Femininities/Chinese Masculinities.* Berkeley: University of California Press.

Burda, Julien. 2007. "Chinese Women after the Accession to the World Trade Organization: A Legal Perspective on Women's Labor Rights." *Feminist Economics* 13(3/4): 259–85.

Çağatay, Nilüfer, Diane Elson, and Caren Grown. 1995. "Introduction." *World Development* 23(11): 1827–36.

Chan, Anita. 2001. *China's Workers Under Assault: The Exploitation of Labor in a Globalizing Economy.* New York: M. E. Sharpe.

Chen, Junjie and Gale Summerfield. 2007. "Gender and Rural Policy reforms in China: A Case Study of Population Control and Land Rights Policies in Northern Liaoning." *Feminist Economics* 13(3/4): 63–92.

Chen, Lanyan and Hilary Standing. 2007. "Gender Equality in Transitional China's Health Policy Reforms." *Feminist Economics* 13(3/4): 189–212.

Cheng, Tiejun and Mark Selden. 1994. "The Origins and Social Consequences of China's Hukou System." *China Quarterly* 139: 644–68.

China Daily. 2003. "Reforms Make Life and Travel Much Easier." August 8. http://www.chinadaily.com.cn/en/doc/2003-08/08/content_252954.htm (accessed May 2007).

Cohen, Colleen B., Richard Wilk, and Beverly Stoeltje, eds. 1996. *Beauty Queens on the Global Stage: Gender, Contests, and Power.* New York: Routledge.

Croll, Elisabeth. 1981. "Women in Rural Production and Reproduction in the Soviet Union, China, Cuba, and Tanzania: Case Studies." *Signs: Journal of Women in Culture and Society* 7(2): 375–99.

——. 2000. *Endangered Daughters: Discrimination and Development in Asia.* London and New York: Routledge.

Davin, Delia. 1998. "Gender and Migration in China," in Flemming Christiansen and Junzuo Zhang, eds. *Village Inc.: Chinese Rural Society in the 1990s*, pp. 230–40. Honolulu: University of Hawaii Press.

Deere, Carmen Diana and Cheryl R. Doss. 2006. "The Gender Asset Gap: What Do We Know and Why Does It Matter?" *Feminist Economics* 12(1/2): 1–50.

Dong, Xiao-yuan. 1996. "Two-Tier Land Tenure System and Sustained Economic Growth in Post-1978 Rural China." *World Development* 24(5): 915–28.

Dong, Xiao-yuan, Fiona MacPhail, Paul Bowles, and Samuel Ho. 2004. "Gender Segmentation at Work in China's Privatized Rural Industry: Some Evidence from Shandong and Jiangsu." *World Development* 32(6): 979–98.

Dong, Xiao-yuan, Jianchun Yang, Fenglian Du, and Sai Ding. 2006. "Women's Employment and Public-Sector Restructuring: The Case of Urban China," in Grace Lee and Malcolm Warner, eds. *Unemployment in China: Economy, Human Resources & Labor Markets*, pp. 87–107. London: Routledge Contemporary China Series.

Du, Fenglian and Xiao-yuan Dong. 2007. Why Women Have Longer Unemployment Durations than Men in Post-Restructuring Urban China? MPIA Working Paper, 2007–23, The Gender Challenge Fund of the Poverty and Economic Policy (PEP) Research Network.

Elliott, Kimberly Ann and Richard B. Freeman. 2003. *Can Labor Standards Improve Under Globalization?* Washington, DC: Institute for International Economics.

Elson, Diane. 1995. *Male Bias in the Development Process*, 2nd ed. Manchester: Manchester University Press.

——. 1999. "Labor Markets as Gendered Institutions: Equality, Efficiency and Empowerment Issues." *World Development* 27(3): 611–27.

Elson, Diane and Nilüfer Çağatay. 2000. "The Social Content of Macroeconomic Policies." *World Development* 28(7): 1347–64.

Elson, Diane and Ruth Pearson. 1981. "'Nimble Fingers Make Cheap Workers': An Analysis of Women's Employment in Third World Export Manufacturing." *Feminist Review* 7: 87–108.

Fan, Gang, Maria Rosa Lunati, and David O'Connor. 1998. Labor Market Aspects of State Enterprise Reform in China. Technical Paper 141, OECD Development Center.

Ford Foundation. 2001. Summary of Gender and Property Rights Workshop (in Chinese), unpublished draft.

Friedman, Barry L. 1996. "Employment and Social Protection Policies in China: Big Reforms and Limited Outcomes," in Gregory K. Schoepfle, ed. *Changes in China's Labor Market: Implications for the Future*, pp. 151–66. Washington, DC: US Department of Labor, Bureau of International Labor Affairs.

Fussell, Elizabeth. 2000. "Making Labor More Flexible: The Recomposition of Tijuana's Maquiladora Female Labor Force." *Feminist Economics* 6(3): 59–80.

Gaetano, Arianne M. and Tamara Jacka, eds. 2004. *On the Move: Women in Rural-to-Urban Migration in Contemporary China.* New York: Columbia University Press.

Gal, Susan and Gail Kligman. 2000. *Reproducing Gender: Politics, Publics, and Everyday Life After Socialism.* Princeton, NJ: Princeton University Press.

Gao, Xiaoxian. 1994. "China's Modernization and Changes in the Social Status of Rural Women," in Christina Gilmartin, Gail Hershatter, Lisa Rofel, and Tyrene White, eds. *Engendering China: Women, Culture, and the State*, pp. 80–97. Cambridge, MA: Harvard University Press.

Guan, Xinping. 2005. "China's Social Policy: Reform and Development in the Context of Marketization and Globalization," in Huck-ju Kwon, ed. *Transforming the Developmental Welfare State in East Asia*, pp. 231–56. Houndmills: Palgrave.

Gertler, Jeffrey L. 2004. "What China's WTO Accession is All About," in Deepak Bhattasali, Shantong Li, and Will Martin, eds. *China and the WTO*, pp. 21–8. Washington, DC: The World Bank.

Giles, John, Albert Park, and Fang Cai. 2006. "Re-Employment of Dislocated Workers in Urban China: the Roles of Information and Incentives." *Journal of Comparative Economics* 34(3): 582–607.

Grapard, Ulla. 1997. "Theoretical Issues of Gender in the Transition from Socialist Regimes." *Journal of Economic Issues* 31(3): 665–86.

Gustafsson, Bjorn and Shi Li. 2000. "Economic Transformation and the Gender Earnings Gap in Urban China." *Journal of Population Economics* 13(2): 305–29.

——. 2003. "The Ethnic Minority-Majority Income Gap in Rural China During Transition." *Economic Development and Cultural Change* 51(4): 805–22.

Haddad, Lawrence, Lynn Brown, Andrea Richter, and Lisa Smith. 1995. "The Gender Dimensions of Economic Adjustment Policies: Potential Interactions and Evidence to Date." *World Development* 23(6): 881–96.

Hannum, Emily and Yu Xie. 1998. "Ethnic Stratification in Northwest China: Occupational Differences between Han Chinese and National Minorities in Xinjiang, 1982–1990." *Demography* 35(3): 323–33.

Hare, Denise, Li Yang, and Daniel Englander. 2007. "Land Management in Rural China and Its Gender Implications." *Feminist Economics* 13(3/4): 35–61.

Hesketh, Therese, Li Lu, and Zhu Wei Xing. 2005. "The Effect of China's One-Child Policy after 25 Years." *New England Journal of Medicine* 353(11): 1171–76.

Ho, Samuel P. S., Paul Bowles, and Xiao-yuan Dong. 2003. "'Letting Go of the Small': An Analysis of Privatizing Rural Enterprises in Shandong and Jiangsu." *Journal of Development Studies* 39(4): 1–26.

Hopkins, Barbara E. 2007. "Western Cosmetics in The Gendered Development of Consumer Culture in China." *Feminist Economics* 13(3/4): 287–306.

Hossfeld, Karen. 1990. "'Their Logic Against Them': Contradictions in Sex, Race, and Class in Silicon Valley," in Kathryn Ward, ed. *Women Workers and Global Restructuring*, pp. 149–78. Ithaca, NY: Cornell University/ILR Press.

International Labour Organization. 2007. "Export Processing Zones by Sector." http://www.ilo.org/public/english/dialogue/sector/themes/epz/stats.htm (accessed March 2007).

Kabeer, Naila. 2004. "Globalization, Labor Standards, and Women's Rights: Dilemmas of Collective (In)action in an Interdependent World." *Feminist Economics* 10(1): 3–35.

Kahn, Jeremy. 2006. "Foreign Ventures Come to Terms with China's Labor Unions." *World Trade* 19(12): 36–40.

Khan, Azizur and Carl Riskin. 2005. "China's Household Income and Its Distribution, 1995 and 2002." *China Quarterly* 182: 356–84.

Koggel, Christine. 2003. "Globalization and Women's Paid Work: Expanding Freedom?" *Feminist Economics* 9(2/3): 163–84.

Lardy, Nicholas R. 1983. *Agriculture in China's Economic Development*. Cambridge, UK: Cambridge University Press.

——. 1994. *China in the World Economy*. Washington, DC: Institute for International Economics.

——. 1998. *China's Unfinished Economic Revolution*. Washington, DC: Brookings Institution Press.

Lastarria-Cornhiel, Susana. 1997. "Impact of Privatization on Gender and Property Rights in Africa." *World Development* 25(8): 1317–33.

Lazreg, Marnia. 2000. Making the Transition Work for Women in Europe and Central Asia. Discussion Paper 411, World Bank.

Lee, Ching Kwan. 2005. Livelihood Struggles and Market Reform: Unmaking Chinese Labour After State Socialism. Occasional Paper 2, United Nations Research Institute for Social Development.

Lee, Hong Yung. 2000. "*Xiagang*, The Chinese Style of Laying Off Workers." *Asian Survey* 40(6): 914–37.

Lim, Linda. 1990. "Women's Work in Export Factories: the Politics of a Cause," in Irene Tinker, ed. *Persistent Inequalities*, pp. 101–19. New York: Oxford University Press.

Lin, Justin. 1987. "The Household Responsibility System Reform in China: A Peasant's Institutional Choice." *American Journal of Agricultural Economics* 69(2): 410–15.

Liu, Jieyu. 2007. "Gender Dynamics and Redundancy in Urban China." *Feminist Economics* 13(3/4): 125–58.

Liu, Minquan, Luodan Xu, and Liu Liu. 2004. "Wage-Related Labour Standards and FDI in China: Some Survey Findings From Guangdong Province." *Pacific Economic Review* 9(3): 225–43.

Liu, Pak-Wai, Xin Meng, and Junsen Zhang. 2000. "Sectoral Gender Wage Differentials and Discrimination in the Transitional Chinese Economy." *Journal of Population Economics* 13(2): 331–52.

Liu, Xiaoyun, Terry Sicular, and Xian Xin. 2006. "Rising Gender Gap in Non-Agricultural Employment in Rural China," in Shunfeng Song and Aimin Chen, eds. *China's Rural Economy After WTO*, pp. 80–94. Aldershot, Hampshire, England: Ashgate Publishing Ltd.

MacPhail, Fiona and Xiao-yuan Dong. 2007. "Women's Market Work and Household Status in Rural China: Evidence from Jiangsu and Shandong in the Late 1990s." *Feminist Economics* 13(3/4): 93–124.

Mahopatra, Sandeep, Scott Rozelle, and Rachael Goodhue. 2007. "Rise of Self-Employment in China: Development or Distress?" *World Development* 35(1): 163–81.

Maurer-Fazio, Margaret and James Hughes. 2002. "The Effects of Market Liberalization on the Relative Earnings of Chinese Women." *Journal of Comparative Economics* 30(4): 709–31.

Maurer-Fazio, Margaret, James Hughes, and Dandan Zhang. 2007. "An Ocean Formed from One Hundred Rivers: The Effects of Ethnicity, Gender, Marriage, and Location on Labor Force Participation in Urban China." *Feminist Economics* 13(3/4): 159–87.

McMillan, John, John Whalley, and Lijing Zhu. 1989. "The Impact of China's Economic Reforms on Agricultural Productivity Growth." *Journal of Political Economy* 97(4): 781–807.

Meng, Xin. 1998. "Male-Female Wage Determination and Gender Wage Discrimination in China's Rural Industrial Sector." *Labor Economics* 5: 67–89.

National Bureau of Statistics (NBS). 1994. *Statistical Yearbook*. Beijing: China Statistical Press.

——. 2005. *Statistical Yearbook*. Beijing: China Statistical Press.

Naughton, Barry. 1996. *Growing Out of the Plan: Chinese Economic Reform 1978–1993*. Cambridge, UK: Cambridge University Press.

——. 2007. *The Chinese Economy: Transitions and Growth*. Cambridge, MA: MIT Press.

Nelson, Julie A. 1995. "Feminism and Economics." *Journal of Economic Perspectives* 9(2): 131–48.

Ngo, Hang-Yue. 2002. "Trends in Occupational Sex Segregation in Urban China." *Gender, Technology and Development* 6(2): 175–96.

Nussbaum, Martha. 2003. "Capabilities as Fundamental Entitlements: Sen and Social Justice." *Feminist Economics* 9(2/3): 33–60.

People's Daily. 2003. "Law Protects Long-Term Land Use of China's Farmers." March 2. http://english.people.com.cn/200303/02/eng20030302_112533.shtml (accessed March 2007).

Power, Marilyn. 2004. "Social Provisioning as a Starting Point for Feminist Economics." *Feminist Economics* 10(3): 3–19.

Pun Ngai. 2005. *Made in China: Women Factories Workers in a Global Marketplace*. Durham, NC: Duke University Press.

——. 2007. "Gendering the Dormitory Labor System: Production, Reproduction, and Migrant Labor in South China." *Feminist Economics* 13(3/4): 239–58.

Qian, Yingyi. 2003. "How Reform Worked in China," in Dani Rodrik, ed. *In Search of Prosperity: Analytic Narratives on Economic Growth*, pp. 297–333. Princeton, NJ: Princeton University Press.

Ravallion, Martin and Shaohua Chen. 2004. China's (Uneven) Progress against Poverty. Policy Research Working Paper 3408, World Bank.

Razavi, Shahra. 1999. "Export-Oriented Employment, Poverty and Gender: Contested Accounts." *Development and Change* 30(3): 653–83.

Ross, Robert J. S. and Anita Chan. 2002. "From North-South to South-South: The True Face of Global Competition." *Foreign Affairs* 81(5): 8–13.

Robeyns, Ingrid. 2003. "Sen's Capability Approach and Gender Inequality: Selecting Relevant Capabilities." *Feminist Economics* 9(2/3): 61–92.

Robinson, Jean C. 1985. "Of Women and Washing Machines: Employment, Housework, and the Reproduction of Motherhood in Socialist China." *China Quarterly* 101: 32–57.

Rodgers, Yana van der Muelen and Günseli Berik. 2006. "Asia's Race to Capture Post-MFA Markets: A Snapshot of Labor Standards, Compliance, and Impacts on Competitiveness." *Asian Development Review* 23(1): 55–86.

Rodrik, Dani. 2003. "Introduction: What Do We Learn From Country Narratives?" in Dani Rodrik, ed. *In Search of Prosperity: Analytic Narratives on Economic Growth*, pp. 1–19. Princeton, NJ: Princeton University Press.

Rozelle, Scott, Xiao-yuan Dong, Linxiu Zhang, and Andrew Mason. 2002. "Gender Wage Gaps in Post-Reform Rural China." *Pacific Economic Review* 7(1): 157–79.

Sen, Amartya. 1990. "Gender and Cooperative Conflicts," in Irene Tinker, ed. *Persistent Inequalities*, pp. 123–49. New York: Oxford University Press.

——. 1999. *Development as Freedom*. New York: Alfred A. Knopf.

Stacey, Judith. 1983. *Patriarchy and Socialist Revolution in China*. Berkeley: University of California Press.

Summerfield, Gale. 1994. "Economic Reform and the Employment of Chinese Women." *Journal of Economic Issues* 28(3): 715–32.

——. 2006. "Gender Equity and Land Reform in Rural China," in Jane Jaquette and Gale Summerfield, eds. *Women and Gender Equity in Development Theory and Practice: Institutions, Resources, and Mobilization*, pp. 137–58. Durham, NC: Duke University Press.

Tan, Lin, Zhenzhen Zheng, and Yueping Song. 2006. "Trade Liberalization, Women's Migration and Reproductive Health in China," in Caren Grown, Elissa Braunstein, and Anju Malhotra, eds. Trading *Women's Health and Rights? Trade Liberalization and Reproductive Health in Developing Countries*, pp. 121–42. London: Zed Press.

Tan, Shen. 1998. "Gender Difference in the Migration of Rural Labor." *Social Science in China* 2: 70–7.

Tinker, Irene and Gale Summerfield, eds. 1999. *Women's Rights to House and Land: China, Laos, Vietnam*. Boulder, CO: Lynne Rienner Publishers.

United Nations Development Programme (UNDP). 1999. *The China Human Development Report 1999*. Beijing: China Financial & Economic Publishing House.

——. 2006. *Human Development Report 2006*. New York: Oxford University Press.

United Nations Development Programme in China. 2003. "China's Ascension to WTO: Challenges for Women in the Agricultural and Industrial Sectors." Report for UNDP, Beijing, China.

Weitzman, Martin and Chenggang Xu. 1994. "Chinese Township Village Enterprises as Vaguely Defined Cooperatives." *Journal of Comparative Economics* 18(2): 121–45.

Wolf, Margery. 1985. *Revolution Postponed: Women in Contemporary China*. Palo Alto, CA: Stanford University Press.

World Bank. 1992. *Strategies for Reducing Poverty in the 1990s*. Washington, DC: IBRD.

——. 1997. *China Engaged*. Washington, DC: The World Bank.

Xu, Gary and Susan Feiner. 2007. "Meinü Jingji/China's Beauty Economy: Buying Looks, Shifting Value, and Changing Places." *Feminist Economics* 13(3/4): 307–23.

Yee, Janet. 2001. "Women's Changing Roles in the Chinese Economy." *The Journal of Economics* 27(2): 55–67.

Zhang, Linxiu, Alan de Brauw, and Scott Rozelle. 2004. "China's Rural Labor Market Development and Its Gender Implications." *China Economic Review* 15(2): 230–47.

Zhao, Yaohui. 2002. "Causes and Consequences of Return Migration: Recent Evidence from China." *Journal of Comparative Economics* 30(2): 376–94.

Zhu, Ling and Zhong-yu Jiang. 2001. "Gender Inequality in the Land Tenure System in Rural China." *World Economy and China* 9(2). http://www.iwep.org.cn/wec/English/articles/2001_02/zhuling.htm (accessed March 2007).

LAND MANAGEMENT IN RURAL CHINA AND ITS GENDER IMPLICATIONS

Denise Hare, Li Yang, and Daniel Englander

INTRODUCTION

China's path towards economic liberalization has gendered impacts in the agricultural sector. As early as the late 1970s, China began to implement reforms that were characterized by rapid growth in the rural industrial sector, creating a situation of labor flight from agricultural to nonagricultural activities.[1] Those who remained to work the land have experienced lower rates of income growth, often coupled with ambiguities surrounding their long-term rights to the land that they cultivate.[2] Women take a great deal of responsibility for the day-to-day work of farming in China. Though a trend towards the "feminization of agriculture" is a popular notion, some would argue that women's labor has always played a dominant role in agricultural work (e.g., Laurel Bossen 2002). In any case, women are an important mainstay of agricultural production in China, though our data suggest that their access to land is increasingly more tenuous than that of their male counterparts.

This paper explores the interplay between gendered patterns of resource access and the design of property rights policy that supports an efficient agricultural sector in which women play an important role. We are particularly concerned with documenting and analyzing gender differences in land allocations within the context of changes to China's rural land management policy. Equity has long been an important consideration of China's agricultural land management policy. Maintenance of equity was achieved during the 1980s and early 1990s through village-level adjustments and contractual reallocations of land among member households. However, the short-term contracts necessitated by such a policy have raised considerable debate about tenure security and production efficiency (Loren Brandt, Jikun Huang, Guo Li, and Scott Rozelle 2002). In practice, efforts to increase land tenure security, beginning in the latter part of the 1990s, paradoxically have had the opposite effect on many women: as contract periods grow longer and the incidence of policy readjustments becomes less frequent, women may be increasingly disadvantaged in their land-use rights and access to land (Li Zongmin 2002; Jennifer Brown 2003).

Based on survey data collected in 2002 from rural households in Hunan and Shanxi provinces, this paper contributes new evidence on China to the growing feminist economics literature on land rights. This literature has documented consistent patterns of women's disadvantage in access to land and possession of land rights in countries around the world. Our paper provides a descriptive account of trends in landlessness in China, by gender. We then examine the determinants of landlessness and its duration, taking into account characteristics of individuals and their communities through multivariate analysis. Our findings suggest that policies implemented coincident to China's WTO accession and meant to improve the efficiency of the agricultural sector have contributed to widening gender inequalities in access to land. On the basis of these findings we call for new or redesigned agricultural land policies that specifically address the emerging relative disadvantages of rural women.

Women's land access and its welfare implications in rural China

With the advent of China's Household Responsibility System in 1978,[3] rights to agricultural land use were returned from the collective to the household level. By the early 1980s, most rural households had entered into contracts with their collectives to farm the parcels of allocated land and to retain surplus production, in return for meeting various obligations such as taxes, fees, and in-kind quotas. The amount of land allocated to a household was determined by the village land endowment as well as the household's labor supply and consumption needs; both the size and the composition of the household population factored into the initial allocation decision. Moreover, commencing in the early 1980s and throughout the first cycle of contracts, which typically had a duration of fifteen years, periodic land readjustments were designed to address household population changes, such as the arrival of new members through marriages, births, or the departure of existing members through out-migration or death. Under these arrangements, household land allocations remained fairly egalitarian within villages. If a woman followed the traditional arrangements of joining her husband's household upon marriage, she could expect that her birth household would lose some land while her husband's household would gain land in the next readjustment.[4] In this first interval of allocations, adjustments could be as frequent as every year, and in any event, one could expect a readjustment within three to five years. Following the demise of the collective, land shares responded to demographic changes and marital transitions and did not have long-lasting impacts on women's land allocations.

During that period, women's actual access to land was critically tied to her association with a household. Land was officially held by the village and contracted to rural households, in accordance with terms set by the state. In practice, the contract was typically negotiated with an individual male household representative whose name appeared on the document record (Jennifer Duncan and Li Ping 2001; Brown 2003). Therefore, a woman's attachment to a household as wife or daughter was essential for her to have access to land. Transfers of land to women through inheritance or in the event of divorce could not be taken for granted and, in fact, seemed more the exception than the rule (Li 2002). Tamara Jacka (1997) makes an interesting argument tying married women's high rates of participation in agriculture to their disadvantaged status with respect to land. Specifically, she proposes that wives were more likely to remain at home and farm, even when their husbands were working in nonagricultural jobs, to demonstrate their claim to the land in the event of a divorce or the death of the husband. Should such circumstances arise, a woman's best chance of retaining access to the land when contested by her husband's family, according to Jacka, was to show a history of active cultivation of the land. This reasoning illustrates that women's rights to land were more tenuous than their male counterparts, even when the allocation policy allowed for adjustments in response to demographic events.

The situation becomes more complicated as we enter the more recent cycle of land allocations and its accompanying legislation. The 1998 Land Management Law extended contract durations to thirty years (from fifteen) and reduced opportunities for villages to exercise land readjustments in response to demographic changes. As such, the possibility that a household would experience an increase in its land allocation with the arrival of a daughter-in-law (or, in fact, any new member) is substantially reduced. At the same time, the household the daughter-in-law left does not necessarily suffer a decline in land. The Rural Land Contract Law, implemented in 2003, specifically preserves women's land allocations in their natal villages until they are able to gain a land allocation through their husband's household. To that end, it may seem, theoretically, that women's net rights to land remain the same but that the household through which their access is realized changes. In practice, the situation seems less balanced. For women who marry outside of their natal village, continuing to farm the land allocated to them through their parents' household is inconvenient, at best. Even among those who remain in the same village, social norms discourage daughters from staking a claim to land through their parents' household. Various sources converge to a common assessment that women, by and large, are hindered by efforts to freeze allocations and reduce readjustments, and their likelihoods of successfully accessing land through their birth households following marriage are very low (Duncan and Li 2001; Li 2002; Brown 2003).

Though much of the attention surrounding the issue of disadvantages in land use rights and access has focused on married women, in fact, there is reason to be concerned about women more generally, independent of their marital status. For instance, Li (2002) notes that there are discrepancies in the amount of land contracted to unmarried men and unmarried women in some villages. Different treatments result from expectations that an unmarried man will marry and bring a wife into the household while an unmarried woman will marry and depart her household. At the same time, divorced and widowed women are particularly vulnerable to losing land (or losing the opportunity to earn income from land) that they accessed through their husbands. Former or late husbands' families may have priority over use of the land or the village may simply take it back. The divorced or widowed woman's natal village is not a likely source of replacement land, even though the woman may have no other choice but to return there. Drawing on fieldwork reports from several sources, Li (2002) concludes that how women fare under such circumstances from place to place varies considerably but suggests that a quick remarriage may often be the best option for regaining land security. It is ironic that marriage emerges as the solution, although it may partly explain why the numbers of unmarried women in rural China are so very low.[5]

The situation of limited land access described here has implications for the well-being of women and their households. Given its key role in agricultural production, a reduction in land holdings can be expected to have a negative influence on household income-earning capacity in agriculture. In a recent analysis of nationwide farm household survey data, Terry Sicular and Zhao Yaohui find that land is the second most important contributing factor to agricultural production (after variable inputs), with an elasticity of 0.32, and it is also shown to have a positive and statistically significant effect on returns to labor in agriculture, as well as to household income generation (2004: 245, 251, 253). Also worthy of consideration is the influence of landlessness and the broader consequences of any status change on women's positions within their households.

Efforts to document and understand the gendered division of property rights arrangements, particularly access to land, contribute importantly towards understanding rural women's positions within their households and their exit options. Examination of whether official land policy treats men and women differently is insufficient, as is well demonstrated in the literature (Bina Agarwal 1994a, 1994b; Carmen Diana Deere 1995; Carmen Diana Deere and Magdalena León 2001, 2003). Traditional practices surrounding, for instance, marriage and inheritance may impede the exercise of legal rights. Examining the situation of women and land in South Asia and pointing specifically to localities where daughters commonly marry outside of their birth villages, Agarwal (1994b) argues that women are deliberately excluded from inheritance of parental land, and the combination of family structures, government institutions that may be open to manipulation, and potentially unsympathetic (male) government officials makes it very difficult for these women to successfully invoke the inheritance laws that would guarantee their land rights. Even in cases where women retain inheritance rights, access to the full value of income generated from the land cannot be assumed, as Agarwal reports: "Pressure on women to sharecrop their land to relatives (at below market rates) is usually high, as are the difficulties of ensuring that they get their fair share of the harvest" (1994b: 532).

Despite the difficulties women may face in inheritance practices, inheritance appears to be the most common route to women's acquisition of land among the twelve Latin American countries studied by Deere and León (2001). However, the authors note that women remain less likely to own land relative to men, that their land holdings are typically smaller in quantity and less desirable in quality, and the same factors that contribute negatively towards women's acquisition of land are likely also to make them more vulnerable to losing land. A strong theme running through this literature is the notion that what may appear to be a small or trivial gender-based disadvantage is compounded through its interaction with other small disadvantages – such as higher transaction costs in input and output markets – so the net outcome reflects severe gender disparities.

To our knowledge only a small body of scholarly work investigates the impacts of gendered land rights with data from China. Using 1996 farm household data from Shaanxi province, Zhu Ling and Jiang Zhongyi (2000) show that the presence of a landless woman significantly increases the household's likelihood of falling into poverty, conditional on the household's days of nonagricultural employment. Zhu and Jiang also note that women without land are more likely to exercise decision-making responsibilities concerning their households' agricultural production activities. They hypothesize that reduced landholdings push many of these households into the nonagricultural sector, which often favors the employment of men over women, thereby increasing women's obligations, and at the same time, their authority within the household's agricultural production sphere. How this may influence women's status more generally within the household is unclear, as disproportionate weight may be attached to males earning income from jobs outside the household. More recently, Junjie Chen and Gale Summerfield (2007, in this volume) explore the interaction of population and land rights policies over several decades of reform, identifying gender disparities in implementations and outcomes, some persisting in spite of efforts made to address explicit gender bias against women.

INCIDENCE OF LANDLESSNESS AND ITS IMPACT

We now turn to examine the evidence on landlessness, including its patterns and its consequences among the households in our data set. Our analysis draws on survey data from 412 farm households in the provinces of Shaanxi and Hunan that was collected by the Research Center for the Rural Economy (RCRE) in August of 2002.[6] These provinces have typical characteristics of the western plains and central hilly agricultural regions, respectively. Hunan is mainly a rice-growing region, whereas Shaanxi households primarily produce wheat, corn, cotton, and fruit. The second cycle of land allocations began as early as 1994 in some of the Hunan survey sites and was completed by 1998 in both Hunan and Shaanxi sites (when the land law that moved to thirty-year leases was passed).

We selected two counties within each province to provide regional representation of each province. Sample counties from Shaanxi include Dali (eastern region) and Baoji (western region), while those from Hunan include Ningxiang (northern region) and Qiyang (southern region). Three villages, stratified by income, were selected within each county. Three groups (formerly called production teams) were selected within villages to represent varying levels of land readjustment frequencies. Finally, households were selected randomly from the groups' household rosters, representing 24 percent of group total household populations and 20 percent of group total contract land areas. Interviews were conducted on site with one or more household members present. Information was gathered about conditions of the household as well as each of its individual members.

Household per capita land area and net income are on the low side, among surveyed households in both provinces, relative to respective provincial averages and national averages (Table 1). For that reason, the inferences drawn from the data will be representative of conditions that

Table 1 Characteristics of sample villages, in comparison with provincial and national averages

	Sample villages in Shaanxi (Obs = 6)	Sample villages in Hunan (Obs = 6)	Shaanxi province	Hunan province	National
Per capita land area $(mu)^a$	1.47	0.86	2.78	1.09	1.69
Per capita net income $(yuan)^b$	1,274	1,779	1,490.8	2,299.5	2,366.4
Workers employed in agriculture (percent)	74.2	68.2	73.9	71.5	67.3
Workers employed in nonagricultural jobs within the county (percent)	20.6	7.8			
Workers employed in nonagricultural jobs outside the county (percent)	5.2	24.0			

Notes: Provincial and national statistics represent rural measurements.
[a]One *mu* is equivalent to 0.067 hectare or 0.165 acres.
[b]One yuan is equivalent to 12 cents (US).
Sources: Sample averages from the Research Center for the Rural Economy (RCRE) (2003); provincial and national averages from the National Bureau of Statistics (2002).

prevail in low- to middle-income regions of China, particularly those with higher population densities than average, in contrast to more prosperous or less densely settled regions. Surveyed villages in both Shaanxi and Hunan display high percentages of labor force employment in agriculture, 74.2 and 68.2 percent, respectively. These figures are well in line with comparable provincial and national statistics. Finally, one important difference between surveyed villages in Shaanxi and those in Hunan deserves attention: nonagricultural employment in Shaanxi is largely local whereas those engaged in nonagricultural employment in Hunan primarily consist of migrants who find their work outside their county of residence. With its more central location, particularly its proximity to Guangzhou and the Pearl River Delta region, coupled with its high population density, it is not surprising to see that Hunan-based respondents tend to be employed outside. Shaanxi is further removed from China's large population centers, and the surveyed villages have more modest levels of local nonagricultural development. The nonagricultural occupations represented in the data from Shaanxi include construction, transportation, and commerce – all typically small-scale, often household-based, ventures. While there is some rural industry organized at the township level, its development falls far short of that observed in more prosperous regions of China (the coastal regions, mostly), so there is less opportunity for a substantial number of households to move out of the agricultural sector entirely.

We can learn more about the breadth of the problem of landlessness and identify who is most likely to experience it through an inspection of the survey data. Table 2 presents information about the proportion of the adults in the sample who report being landless at the time of the survey. We use the term "landless" to indicate that an individual has no share of the village contract land, though she may reside in a household where other members possess contract allocations. Therefore she may well have access to the land allocated to other members of her household, despite her individual landless status. Among men and women between the ages of 20 and 59, we find that more than 5 percent of those interviewed currently lack a contract land allocation. Moreover, it is clear that the problem is concentrated among the women and is particularly severe for those aged 20 to 29; more than one-third of those interviewed report that they are landless. The only other demographic group with any notable degree of landlessness is the set of women aged 30 to 39. Their landless proportion, however, is only 6.9 percent. Because a loss of land is usually associated with marriage, few adult single women are observed to be landless. Among landless women represented in Table 2, only four are unmarried. Among the married women in our sample who are currently landless, as well as those who have experienced landlessness in the past, the year they lost contract responsibility land coincides with their year of marriage in all but a few cases. Therefore, our subsequent analysis and discussion will focus on married women, exclusively.

We can infer recent trends in landlessness among married women from retrospective data collected in our survey. Individuals were asked to report previous incidence of landlessness, including the duration and explanations for their occurrence. Combining data on landless spells with individuals' reported age and year of marriage, we construct ratios of landlessness to the total number of married women. Figure 1 demonstrates

Table 2 Proportion of sample currently landless, by age and sex (964 observations)

Age	Female	Male	Total
20–9 years	35.96	0	17.30
30–9 years	6.90	0.81	3.75
40–9 years	0	0	0
50–9 years	0.78	0	0.41
Total	10.37	0.21	5.29

Source: RCRE (2003).

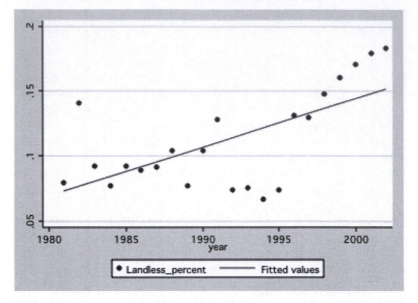

Figure 1 Landless women as a percent of married women, 1981–2002
Source: RCRE (2003).

the general upward trend in this ratio, showing a sharp increase in recent years. By 2002, nearly one in five married women did not have a land allocation. Further evidence about the growing seriousness of the problem is provided by the All-China Women's Federation, which reports an average annual increase of ten percent or more in the number of letters received registering complaints about violations of women's land rights between 1999 and 2002 (Fang Yuzhu 2003).

While our data do not allow us to calculate married women's rates of landlessness beyond 2002, we may draw some information about future trends from responses to other survey questions. Among the thirty-six village-groups in our sample, 39 percent revealed that they do not intend to conduct any subsequent land reallocations or readjustments. Therefore, for a noteworthy portion of the sample, landlessness is a permanent condition. The proportion of communities in our data intending no future land changes is consistent with that reported by other studies. In a 2003 RCRE study, the comparable figure is 36 percent (of ninety-six village-groups surveyed); and more recently, among a sample of seventy-eight villages, 40 percent had ceased to change land allocations (Qian Wenrong and Mao Yingchun 2005). In the longer term, if children born to rural households no longer acquire land through reallocations, then opportunities to inherit family land will take on even greater importance. Among the households in

42

our survey, 83 percent expect that their land holdings will be passed on only to sons, not to daughters. One might also consider the case of Meitan county, in Guizhou province, where land allocations were frozen in 1987 with no subsequent policy-led reallocations or readjustments.[7] In households where there are no sons, daughters routinely partition land from their parents' households: they claim their share of land, farm it, and can even collect rental income from their land share. If a household has sons, however, it is less likely that a daughter will partition her share, and if she does (at the initiative of her father or brothers), it is even more rare for her to be able to collect rent from leasing it out.[8]

Other noteworthy trends in the experience of landlessness emerge by considering the rates among women married before and after the second cycle of land allocations, as well as the duration of their landless spells (Table 3). Among married women in their twenties and thirties, about half have experienced a period of landlessness in conjunction with their marriage. However, the incidence is much greater for those who married following the second cycle of land allocation in their husbands' respective villages or groups. Interestingly, the measured duration of the landless spell appears nearly identical between those who married before and after the second cycle land allocation. However, this measure understates the difference in true length of landlessness, as among the fifty-three who married earlier, only eight remained without land at the time of the survey. Among the group marrying later, thirty-three of the thirty-eight observed periods are censored because these women remained landless; therefore we cannot observe the true duration of their landless state, and the reported values understate the length of their landless spells.

Table 3 Married women's probabilities of landlessness and landless spell durations

		Married women, aged 20–39	
	Total	Married before second cycle land allocation	Married after second cycle land allocation
Probability of permanent landlessness (percent)	51.91 ($n=183$)	39.85 ($n=153$)	84.00 ($n=50$)
Duration of landless spell (years)	3.58 ($n=91$, 41 cases censored)	3.55 ($n=53$, 8 cases censored)	3.63 ($n=38$, 33 cases censored)

Notes: The second row of figures is calculated using only those women who report some period of landlessness subsequent to their marriage (four observations are lost here due to missing data). Censored observations represent women who remain landless.
Source: RCRE (2003).

Table 4 provides further information about how women experience landlessness by comparing the responses of those who remain landless to those who experienced landlessness but now have land. For both groups, having missed their village-group's reallocation is the key reason for lacking contract land. Nearly 80 percent of those whose condition of landlessness was resolved report obtaining their land allocation through a village-group readjustment. Among those currently landless, nearly two-thirds are uncertain, doubtful, or have no expectations of getting land in the future, while only a little more than a third report any positive expectation about obtaining a land allocation. The vast majority (greater than 80 percent) is unable to predict the year in which they expect to receive a land allocation.

Table 5 illustrates the economic impact of losing land on the households with landless women compared with other households. Households are

Table 4 Reasons for married women's landlessness and their expectations for obtaining land (in percentages)

	Ever landless married women, aged 20–39	
	Continue to be landless (41 observations)	Now have land (50 observations)
Why do/did you have no land?		
Missed the land reallocation	85.37	94.00
Present for reallocation, but land allocation delayed	2.44	4.00
Other reasons	12.20	2.00
Total	100	100
Do you believe that you will get land?		
Certain	17.95	
Likely	20.51	
Unlikely	2.56	
Impossible	17.95	
Do not know	41.03	
Total	100	
In what year do you expect to get land?		
This year	11.54	
At expiration of current thirty-year contracts	7.69	
Do not know	80.77	
Total	100	
How did you get your land?		
Small land readjustment		54.00
Big land readjustment		24.00
Reserve land		20.00
Other means		2.00
Total		100

Source: RCRE (2003).

Table 5 Economic impact of women's landlessness on their households' output and income

| | Low-income group (<1,000 yuan) | | Middle-income group (1,001–1,700 yuan) | | High-income group (>1,700 yuan) | |
	Households with a landless married woman (Obs = 9)	Other households (Obs = 52)	Households with a landless married woman (Obs = 17)	Other households (Obs = 44)	Households with a landless married woman (Obs = 19)	Other households (Obs = 42)
Per capita contract land area (*mu*)	0.71	1.11	0.46	0.90	0.64	1.02
Per capita income from agriculture (yuan)	362	388	301	405	453	652
Per capita net income (yuan)	588	628	1,336	1,327	3,124	2,732
Agricultural income share of total income (percent)	0.72	0.67	0.24	0.33	0.17	0.26

Source: RCRE (2003).

45

divided into three groups of sixty-one households each, based on annual income. Within each of the income groups, households with landless women report lower levels of per capita contract land area and per capita income from agriculture, as would be expected. However, the middle- and high-income group seems better able to compensate for their lack of land by supplementing their income with earnings from other (nonagricultural) sources, such that their per capita total (net) incomes reflect little difference in response to the presence of a landless woman. Households with landless women in the low-income group, however, are consistently worse off relative to other households in their income group, as well as to households with or without landless women in all other income groups. Worthy of note is the high proportion of agricultural income to total income of the low-income households – 72 and 67 percent, respectively – for households with landless women and other households. There is no doubt that the lack of nonagricultural income sources imposes a heavy penalty on household incomes, regardless of their land endowments. Reliance on agriculture leaves little opportunity to overcome land deficiencies, and therefore we find the greatest evidence for negative impacts of landlessness on household incomes among low-income households.

While the actual income discrepancy among low-income households is relatively modest (40 yuan, or 6.5 percent of the average household income of the low-income group as a whole), the perception that having a landless woman contributes negatively to household economic well-being is widely held. Among the households in our survey, 82 percent report the belief that women's landlessness will decrease the household's income. Respondents also noted the concern that reduced capacity to grow food can have a negative impact on the expenditure side of the budget, as food that must be purchased in the marketplace is more costly than food produced in-kind.

The figures in Table 6 demonstrate how women's landlessness influences their participation in household and agricultural decision making. Once again, households are categorized by low-, middle-, and high-income groups. Across the board, in households with landless women, women are less likely to take part in decision making regarding agricultural production (note this result is contrary to the findings of Zhu and Jiang [2000] reported earlier in this paper). These disparities are widest among the low-income group and narrow as incomes rise. Among the high-income group, women have more prominent decision-making roles in all categories and may reflect their residual responsibilities in agriculture and in their households in cases where men have deeper engagement in the nonagricultural sector. Landless women among the low-income group of households display a notable lack of say, except in decisions about daily family expenditures, where women generally appear to have more clout.

Table 6 Women's landlessness and their participation in decision making

Percent of households where women participate in decisions about	Low-income group (<1,000 yuan)		Middle-income group (1,001–1,701 yuan)		High-income group (>1,700 yuan)	
	Households with a landless married woman (Obs = 9)	Other households (Obs = 52)	Households with a landless married woman (Obs = 17)	Other households (Obs = 44)	Households with a landless married woman (Obs = 19)	Other households (Obs = 42)
Crop choice	11.1	51.9	33.3	51.2	41.2	48.8
Fertilizer application	0	40.4	33.3	43.9	35.3	34.1
Farm chemical use	0	48.1	33.3	43.9	35.3	31.7
Long-term investment	22.2	43.2	31.3	35.1	35.7	36.1
Raising livestock	37.5	54.1	64.3	58.3	69.2	62.9
New seed varieties/new technology	22.2	51.3	35.7	38.2	30.0	41.4
Product sales	25.0	48.9	62.5	46.2	40.0	61.5
Daily living expenditures	77.8	74.5	83.3	74.4	82.4	82.9
Big ticket purchases	44.4	53.3	55.6	42.9	64.3	53.5
Children's education	44.4	66.7	71.4	58.5	66.7	59.0
Other family issues	44.4	66.7	61.1	46.5	68.8	53.7

Source: RCRE (2003).

47

Without a doubt, landlessness among women in China's low-income households is associated with less decision-making authority and suggests a reduced status within their households. Among middle- and high-income groups, the evidence is mixed but is not inconsistent with notions about the gendered division of labor and, as the nonagricultural sector expands, the shifting of agricultural tasks to women's domain, as suggested by Jacka (1997).

Narrative accounts from survey participants about their experiences with landlessness supplement the statistical description presented above. Most women commented on the sense of insecurity that accompanies their landlessness. Among these, some found sufficient opportunities to earn income even without their own land, and as such, their lack of land did not appear to constrain current household income. Others, particularly those who depended in large part upon agriculture for their incomes, reported substantial concern about their immediate economic situation, suggesting that a lack of land contributes to food insecurity and to worries about meeting basic subsistence needs. Regardless of whether current income (and production in-kind) from land was a critical issue, respondents sought the long-term assurance associated with one's own land allocation.

In addition to concerns about security, women respondents also commented that lack of land contributed to tensions within the household – particularly in cases when finances were already tight – potentially fueling domestic disputes. Some felt that their husbands and husbands' families looked down on them; others felt a sense of inferiority in comparison with other women in the village who had land allocations. They expressed a general sense of unfairness and denial of due rights, along with suggesting that landless women resented tax and fee assessments that did not fully take into account their differential status in connection to land.

Given the broad array of implications that can arise from the condition of women's landlessness, we believe that greater attention to intrahousehold disparities and how those may be exacerbated by patterns of gendered rights in access to land is in order. Unfortunately, because our data do not allow any quantitative inspection below the household level, we are unable to test any hypotheses concerning the relationship between landlessness and intrahousehold resource allocation. However, it seems clear, from the qualitative responses, that women's landlessness is an issue of concern to households and particularly to the women who experience it. Moreover, the condition of landlessness is associated with substantially lower rates of participation in decision making for women in low-income households. Further exploration into the welfare impacts experienced by individuals, and appropriate policy responses, is worthy of future scholarly attention.

EMPIRICAL RESULTS

Given our understanding of the relationship between marriage and landlessness, our objective is to explore more deeply the circumstances under which adult married women are likely to experience landlessness. Because the condition of landlessness is largely concentrated among women below 40, we will restrict our analysis to married women between the ages of 20 and 39.[9] As such, we will utilize econometric techniques in order to identify factors associated with observed landlessness and with the duration of the landless spell, including among our considerations both personal characteristics as well as variables that represent economic conditions of the communities in which the women reside. We will employ logit models to estimate the probabilities that married women are observed to be landless, while utilizing a Cox proportional hazards model to analyze determinants of the length of the landless spell.

Table 7 provides the means and standard deviations of the variables that we will include in our analysis. At the individual level we consider both the woman's age and the number of years that she has been married. We measure years since marriage separately for those married before and those married after their community's second cycle land allocation. We also control for whether the woman's natal household is located in the same

Table 7 Descriptive statistics of logit model variables, married women, aged 20–39 (183 observations)

	Mean	St. dev.	Minimum	Maximum
Dependent variable				
Possession of a land allocation (yes = 1)	0.7541	0.4318	0	1
Independent variables				
Village flat agricultural land (mu per capita)	0.9815	0.5789	0.0435	2.3250
Proportion of village workforce engaged in migration (outside of home county)	0.1578	0.1711	0	0.6000
Proportion of village workforce employed in nonagricultural jobs (inside home county)	0.1470	0.1496	0	0.6154
Resident of Shaanxi province	0.5355	0.5001	0	1
Lower secondary school completion or better	0.6230	0.4860	0	1
Age (years)	31.2678	4.9591	20	39
Years married	9.5082	5.3152	0	21
Married after second cycle reallocation (years)	0.9235	1.8737	0	7
Moved to new village upon marriage	0.6885	0.4644	0	1

village as her husband's or in a different village. Finally, we include a dummy variable to represent whether the woman has completed the lower secondary level of schooling. At the community (village-group) level, we include the per capita endowment of flat, arable land and its square, in addition to two variables representing local labor market conditions. The first is a measure of what proportion of the labor force is employed in local (within the county) nonagricultural jobs. The second measures the proportion of the labor force that engages in migration, defined as employment outside the county.

Table 8 provides the estimation results from two logit regression models of whether the respondent is in possession of a land allocation. The second model contains all variables in the first and adds the two community-level variables representing nonagricultural labor market opportunities. Table 9 shows the marginal effects derived from the coefficient estimates. Many results are highly similar across the two specifications, and the discussion here will focus mainly on the results derived from the second model.

Table 8 Logit regression results

	Model 1		Model 2	
	Coef	s.e.	Coef	s.e.
Dependent variable				
Possession of a land allocation (yes $=1$)				
Independent variables				
Village flat agricultural land (mu per capita)	3.48	2.07	4.92	2.40
Village flat agricultural land squared (mu per capita)	-1.47	0.92	-1.76	1.03
Proportion of village workforce engaged in migration (outside of home county)			-3.80	2.50
Proportion of village workforce employed in nonagriculture (inside of home county)			6.32	2.72
Resident of Shaanxi province	2.11	0.83	0.66	1.03
Lower secondary school completion or better	-0.37	0.60	-0.49	0.66
Age (years)	0.08	0.10	0.05	0.11
Years married	0.44	0.13	0.51	0.14
Married after second cycle reallocation (years)	-0.29	0.12	-0.31	0.13
Moved to new village upon marriage	0.04	0.62	-0.47	0.75
Constant	-5.83	3.02	-5.66	3.31
Log likelihood	-45.3501		-40.6816	
Pseudo R-squared	0.5557		0.6015	

Table 9 Marginal effects of changes in independent variables on the probability of possessing a land allocation

	Model 1 dP/dx	Model 2 dP/dx	Unit of change
Dependent variable			
Possession of a land allocation (yes $= 1$)			
Independent variables			
Village flat agricultural land	0.0308	0.0572	*Mu* per capita (evaluated at the sample mean)
Proportion of village workforce engaged in migration (outside of home county)		-0.1480	Percentage point in ratio of outmigrants to total village workforce
Proportion of village workforce employed in nonagricultural jobs (inside home county)		0.2463	Percentage point in ratio of locally employed nonagricultural workers to total village workforce
Resident of Shaanxi province	0.1300	0.0266	Discrete change from Hunan resident to Shaanxi resident
Lower secondary school completion or better	-0.0186	-0.0181	Discrete change from non-completion to completion
Age (years)	0.0039	0.0021	Years since birth
Years married (married before second cycle land allocation)	0.0225	0.0199	Years since marriage
Years married (married after second cycle land allocation)	0.0074	0.0076	Years since marriage
Moved to new village upon marriage	0.0023	-0.0170	Discrete change from remained in native village to moved

We find that the number of years a woman was married is the key personal characteristic affecting whether she was allocated land. Each additional year of marriage increases the probability of a contract responsibility land allocation by about 2 percentage points for those who were married prior to the second cycle land allocation, and this result is significant at 1 percent. However, the likelihood of obtaining land is predicted to be much lower for those who married later, after their community's second cycle land allocation. For this group of women, the probability of gaining a land allocation increases by only 0.7 percentage points for each year married, and the reduction in magnitude is significant at 1 percent. That the incremental probability of obtaining land associated with each year of marriage falls by greater than 50 percent for women married after the second cycle land allocation is one of the key empirical findings of this paper. Consider two women, one married just prior to the second cycle allocation and the other just afterwards. Five years down the road, the first will have an additional 10 percentage points added to her baseline probability of possessing a land allocation. The second woman's probability of having land will have increased by only 3.5 percentage points. And this gap only widens with each passing year, underscoring our prediction that landlessness among women will persist and increase over time.

Aside from the number of years married, other personal characteristics for the women in the sample demonstrate no statistically significant correlations with their land allocation outcomes. Notably, the likelihood of a land allocation for women who have married in from another village is not significantly different (at any conventional confidence level) from that of a woman who remains in her natal village after marriage.[10] Variables representing the woman's educational background also lack statistical significance in this model. We tested many different specifications of this variable, including a simple measure of years of schooling, and absolutely no evidence of any statistical correlation could be found.

Turning to community-level variables, we find evidence to suggest that landlessness predominates in the sample when there is greater pressure on local land resources. Women's access to land increases with her group's per capita (flat agricultural) land endowment, peaking at a per capita endowment of 1.40 *mu*. Beyond this point, the probability of having a land allocation decreases. An interpretation we offer for this result draws from work by Yang Yao (2002), who suggests that the frequency of land readjustments may have a quadratic relationship with village land endowments. We do not know if the influence of the size of the village land endowment on village readjustments drives this result, but our data is consistent with this explanation.

We find, in Model 1, that women in Shaanxi province have a 13 percentage point advantage in gaining a land contract over women in Hunan. Model 2 adds the nonagricultural employment structure variables and indicates that women's access to land increases with local nonagricultural employment and it declines with the share of local labor engaged in migration. A greater abundance and diversity of local opportunities may reduce pressure on land, increasing the opportunities for women to obtain an allocation after marriage through a village readjustment. On the other hand, when the community is more dependent on migration as a means of employment, there appears to be a lower likelihood that women possess a land allocation, suggesting greater competition for land as a source of income or security. Though statistically significant, the actual magnitudes of these effects are rather small. A 1 percentage point increase in migrant

52

labor (relative to the total village labor force) reduces women's probabilities of having a land allocation by 0.15 percentage points. Meanwhile, a 1 percentage point increase in local nonagricultural employment (again relative to total village labor force) increases women's chances of having a land allocation by 0.25 percentage points. Controlling for these differences in nonagricultural employment structure, we see that the advantage held by Shaanxi women in obtaining land has disappeared, now yielding less than a 3 percentage point difference. Perhaps other unobserved factors come into play here – such as quality and attitudes of local leadership – that influence both the development direction of the local economy as well as attitudes towards land management. Exploration of those issues is undoubtedly a worthwhile area of future inquiry.

As a final exercise, we analyze the length of time that women are without land contracts, employing a Cox proportional hazard model to estimate the duration of the landlessness.[11] This exercise allows us to examine how the factors we considered previously impact the duration of the landlessness experienced among women in our sample. The model estimates the hazard rate of exiting the landless state. In the current context, the hazard rate can be understood as the woman's chance of getting land this year, given that she did not get it prior to this year. Variables that exert a positive (negative) effect on the hazard rate therefore increase the likelihood of an earlier exit and are correlated with shorter (longer) landless spells. As we do not have retrospective data at the community level, all the community-level variables have been dropped because we cannot be sure they would be representative of conditions at the points in time when the women in our survey were experiencing landlessness. The set of individual variable characteristics included in the model are provided in Table 10. Our sample size has been reduced to include only those who have experienced some landlessness. The mean observed landless spell is about three and a half years, although recall from Table 3 that forty-one of the ninety-one observations are right-censored. Each individual-level variable used in the logit estimation has a counterpart here, though specifications are sometimes changed due to the nature of the analysis. We measure age at the year of marriage, while marriage enters directly as the year married. The results (Table 11) are consistent with our earlier findings. Shaanxi residence increases the hazard ratio relative to the baseline by 80 percent, thereby reducing the length of the landless spell (this result is significant at 10 percent). Notably, marriage in a later year decreases the hazard ratio by 10 percent for each year that passes before the marriage takes place, indicating longer spells of landlessness for those married more recently (significant at 1 percent). Once again the data provide strong support for the notion that women's landlessness is trending upwards – in this case with evidence that more recently married women experience landlessness more deeply, as manifested in their longer spells. A full accounting of the

Table 10 Descriptive statistics of Cox proportional hazards model estimation of married women, aged 20 – 39, who have experienced a landless spell (91 observations)

	Mean	St. dev.	Minimum	Maximum
Dependent variable				
Length of landless spell in years	3.5824	1.9440	1	11
Independent variables				
Resident of Shaanxi province	0.5055	0.5027	0	1
Lower secondary school completion or better	0.6264	0.4864	0	1
Age at marriage	21.8462	2.6622	18	33
Year married	1993.659	5.0820	1981	2001
Moved to new village upon marriage	0.7143	0.4543	0	1

Table 11 Cox proportional hazards model results

	Hazard ratio	s.e.
Dependent variable		
Length of landless spell in years		
Independent variables		
Resident of Shaanxi province	1.8118	0.6256
Lower secondary school completion or better	0.7410	0.2136
Age at marriage	0.9965	0.0655
Year married	0.9039	0.0305
Moved to new village upon marriage	1.0058	0.3270
Log likelihood	-188.6071	

economic loss associated with the predicted growth in the duration of women's landlessness requires quantification of its welfare impacts on women and their households – an exercise which is beyond the scope of this paper. None of the other variables entered in the Cox model yield a statistically significant result.

POLICY IMPLICATIONS AND CONCLUSIONS

Our analysis of household data reinforces the key role of marriage customs in women's landlessness in rural China. Those who married more recently and missed the second cycle of land allocations have a substantially greater likelihood of being landless, and the timing of marriage is the only personal characteristic that demonstrates a significant statistical correlation with our measures of landlessness. Interestingly, village exogamy itself – whether the woman marries outside her village – is not relevant to landlessness because women's likelihood of having a land allocation and the duration of any landless spell are unaffected by the village of residence after marriage. Apparently the loss of access to land through one's birth household upon marriage is not predicated on the distance or inconvenience of returning to the natal village to farm the land. If that were true, we would have expected to find that those who married inside their native village to be more likely to have land. The marriage event is therefore the key trigger of landlessness.

The other key insight arising from our empirical investigation is the importance of resources in determining the impact of landlessness. The evidence suggests that women's landlessness bears most heavily on households in the lowest income group who are typically heavily dependent on agriculture as their income source. It is in these households that concerns about women's status and both individual- and household-level welfare outcomes should be focused. Resources also matter with respect to the prevalence of the problem. Extreme scarcity in land at the community level leads to a higher incidence of women's landlessness. Counter-intuitively, relative abundance in land may also hurt women's opportunities to gain land, as the need for frequent adjustments may be lessened. More diversified local economies are associated with a lower likelihood of landlessness. These findings suggest that efforts to raise rural incomes and to develop rural economies, commonly advocated as good solutions to a broad range of economic and social concerns, are also likely to be effective in addressing women's landlessness.

The structural change accompanying China's recent WTO accession will undoubtedly lead to fundamental changes in employment patterns and income-earning opportunities in agriculture and other sectors, perhaps reducing some households' dependence on land as an income source. Increased exposure to global markets will push China in the direction of its comparative advantage – towards more labor-intensive production and away from the relatively more land-intensive agricultural sector. Some scholars project that textiles and apparel will be big winners in terms of both output and employment (Elena Ianchovichina and Will Martin 2004). At the same time, concern is expressed about the welfare of rural households, particularly those that are heavily reliant on agricultural income sources. This concern arises on two fronts. Jikun Huang, Scott Rozelle, and Chang Min (2004) suggest that China's relatively well-integrated markets put many farmers in a good position to take advantage of export opportunities arising from exposure to world markets. But they caution that this exposure is likely to work against producers of crops such as feed grains and cotton, as those products will undoubtedly face very substantial import competition. At the same time, analysis of rural household labor supply and its allocation across agricultural and nonagricultural employment suggests a relatively low level of responsiveness to changes in marginal returns to labor across sectors. More important determinants include structural factors such as human capital and household family composition, variables that are unlikely to be influenced by WTO accession in the short run (Sicular and Zhao 2004). As such, prices and wages may be quick to adjust, even in the more remote regions, with impeded labor mobility locking some households into a situation of substantial income loss. Households lacking access to employment in the growth sectors, either locally or through migration, are most worthy of concern in this regard (Kym Anderson, Jikun Huang, and Elena Ianchovichina 2004).

The adjustment of China's domestic economy precipitated by WTO accession likely will lead to a net decline in the returns to land. As such, one may speculate about the future value of land and its attractiveness to rural households, raising the question of whether one should attach serious concern to the situation of landless women. Two points can be made in this regard. First, central authorities are taking concrete steps to ease farmers' fiscal burdens and to support their earnings from agricultural production (Joseph Kahn 2005). Reductions and subsequent elimination of agricultural taxes, coupled with some subsidies for grain production, are meant to enhance the value of farmland and the livelihood it can support. These policies may come partly in response to WTO-induced structural change but certainly also respond to long-standing concerns about rural–urban disparities (and the ever widening gap between the two sectors). Second, land valuation serves an insurance function. Athar Hussain (2004) includes land allocations as one of only three income-maintenance schemes in place to help residents of rural China cope with earnings declines associated with WTO accession. Of the three, the allocation of land plots is the most broad-based scheme and covers the largest proportion of the rural population, in contrast to the narrow (and, according to Hussain, often inaccurately targeted) beneficiary bases of the other two. Press reports about the discontent and social unrest generated when land is confiscated confirm the strong sentiments that farmers in rural China hold towards their land (Elisabeth Rosenthal 2003; Howard French 2006).

In sum, in spite of the relatively low incomes typically associated with the agricultural sector, establishment of gender parity in access to farmland is a worthwhile goal, as there are benefits to secure access to land. Attention to women's needs (including their access to land, as well as training, credit, insurance, and markets) in the agricultural sector must not be neglected, as substantial numbers of households, and their women members in particular, can be expected to remain in the agricultural sector for the foreseeable future. Strengthening women's positions within their households, moreover, may have positive spillover effects on their bargaining power in nonagricultural labor markets.

Among our two survey sites, households in Hunan can be expected to have better access to new job growth, most immediately through migration channels. Though migration rates may rise, the new job growth cannot be expected to quickly ease conditions of land scarcity, as households likely will continue to diversify their employment portfolios in multiple sectors (and locations). And some households certainly will be left behind, whether due to inadequate levels of schooling, high dependency ratios, or some other factor. Meanwhile, households in Shaanxi may well experience lower commodity prices for many of their farm products prior to enjoying any employment growth outside of agriculture. Given the pressures created by the terms of trade moving against agriculture, coupled with dependence on land for both income-generating and insurance purposes, it is unlikely that the circumstances leading to women's landlessness will resolve of their own accord in either locale.

Denise Hare, Reed College,
Department of Economics, 3203 S.E. Woodstock Blvd., Portland, OR 97202, USA
email: dhare@reed.edu

Li Yang, Ministry of Agriculture, Research Center for the Rural Economy,
No. 56 Xisi Zhuantahutong, Beijing, China 100810
e-mail: li.yang@rcre.org.cn

Daniel Englander, Mayer, Brown, Rowe & Maw LLP,
1909 K Street NW, Washington, DC, 20006, USA
daniel.englander@gmail.com

ACKNOWLEDGMENTS

We wish to acknowledge financial support from the Ford Foundation as well as the Bernard Goldhammer Grant for Research on Economics and Natural Resources (Reed College). We are also grateful for suggestions and comments received following presentations of earlier drafts of this paper at the Workshop on Gender, China, and the WTO (Rice University, April 2006) and the International Workshop on Gender and Development (Beijing, June 2004), and for the helpful comments of three anonymous reviewers, the three guest editors of this volume, and the editorial staff of *Feminist Economics*.

NOTES

[1] The process of labor transfer out of agriculture in post-reform China has been treated extensively in the literature. Recent overviews of reform era employment trends are provided in pieces by Ray Brooks (2004) and Terry Sicular and Zhao Yaohui (2004). For discussions on issues related to labor migration, see, for example, Scott Rozelle, Guo Li, Mingao Shen, Amelia Hughart, and John Giles (1999), Dorothy J. Solinger (1999), Loraine A. West and Zhao Yaohui (2000), or Zhang Li (2001). Sources on rural industrialization and its employment implications include William A.

Byrd and Lin Qingsong (1990), Samuel P. S. Ho (1994), Albert Nyberg and Scott Rozelle (1999), and Justin Yifu Lin and Yang Yao (2001).

[2] See Xiwen Chen (2004) or Sicular and Zhao (2004) for evidence on farm income patterns. Nyberg and Rozelle (1999) provide a nice discussion of the rural land management policies and procedures that were in effect at the onset of our study period.

[3] For general discussion and description of China's Household Responsibility System, see Robert F. Ash (1988) and Reeitsu Kojima (1988). Details about its implementation, with a focus on regional variations as drawn from scholars' local fieldwork experiences, are provided in William L. Parish (1985). For attention to policy impacts on women, see Tamara Jacka (1997), Jennifer Duncan and Li Ping (2001), or Bossen (2002).

[4] Brandt et al. (2002) note that landholdings allocations made in response to changes in household size do not necessarily require a village-wide reallocation, and they report that about a quarter of the landholdings changes in their study (of the 1983–95 period) consist of smaller-scale readjustments. A readjustment would typically affect only the subset of households who had experienced a recent death, birth, or marriage, with each household giving up or receiving a parcel of land commensurate to its population change, and the balance taken up by village reserve land set aside specifically for this purpose.

[5] Our main empirical discussion begins in the next section; however, it may be useful to note here that among the 508 women in our sample between the ages of 20 and 59, 88 percent report being married. Only slightly more than 1 percent of the sample report divorced or widowed as their marital state. Carmen Diana Deere (1995) makes a similar observation that relates women's need to marry in order to have access to land to the subsequent stability in household relations observed in the highlands of Peru in the early twentieth century.

[6] The RCRE is located within the Ministry of Agriculture in Beijing. The survey team was headed by Li Yang.

[7] Li Yang's observation based on fieldwork carried out in Guanyin village (Meijiang township), Dazhai village (Huangjiaba township), and Zaojiao village (Tiancheng township), Meitan county, Guizhou province, July 2005.

[8] Note that this pattern of land access bears striking similarity to Agarwal's (1994b) discussion about women's difficulties inheriting land in South Asia, mentioned in the previous section. Reporting on similar developments in Vietnam, Steffanie Scott (2003) suggests that the pressures of a growing population coupled with a fixed supply of land may lead to increased favoritism towards males in land bequests.

[9] The only married woman over 40 reporting landlessness in our sample is a 53-year-old woman from the Hunan province who also reports a cadre appointment as her primary occupation and is an upper secondary technical school (*zhong zhuan*) graduate to boot. Given her education and the position she has achieved, her lack of land is undoubtedly associated with a relatively wide choice set that includes opportunities that typically would not be available to many of the other women in the sample.

[10] None of the surveyed landless women go back to farmland in their parents' household subsequent to marriage, even if they remain in the same village. Hence, it would seem that location of residence after marriage plays no role in either formal allocations or in patterns of access to land held prior to being married.

[11] We chose to report the Cox proportional hazard model results here, as this model is often deemed desirable due to its nonparametric form. Tests of the proportional hazards assumption yielded no evidence of any violation. Furthermore, the results are highly consistent across a broad range of parametric model estimations. William H. Greene (2000) provides a useful discussion of the Cox and other methods used to estimate duration models.

REFERENCES

Agarwal, Bina. 1994a. *A Field of One's Own: Gender and Land Rights in South Asia.* New York: Cambridge University Press.

———. 1994b. "Gender and Command Over Property: A Critical Gap in Economic Analysis and Policy in South Asia." *World Development* 22(10): 1455–78.

Anderson, Kym, Jikun Huang, and Elena Ianchovichina. 2004. "Will China's WTO Accession Worsen Farm Household Incomes?" *China Economic Review* 15(4): 443–56.

Ash, Robert F. 1988. "The Evolution of Agricultural Policy." *China Quarterly* 116: 529–55.

Bossen, Laurel. 2002. *Chinese Women and Rural Development.* Lanham, MD: Rowman & Littlefield.

Brandt, Loren, Jikun Huang, Guo Li, and Scott Rozelle. 2002. "Land Rights in Rural China: Facts, Fictions and Issues." *China Journal* 47: 67–97.

Brooks, Ray. 2004. "Labor Market Performance and Prospects," in Eswar Prasad, ed. *China's Growth and Integration into the World Economy,* pp. 51–64. Washington, DC: International Monetary Fund.

Brown, Jennifer. 2003. Protecting Women's Land Rights Through RLCL Implementing Regulations. Rural Development Institute.

Byrd, William A. and Lin Qingsong. 1990. *China's Rural Industry: Structure, Development, and Reform.* New York: Oxford University Press.

Chen, Junjie and Gale Summerfield. 2007. "Gender and Rural Reforms in China: An Ethnographic Case Study of Population Control and Land Rights Reforms." *Feminist Economics* 13(3/4): 63–92.

Chen, Xiwen. 2004. "China's Agricultural Development and Policy Readjustment After its WTO Accession," in Deepak Bhattasali, Shantong Li, and Will Martin, eds. *China and the WTO,* pp. 69–80. Washington, DC: World Bank.

Deere, Carmen Diana. 1995. "What Difference Does Gender Make? Rethinking Peasant Studies." *Feminist Economics* 1(1): 53–72.

Deere, Carmen Diana and Magdalena León. 2001. *Empowering Women: Land and Property Rights in Latin America.* Pittsburgh, PA: University of Pittsburgh Press.

———. 2003. "The Gender Asset Gap: Land in Latin America." *World Development* 31(6): 925–47.

Duncan, Jennifer and Li Ping. 2001. *Women and Land Tenure in China: A Study of Women's Land Rights in Dongfang County, Hainan Province.* RDI Reports on Foreign Aid and Development 110, Rural Development Institute.

Fang Yuzhu. 2003. Protect Women's Legal Land Rights. Materials compiled for the Women's Land Rights Training Seminar sponsored by the All-China Women's Federation and the Ford Foundation – Beijing, December 2–5.

French, Howard. 2006. "Police in China Battle Villagers in Land Protest." *New York Times,* January 17.

Greene, William H. 2000. *Econometric Analysis,* 4th ed. Upper Saddle River, NJ: Prentice Hall.

Ho, Samuel P. S. 1994. *Rural China in Transition: Non-Agricultural Development in Rural Jiangsu, 1978–1990.* New York: Oxford University Press.

Huang, Jikun, Scott Rozelle, and Chang Min. 2004. "The Nature of Distortions to Agricultural Incentives in China and Implications of WTO Accession," in Deepak Bhattasali, Shantong Li, and Will Martin, eds. *China and the WTO,* pp. 81–98 Washington, DC: World Bank.

Hussain, Athar. 2004. "Coping with and Adapting to Job Losses and Declines in Farm Earnings in China," in Deepak Bhattasali, Shantong Li, and Will Martin, eds. *China and the WTO,* pp. 305–24. Washington, DC: World Bank.

Ianchovichina, Elena and Will Martin. 2004. "Economic Impacts of China's Accession to the WTO," in Deepak Bhattasali, Shantong Li, and Will Martin, eds. *China and the WTO*, pp. 211–36. Washington, DC: World Bank.

Jacka, Tamara. 1997. *Women's Work in Rural China*. New York: Cambridge University Press.

Kahn, Joseph. 2005. "China to Cut Taxes on Farmers and Raise Their Subsidies." *New York Times*, February 3.

Kojima, Reeitsu. 1988. "Agricultural Organization: New Forms, New Contradictions." *China Quarterly* 116: 706–35.

Li Zongmin. 2002. *Women's Land Rights in Rural China: A Synthesis*. Beijing: Ford Foundation Office.

Lin, Justin Yifu and Yang Yao. 2001. "Chinese Rural Industrialization in the Context of the East Asian Miracle," in Joseph E. Stiglitz and Shahid Yusuf, eds. *Rethinking the East Asian Miracle*, pp. 143–96. New York: Oxford University Press.

National Bureau of Statistics. 2002. *Zhongguo tongji nianjian* [China Statistical Yearbook]. Beijing: Zhongguo tongji chubanshe [China Statistics Press].

Nyberg, Albert and Scott Rozelle. 1999. *Accelerating China's Rural Transformation*. Washington, DC: World Bank.

Parish, William L., ed. 1985. *Chinese Rural Development: The Great Transformation*. Armonk: M.E. Sharpe.

Qian Wenrong and Mao Yingchun. 2005. "Zhongguo nongcun tudi quanli wenti shizheng yanjiu [Research on the Question of China's Rural Land Rights]." Collected Papers of the International Symposium on Incorporating Women in Small Town Development, organized by Zhejiang University, University of Nottingham, and Zhongguo nongcun jingji zazhishe and held in Hangzhou, China.

Research Center for the Rural Economy (RCRE). 2003. *Zhongguo nongcun tudi chengbao zhidu yanjiu* [Research on China's Rural Land Contract System]. Beijing: Zhongguo caizheng jingji chubanshe.

Rosenthal, Elisabeth. 2003. "Factories Wrest Land From China's Farmers." *New York Times*, March 23.

Rozelle, Scott, Guo Li, Mingao Shen, Amelia Hughart, and John Giles. 1999. "Leaving China's Farms: Survey Results of New Paths and Remaining Hurdles to Rural Migration." *China Quarterly* 158: 367–93.

Scott, Steffanie. 2003. "Gender, Household Headship and Entitlements to Land: New Vulnerabilities in Vietnam's Decollectivization." *Gender, Technology and Development* 7(2): 233–63.

Sicular, Terry and Zhao Yaohui. 2004. "Earnings and Labor Mobility in Rural China: Implications for China's Accession to the WTO," in Deepak Bhattasali, Shantong Li, and Will Martin, eds. *China and the WTO*, pp. 239–60. Washington, DC: World Bank.

Solinger, Dorothy J. 1999. *Contesting Citizenship in Urban China*. Berkeley: University of California Press.

West, Loraine A. and Zhao Yaohui, eds. 2000. *Rural Labor Flows in China*. Berkeley: Institute of East Asian Studies, University of California.

Yao, Yang. 2002. *Ziyou gongzheng he zhidu bianqian* [Freedom, Justice, and Institutional Change]. Zhengzhou, China: Henan People's Press.

Zhang Li. 2001. *Strangers in the City*. Palo Alto, CA: Stanford University Press.

Zhu Ling and Jiang Zhongyi. 2000. "Gender Inequality in the Land Tenure System of Rural China." *Jingji yanjiu* [Economic Research] 9: 34–42.

GENDER AND RURAL REFORMS IN CHINA: A CASE STUDY OF POPULATION CONTROL AND LAND RIGHTS POLICIES IN NORTHERN LIAONING

Junjie Chen and Gale Summerfield

INTRODUCTION

Grounded in fieldwork carried out in 2002 and 2004–5, this paper provides an ethnographic case study of the gender aspects of population control and land tenure policies as they developed during two phases of the reform period (1980–mid-1990s and mid-1990s–2005) in River Crossing, a pseudonym for a village in northern Liaoning Province in Northeast China.[1] Population and land tenure policies have a strong impact on life in the village and important implications for gender equity. This case study illustrates how the policies have acted together to either reinforce or offset gender disparities and influence the well-being and agency of River Crossing residents. Together they provide a richer representation of the gendered experience of living in River Crossing than discussion of either could alone.

The one-child policy has relied mainly on a quota restricting births that reflects substantial state intervention in decisions of the family unit. While population pressures on China are obvious, it is not as clear that the urgency for limits is justified, especially since the policy imposes significant costs on unwanted girls, their mothers, and in some ways, boys (Amartya Sen 1997, 1999; Elisabeth Croll 2000; Susan Greenhalgh 2003b; Gale Summerfield 2006). As per capita income has increased since the 1980s, so has the sex ratio (male/female). The restriction has eased since the late 1980s and is currently commonly referred to as the "one-and-half-children" policy.

Land tenure reform has been central to the decollectivization of farming and rural reform more broadly. Most of the mainstream economics literature that examines transition policies in China has overlooked gender aspects of the huge transfer of resources occurring as land-use rights were contracted to families, with tenure increasing over time from a few years to thirty years. Feminist economists have paid more attention to land rights, but most of their studies have focused on countries where land markets exist and land allocation is extremely unequal.[2] Land ownership predominately provides wealth for rural residents in most countries and can be as important as income in influencing women's capabilities and agency (Carmen Diana Deere and Cheryl R. Doss 2006).[3]

Because private land ownership is not permitted in China, this paper focuses on the gendered implications of use rights to land. China's land policy has been much more egalitarian than in most developing countries, stipulating land rights for women. Yet, this paper illustrates how implicit gender biases resulted in smaller land allocations for families with daughters in the land reforms of the 1980s. While overt gender discrimination was reduced in the late 1990s and early 2000s, Chinese women's rights have become less secure, particularly because with the end of land reallocations, marriage has now become a source of landlessness for women (Summerfield 2006; Denise Hare, Li Yang, and Daniel Englander 2007, in this volume).

Access to land is central to livelihoods in River Crossing, which is heavily dependent on maize farming. In rural China, WTO accession is expected to be felt through the decline in grain prices partly with the consequent impoverishment of farm households and rise of income inequality between rural and urban areas (for example, Kym Anderson, Jikun Huang, and Elena Ianchovichina 2004). In River Crossing, as well as elsewhere, the predicted fall in grain prices took place in the years leading up to the WTO accession, which resulted in demonstrations by farmers in many areas of China (Ray Yep 2002; Xiwen Chen 2004).[4] A good harvest in River Crossing in 2004 and the subsequent government subsidies to support the price of maize cushioned the impact of rising imports and made possible slow growth in per capita income in the village. Future maize price levels along with size of landholdings, however, will be central in shaping farm incomes and the fortunes of village residents. While migration out of the village is limited thus far, it is likely to pick up with the continued growth of non-agricultural employment ushered by the reform process associated with China's WTO membership. Likewise, the village itself may become a site of new, export-oriented, nonagricultural employment opportunities. Both field visits to the village took place after WTO accession; so, although we explore the post-WTO period, we cannot directly assess the impact of WTO accession in River Crossing.

This paper illustrates that the population and land rights policies have been gender biased in either the local implementation or outcomes, even if government policy may not have been biased by design. Over time, reliance on incentives, instead of authoritarian mechanisms, has helped reduce the bias in population policy, and explicit bias in access to land-use rights has also been removed. Yet, the persistence of traditional values and practices that discriminate against women continue to shape less favorable outcomes for women, and new distortions arise in implementation requiring ongoing adjustment. By linking the examination of land rights and population policy over two phases of land and population policies, we demonstrate how disparities in power, class, and health intersect with gender bias to shape villagers' experiences of everyday life. Population and land policies in China influence the control over one's own body and control over important social resources. The policies have reinforced each other over many of the reform years, but at times, they have worked in opposite directions in creating the gendered experience of rural life. They impact women's bargaining power within the home, as well as status in the community, and the provision of social security for old age and a safety net in case of divorce, death of the spouse, abandonment, or other crises.

POPULATION AND LAND TENURE POLICY REFORMS AT THE NATIONAL LEVEL

The one-child policy

The national government began implementing the rigorous one-child policy in rural and urban areas in 1980, in order to reduce the population growth rate, and eventually the size of the population, and to promote modernization. The policy was strictly enforced among both the majority Han, who comprise some 93 percent of the nation's population, and large ethnic minorities such as the Manchu. Smaller minority populations, such as the Daur and Ewenki, were encouraged but not compelled to have only one child (Junhong Chu 1995; Dezhi Zhao 1995; Peiyun Peng, Kuifu Yang,

Jimin Liang, and Honggui Li 1996; Susan Greenhalgh 2003a). The authoritarian nature of the policy, which combines a limit on births with some economic incentives and disincentives, stands in stark contrast to the market-oriented reforms that have stressed deregulation and the use of economic incentives much more than state planning. Although many Chinese are sympathetic to the goal of slowing the country's population growth, the policy is unpopular, particularly in rural areas, and excesses in enforcing it have frequently been reported, especially in the early 1980s (Tyrene White 1990, 1994; Susan Greenhalgh 1994; Ann Anagnost 1997).[5]

The policy has been unevenly enforced in rural areas depending on the approach of local authorities. In the late 1980s, the central government eased the population policy to make it more acceptable to villagers. In 1987, they allowed rural families, whose first child was a girl, a second chance to bear a son, usually after an interval of four to six years. In the following year, the central government further permitted rural couples, as long as one of the spouses was an only-child, to have a second child regardless of the sex of their first baby (Greenhalgh 1994; Chu 1995; Zhao 1995; Zhongtang Liang, Kejian Tan, and Shiming Jing 1999).

After 1992, the government further endeavored to create an enabling environment for its population policy by emphasizing the economic incentives of having fewer children, using the slogans: "Enable women to make a fortune" (*bangzhu funu zhifu*) and "Bear fewer children, prosper quickly" (*shaosheng kuaifu*) (Edwin A. Winckler 2002). Officials stressed off-farm work for rural women, so they could procure "a relatively comfortable life" by engaging in market labor (Editorial Department of China Population Press 2000: 90). The logic underlying the emphasis on women's off-farm work was that women would want to increase household income and would thus realize that having more than one child is an obstacle to their employment.

The one-child policy is a sensitive topic in China in part because it has received so much external criticism. In the late 1990s, Chinese officials began to use population policy reforms to increase the nation's international stature and facilitate its WTO accession. Officials advocated that having fewer children was "civilized" behavior. They argued for transforming the old "fertility culture" (*shengyu wenhua*) into a new, "civilized" one that promotes small family size and gender equality (Kuifu Yang, Jimin Liang, and Fan Zhang 2001: 420–1).[6] Promising to provide rural women with more "high-quality services" (*youzhi fuwu*) for their reproductive health, the government advised rural residents to emulate the urban, middle-class lifestyle emphasizing nuclear family values, in particular following the trend toward fewer children and more investment in education and consumption for each child. By so doing, the government hoped rural people would accept a "scientific and progressive notion of marriage and childbearing," creating "civilized and happy families" (Baochang Gu 2002: 3).[7]

To further promote an internationally acceptable image of China's population control policy, officials continue to transform the policy through economic incentives and better reproductive health services (Peng, Yang, Liang, and Li 1996: 252–4; Gu 2002). On December 29, 2001 the Chinese government legislated the National Population and Family Planning Law. This revised policy, rather than blocking villagers from having an additional child, required them to pay a Social Nurturance Fee (*shehui fuyang fei*) to the county government. The fee was intended to compensate the country for the additional costs incurred for the child. In the early 2000s, the central government promised pensions to rural couples who agreed to comply with the population policy (State Commission of Population and Family Planning and Ministry of Finance 2004).

Land tenure reform

The Household Responsibility System (HRS) was officially instituted by the central government in 1978. Rural areas immediately began experimenting with decollectivization; the conversion was nationally mandated in 1983.[8] One of the most visible changes of this period was the creation of more than 200 million small, fragmented family farms when the communes were broken up. Although there were many variations across Chinese villages, land was usually divided on a per capita basis with individuals – women as well as men – receiving several small plots of land of varying quality (Qisheng Gong and Feizhou Zhou 1999). Most land was categorized as household responsibility land (used to deliver output quotas to the state and whatever else the family decided to grow), and a small amount was set aside for minor redistributions necessary because of marriages, births, and deaths.[9] Total household holdings typically added up to less than half a hectare.

By the mid-1980s, land tenure leases were extended from just a few years to fifteen years, but frequent redistributions created tenure insecurity and discouraged investment in land (Zongmin Li 1999; Hanan G. Jacoby, Guo Li, and Scott Rozelle 2002). Moreover, the policy of land reallocation in response to demographic changes created incentives in conflict with the one-child policy. Under the egalitarian redistribution policy, rural families gained from having more children, especially sons who were expected to continue to support their parents after they married, which contradicted the government's effort at rigorous birth control.

In 1998, contracts were extended to thirty years, and redistributions could only be made when two-thirds of the villagers voted in their favor. With the extension of leases to thirty years, parents of daughters who married out of a village implicitly received a windfall gain, but women marrying into a village no longer had access to land adjustments. In 2003, the Rural Land Contract Law (RLCL) reinforced the thirty-year leases and prohibited readjustments (Ping Li 2003).[10] It addressed women's land rights by stating that a woman should retain rights to her natal family's land upon marriage until she receives a share from her new husband's village. In practice, patrilineal, virilocal customs prevail in rural China. It is difficult for a woman to retain land rights in her natal family if she marries outside the village. She cannot easily farm the land if she does not live in the same area, and her family will not be eager to return her land share if she returns to her natal village because of divorce. Often it is difficult to retain control of output from the land with her original family after she marries, even if a woman remains in the same village.

The return to traditional, patriarchal family farming arrangements with decollectivization and allocation of different quality land posed potential sources for gender and other forms of discrimination. But several key differences from earlier periods of household farming worked against traditional biases: women did receive explicit shares of land, off-farm opportunities were growing, and a set of laws guaranteed women use rights to land even if these laws were not always enforced.[11] The frequent revisions of laws regulating land rights have had the unintended effect that women who marry into a village at different times may have different rights. The ending of land reallocation raises the possibility of a market for use and ownership rights; however, it also makes women's rights to land less secure.

THE CASE STUDY

The data for this project were gathered mainly through ethnographic fieldwork in River Crossing in rural Liaoning Province in Northeast China from May to June 2002 and August 2004 to August 2005.[12]

The setting: Liaoning province

Liaoning was selected to explore some aspects of regional variation. It is the only coastal province that has stagnated. (The only exception for this province is the Liaodong Peninsula, where both industry and agriculture are thriving). This is attributed mainly to the region's earlier reliance on heavy industry, which has lost its importance since the reforms (see Chen [2004] and Dwight Perkins [2004]). Layoffs from state-owned enterprises in the cities have been extensive. Years of heavy industrial production have resulted in environmental pollution, especially serious for air and water reserves. Rural areas in Liaoning are neither particularly well-off compared to Jiangsu, Zhejiang, and Guangdong nor are they especially poor compared to inland provinces such as Gansu, Guizhou, and Yunnan. In most of the reform years, rural Liaoning has had slightly above average per capita income for rural China.[13]

The village of River Crossing in northern Liaoning province

River Crossing was chosen as the fieldwork site because it represented a typical village that did not have significant rural industry or outward migration, partly due to declining state-owned industry in the surrounding major cities.[14] Approximately 95 percent of the land is planted with maize, the main cash crop. The rest is devoted to millet, soybeans, and other pod-bearing plants, primarily used for family consumption. In 2004, annual per capita income in River Crossing was about 3,300 yuan (River Crossing Township Government Statistics 2004), close to the provincial average and higher than the national average.[15] On the other hand, River Crossing stands out in several ways. With 446 households and about 1,450 residents, it is the largest village in a township of 4,213 households (see Table 1). It has a large minority population (48 percent Manchu) and houses the township government.[16]

During the first half of the 1980s in River Crossing, as in other parts of rural Liaoning and China as a whole, the introduction of the HRS brought about rapid growth in agriculture. However, growth slowed in the 1990s. Liaoning was one of six provinces that experienced a drop in per capita income at the end of the 1990s owing to a drop in crop prices, partly due to the government's steps to prepare for WTO accession (Chen 2004; Qingjie Xia and Colin Simmons 2004).

Table 1 Basic data on the administrative village (River Crossing plus five small villages), end of 2003

Population	
Total	2,192
Women	1,027
Men	1,165
Families/households	
Farm households	571
Housholds with urban hukou	80
Age sets	
0–17	384
18–35	632
36–59	942
60 and above	234
Average family size	3.37
Average farmland per person	2.5 *mu*
Average per capita income in the area	
2002	2,800 yuan
2004	3,300 yuan

Source: River Crossing Township Government Statistics 2003, 2004.

As of 2005, China's accession to the WTO had not yet produced much change in village life. The most notable differences in the village between fieldwork conducted in 2002 and 2004–5 were economic improvement due to a good harvest in the fall of 2004 and government subsidies that contributed to an increase in the price of maize in 2004. Per capita rural income continued to grow in the early 2000s, but it has remained significantly below that of urban areas.

The interviews

The goal of in-depth interviews was to find out about residents' views on their current experiences with childbearing and land tenure as well as recollections about these issues in the first reform period (1980 to mid-1990s). Interviews, with open-ended questions, were conducted with sixty-two married women (ranging in age from 18 to 99) and fifty-three of these women's husbands (ranging in age from 19 to 86).[17] Up to ten sessions were held with each respondent to obtain information and clarify inconsistencies. River Crossing has seven villager groups that officially own the farmland. Two of these groups were the focus of this study, which reflected the general composition of River Crossing population because there was a fairly equal mixture of Han and Manchu residents and a common interethnic marriage pattern. Approximately 45 percent of the residents in these areas were interviewed. Additional interviews were conducted with residents of other neighborhoods. Respondents were selected to represent a diversity of ages, ethnicities, classes, and kinship backgrounds. To compensate for any limitations in exploring sensitive topics that might be caused by the interviewer being male, born in a different province, and a graduate student in the US, a local Manchu woman was hired as a research assistant. Most interviews were semi-structured. Village, township, county, prefecture, and provincial officials were also interviewed; archival research for statistics and policy documents was carried out in county, township, and village government offices; and extensive participant-observation research was conducted. To express gratitude for the community's participation, the researcher tutored several junior and senior high school students.

THE FIRST PERIOD: POPULATION AND LAND TENURE POLICY IN RIVER CROSSING, 1980 TO MID-1990S

The one-child policy and the easing of population policy in the late 1980s

After the 1980 implementation of the one-child policy in River Crossing, local officials encountered varying degrees of resistance from residents. Most families wanted more children, especially sons who would contribute financially to the family, even after they married, and continue to care for the parents in old age. Traditional cultural values and the system of ancestor worship are also strong in River Crossing and contribute to a preference for sons (Chu 1995; Junjie Chen and Guangzong Mu 1996; Junjie Chen 1998).[18]

To implement the one-child policy rigorously, the local township administration established "small shock brigades of the family planning program" to "catch big wombs" (zhua daduzi). Their job was to detect – largely through unannounced examinations – "unexpected" pregnancies that occurred outside the township government's annual population plan and then to require illegally pregnant women to have abortions. A local female official recalled that, during the early 1980s, an administrative village (then called a production brigade) in the township had on average eight to ten pregnancies that did not conform to the population plan each year. To enforce the one-child policy, all married women in River Crossing were required to undergo sterilization surgery if they had more than one child or have IUDs inserted if they had only one child. Families were fined not only for having more than one child but also for refusing sterilization surgery. When families were too poor to pay cash, local officials seized their livestock – horses, cattle, pigs, or goats – or other property. During an interview, one woman expressed a common view: "That thing [birth control] was really strict (yan) in those years (from 1980 to the mid-1980s)." Respondents recalled that in 1980, about ten families out of about 360 households living in the village at that time were fined for noncompliance with the policy. A case in point is Liu Dajie, who had her second daughter in June 1980, just before the one-child rule was implemented in the village. Three months after her delivery, she was ordered to have sterilization surgery but refused, stating that she was still too weak. To punish her defiance, her family was forced to pay a fine of 450 yuan in cash, and she was compelled to have an IUD inserted so she would not try to get pregnant again to have a son. Since the family could not afford the full fine of 450 yuan, which was more than an ordinary family's annual cash income at that time, township and village officials confiscated some of the family property including a wardrobe. Two and a half years later, Liu Dajie had to undergo the sterilization surgery anyway because her family could not pay an additional fine to postpone the surgery further. Liu Dajie's experience was not unusual during those years.

Mandatory abortion became a major tool for maintaining annual quotas. According to the township's 1980 annual report, seventeen women underwent abortions in the administrative village, with fifteen in the first trimester, one in the second trimester, and one in the third trimester. At the township level (which includes River Crossing), ninety women had abortions, sixty-one of them in the first-trimester, twenty in the second trimester, and nine in the third trimester. Li Juanjuan, a River Crossing woman, recalled having an unapproved pregnancy in 1987 that was detected in the second trimester. Township and village leaders sent three officials – two men and a woman – to stay with her and persuade her to undergo the mandatory abortion. After being confined to her house for several days, Li Juanjuan succumbed to the pressure.

The one-child policy was eased in River Crossing in 1987 and 1988, in line with policy adjustment at the national level. Couples were permitted to have a second child if their first was a girl; when at least one of the spouses was an only child, they could have a second child regardless of the sex of the first.[19] In this area, families were required to wait for at least four years after the birth of their daughter or until the mother had reached the age of 28.

Villagers deemed a family fortunate if the second child was male. For example, Song Dajie had a son in 1991 when her first child (a girl) was eight. During a 2004 interview, she said, "My husband and I were very upset when our first child was a girl, yet now we feel very pleased because we have both a son and a daughter. It is even better than those who only have a son." Her sister-in-law, Ma Sansao, gave birth to a second daughter in 1988 and was sterilized soon afterwards. The birth of a second daughter was considered unpleasant, even disastrous. The family, especially Ma Sansao's husband, was not satisfied with two daughters. He was the only one of four brothers without a male descendant. Sometimes when he became drunk at home, he cried and yelled at his wife. "That became the end of my world – when he got drunk and yelled at me," Ma Sansao sighed.

By easing the one-child policy only for families who had a single girl, the government accommodated, rather than challenged, traditional patriarchal gender stereotypes. Disappointment over the birth of a daughter remained common in the village.

Use rights to land: Gendered access

Because agriculture is the major source of income in River Crossing, land allocation has been a delicate issue of dispute and competition. In spring 1981, the administrative village government began the process of decollectivization by dividing each of the twelve villager groups, composed of approximately fifty households, into two to three smaller, temporary working groups that still had collective rights to land.[20] Mr. Pang, a township leader since the late 1970s, recalled that the villagers had worked harder when the smaller working units were introduced because their effort could be more easily observed and compensated. As a result, by the end of 1981, the whole village experienced a considerable increase in both harvest and annual income.

Following the first step toward decollectivization, the local government introduced the HRS in early spring of 1982, allocating farmland to individual households. In River Crossing, the villager group (and the farmland it collectively owned) was the basic unit for land redistribution; because there were seven groups in River Crossing with different amounts of land holdings, this process resulted in some variation in the size of land allocated to villagers, although land was distributed equally within groups. Collective land was separated into four categories by quality ranging from class I (the best land) to class IV (the least productive land), and each villager received a plot of each quality. For example, in the seven-member Er Ma family (two parents, four daughters, and one young son), each person received 0.6 *mu* of class I land, 0.5 *mu* of class II, 0.36 *mu* of class III, and 0.1 *mu* of class IV.[21] Each also received 0.45 *mu* of top quality self-sufficiency land for a total of 2.01 *mu* per capita. Altogether, the Er Ma family received about 14 *mu* of land of differing quality.

In River Crossing, with families receiving an average of six separate plots, allocations were less fragmented than in many places. Yet, some residents received eight to ten small plots, making farming very inconvenient; during interviews, these families always complained about the difficulty of working on scattered plots, noting that some plots were more than two miles apart. In 1982, leases lasted only one year, though they were renewable. This very short-term lease made farmers unwilling to invest in improving the land. Each villager group retained about 20 percent of the worst quality land as reserve for villagers to lease. To encourage the use of extremely low quality land, the local government sometimes waived taxes and fees associated with these leases.

A major redistribution of farmland was held in 1985. Farmland was pooled within the villager groups and reallocated to individual households. This time villagers were given fifteen-year leases to encourage improvements on the land. To avoid disruptive adjustments for marriages, births, and deaths, officials decided to estimate the average size of each household for the fifteen-year period and make the allocation in advance. Their method was based on prevailing patriarchal ideas about gender relations and virilocal marriage patterns. In River Crossing, the dominant marriage pattern occurs between villages, but since it is a large village with seven major lineages, approximately 15–20 percent of marriages happen within the village (Director of the Township Women's Federation, personal communication, April 4, 2005). Uxorilocal marriage, in which the man moves into his wife's residence upon marriage, is rare and is usually stigmatized. Among the respondents interviewed, only one man, Da Chen, could be classified as having a somewhat uxorilocal post-marriage residence.[22] Informal partnerships, however, have become more common.[23]

Under the fifteen-year lease regime, all married, widowed, and divorced adults were entitled to rights to a full share of land, about 2–2.5 *mu*. For families with unmarried children, a different rule was used for boys and girls. The township and village leaders reasoned that since an unmarried son would be expected to marry and have a child, he should be allocated a larger share of farmland than a daughter to support his future family, who would reside with or near his parents. In contrast, since an unmarried daughter would eventually marry out of her natal family and usually leave the village, she was, therefore, only allowed a smaller share of farmland. Local officials further assumed that a villager would get married once he/ she reached the minimum legal age for marriage: 22 years for men and 20 years for women.

Based on these guidelines, boys received a full share of land plus an adjusted allocation for their future family based on their present age (those over 16 received an additional full share; boys under 16 received smaller additions commensurate with age). A further qualification was also based on age. Locals believe that a man, who has not married by age 30 (due to poverty in most cases), will probably stay single for the rest of his life; so single men over 30 were not given the additional share of land.

Unmarried girls of all ages received much smaller land allocations. The closer a girl was to the legal age of marriage, the smaller the share of land she would be allotted. Moreover, a girl did not receive an additional share for her future husband and child. The only exception was for a family with two unmarried daughters and no sons. Local officials assumed that, to continue the patriarchal family line, the parents would manage to have one of their daughters and her husband live with them. Under such an arrangement, one daughter would receive a larger allocation, as if she were a boy entitled to have land, for herself and her future husband and child.

This gender-biased approach to land redistribution had two far-reaching effects. First, although land allocation was ostensibly equal in size for adult women and men, families with sons immediately had more land than those who only had daughters. For example, in 1985 the Ren family with six members – comprised of parents, an unmarried daughter, and three unmarried sons (two in their 20s and one teenager) – was allotted about 19 *mu* of farmland. By contrast, the Er Ma family, which had seven members (parents, four daughters, and a son), received only 15.4 *mu*. The overtly stated ideal of equal distribution of land was thus undermined by entrenched gender bias in the attempt to avoid the disruption of frequent redistributions. The second major effect was that the gender-based, unequal land reallocation reinforced villagers' traditional preference for sons. During an interview with the Zhang family, which had two daughters (the first born in 1984 and the second in 1990), the father complained: "Having a son is always lucky in all aspects; he will earn you land even when he is still a boy."

The land lease of 1985 remained in place until spring 2001, a year longer than the fifteen-year contract, because the local government needed extra time to prepare for the next redistribution. During this period, most families' allocation remained largely unchanged except for a few "minor adjustments" made from reserved land of about 30–50 mu per villager group. Minor adjustments were supposed to be applied when new wives married into the village or local girls married out of the village, after births and deaths, and when registrations changed. In practice, however, very few adjustments were made. The negative impact fell hardest on women who married into the village and on families with new babies. An inadequate amount of reserve land had been set aside in the original distribution, and families who had lost members through marriage out of the village, migration, or death, did not always relinquish the land allocation as they were supposed to. For example, when the daughter of the Ren family married out of the village in 1995, the family retained her quota until spring 2001, a typical practice.

Respondents indicated that in many cases local power and class inequality dictated who was allowed to ignore the rules. After the eldest daughter in the Er Ma family married out of the village in 1992, the family kept their whole plot of 15.4 mu even beyond the next round of land redistribution in 2001. Some villagers noted in interviews that the father had a close relative in the village administration. The Zhang family, in contrast, lacked ties to officials, and when their second daughter was born in 1990, they did not receive any land adjustment. Of course, as some villagers revealed, families without connections might get their due allocation, on the condition that they "do something" – which implied sending some gifts to local officials.

Families with members who migrated to other places or went to work in local nonagricultural jobs – seasonal or long-term – retained the land allocation for that person, as long as the person's official rural registration did not change. Among the sixty-two families interviewed on land issues, eight had members working in the city (for periods ranging from two years to more than ten years). All the families retained land quotas of absent members. In the mid-1990s, for example, Uncle Lin's second, unmarried daughter migrated to Shenyang, the provincial capital, to work as a salesperson. Her land quota was retained by her family, even during the next major land redistribution in spring 2001; no one in her villager group has questioned her eligibility.

According to many respondents, minor land adjustments have been carried out in River Crossing mainly as a reward for compliance with the one-child policy. On the promise not to have a second child, a family was rewarded with an extra mu of good quality land for their only child.

An unmarried boy, who had received an age-adjusted partial share for his future wife in the 1985 distribution, could not apply for a larger share of land when he married. For example, in 1985, the 15-year-old Da Su was allotted 3.5 mu, 60 percent more than a standard quota in his villager group. He married in 1989 and had a son in 1991, but his land size did not increase. Because he married younger, at three years under the legal age of 22, he was not granted an extra *mu* for the birth of his son until he sent some gifts to village officials. During an interview in summer 2005, Da Su said that his experience with land allocation was "common" to most ordinary families. "Of course, a few families with connections [to officials]," he added, "could find various excuses for minor adjustments." Da Su's comments illustrate how class differentiation (connections, power, and income level) has conditioned land distribution and added a further layer of inequality to gender inequality.

Qing Laotai, an old woman in her eighties, was one of the poorest respondents. Her husband had died at the age of 45 in 1968, leaving her with four sons and one daughter. Her two oldest sons could not get married before 30 because of poverty. Her eldest son, Da Kuan, born in 1944, married a divorced woman in 1976; her second son, born in 1951, married a widow in her mid-forties in 1995, who had undergone sterilization surgery during her previous marriage. Both marriages were deemed disgraceful from a local perspective, further reinforcing the family's low socioeconomic status in the village. Qing Laotai's third son, born in 1962, was disabled because of delayed and insufficient medical care in his childhood. In 1985, this son was 23 and should have been given a full allocation for his prospective wife according to the local practice. However, he was deprived of his rights. When Qing Laotai appealed to village leaders for her son's due land quota, she was told that local officials believed that her son would not be able to get married because of his disability, and therefore he was not qualified to receive the land allocation for a prospective wife. When Qing Laotai recounted her story in July 2005, she complained: "I was humiliated. Tears were in and around my eyes. Anger was rising at the bottom of my heart, but I had to keep it there...How much I had hoped that I could have someone listen to me and who would speak for me with the officials!"

A closer look at Qing Laotai's story reveals complex discrimination prevailing in River Crossing. In the 1985 land redistribution, males (and their natal families) were clearly favored, receiving extra allocations for future wives potentially years before marriage. Qing Laotai implicitly accepted the bias in favor of males. She did not question why families with daughters were denied an extra share of land. Based on the difficulties that her two older sons had in getting married, there was indeed serious doubt that her disabled son would be able to marry. But this realization did not appear in her narrative. The source of her indignation was her experience of class-based discrimination (reinforced by bias against those with disabilities and poor health) and her perception that if she had better connections her son would have received an allocation for a prospective (though unlikely) wife.

Population and land policies

Together the population and land policies – the two major policies impacting daily life – in this early phase of the reforms sent a clear message to women that they were not equal to men in the village. This bias against women was rooted in traditional values, but it also flourished with some aspects of the reforms. The local method of land allocation dismayed families with relatively more daughters since they received less land. Although the allocation process was much more equitable than in many other countries, it was becoming observably less equitable than in the pre-reform period in China. It reinforced discrimination against girls just as the extra child exemption for families "unfortunate enough" to have a baby girl did with the population policy in this phase. Although the families who received less land complained about the allocation and those with daughters lamented the population policy, they usually favored the reforms overall because incomes were increasing.

THE SECOND PERIOD: POPULATION AND LAND TENURE POLICY IN RIVER CROSSING, 1995 – 2005

The "enabling" environment: "Have fewer children, prosper quickly"

In the mid-1990s, the Chinese government began to emphasize the economic rationality of having one child, moving away from the punitive elements of the one-child policy. In accordance with the shift in the national policy toward greater use of incentives, the local government publicized growing employment opportunities for women in silk flower production as a means of lowering fertility rates.[24] Officials announced that this work was an exemplary way of both "enabling women to make a fortune" (*bangzhu funu zhifu*) and limiting family size.

Although they did not become wealthy from the work, local women were able to augment family incomes substantially through this employment, earning about 8 – 10 yuan per day for ten to twelve hours of work. This work was likely to increase their status and bargaining power in the family. Working conditions, however, were problematic, and stress injuries were common. Silk flower assembly work was generally only available four to six months a year, but it would be difficult to work continuously more than half a year, even if additional opportunities were available. Only young women could endure the highly intense labor required to earn more than 300 – 400 yuan a month.

In 1998, the Liaoning provincial government, like many other local governments across China, banned violence and the confiscation of property in implementing population policy. In response to the national effort to integrate into the global economy, the local government disseminated the "civilized" view of family and childbearing among rural residents.

Following the 2001 National Population and Family Planning Law, the Liaoning provincial government updated its regulation on population control on January 16, 2003. In this policy revision, villagers were still strongly discouraged from having unapproved pregnancies; yet if they insisted on doing so, they were required to pay the standardized Social Nurturance Fee (*shehui fuyang fei*) to the county government instead of being compelled to pay arbitrary fines. In 2005, in River Crossing and other villages in the same county, the fee for the first additional child was about 5,000–6,000 yuan.

The reduction in the use of force was welcomed. As Lingling, mother of a three-year-old boy, said during an interview "now the [population control] policy is not as harsh as before. If I become pregnant again, they [local officials] would try to dissuade me. Yet if I insist, they won't come to catch me and send me to the hospital for an abortion. Instead, they will ask me to pay a lot of money for an out-of-plan child."

Land tenure reform in 2001

As land leases of the mid-1980s expired, a new round of land tenure reform was launched in River Crossing in spring 2001. The main goal was to extend leases to thirty years following the national Land Management Law of 1998, a goal that was generally welcomed by River Crossing residents as was the case elsewhere in rural China.

A new method was used for allocating land-use rights that no longer overtly discriminated against girls and their families. All land owned by the villager group and leased in 1985 was first pooled for redistribution.[25] Then, about 5 percent of the land was put aside for minor adjustments, farming contracts, or nonagricultural commercial contracts, with rental fees paid to the administrative village authorities.[26] Land was reallocated to the current members of each villager group regardless of sex or age. In this round of land tenure reform, two types of villagers were denied access to land: convicted criminals and married couples who had over-quota births and had not paid the associated fine. According to village officials, each villager received about 2 to 2.5 *mu* in the 2001 land redistribution, basically the same as in 1985. While commitment to maintaining equality of land quality continued, most villager groups also sought to reduce the number of plots allocated to individual families in order to make farming more convenient. Thus, each family received either class I (the best land) combined with class IV (the worst land), or a combination of class II and III, and a total of about three to five parcels.

In this round, families of unmarried boys did not receive extra shares for future wives. Those who had received extra shares for potential daughters-in-law in 1985 lost them if the young men had not married. Families with unmarried daughters were not penalized in this round and could expect to hold on to the daughter's land allocation after marriage. The elimination of overt discrimination against girls in the 2001 land distribution represents a windfall gain for girls' families. Although the land allocation could be used to increase the dowry of a young woman when she marries, the land tends to be viewed as belonging to her natal family, and the new policy is not likely to change the relative value of daughters.

Actual land use tends to be greater than the official allocation. River Crossing lies in a mountainous area. Land on nearby hillsides is called wasteland and restricted for forestry and environmental reasons. During the 1990s, however, many villagers with plots of land at the base of the hills (and a few others) illegally expanded their plots partway up nearby hills. As a result, quite a few families farmed more than 3 *mu* per person. Because of the primary importance of agriculture in the local area, expanding the farmland in this manner has significantly increased family income.

Such wasteland development is coveted, and the resulting gains in income reflect connections to officials and have gender implications. Illegal expansion to the hillsides is mainly available to people who either have adjacent plots of land or receive permission to do so. The location of land in the redistribution process is important, and much negotiation has gone into this process. Hillsides are not terraced, and breaking new ground on the slopes requires intense manual labor. Few machines are available to assist with this task, which is done almost exclusively by men. Thus developing wasteland became a highly gendered process, and the resultant gains in income also boost male power and status.

Illegal use of restricted land has become institutionalized to some extent. In order to be protected by local officials for farming the wasteland, ordinary villagers have to make illegal annual payments, usually between 40 and 60 yuan/*mu*, to the village authority, depending on the quality of the land. Some families with connections to local officials, however, pay smaller amounts or avoid them altogether.

For example, Liu Sao, a woman who is a leader in the village and a close friend of a village official, has developed 3 *mu* of wasteland since the late 1980s but has never paid a protection fee to the village authority. In 2001, she further leased about 20 *mu* of wasteland from village authorities at the lower hill of a mountain near the village at a very low price (400 yuan for the next thirty years). Soon thereafter, Liu Sao's family began to turn the wasteland into farmland. By the end of 2003, the family had developed about 15 *mu* of this land. In 2004, this parcel produced about 18,000 *jin* of maize and a net income of over 4,000 yuan.[27] As stated above, it is unusual for a woman to have control over illegally farmed land. In Liu Sao's case, her position in the village gave her family access to the land, which she farmed along with her male family members. Having access to land in her name gave her more control over income from the land. The impact on her status in the village is not clear, however, since many villagers expressed resentment toward her for using her power and connections to get access to so much extra land.

Gender, connections, and virilocal marriage patterns also resulted in the uneven implementation of the 1998 national law on land rights. Under this law, a woman marrying out of River Crossing could keep her registration in the village until she received a land allocation in her husband's village. Practice in River Crossing, however, was inconsistent. A few women were allowed to keep their land allocations even though they transferred their registration to their husbands' villages when they married out of River Crossing. The Er Ma family had two daughters who left the village in the 1990s: the elder one married and transferred her registration out of the village in 1992, and in 1996 the third became a college student who therefore received an urban *hukou*. Neither should have retained land in River Crossing. However, their father's connections to local officials helped the family retain the land quota for both daughters. Income from this land most immediately benefited the father rather than his daughters who had left the village.

The experience of Da Kuan, Qing Laotai's eldest son and one of the poorest village residents, presents a contrast. His daughter (born in 1977) married out of the village in 1995 but could not transfer her registration out of River Crossing because she was younger than the legal age of marriage. Da Kuan was only able to retain her land allotment until the 1985 land lease ended. In the redistribution of 2001, his daughter was denied a land quota in River Crossing. When the father asked village officials for her due quota, he was told that his daughter's marriage out of the village so many years earlier eliminated the village's obligation to her. His daughter could not transfer her registration to her husband's village to get land there because they could not afford the fine. Da Kuan lamented the consequences of his daughter not receiving land in her own name: "Because she could not have her land either here or in her [husband's] village, she has to listen to their (her husband's family's) complaints [about her landlessness] and can never speak back."

The virilocal marriage pattern and thirty-year leases established by the land redistribution in 2001 have also left some women marrying into families in River Crossing landless. While they work on their husbands' small land allotment, neither they nor their family received a share of land to support them. Reserve land is supposed to provide allocations to these new wives and others who qualify, but administrative village officials have already given out thirty-year leases for essentially all of this land. Women who married into River Crossing after 2001 without any entitlement to village land complain that this has not only reduced their (per capita) family income but also their status in the family and their feelings of self-worth. Sometimes their husbands call them "eating rice with an empty hand" (taking more than they give to the family). Thus, after the 2001 redistribution, as overall tenure security for families increased, young women's land rights became less secure[28] (see also Hare, Li, and Englander [2007], in this volume).

The Hu sisters

Hu Lili and Hu Lihua are sisters (Liu Dajie's daughters) who grew up in River Crossing, and both married men who live in the village. Hu Lili married in 2000 and had a son in 2002. Her natal family had received a share of land for her in the 1985 allocation, which they retained and farmed themselves during the first year of her marriage. In the 2001 land redistribution, however, her parents had to relinquish her share of land, and Hu Lili received a new share of land from her husband's villager group, certified under the name of her father-in-law as head of the household. Together, her parents-in-law, Hu Lili, and her husband, received a thirty-year lease for 8.6 mu of land, and they also farmed about 2 mu of illegally developed wasteland. No additional land was allocated to the family when Hu Lili's son was born in 2002, but her in-laws were delighted to have a grandson and that elevated her status within the family.

Hu Lili's status in the household was further enhanced when she became an outstanding worker in the new silk flower assembly plant in 2004 and contributed to the family income. She earned about 3,500 yuan for her first six months of work. In her neighborhood, no young woman could match her record. She commented in an interview that her mother-in-law stopped complaining about her absence during meal preparation. Unfortunately, after six months, the repetitive stress of flower assembly resulted in swelling and bruising of her wrists and finger joints, which was a common complaint among women assemblers interviewed. Despite a lengthy break from the work, she could no longer be as productive as before because, in her words, "my hand is no longer skillful."

Hu Lili's younger sister, Hu Lihua, married in 2001 and had a son in 2003. Hu Lihua's husband belongs to the same villager group as her parents, and they live only a few blocks apart. During the land redistribution of 2001, she had not yet married and therefore received a share in her natal family's allotment. After her marriage her parents retained her land share, certified under her father's name, and farmed it themselves. Hu Lihua and her husband farm the meager allocation of 2.5 mu, which he received in the 2001 redistribution, plus less than an additional *mu* of illegal wasteland. The couple did not receive any land after the birth of their son. Not having land in her own name is an embarrassment for Hu Lihua. During an interview, she commented: "This piece of land is really too tiny; sometimes my husband complains to me that we're almost landless. When he complains, I feel inferior in my heart, but I never have the nerve to speak back."

The arrival of her son improved Hu Lihua's intrahousehold status. Moreover, in 2004, like her sister, she became an outstanding paper flower assembler, which further improved her status. She even arranged for her father-in-law to take care of her one-and-a-half-year-old son without any explicit complaint from him. In this village, childcare is viewed almost exclusively as a woman's job. Many villagers expressed amazement that this young woman could get her husband's father to take care of her child; during an interview, she expressed pride in the arrangement.

In 2005, Hu Lihua's father injured his back and could no longer farm. Since they live in the same village, Hu Lihua and her husband agreed to lease the land from her parents and pay them 400–500 yuan annually in addition to providing the equivalent value in flour for their subsistence. Although legally Hu Lihua is entitled to farm her allocation from 2001 since she did not receive land as part of her husband's family, in practice she had no access to this land until her father's injury. At present, she and her husband are paying to lease her original share plus that of her parents and the unofficial wasteland the family farmed. Thus, Hu Lihua and her husband, now farm more than 12 *mu* of land. During a conversation in summer 2005, she said: "This year my husband looks content. He never says 'landless' anymore."

The experiences of the Hu sisters are interesting because they both married within their natal village, and yet they have different land rights. Hu Lili married right before the last land redistribution in 2001 and received a share in her husband's family. Hu Lihua received her land allocation in her natal family, but even though she lives in the same village, she had no access to it or income from it until her father was injured in 2005 and could no longer do farm work. Then she and her husband had to pay to lease her parents' land (including her own share), but this still increased their income. Access to land rights increased her status and bargaining power.

Hu Lili and Hu Lihua are both considered very fortunate to have given birth to sons. This not only significantly improved their status within their husbands' families, it has also made it easier for the sisters to work off-farm in silk flower production. They both stated that they preferred this work to farming, partly because they could control their income much more easily. Although having a son partly compensates for the adverse effect of being landless on an individual level, the interactions of the land

and population policies are not just individual matters. The cumulative impacts of land and population policies affect the perceptions of women in the community. Women are not yet treated as equals, and traditional and new forms of gender discrimination keep emerging. Having a woman's status within the household tied to giving birth to a son is itself quite contradictory.

To some extent, the village has succeeded in reducing bias, especially by changing from an overtly discriminatory version of land distribution in 1985 to a more equal version in 2001. Yet, landlessness still hits women first, as Hu Lihua's experience demonstrates. Moreover, their sons, both born after 2001, have no land allocations. When the sons marry in their twenties, their parents and grandparents are likely to still be alive and may depend on the same parcels of land that they have now. The continuing crowding of these tiny farms will provide strong incentives for looking for other ways of earning an income including migrating to urban areas, especially as farming becomes increasingly costly due to low grain prices in the liberalized trade regime.

Land and population in the second period

Land tenure and incentives to have children

When the HRS was introduced, policy-makers largely ignored the incentive to have more children implicit in the system. However, at times they expressed concern that short-term leases with frequent redistributions promoted noncompliance with the population control efforts because they provided additional land allotments for newborns (Junjie Chen 1992; James Kai-sing Kung 2006). The increase in tenure to thirty years following the series of laws initiated in 1998 reduced this incentive. River Crossing has shown a tendency toward secure tenure throughout the two reform periods. Most farmers have received leases, and land has not been confiscated. Thus, in this village, land tenure policy is moving steadily in the direction of greater consistency with the one-child policy.[29]

Intrahousehold bargaining power

The stress on expanding women's off-farm work and achieving prosperity through fertility reduction and the end of explicit bias against women in allocating land appear to have improved intrahousehold bargaining power for women in the village over time as respondents expressed.

The increasing need for women to gain access to land as dependents of men, however, offsets these gains. Now that the land has been distributed in long-term leases, new wives are not receiving shares, and as noted above, they complain that this lowers their status and ability to make household decisions. When the current thirty-year leases were set up, all household members received land allotments. Yet, in River Crossing, and many other places in China, women are not explicitly listed as joint lease holders, although the law permits this.[30] When asked if his wife could co-sign the land lease with him, Da Su almost jumped up in response: "That's ridiculous! If I let my wife do so, my neighbors will all be laughing at me!" Leases are signed by a local government representative and the household head and then given an official seal. As long as the husband is alive, he – not the wife – is always considered the head of the household. Even after the death of a husband, it is not unusual to have his name remain for a number of years on the village government's household index as the symbolic representative of his family. Not having her name on the lease affects how a woman's land rights are treated by the courts in divorce proceedings or if her husband dies. With the end of redistribution, the lack of clarity in rights is becoming more serious.

Having fewer children and the emphasis on nonagricultural employment can lead to higher incomes for women, which is usually positively correlated with bargaining power within the household. The source of income often matters though; for example, the Hu sisters had more control over their non-farm income (also see Fiona MacPhail and Xiao-yuan Dong [2007], in this volume). Thus, in some ways, the recent land and population policies are less reinforcing of bias against women.

Land and children as social security

In rural areas of China, as in other developing countries, children – primarily sons – and land rights provide social security for crises and old age. Middle-aged, married women often remain on the farm when their husbands move to the city to work to retain the land rights for security and to care for the child and the husband's parents. Having fewer children and less secure land rights undermines traditional security arrangements, especially for women. In the early 2000s some effort was made to redress the decline in old age security by providing pensions for those who adhere to the population policy. In spring 2004, the Chinese government initiated a project that would provide some security in old age for those who complied with the birth control policy in selected rural areas (State Commission of Population and Family Planning and Ministry of Finance 2004). In 2005, the Liaoning provincial government launched this project in a test area and the following year implemented it across rural Liaoning. With this project, if husband and wife both have rural registrations, were born after January 1, 1933, and have either one child or two daughters, then they are entitled to receive 600 yuan/year per person after they reach age 60. This policy provides a basic pension for rural residents and may reduce their desire to have more than one child.

WTO: Off-farm work and migration opportunities

Growing population pressures on small plots of land combined with increasing landlessness motivate off-farm work and migration. China's accession to the WTO provides further incentive to make these moves out of agriculture for women and men (Audra J. Bowlus and Terry Sicular 2003; Deepak Bhattasali, Shantong Li, and Will Martin 2004). Village officials noted in interviews that exports of silk flowers to Japan and South Korea are expected to increase now that China is a WTO member, so job opportunities for local women and men should increase. At present, young women appear to have an advantage because they are preferred for low-level assembly work that requires much dexterity.

Migration may well accelerate over the next few years. The expiration of the Multi-Fiber Arrangement at the end of 2004, which has already increased demand for Chinese textiles and apparel, may provide more jobs for rural women from River Crossing who migrate to the cities. Furthermore, population and land policy reforms may improve the chances of women as well as men to gain from the new trade opportunities. The growth in nonagricultural employment opportunities following China's entry to WTO should help to mitigate the impact of growing landlessness among rural women and dampen the desire to have more than one or two children.

CONCLUSION

The reform period has brought dramatic improvements for women and men in rural China accompanied by great social tensions. In the implementation of population and land rights policies gender disparities have surfaced, almost always to women's disadvantage, although these disparities vary with age, education, class, health status, and social connections. This paper has examined gender aspects of population and land-use rights policies in the village of River Crossing in northern Liaoning since 1980. Taking into account the complexity of regional variations, we believe observations from this case study are informative, if not representative, of rural conditions in Liaoning and some parts of China, particularly the northeastern provinces of Jilin and Heilongjiang, which share geography and to a large degree socioeconomic history with northern Liaoning.

Gender biases were explicit in the village implementation of both policies in the 1980s, and the policies together reinforced the biases. The one-child policy was enforced harshly, women's bodies became the target of enforcement, and verbal or physical abuse by officials was frequently directed at women for exceeding planned births. Even the easing of the policy in the late 1980s played into traditional gender biases since only families "cursed" with a daughter were allowed a second child. Traditional discrimination against women was also manifested in the distribution of land leases. Families with sons received larger allocations than those with daughters based on the virilocal marriage patterns, and this further reinforced son preference; access to more land for families with boys augmented their income and contributed to income inequality until the land redistribution of 2001.

Explicit biases against women were reduced in both policies from the mid-1990s onward, but the changes did not completely prevent gender inequitable outcomes. Although men and women received equal land shares in the reallocation of 2001, women have less secure rights to land than men. The extended tenure mandated by the RLCL in 2003 – and reiterated in the draft Property Rights Law of 2005 – has already contributed to landlessness among women marrying into the village; although they may work on their husband's land, their own rights to the land are not clear, and they lose status in the family and village.

The reform environment in both periods created challenges to women's well-being and agency in River Crossing, but the emergence of new opportunities offset some of the biases. Incomes were increasing, and women helped create those larger incomes not only through their farm-based work but also by engaging in off-farm opportunities. Having fewer children freed women's time for off-farm, income-generating activities in the village where women were the preferred employees. Although migration overall is still quite low in this area, women are increasingly among those who leave for employment in the cities.

Comprehending gender experiences of daily life under land and population reforms in River Crossing resembles looking into a cracked mirror; combining the impacts of the two policies represents a larger fragment where you can see most of the image, but the typical single policy analysis gives you only a sliver of the image and may be more distorted.

Junjie Chen, University of Illinois at Urbana-Champaign, Anthropology
109 Davenport Hall, 607 South Mathews Ave., Urbana, IL 61801, USA
e-mail: jchen1@uiuc.edu

Gale Summerfield, University of Illinois at Urbana-Champaign,
Women and Gender in Global Perspectives, 320 International Studies Building,
910 S. Fifth St, Champaign, IL 61820, USA
e-mail: summrfld@uiuc.edu

ACKNOWLEDGMENTS

We would like to thank Günseli Berik, Xiao-yuan Dong, participants in the Rice University workshop, and several anonymous referees for their insights on the draft of this paper. We would like to thank the Werner-Gren Foundation and the Goodman Fellowship for support of the fieldwork that provided data for this publication.

NOTES

[1] To keep the identities of research participants anonymous, pseudonyms are used for the village and participants.

[2] Bina Agarwal (1994, 2003); Shahra Razavi (2003); Carmen Diana Deere and Cheryl R. Doss (2006). For China, see Irene Tinker and Gale Summerfield (1999); Zongmin Li (1999, 2003); Laurel Bossen (2000); Jennifer Duncan and Ping Li (2001); Ling Zhu and Zhong-yu Jiang (2001).

[3] Because rural housing has continued to be privately owned since the founding of the PRC, while only use rights to land are contracted to individuals, farmers have invested in their homes to store wealth. Longer-term leases are designed to encourage more investment in the land itself.

[4] According to villagers, no demonstrations occurred in River Crossing, and none were observed during fieldwork.

[5] Tracking women's periods, forced abortions, and forced sterilizations target women's bodies. Unwanted girls are often put up for adoption, hidden, or abandoned in hopes that the family can still have a boy without paying large fines. In these and many other ways, women and girls are reminded that they are unwanted, a burden on their families, and second-class citizens. The Malthusian-based one-child policy, however, is not the only possible policy approach to reducing population growth rates. As Sen (1997) points out, even when Malthus was alive, Condorcet stressed that people can be educated to understand the value of having fewer children rather than being subjected to coercion.

[6] The pejorative implication of the word "civilized" in this context is hard to miss. It emphasizes the conception of rural residents as somehow "backward" and "inferior" to the citizens who reside in the cities. The directive to become more "civilized" is focused on women who continue to be the target of population control policy.

[7] The expressions are: "scientific and progressive notion of marriage and child-bearing" (*kexue wenming de hunyuguan*) and "civilized and happy families" (*wenming xinfu jiating*).

[8] Under the HRS, although the villager group or administrative village collectively owns land, the individual household has exclusive power over its management. In the 1980s and early 1990s, families were required to sell a quota of agricultural products such as grains or cotton to the national government but controlled the rest themselves (Barry Naughton 1995).

[9] Surveys in 1992 and 1995 of more than 270 villages indicated that over 90 percent of farmland was categorized as collective land (*jiti di*), with most of the rest denoted as private/self-sufficiency plots (*ziliu di*). Collective land, which was subject to redistribution at the time, was subdivided into three categories: responsibility land (*zeren tian*) with requirements to deliver part of the output as a quota to the state (usually 75–85 percent of collective land), contract land (*chengbao tian*) leased by the village to farmers for a fee, and a small amount of subsistence/ration land (*kouliang tian*) (Loren Brandt, Jikun Huang, Guo Li, and Scott Rozelle 2002).

[10] The National People's Congress passed the RLCL on August 29, 2002, which was implemented on March 1, 2003.

[11] The most relevant laws for women's land rights in the reform period are as follows: The Marriage Law of 1980 states that property "earned during marriage is jointly owned by husband and wife unless otherwise provided in an agreement" (Duncan and Li 2001:

20); the 1992 Law on Women's Rights; the 1998 Land Reform Law assures leases for thirty years unless two-thirds of the villagers vote to redistribute them; the updated Marriage Law of 2001 confirms land rights for divorced women; and the 2003 Rural Land Contract Law reaffirms thirty-year leases and puts an end to redistributions. It also stipulates that women should not lose rights to land in their natal family until they receive land in new marriage and that divorced and widowed women should retain land rights where they live (Roy Prosterman, Brian Schwarzwalder, and Jianping Ye 2000; All-China Women's Federation [ACWF] 2003).

[12] The fieldwork for this project was carried out in Liaoning Province by Junjie Chen, with support from the Wenner-Gren Foundation for Anthropological Research and a Rita and Arnold Goodman Fellowship from the Women and Gender in Global Perspectives Program at the University of Illinois at Urbana-Champaign.

[13] Per capita income in rural Liaoning in 2002 was 2,751 yuan compared to the national average of 2,476 yuan (and per capita urban income of 7,703 in China) (National Bureau of Statistics of China 2004).

[14] Nearby cities include Shenyang, Fushun, Anshan, Benxi, and Tieling. About 175–200 people can be considered migrants from the village; most of them are temporary male migrants doing manual labor in off-farm jobs, such as urban construction, for several weeks to two or three months each year. The construction work availability corresponds with some of the busiest times in agriculture, so the farm work is picked up mainly by spouses. Increasingly, women are also migrating to work one or two years in hotels or restaurants in the cities. A small number of migrants have worked in the city for several years and can be considered long-term migrant workers. Among the families of respondents, six men and five women were long-term migrants.

[15] In 2003–4, US$1 = 8.28 yuan.

[16] The township is composed of twelve "administrative villages," and each of these is made up of several natural villages (just called villages). There are six villages in River Crossing's administrative village; River Crossing is the largest with seven villager groups and 446 households. The other five combined have 205 households and only one villager group each. Hosting the township government also provides a base for market activities in River Crossing. Terminology for administration changed from the pre-reform terms in 1983: township used to be commune; administrative village was the production brigade; and villager group was the production team. This paper uses the new terms.

[17] Several of the women's spouses had died, and others were not available during the fieldwork period.

[18] The forced implementation of the one-child policy led to numerous abuses and acts of violence nationwide, mainly directed against women (Jeffrey Wasserstrom 1984: 371; Ann Anagnost 1988). These excesses included: emotional humiliation and/or physical abuse meted out to rural women and men and sometimes to their immediate relatives; forced abortions; and appropriations and demolition of villagers' property, ranging from taking away some of their livestock and furniture to razing part of their houses. Women bore the brunt of the blame for the extra births.

[19] For villagers who entered their reproductive years in the 1980s, almost everyone had at least one sibling. Thus, the policy revision was hardly noticed by River Crossing villagers. It will become more influential when rural only-children (most of whom are men) come to their reproductive ages during the 2000s.

[20] The state owns urban land, but the village, village cooperative, or villager group owns rural land. However, the state has power to make key decisions about land in rural areas. Villages that wanted to retain collective farming during the 1980s, for example, were not permitted to do so.

[21] A *mu* is 1/15 of a hectare; a hectare is 2.47 acres.

[22] In the early 1980s, through matchmaking, Da Chen, whose first marriage failed, re-married and moved to his new wife's house. His wife's first husband had died, leaving her to take care of their four-year-old son. In order to continue the husband's family line, his parents and siblings encouraged the woman to marry a man who would be willing to come to live with her to raise her son, who would carry his father's family name.

[23] For women who are divorced or widowed, lack of male labor is a serious practical challenge, and help from their kin is usually insufficient. Although rural widows and divorced women frequently remarry, this is not a likely option for women who are older or have several unmarried children. Informal partnerships with men have become more common but still contribute to a woman losing face in the village. At least part of the increase in the incidence of informal partnerships can be attributed to women wishing to retain land-use rights in their own names. A case in point is Gui Xiuqing, who is a 47-year-old widow. She has a 23-year-old daughter, now married to a man in a different village, and a 9-year-old son. In winter 2003, Gui Xiuqing became involved with Laoqu, a 54-year-old widower living in a village about 25 kilometers from River Crossing, who helped with her farm. They discussed marriage, but Gui Xiuqing did not want to move to Laoqu's village because she and her son would lose the rights to her land and would not get land rights in their own names in the new village. Laoqu was not willing to endure the infamy of moving to her home, so they have remained informal partners and Gui Xiuqing's reputation suffers.

[24] Through the coordination of local middlemen and the township government, outside entrepreneurs began to subcontract the assembly of these inexpensive handicrafts to local women in River Crossing. In 2003, the subcontracting opportunities for paper and silk flower assembly were supplemented when outside investors opened two artificial flower assembly plants. They employed between fifty and seventy village women, part-time or full-time, depending on demand for the product.

[25] They no longer divided collective land into the responsibility, contract, and subsistence/ration categories.

[26] In River Crossing only 3.4 percent of the land was reserved, and all of it was leased out. So changes in allocations after 2001 were extremely limited.

[27] One *jin* is equal to 500 grams or 1.1 pounds.

[28] Based on a 2001 survey in twenty-two villages across fifteen provinces, excluding Liaoning, Zhibin Lin (2001) found that women were more likely to become landless than men. Among 19,163 respondents, 5 percent of women were landless; by contrast, only 2 percent of men were landless. Lin's finding is widely supported by other research (see Zhonggen Zhang and Shanhu Wu 2002; Ling Zhao 2002; Wei Liu 2003).

[29] However, as of 2006, land laws were not yet uniformly implemented. In some areas redistributions continue; in others titles for the thirty-year leases have not been officially issued to many farmers, and land is being confiscated by local officials for nonagricultural use without adequate compensation to the farm family or the village (Xinhua News Agency 2006; Keliang Zhu and Roy Prosterman 2006).

[30] The language on joint ownership, however, is complicated in the legislation and could be open to different interpretations by the courts; moreover, the contracts for land titling often have only one line for a signature based on the expectation that the head of the household will sign.

REFERENCES

Agarwal, Bina. 1994. *A Field of One's Own: Gender and Land Rights in South Asia.* New York: Cambridge University Press.

———. 2003. "Gender and Land Rights Revisited: Exploring New Prospects Via the State, Market, and Family." *Journal of Agrarian Change* 3(1/2): 184–224.

All-China Women's Federation (ACWF). 2003. "Women's Rights in Land Contract Are Outlined in the Law." http://www.women.org.cn/english/english/whatisnws/2002-4.htm (accessed March 2007).

Anagnost, Ann. 1988. "Family Violence and Magical Violence: The Woman as Victim in China's One-Child Policy." *Women and Language* 11(2): 16–21.

——. 1997. *National Past-Times: Narrative, Representation, and Power in Modern China.* Durham, NC: Duke University Press.

Anderson, Kym, Jikun Huang, and Elena Ianchovichina. 2004. "Will China's WTO Accession Worsen Farm Household Incomes?" *China Economic Review* 15(4): 443–56.

Bhattasali, Deepak, Shantong Li, and Will Martin, eds. 2004. *China and the WTO: Accession, Policy Reform, and Poverty Reduction Strategies.* Washington, DC: The World Bank.

Bossen, Laurel. 2000. "Women Farmers, Small Plots, and Changing Markets in China," in Anita Spring, ed. *Women Farmers and Commercial Ventures: Increasing Food Security in Developing Countries*, pp. 171–89. Boulder, CO: Lynne Rienner Publishers.

Bowlus, Audra J. and Terry Sicular. 2003. "Moving Toward Rural Markets? Labor Allocation in Rural China." *Journal of Development Economics* 71(2): 561–83.

Brandt, Loren, Jikun Huang, Guo Li, and Scott Rozelle. 2002. "Land Rights in Rural China: Facts, Fictions and Issues." *China Journal* 47: 67–97.

Chen, Junjie. 1992. "China's Rural Labor Mobility and Its Prerequisites: A Field Study in Four Villages in Hebei Province" [in Chinese]. *Sociology and Social Survey* 4(2): 35–40.

——. 1998. *"Guanxi" and Non Agriculturalization in Rural China: A Field Study in the Village of Yue* [in Chinese]. Beijing: Chinese Social Sciences Press.

—— and Guangzong Mu. 1996. "Chinese Peasants' Childbearing Needs" [in Chinese]. *Social Sciences in China* 17(2): 126–37.

Chen, Xiwen. 2004. "China's Agricultural Development and Policy Readjustment after its WTO Accession," in Deepak Bhattasali, Shantong Li, and Will Martin, eds. *China and the WTO: Accession, Policy Reform, and Poverty Reduction Strategies*, pp. 69–79. Washington, DC: The World Bank.

Chu, Junhong. 1995. "The Development of Population Studies and the Establishment of Demographic Science in China" [in Chinese]. *Peking University Learned Journal* (5): 74–80.

Croll, Elisabeth. 2000. *Endangered Daughters: Discrimination and Development in Asia.* London and New York: Routledge.

Deere, Carmen Diana and Cheryl R. Doss. 2006. "The Gender Asset Gap: What Do We Know and Why Does It Matter?" *Feminist Economics* 12(1/2): 1–50.

Duncan, Jennifer and Ping Li. 2001. "Women and Land Tenure in China: A Study of Women's Land Rights in Dong Fang County, Hainan Province." RDI Reports on Foreign Aid and Development 110, Rural Development Institute.

Editorial Department of China Population Press. 2000. *An Essential Pamphlet for Leaders of the Family Planning Program* [in Chinese]. Beijing: China Population Press.

Gong, Qisheng and Feizhou Zhou. 1999. "Institutions of Land Adjustment in Contemporary Rural China: A Case Study" [in Chinese]. *The 21st Century* 10(5): 136–47.

Greenhalgh, Susan. 1994. "Controlling Births and Bodies in Village China." *American Ethnologist* 21(1): 3–30.

——. 2003a. "Science, Modernity, and the Making of China's One-Child Policy." *Population and Development Review* 29(2): 163–96.

——. 2003b. "Planned Births, Unplanned Persons: 'Population' in the Making of Chinese Modernity." *American Ethnologist* 30(2): 196–215.

Gu, Baochang. 2002. "On the Reform of China's Family Planning Program" [in Chinese]. *Population Research* 26(3): 1–8.

Hare, Denise, Li Yang, and Daniel Englander. 2007. "Land Management in Rural China and Its Gender Implications." *Feminist Economics* 13(3/4): 35–61.

Jacoby, Hanan G., Guo Li, and Scott Rozelle. 2002. "Hazards of Expropriation: Tenure Insecurity and Investment in Rural China." *American Economic Review* 92(5): 1420–47.

Kung, James Kai-sing. 2006. "Do Secure Land Use Rights Reduce Fertility? The Case of Meitan County in China." *Land Economics* 82(1): 36–55.

Li, Ping. 2003. "Rural Land Tenure Reforms in China: Issues, Regulations, and Prospects for Additional Reforms." *Land Reform, Land Settlement and Cooperatives,* Special Edition, 3: 59–72. http://www.rdiland.org/PDF/PDF_Publications/LP-RuralLandTenure Reforms.pdf (accessed March 2007).

Li, Zongmin. 1999. "Changing Land and Housing Use by Rural Women in Northern China," in Irene Tinker and Gale Summerfield, eds. *Women's Rights to House and Land: China, Laos, Vietnam,* pp. 241–64. Boulder, CO: Lynne Rienner Publishers.

———. 2003. *Women's Land Rights in Rural China: A Synthesis.* Beijing: Ford Foundation Office.

Liang, Zhongtang, Kejian Tan, and Shiming Jing. 1999. "On the Adjustment of the Population Control Policy" [in Chinese]. *Learned Journal of the Party School of the CPC (The Communist Party of China) Shanxi Provincial Committee* (4): 33–6.

Lin, Zhibin. 2001. "Gender Biases in the Application of Rural Land Policy: A Preliminary Survey in 22 Villages across 15 Provinces" [in Chinese]. *Rural China Observation* (4): 49–52.

Liu, Wei. 2003. "An Analysis of Difficulties Encountered by Rural Women Who Moved Out of Their Paternal Village After Marriage" [in Chinese]. *Liaowang News Weekly* (4): 46–7.

MacPhail, Fiona and Xiao-yuan Dong. 2007. "Market Labor and Women's Household Status in Rural China." *Feminist Economics* 13(3/4): 93–124.

National Bureau of Statistics of China. 2004. *China Statistical Yearbook.* Vol. 23. Beijing: China Statistics Press.

Naughton, Barry. 1995. *Growing Out of the Plan: Chinese Economic Reform 1978–1993.* Cambridge: Cambridge University Press.

Peng, Peiyun, Kuifu Yang, Jimin Liang, and Honggui Li, eds. 1996. *A Complete Compilation of Documents of China's Family Planning Program* [in Chinese]. Beijing: China Population Press.

Perkins, Dwight. 2004. "Declining Growth in Farm Output and Employment: Implications for China's Economy and Society" (draft). http://post.economics .harvard.edu/faculty/perkins/papers/farmoutput.pdf (accessed March 2007).

Prosterman, Roy, Brian Schwarzwalder, and Jianping Ye. 2000. "Implementation of 30-Year Land Use Rights for Farmers Under China's 1998 Land Management Law: An Analysis and Recommendations Based on a 17 Province Survey." RDI Reports on Foreign Aid and Development 105, Rural Development Institute.

Razavi, Shahra. 2003. "Introduction: Agrarian Change, Gender, and Land Rights." *Journal of Agrarian Change* 3(1/2): 2–32.

River Crossing Township Government Statistics. 2003, 2004. Liaoning, China.

Sen, Amartya. 1997. "Population Policy: Authoritarianism Versus Cooperation." *Journal of Population Economics* 10(1): 3–22.

———. 1999. *Development as Freedom.* New York: Knopf.

State Commission of Population and Family Planning and Ministry of Finance. 2004. "Tentative Proposal to Reward and Assist Some Rural Families Who Have Complied with the Family Planning Policy" [in Chinese]. *Population and Family Planning* 12(7): 4–6.

Summerfield, Gale. 2006. "Gender Equity and Land Reform in Rural China," in Jane Jaquette and Gale Summerfield, eds. *Women and Gender Equity in Development Theory and Practice,* pp. 137–58. Durham, NC: Duke University Press.

Tinker, Irene and Gale Summerfield, eds. 1999. *Women's Rights to House and Land: China, Laos, Vietnam.* Boulder, CO: Lynne Rienner Publishers.

Wasserstrom, Jeffrey. 1984. "Resistance to the One-Child Policy." *Modern China* 10(3): 345–74.

White, Tyrene. 1990. "Postrevolutionary Mobilization in China: The One-Child Policy Reconsidered." *World Politics* 43(1): 53–76.

———. 1994. "The Origins of China's Birth Planning Policy," in Christina K. Gilmartin, Gail Hershatter, Lisa Rofel, and Tyrene White, eds. *Engendering China: Women, Culture, and the State*, pp. 250–78. Harvard Contemporary China Series 10. Cambridge, MA: Harvard University Press.

Winckler, Edwin A. 2002. "Chinese Reproductive Policy at the Turn of the Millennium: Dynamic Stability." *Population and Development Review* 28(3): 379–418.

Xia, Qingjie and Colin Simmons. 2004. "Diversify and Prosper: Peasant Households Participating in Emerging Markets in Northeast China." *China Economic Review* 15(4): 375–97.

Xinhua News Agency. 2006. "China Grapples with Thorny Issue of Rural Land Rights." *People's Daily*, September 19. http://english.people.com.cn/200609/01/eng20060901_298824.html (accessed March 2007).

Yang, Kuifu, Jimin Liang, and Fan Zhang. 2001. *A Concise Chronological Outline of the Major Events of China Population and Family Planning* [in Chinese]. Beijing: China Population Press.

Yep, Ray. 2002. Maintaining Stability in Rural China: Challenges and Responses. Center for Northeastern Asian Policy Studies, CNAPS Working Paper, The Brookings Institution. http://www.brookings.edu/fp/cnaps/papers/2002_yep.pdf (accessed March 2007).

Zhang, Zhonggen and Shanhu Wu. 2002. "Protecting Rural Women's Use Rights to Land Who Moved Out of Their Paternal Villages After Marriage" [in Chinese]. *Rural Economy* (8): 13–5.

Zhao, Dezhi. 1995. "Some Thoughts on the Cause of Family Planning in the Era of Socialist Market Economy" [in Chinese]. *Journal of Nanjing College for Population Programme Management* 11(3): 10–7.

Zhao, Ling. 2002. "An Institutional Analysis of Problems Concerning Use Rights to Land Encountered by Rural Women" [in Chinese]. *Chinese Women's Movement* (7): 28–30.

Zhu, Keliang and Roy Prosterman. 2006. "From Land Rights to Economic Boom." *China Business Review* 33(4): 44–8.

Zhu, Ling and Zhong-yu Jiang. 2001. "Gender Inequality in the Land Tenure System in Rural China." *China and World Economy* 9(2). http://en.iwep.org.cn/info/content.asp?infoId=887 (accessed May 2007).

Women's Market Work and Household Status in Rural China: Evidence from Jiangsu and Shandong in the Late 1990s

Fiona MacPhail and Xiao-yuan Dong

INTRODUCTION

Analyses of the gendered impact of structural adjustment policies and trade liberalization in developing countries and market reforms in transition economies tend to focus upon changes in employment, wages, and access to publicly provided services. While such outcomes are critically important, it is often assumed that increases in female employment and wages will automatically translate into improvements in welfare.[1] In the context of rural China, for example, Linxiu Zhang, Alan de Brauw, and Scott Rozelle state:

> [W]e assume, as do Thomas, Contreras, and Frankenberg (1997) and Quisumbing and Malluccio (2000), that increased participation in the

off-farm labor market and higher wages for those with off-farm jobs are metrics that are positively correlated with women's welfare. These authors argue that as women take jobs, the income generated is directly attributable to their labor, which increases their decision-making power within the household. (2004: 232)

Feminist economists carefully qualify conclusions about the impact of employment changes on women. As early as 1981, Diane Elson and Ruth Pearson noted that while Export Processing Zones in developing countries resulted in increased employment opportunities for young women, this alone would not improve women's subordinate position, since this position is not "constituted purely at the economic level" (1981: 98). Many feminist economists have demonstrated how increased employment may be associated with decreased leisure, increased work intensity, and lower well-being (Lourdes Benería 1995; Diane Elson 1995; Maria S. Floro 1995; Christine Koggel 2003).

In this paper, we analyze how women's market work affects their household status in rural China, which has experienced growth in paid employment in rural industries known as township and village enterprises (TVEs). Specifically, we address the question: within a household bargaining framework, does market work (time and/or wages) improve women's household status? An improvement in women's household status should result in a decrease in women's domestic labor hours, a decrease in women's responsibility for domestic tasks, or an increase in their influence over household decisions. We use the term household status to refer collectively to these three indicators. We prefer it to the term welfare because we are interested in how women fare relative to men in the household in terms of specific indicators that go beyond conventional notions of welfare. Our choice of indicators is consistent with the feminist capability literature, which advocates moving beyond proxies for welfare, such as income and commodities, to specific capability indicators (see Ingrid Robeyns [2003], for example).

This paper draws upon a survey of over 750 people working in TVEs and twenty in-depth qualitative interviews with people in this sample that were carried out in 1999 and 2000, in rural areas of the provinces of Jiangsu and Shandong. Given that the survey was designed with these research questions in mind, the data set offers a rich source of information, and the sample size is quite large compared to other case studies. Jiangsu and Shandong are major provinces with a high proportion of the rural labor force working in township and village enterprises, and they are located in the eastern coastal region, which is an area relatively open to trade. Thus, they are ideal provinces to study the impacts of market reforms and trade liberalization.

We develop and estimate models to explain the absolute amount of domestic labor, responsibility for domestic tasks, and household decision-making influence. We find that women in China have lower household status than men based upon their greater domestic work burden, greater responsibility for (undervalued) domestic tasks, and lesser influence over household decisions. Further, based upon the multivariate analysis, we find that women's market wages, rather than just participation in waged employment, enable them to reduce domestic labor time and affect the gender division of labor. The results provide mixed support for the hypothesis that Chinese women's market work will enable them to gain greater control over household decisions. The main implication of this study is that greater access to market work through market reforms and trade liberalization, such as is expected to occur with WTO membership, could improve some, but not all, dimensions of Chinese women's household status, and thus, initiatives supporting gender equity are required.

A FRAMEWORK FOR ANALYZING THE IMPACT OF MARKET WORK ON WOMEN'S HOUSEHOLD STATUS IN RURAL CHINA

Gender differentiated employment impacts of market reforms and trade liberalization in China

The impact of China's market reforms, underway since 1978, and rapid economic growth has not been gender neutral,[2] which is consistent with evidence from other post-socialist countries (Nahid Aslanbeigui, Steven Pressman, and Gale Summerfield 1994) and developing countries (Susan Joekes 1999). In urban areas, market reforms resulted in the layoff of about one-third of state-owned-enterprise (SOE) employees (about 36 million workers) between 1992 and 2001 (Nicholas R. Lardy 2002). By 2001, the SOE sector accounted for only 12 percent of total national employment (International Labour Organization [ILO] 2004).Women have disproportionately experienced layoffs from the SOEs (ILO 2004). Further, the liberalization of the economy was associated with increased wage discrimination against women (Margaret Maurer-Fazio, Thomas Rawski, and Wei Zhang 1999; Margaret Maurer-Fazio and James Hughes 2002) and women having greater difficulty gaining re-employment after layoffs (Gale Summerfield 1994; Xiao-yuan Dong, Jiangchun Yang, Fenglian Du, and Sai Ding 2006).

In rural areas, market reforms involved the switch from a collective system of agriculture to household responsibility system and the rapid expansion of rural industries owned by township and village governments.[3] The TVEs became an important source of wage employment. In 1996, about 41 percent of total employment in TVEs was female, amounting to

93

54.4 million women (United Nations Development Programme [UNDP] 1999b: 48); by 2001, the TVEs accounted for 18 percent of overall national employment (ILO 2004).[4] In the late 1990s, the collectively owned TVEs were sold to private investors in accordance with national policy.[5] China's accession to the WTO in 2001 will likely accentuate the growth of private enterprises and labor intensive manufacturing (Mo Rong 2002).

Privatization of TVEs has accentuated gender divisions within the workplace by widening the gender gap in income, wealth, and decision making and increasing discrimination against women in terms of earnings and employment opportunities, although it is also associated with increased absolute wages for all workers who were not laid off (Xiao-yuan Dong, Fiona MacPhail, Paul Bowles, and Samuel P. S. Ho 2004). While it is too early to assess the employment effects in China of its WTO membership, the main prediction is that industrial employment in labor-intensive industries will rise and that this shift may promote employment opportunities for women (UNDP 2003: 75–7).[6] The employment gains for women may be smaller, however, if men move into this sector after being laid off from the more capital-intensive or SOE sectors or if women are forced (or choose) to return to the home.[7] Further, the increase in private ownership in the economy, expected to occur under the WTO, may result in increased employment and wage discrimination against women.

The impact of women's market work on household status

Within a household bargaining model, a positive relationship is predicted to exist between employment and welfare.[8] In terms of measuring intrahousehold welfare, empirical studies using a bargaining model tend to focus on the allocation of the household's goods and services among household members (Duncan Thomas 1990; Harold Alderman, Pierre-Andre Chiappori, Laurence Haddad, John Hoddinott, and Ravi Kanbur 1995; John Hoddinott and Lawrence Haddad 1995). In rural China, for example, Lina Song (2000) shows that the higher a woman's education relative to her partner's, the greater the share of household income is spent on children's education and clothing, and the lower the share on alcohol and cigarettes.

In this paper, we adopt a bargaining model of the household for examining the impact of market work on women's household status. First, we recognize that the bargaining may be limited by gender-biased social norms, structures, and ideologies (Bina Agarwal 1997; Deniz Kandiyoti 1998). Norms, as Agarwal argues, can limit what can be bargained over, constrain bargaining power, be the "subject of negotiation," and influence "how the process of bargaining is conducted" (1997: 15). For example, the gendered division of housework often does not adjust to changes in the time allocation between men and women in the workplace (Diane Elson 1999), with the outcome that women in the labor force have less time for leisure than their male counterparts (UNDP 1999a). Thus, women's ability to use their employment to negotiate more favorable outcomes in the household may be constrained by the overarching patriarchal system of gender-biased social norms which vary by location.[9] Therefore, similar increases in resources for men and women may not generate equal improvements in outcomes and may even be negligible for women if it requires altering perceptions of appropriate gender roles that may be strongly held.

Second, in estimating the model, we use three specific indicators, namely, individual's domestic work hours, responsibility for domestic tasks, and control over household decisions. Since this bargaining approach considers these indicators for both men and women, the first two indicators capture the gendered division of labor and the third indicator captures the gender division of control over household decisions. While the term, status, is used in a variety of ways in the literature to reflect not just well-being but also power, we use the term household status to refer collectively to the three indicators specified above.

These indicators go beyond the conventional view of intrahousehold welfare in two ways. The feminist capability literature informs this choice, as researchers have argued that, rather than focusing upon income or commodities as measures of welfare, the focus should be on capabilities since these reflect the freedom to achieve something (see, for example, Amartya Sen [1985]; Vegard Iversen [2003]; Martha Nussbaum [2003]; and Robeyns [2003]). Robeyns (2003), for example, offers a set of capabilities useful for studying gender inequality where the specific indicators include non-market measures and recognize the individuals are interdependent.[10] Our indicators go beyond the market since we focus on domestic labor time, and we recognize that the outcomes will depend upon the presence of other household members.

Also, we refer to three indicators collectively as household status, rather than welfare or well-being. Domestic labor time has a relationship to welfare because for a given amount of market work time, leisure is inversely related to domestic labor time. However, domestic labor time goes beyond welfare because the valuation of domestic labor is socially constructed, and this has implications for control over household resources (see Ann Whitehead 1984). Further, we focus directly on control over household decisions, which by themselves do not proxy for welfare, although they may have subsequent impact on an individual's welfare.

These specific indicators are relevant in the rural Chinese context. A higher domestic burden of women, relative to men, is taken to reflect lower status because, while some domestic tasks can be personally rewarding, many are onerous and time-consuming, leaving little time for leisure. The adverse implications for women's status is accentuated in a situation where domestic labor is undervalued compared to other forms of labor. Tamara Jacka (1997: 101–2), for example, reports that in interviews, peasants and rural cadres in China indicated that domestic work is viewed as less important than other work because it is unproductive, unremunerated, and conducted on the inside, rather than on the outside.[11]

From the literature, it is clear that women in China have a greater domestic work burden;[12] for example, women and men report domestic labor times of 5 and 2.8 hours per day, respectively (W. P. Cheung and C. F. Tao 1993, cited in Sam Wai Kam Yu and Ruby Chui Man Chau 1997: 615).[13] The amount of time and gendered division of labor within the household may change over time, as a result of family size, composition, and household technologies, although not always in obvious ways. For example, the one-child policy may have reduced the total number of children per family (with varying impacts in rural and urban areas), total amount of childcare required, and overall domestic labor. Yet, since it ultimately reduces the number of carers and domestic workers, it can increase the domestic burden for individual women. Also, domestic labor time may decline due to the provision of electricity and running water and the use of appliances for those women with access (Jacka 1997: 106).[14]

Women have increased their role in the family's decision making, compared to the past when the men made most of the major decisions. A recent national survey conducted by the All-China Women's Federation (ACWF), as cited by Xinyan Bao (2002), shows that 57 percent of wives have greater control than their husband over daily expenditure items. However, on bigger items only 7 percent of wives had the greater control over the decisions (Bao 2002); and decision-making patterns of married men and women were further complicated by the influence of fathers and other older relatives. Weiguo Zhang (2002: 163) argues that the proportion of family income controlled by women is greater among younger generations than older ones and, also, that women are increasingly involved in making decisions about the sale of agricultural products, purchasing large items such as houses, and consumer durables and investments.

DATA

In this paper, we use data derived from a survey and in-depth interviews undertaken in three counties in the provinces of Jiangsu and Shandong in 1999 and 2000.[15] Both provinces had been leaders in the development of collective rural industries prior to their privatization in the late 1990s. The three counties, Penglai and Yanzhou in Shandong and Wujin in Jiangsu, are above the national and their respective provincial average per capita income levels, although the income levels of the three counties vary, with Wujin being the highest and Yanzhou the lowest. For a variety of reasons, including slowing output and employment growth and increased competition from the private sector, the local governments, to conform to national policy, undertook major privatization programs of their TVEs in the period 1996–8.

The survey includes twenty-five employees in each of the forty-five TVEs selected.[16] The employees in each enterprise were selected randomly from the payroll list subject to the following conditions: (a) five of the selected employees must have been mid-ranked managerial or technical personnel and (b) all of the selected employees must have worked at the enterprise both before and after privatization. Our analysis focuses on those who were married (accounting for 79 percent of the total of 1,125 employees in the sample).[17] In-depth interviews were conducted with five married men and fifteen married women selected from the sample of completed employee questionnaires at each of the TVEs, in four sample enterprises in the two counties of Shandong province, with two in light industry and two in heavy industry.

Based upon the survey questionnaire, we obtained information on workers in four broad categories. For demographic characteristics, we gathered data on each worker's age, marital status, number of children, years of education, and work history. Concerning market work, we collected data on the number of hours of paid labor and wages in the TVE. For domestic labor, the data collected included the distribution of household tasks among household members, hours spent on household tasks, and how household decisions are made. We collected data on specific tasks that we thought are important in this context based upon our review of selected anthropological studies (see Jacka [1997: 101], for example).

The follow-up interviews that were conducted with selected workers who responded to the questionnaire used an open-ended question format to seek information on the importance of market work, views about domestic labor (which tasks are onerous or enjoyable), reasons for a particular form of domestic division of labor, views about the pattern of household decision-making, and how the division of labor and pattern of decision making are different from their parents.

The strengths of the data are twofold. First, the follow-up interviews provide information helpful for interpreting survey results and useful examples. Second, both types of data collection methods sought responses from both men and women, and thus, we are able to make gender comparisons.

There are several limitations of the data viewed for the purposes of this study. First, the sample is comprised of workers in the TVE sector, and therefore, there is less variation in earnings among the respondents than if the sample also included people working in the agricultural sector or sideline activities and those without income-generating work.[18] However, our sample is representative of married workers in China's rural industrial sector, and it is workers in the industrial sector who are most likely to be

97

affected by changes arising from accession to the WTO. Second, the sample does not include matched husbands and wives. Therefore, it is not possible, for example, to explore gender-time gaps of a matched husband and wife within a given household, and we rely upon differences between married men and women in general.[19] Third, the indicators of domestic responsibilities and household decision-making influence are measured by respondents' own statements. While peoples' perceptions of domestic labor and decision-making influence are shaped by norms or value judgements, we think that systematic variations in these indicators provide useful information about the actual division of labor and decision-making patterns.

Descriptive statistics for this sample are presented in Table 1. Female workers comprise 39 percent of the sample, which reflects their representation in the TVE workforce. Nearly half (46 percent) of the workers live in extended households, either with parents or parents-in-law. Women and men in this sample have on average similar levels of education. In terms of income, female workers contribute an average of 44 percent of the combined income from husband and wife and 40 percent of the total household income.[20]

Table 1 Descriptive statistics of the sample of married TVE workers[a]

	All	Men	Women
Age (years)	35.39	36.16	34.10
	(8.21)	(8.72)	(7.08)
Number of children	1.19	1.27	1.06
	(0.62)	(0.68)	(0.47)
Living with parents or in-laws (%)	46	46	45
	(0.50)	(0.50)	(0.50)
Education (years of schooling)	9.12	9.34	8.76
	(2.19)	(2.24)	(2.07)
Spouse's education (years of schooling)	8.12	7.82	8.89
	(2.24)	(2.21)	(2.13)
Relative education (%)[b]	53	54	49
	(8.5)	(9.0)	(6.0)
Annual income (yuan)	6,833	7,701	5,486
	(4,430)	(5,173)	(2,367)
Wage rate (yuan/hour)	2.75	2.21	3.11
	(2.07)	(0.063)	(0.11)
Spouse's annual income (yuan)	5,204	3,634	7,843
	(5,443)	(3,048)	(7,267)
Relative household Income (%)[c]	58	68	44
	(18.0)	(14.0)	(14.0)
Observations	717	436	281

Notes: [a]Figures in parentheses are standard deviations. [b]Relative education shows a worker's years of schooling divided by the sum of his/her and his/her spouse's years of schooling times 100. [c]Share in family income is the annual earnings of a worker divided by the sum his/her and his/her spouse's annual earnings times 100.
Source: Calculated from the survey of TVE workers.

RESULTS

Perceptions of women's status and meanings of market work

We start by analyzing men's and women's perceptions of women's status in society, their families, and their workplaces. We also examine three specific workplace issues relating to women's opportunities to receive training and promotions, opportunities to participate in enterprise's decision making, and the meanings respondents attached to their market work in the TVE sector. Through the survey, we collected data on respondents' perceptions of women's status in these areas, and while status in these survey questions is more broadly conceived, compared to our definition of household status used in the remainder of the paper, the results contribute to the context for the paper.

To assess the general perceptions of women's status, we asked respondents: "In your opinion, which of the following statements best characterizes the condition faced by men and women," to which workers responded using a three-point scale, where 1 indicates women's status is lesser than men's, 2 indicates status is the same as men's, and 3 indicates women's status is greater than men's.[21] The first part of Table 2 presents the average rankings derived from responses regarding women's status

Table 2 Perceptions of the status of women[a]

	Mean Score[b]		
	All	Women	Men
Status in society	1.98	1.94	2.00
	(0.001)*	(0.002)***	(0.001)
Status in family	2.05	2.01	2.07
	(0.011)***	(0.008)	(0.014)***
Status in work place	1.95	1.89	2.00
	(0.015)***	(0.024)***	(0.001)
Specific workplace issues			
Opportunity to receive training	1.91	1.89	1.91
	(0.017)***	(0.033)***	(0.023)***
Opportunity for promotion	1.75	1.69	1.79
	(0.020)***	(0.032)***	(0.025)***
Opportunity to participate in	1.78	1.69	1.83
enterprise's decision making	(0.018)***	(0.031)***	(0.022)***
Observations	759	300	459

Notes: [a]Workers' perceptions of women's condition in each situation with 1 indicating less (or lower) than men, 2 indicating same as men, and 3 meaning greater (or higher) than men. [b]Figures in parentheses are the standard errors of the test for the null hypothesis that the mean score is equal to 2. * denotes statistical significance at the 10 percent level; ** denotes statistical significance at the 5 percent level; *** denotes statistical significance at the 1 percent level for a two-tailed test.
Source: Calculated from the survey of TVE workers.

relative to men in society, family, and workplace. From women's perspectives, their status is lower than men's in society and the workplace and equal with men in the family. By contrast, men perceive that women have an equal status with men in society and the workplace and a higher status in the family.

The second part of Table 2 reports the perception scores with respect to specific workplace issues. For all workers (men and women combined), the general perception is that women experience a lower status than men on the three workplace issues. Examining the results separately for men and women indicates that women perceive a lower condition for themselves, compared to men's assessment of women's situation.

The information provided by female workers in the follow-up interviews illustrates the importance women attach to being able to contribute financially to their families. Below, are some sample responses:

- "Our family life would be worse without this job."
- "My income lightens my family's burden."
- "Working is necessary for buying food for my child and other family members."

The in-depth interviews also reveal the importance of market work to women's status, as shown in the following extracts:

- "If I did not have a job, I would feel shame staying at home living off of my husband."
- "My position is higher with a job, and I would be under some pressure without work."
- "Without a job people will look down on you, even if your husband does not."
- "With your own income, other members of the family do not look down on you."
- "Without a job, I would look down on myself, although my husband and son would not."

In addition, women expressed a preference for waged work over agricultural work and indicated that they derived personal satisfaction from working:

- "I could do farm work, but work in the enterprise is less gruelling and I can make friends."
- "I do not need to work because my family is well-off, but working can satisfy my spirit."
- "If I do not work, my life would be meaningless. I would feel I had nothing to depend on."

Domestic labor time and gender division of domestic labor

Patterns of domestic labor time and gender division of labor

Overall, women have heavier work burdens than men, as shown in Table 3. First, in terms of market work, women and men both work a large number of hours per week in the TVEs; on average, women work 56.61 hours per week and men work 55.42 hours per week, although the difference is not statistically significant. Second, in terms of domestic labor (time spent on activities such as cleaning, shopping, cooking, laundry, and care of children and elders), women reported undertaking an average of 22.43 hours per week, compared to men's reported contribution, which averaged 14.93 hours per week. The gender time gap for domestic labor is about 7.5 hours per week (a statistically significant difference) which is a sizeable gap amounting to more than 50 percent of the average male domestic labor.[22] Thus, women have comparable hours of paid labor but because they perform more hours of unpaid domestic labor, their overall work burden is higher (by nine hours per week).

In addition to gender differences in the amount of time allocated to domestic tasks, we are interested in whether a gendered division of domestic labor exists. People were asked to assess who in their household did various household tasks, using a six-point scale, where 5 indicated self, 4 mostly self but with some help from spouse, 3 equally shared between self and spouse,

Table 3 Time allocated to market and domestic labor

	Women	Men	Test score[a] & standard error
Market labor			
Hours per week	56.61	55.42	1.19
	(12.81)	(9.63)	(0.83)
Months per year	11.56	11.62	−0.06
	(0.91)	(0.74)	(0.05)
Hours per year	2,632.87	2,584.14	48.73
	(682.96)	(516.91)	(44.71)
Domestic labor			
Hours per week	22.43	14.93	7.50***
	(11.47)	(8.95)	(0.66)
Total labor			
Hours per week	79.18	70.14	9.04***
	(15.16)	(12.55)	(0.78)
Observations	303	460	

Notes: [a]Figures in parentheses are standard deviations in the first two columns and standard errors in the last column. The test score is the between-group difference with *** denoting the significance level of 1 percent for a two-tailed test.
Source: Calculated from the survey of TVE workers.

2 equally shared by all family members, 1 mostly spouse but with some help from self, and 0 spouse alone or parents or in-laws.

The frequency results indicate that the majority of respondents reported the various sets of household tasks are shared equally between self and spouse, see Table 4. Notice that respondents reported the highest percentages for option 3 (equal sharing of tasks between self and spouse). This result appears to overstate the contribution of men to domestic tasks, compared to the previously reported estimates of hours spent on household tasks, which showed that, on average, men performed about two-thirds of the domestic labor time of women. A possible explanation for the difference between the two sets of findings is that respondents may answer the questions on responsibility for domestic tasks in terms of norms about who should undertake these tasks, rather than on how these tasks are actually undertaken in their households.[23] Since the measure of domestic hours is less affected by the subjective interpretation of equal sharing responsibilities, it is more reliable.

For each of the three categories of tasks, the mean score for women is higher than that for men, and the differences are statistically significant. The mean score is higher for women than men because a higher percentage of women undertake these tasks by themselves or mostly by themselves with some help from their spouse (categories 4 and 5). For example, in the "food shopping, cooking, laundry, and housecleaning" set of tasks, 32.5 percent of women, compared to 4.3 percent of men, reported performing this tasks by themselves or mostly by themselves. Thus, in terms of the gendered division of domestic tasks, women are more likely than men to have primary responsibility for domestic tasks, and this is particularly the case for the food and cleaning set of tasks.

The interview comments illuminate possible reasons why, in the gender division of domestic labor, women are more likely to have primary responsibility for domestic tasks and undertake greater amounts of domestic labor time compared to men. The comments also illustrate the nature of the system of gender-biased norms and values in which negotiations about time allocation and household decision-making occur. Women perceive that housework is their duty, as shown by the following responses:

- "I do not like housework but have to do it. My husband does a little, but I do not think men should do housework. Doing housework is women's duty."
- "Housework is a duty whether you like it or not."

There is also a sense that women perceive their domestic work to be easier than that of their mothers'. For example, one respondent said:

102

Table 4 Gender Division of Domestic Labor[a]

	Women	Men	Test score[b] & standard error
Food shopping, cooking, laundry, and housecleaning			
Frequency (%)			
0	1.7	10.0	
1	0.3	29.4	
2	11.1	7.6	
3	54.4	48.6	
4	18.6	2.6	
5	13.9	1.7	
Mean score	3.27	2.09	1.18***
	(0.06)	(0.06)	(0.08)
Caring of elderly and children			
Frequency (%)			
0	3.4	6.7	
1	0.7	15.5	
2	12.8	8.1	
3	64.5	66.9	
4	12.5	2.2	
5	6.1	0.6	
Mean score	3.00	2.45	0.55***
	(0.05)	(0.05)	(0.07)
Work on private plot and care of livestock			
Frequency (%)			
0	16.4	16.9	
1	5.2	18.3	
2	6.1	4.2	
3	61.9	55.5	
4	6.1	4.4	
5	4.2	0.7	
Mean score	2.49	2.14	0.35***
	(0.09)	(0.06)	(0.11)
Observations	296	459	

Notes: [a]Workers' assessments of who does each household task, with 5 indicating self, 4 mostly self but with some help from spouse, 3 equally shared between self and spouse, 2 equally shared by all family members, 1 mostly spouse but with some help from self, and 0 spouse alone or parents or in-laws.
[b]Figures in parentheses are standard deviations in the first two columns and standard errors in the last column. The test score is the between group difference with *** denoting the significance level of 1 percent for a two-tailed test.
Source: Calculated from the survey of TVE workers.

"My mother did more than me. She had more children, no running water and no electricity."

Men feel that, in comparison to their fathers, they do more housework. But they may have freedom as to which household tasks to undertake. For example, one man stated: "I do the cooking sometimes but not washing. I do not like it because it is too time consuming. My father never did any housework."

Determinants of domestic labor time

In our model, an individual's domestic labor time, measured by average weekly hours spent on domestic labor (reported in Table 3), is a function of the person's predicted wage rate, predicted number of hours of market work, relative income share, number of children, living arrangement, and age, as well as regional variables. The wage rate reflects the opportunity costs of leisure and home production time, and thus, an increase in the wage rate is expected to reduce the number of hours the person allocates to leisure and home production by inducing her/him to supply additional hours to the labor market. A higher wage rate, for a given amount of market work hours, also implies a higher level of income, enabling the worker to enjoy more leisure. Overall though, we expect a negative relationship between the wage rate and domestic labor time. We use the predicted market wage rate, rather than the actual market wage rate, in order to avoid potential endogeneity between market wage rate and domestic labor time. The endogeneity problem arises because the market wage rate is calculated as total annual earnings divided by annual market work hours and the number of market work hours may be determined simultaneously by the amount of domestic labor time.[24]

We introduce the number of hours of market work in order to test for the substitutability of market work time for domestic labor time. Neoclassical economic theory considers home production a close substitute to market work (Reuben Gronau 1986). If, however, the allocation of time between housework and market work is dictated by social conventions in the short run, then the substitution effect may be observed only for men, and women who allocate more time to market work may do so at the expense of their leisure instead of domestic labor, which is confirmed by empirical studies on gender and time allocation in developing countries (Floro 1995). The number of hours of market work is measured by the predicted market work hours, rather than the actual hours of work, in order to avoid simultaneity between domestic labor time and market work time.[25]

The individual's relative household income contribution, defined as the ratio of the individual's earnings to the sum of the earnings of that individual and his/her spouse, is introduced as a proxy for a worker's relative contribution to household income. An increase in the individual's visible financial contribution is expected to raise his/her ability to bargain for a reduced domestic work burden, at a given market wage rate; and thus, we expect a negative relationship between the relative income contribution variable and domestic labor time. When market work hours are controlled for, the effect of financial resources on domestic labor time reflects the reallocation of time between domestic labor and leisure.

We control for other socioeconomic factors related to domestic labor time, including the presence of children, living arrangements, age, and locality. We expect married workers who live in households with children will undertake greater amounts of household labor. Living in an extended family situation with older adults increases the possibility of sharing domestic labor, as well as the responsibility of taking care of the elderly; hence the impact of living with parents or parents-in-law on domestic labor cannot be determined a priori.[26] The presence of children and living in an extended family situation may not affect the domestic labor burden equally for men and women because the sharing of work burdens is set within an overarching patriarchal structure which values the contributions of men, including men's leisure, more highly than the contributions of women. Specifically, the presence of children may increase the domestic labor time for women but not for men; living with parents may reduce the domestic labor time for men but not for women.

We include the age of the respondent because of norms associated with respect for the elderly. This may mean that older men are less likely to be involved in domestic labor, although, age may have little bearing on women's domestic labor time. Finally we include regional dummy variables to reflect differences among the three counties.

The determinants of weekly hours of domestic labor time are estimated by a Tobit regression and the results are presented in Table 5. As indicated by the χ^2 test scores at the bottom of the table, all the regressions are highly significant. We report the estimates of marginal effects instead of the coefficients because the former estimates are more intuitive. The first column reports the regression results for all workers with a dummy variable included for the sex of the worker and it takes the value of 1 if the worker is a man. Note that the dummy variable for male workers is negative and significant and the estimates indicate that men, on average, perform 2.2 hours per week less domestic labor after controlling for other variables, a result which is consistent with the descriptive statistics reported in Table 3.

For men, financial resources are associated with lower domestic labor time commitments. The estimated elasticities indicate that domestic labor time will fall by 0.39 percent with respect to a one percent increase in the wage rate and by 0.52 percent with respect to a one percent increase in the relative household income contribution. The predicted market work hour variable also has a negative sign and is statistically significant. For men, market work and domestic labor time appear to be highly substitutable with a one percent increase in market hours resulting in a decline of housework hours by 2.14 percent.[27] In terms of age, older men provide less domestic labor than younger men, given that the age variable is negative and statistically significant. Quantitatively, the estimate indicates that a man would provide 1.5 hours less domestic labor per week than a man aged ten

Table 5 Tobit regressions of the determinants of weekly domestic labor hours[a]

	All workers marginal effect	Elasticity[b]	Women marginal effect	Elasticity[b]	Men marginal effect	Elasticity[b]
Male	−2.236 (1.349)*		−		−	
Predicted wage	−9.647 (2.815)***	−0.52	−9.793 (4.372)**	−0.43	−6.045 (3.179)**	−0.39
Relative household income	−7.321 (2.454)***	−0.39	−1.159 (4.331)	−0.05	−8.231 (2.939)***	−0.52
Predicted market−work hours	−0.631 (0.196)***	−1.90	−0.119 (0.234)	−0.29	−0.610 (0.273)***	−2.14
Number of children	0.734 (0.843)		3.027 (1.545)**		−0.152 (0.944)	
Living with parents/ Parents-in-law	0.791 (0.711)		1.241 (1.207)		0.304 (0.843)	
Age	−0.154 (0.065)***		−0.018 (0.105)		−0.154 (0.075)**	
Wujin	0.954 (2.316)		−8.328 (3.737)**		1.404 (2.237)	
Yanzhou	−1.931 (1.139)**		−3.489 (1.947)***		−0.541 (1.348)	
Constant	79.618 (11.914)***		37.752 (14.876)**		75.585 (16.154)***	
χ^2 test − zero slope	214.85		84.74		58.96	
p-value	0.00		0.00		0.00	
Pseudo R^2	0.038		0.037		0.018	
Observations	748		296		452	

Notes: [a]The table presents the estimated marginal effects of the Tobit regressions with standard errors reported in parentheses. [b]The estimates of elasticities are derived at the sample mean values of the variables involved. * denotes statistical significance at the 10 percent level; ** denotes statistical significance at the 5 percent level; *** denotes statistical significance at the 1 percent level.
Source: Calculated from the survey of TVE workers.

years younger. Finally, for men, the presence of children is not statistically significantly associated with domestic labor time and neither is the living arrangements variable.[28]

For women, the predicted wage and the relative household income contribution variables both have negative signs, but only the predicted wage is statistically significant. As with men, a higher wage rate induces women to substitute market work for domestic work and also affords women more leisure time, with the size of wage elasticity slightly higher than for men. Notice that the estimated elasticity indicates that domestic labor time will fall by .43 percent with respect to a one percent increase in the wage rate. However, unlike for men, a rise in relative household income contribution has no effect on women's time commitment to domestic labor, at a given wage rate. Moreover, women's market work time does not have significant effect on their domestic labor time and unlike for men, age has no significant effect on women's domestic labor.

Why do men substitute market work time for domestic labor time and women do not? The comments from the in-depth interviews suggest that women undertake domestic labor because they and others view domestic labor as their duty. The lack of substitution of market hours for domestic hours among women is consistent with a bargaining model in which increased market work time is still insufficient to enable women to negotiate a reduced domestic work burden given cultural norms about who should be undertaking domestic labor. This idea is also supported by the results for the presence of children. For women, unlike for men, the presence of children does increase their domestic labor time (three hours per week), as indicated by the positive and statistically significant coefficient on the number of children variable.

In addition to cultural norms, gender wage inequality may well contribute to the weak response of women's domestic hours to market hours relative to men's. In our sample, the wage rate of women is 40 percent lower than that of men. Thus, at a given wage rate, an additional market work hour enables a male worker to purchase more goods and services to substitute for domestic labor than it does for a female worker. Moreover, given the traditional marriage pattern that a husband's wage is higher than a wife's wage as in the case of our sample (see statistics on income and spousal income in Table 1), the lack of responsiveness between market and domestic work time for women is also consistent with a bargaining framework in which women are unable to negotiate a reduction in their domestic work hours even if their market work hours increase because their wages are still lower than men's wages. This may explain why women's domestic hours are responsive to wages but not market hours. Thus, reducing gender wage differentials would increase women's ability to substitute market work time for domestic labor.

Determinants of the gender division of domestic labor

We examine the determinants of the gender division of domestic labor with respect to selected domestic tasks, using a modified version of the above model. The dependent variable is the gender division of domestic labor for three sets of tasks, which were presented in descriptive terms in Table 4. Since the dependent variable is defined in a relative manner, we include the relative household income contribution variable to proxy access to financial resources and omit the predicted wage. The variables for education and spouse's education are added to the list of explanatory variables to examine if education fosters a value of gender equality within the household. Since the dependent variable is an ordinal variable, with six numerical values which are ordered in terms of increasing responsibility for the domestic task, the model is estimated using an Ordered Probit Regression, instead of using Ordinary Least Squares (William H. Greene 2003). We present the results separately for men and women in Table 6.

For women, the hypothesis that the greater the individual's financial resources the less likely she is to be responsible for certain domestic tasks is supported for two sets of tasks, namely the cooking, cleaning, and laundry set and the care of the elderly and children. Note that for these two dependent variables, the relative household income variable is negative and statistically significant. Although the variable is significant indicating that relative household income influences the gendered division of labor, we cannot assess the empirical impact. The dependent variable in the regressions is a rank-ordered variable, and thus, we cannot directly evaluate whether a given change in an independent variable, such as women's relative household income, would have a large or small impact on shifting the responsibility for a set of domestic tasks away from women to men.

As with the time allocation regression, the number of predicted market work hours has no significant effect on women's responsibility on any of the three selected activities. Thus, it appears that the actual financial contribution has the impact on allocation or negotiation of the gendered division of labor, rather than just involvement in market work. In terms of household composition, living with parents-in-law is associated with a lower probability of responsibility for the domestic tasks of cooking, cleaning, and laundry, as well as tending plots and livestock, but it is not statistically related to care for children and elderly. Education reduces women's responsibility for taking care of private plot and livestock but has no effect on the other two sets of tasks, and spouse's education is not statistically significant for any of three domestic activities.

Compared with the regressions for women, the explanatory power of the regressions for men is low. Further, only two variables, education and living arrangement, are statistically significant in some models.[29] The finding that relative household income contribution and predicted market work hours variables are not significant may indicate that men can choose whether to participate in these domestic tasks as suggested by the data from the in-depth interviews reported upon above, rather than having to negotiate with their spouse based upon their involvement in the market.

In summary, women have a greater work burden than men, given that men and women on average allocate similar amounts of time to market

Table 6 Ordered probit regressions of the gender division of domestic labor tasks[a]

	Female workers			Male workers	
	Cooking, cleaning, etc.	Caring of elderly & children	Taking care of private plots & livestock	Cooking, cleaning, etc.	Caring of elderly & children	Taking care of private plots & livestock
Relative household income	−0.965	−1.083	−0.479	−0.569	0.406	0.243
	(0.491)**	(0.510)**	(0.623)	(0.376)	(0.402)	(0.414)
Predicted market work hours	−0.021	−0.021	−0.050	−0.028	−0.035	−0.051
	(0.025)	(0.026)	(0.031)	(0.027)	(0.030)	(0.032)
Education	−0.003	−0.018	−0.122	−0.076	0.008	−0.098
	(0.036)	(0.037)	(0.050)*	(0.025)***	(0.028)	(0.029)***
Spouse's education	−0.008	−0.052	−0.024	0.032	0.005	0.031
	(0.035)	(0.036)	(0.046)	(0.026)	(0.029)	(0.029)
Age	0.012	0.027	0.050	0.001	0.004	0.005
	(0.012)	(0.012)**	(0.014)***	(0.009)	(0.010)	(0.010)
Living with parents/in-laws	−0.389	−0.070	−0.375	0.268	0.010	−0.022
	(0.136)***	(0.139)	(−2.20)**	(0.107)**	(0.115)	(0.116)
Number of children	−0.055	−0.043	−0.134	0.055	−0.012	0.001
	(0.171)	(0.179)	(0.230)	(0.119)	(0.129)	(0.134)
Wujin	−0.400	−0.127	0.461	0.358	0.345	0.265
	(0.403)	(0.414)	(0.510)	(0.220)*	(0.239)	(0.249)
Yanzhou	−0.191	0.164	0.344	0.017	0.082	−0.187
	(0.192)	(0.199)	(0.287)	(0.143)	(0.155)	(0.161)
χ^2 test – zero slope	50.09	37.96	54.99	24.96	4.73	29.31
p-value	0.00	0.00	0.00	0.00	0.85	0.00
Scaled R^2	0.068	0.057	0.106	0.021	0.005	0.030
Observations	297	296	212	456	453	403

Notes: [a]The table reports the estimates of the ordered probit regressions with standard errors presented in parentheses. * denotes statistical significance at the 10 percent level; ** denotes statistical significance at the 5 percent level; *** denotes statistical significance at the 1 percent level.
Source: Calculated from the survey of TVE workers.

work but women undertake greater amounts of domestic labor, which the secondary literature indicates is not as highly valued as work undertaken outside of the home (see Jacka [1997]). Further, while the amount of domestic labor time and gender division of domestic labor are influenced by market work, for women the market wage and the relative household income contribution are important determinants respectively, rather than the number of hours contributed to the market work. For men, domestic labor hours respond to all three determinants of market work, namely, the wage, relative household income, and market work hours.

Gender division of household decision-making

Patterns of household decision making

To investigate the gendered pattern of household decision making, workers were asked to assess how three types of decisions are made in their households: with 4 indicating by oneself, 3 mostly self in consultation with spouse, 2 self and spouse equally, 1 mostly spouse in consultation with self, and 0 spouse, parents, or in-laws alone. As shown in Table 7, men tend to

Table 7 Gender division of household decision-making[a]

	Women	Men	Test score & standard error
Mean score[b]			
Major purchases	1.98	2.16	-0.18^{***}
	(0.53)	(0.72)	(0.04)
Children's education	2.01	2.15	-0.14^{***}
	(0.56)	(0.62)	(0.04)
Own employment	2.81	3.01	-0.20^{***}
	(1.01)	(0.95)	(0.07)
Frequency			
Major purchase Choice			
0	2.9	3.7	
1	4.0	2.8	
2	86.1	72.1	
3	4.6	16.2	
4	1.7	5.0	
Observations	301	458	

Notes: [a]Workers assessment of how the following decisions are made in their household with 4 indicating self, 3 mostly self in consultation with spouse, 2 self and spouse equally, 1 mostly spouse in consultation with self, and 0 spouse, parents or in-laws alone. [b]Figures in parentheses are standard deviations in the first two columns and standard errors in the last column. The test score is the between-group difference with *** denoting the significance level of 1 percent for a two-tailed test.
Source: Calculated from the survey of TVE workers.

have greater control over household decisions, compared to women. Note that the mean score for decision-making influence in each of the three categories is higher for men than women and the difference is highly significant. This result arises because men are more likely to view decisions as being taken either by themselves or mostly by themselves with some consultation with their spouse. This is consistent with the reports from women who indicate that decisions are taken mostly by their spouse or in consultation with them. The frequency distribution for major purchases in Table 7 shows this point as well. Thus, the difference of 0.18 between the mean scores for women and men with respect to major purchases occurs because 21.2 percent of men view decisions about major purchases being made by themselves or mostly by them in consultation with their spouse (sum of options 3 and 4), compared with 6.3 percent of women.[30]

Comments made by workers in the interview reflect the tendency for men to have more control over household decision-making. The comments also suggest that even with increased financial resources there are limits to women's bargaining power. For example, women stated:

- "My husband has the final say. I can buy inexpensive things with no interference, but we discuss expensive things."
- "My husband makes more decisions; we discuss but he decides. I am not much different from my mother."
- "On more important issues, my husband decides; I have no say in the important issues and I feel that my position is lower than my husband's."
- "My husband makes the final decisions; he is more experienced and reasonable. I do not hope to have more say in this matter, and his eldest brother also makes decisions that affect us."
- "My position is the same as my mother's. She decided all household affairs, and my father decided external ones."
- "My position is higher than my mother's: she had no say over building our house, where and how much to save, and whether to send children to school."

Interestingly, men reported that:

- "I have the final say in how big money is spent and how to treat my parents well."
- "We generally discuss things, but I can decide."
- "I have a more important role: I can persuade her."
- "My position is lower than my father's: he had more say."
- "My father decided all family affairs and we feared him."

Determinants of the gender division of household decision-making

Turning now to determinants of the gender division of household decision making, we assess factors that may affect decision-making control using the model developed above. Here, the dependent variable is the gender household decision-making variable with respect to the three types of decisions, namely major purchases, children's education, and personal employment. We have added an individual's education relative to his/her spouse's education to the model because relative education levels may be perceived to affect one's right or ability to make decisions. Predicted market hours and number of children were not statistically significant variables in the estimated model of the gendered division of domestic responsibilities, and consequently, these two variables have been excluded from this model. The model is estimated by an Ordered Probit Regression and the results are presented separately for men and women in Table 8.

Starting with men, financial resources and education are both important determinants of male decision-making control. For example, the relative household income contribution variable is positive and significant in the equations explaining decision-making control over major purchases and own employment, and relative education has positive effects on the probability of higher degree of decision-making control over all three types of decisions. Based upon the regression results, we cannot directly infer the quantitative impact of a given change in relative education on the gender division of household decision-making.

For women, surprisingly, the financial resources hypothesis, that an increase in women's relative household income contribution will enable them greater household decision-making control, is not supported by any regression results; note that the relative household income contribution variable is significant but is negative in two equations. However, relative education does give women more control over decisions regarding their children's education. For women, living with parents-in-law reduces their decision-making influence over major purchases and own employment. This supports the idea noted in the literature that a move to nuclear families is associated with a decline in patriarchal control. In general, the regressions of household decision-making are less statistically significant for women than for men, judging by the χ^2 tests reported at the bottom of Table 8.[31]

The finding that men's relative household income affects their control over household decisions indicates indirectly that women's income does influence women's own control over household decisions. For example, if women's incomes decline, then men's relative household income contribution increases resulting in a decrease in women's own control over household decisions and an increase in men's control. The regression

112

Table 8 Ordered probit regressions of the gender division of household decision-making[a]

	Women				Men			
	Major purch.	Children's educ.	Own emp.	Major purch.	Children's educ.	Own emp.
Relative household income	−1.194	−1.384	−0.097	1.127	0.219	0.674
	(0.619)*	(0.638)**	(0.483)	(0.402)***	(0.446)	(0.345)*
Education relative to spouse	0.906	3.937	0.891	1.391	2.129	1.629
	(1.325)	(1.356)***	(1.048)	(0.657)**	(0.687)***	(0.650)**
Age	−0.012	0.001	−0.011	−0.003	0.006	−0.004
	(0.012)	(0.012)	(0.009)	(0.007)	(0.007)	(0.006)
Living with parents/in-laws	−0.372	−0.034	−0.269	−0.029	−0.108	−0.009
	(0.177)**	(0.179)	(0.136)**	(0.116)	(0.126)	(0.110)
Wujin	0.237	0.049	0.131	0.323	0.528	0.133
	(0.196)	(0.196)	(0.152)	(0.154)**	(0.171)***	(0.146)
Yanzhou	−0.161	−0.295	−0.297	0.139	0.587	0.028
	(0.226)	(0.243)	(0.178)*	(0.141)	(0.158)***	(0.132)
χ^2 test–zero slope	11.94	14.45	11.43	17.58	34.46	11.49
p-value	0.063	0.025	0.076	0.007	0.00	0.074
Scaled R^2	0.037	0.046	0.016	0.021	0.051	0.011
Observations	301	295	296	455	451	451

Notes: [a]The table reports the estimates of the ordered probit regressions with standard errors presented in parentheses. * denotes statistical significance at the 10 percent level; ** denotes statistical significance at the 5 percent level; *** denotes statistical significance at the 1 percent level.
Source: Calculated from the Survey of TVE workers.

results for the sample of women surprisingly does not support the hypothesis, but the results may suggest that there is not a straightforward linear relationship between relative household income contribution and bargaining power and the outcome of control over household decision-making exists. The relationship between income and decision-making control remains an area for further exploration through qualitative studies of the bargaining process and determinants, and quantitative analysis which would test some new hypotheses, as well as alternative indicators of control over household decisions.

CONCLUSION

This study of market work and household status draws upon a sample of married men and women who work for wages in the Township and Village Enterprise sector in the provinces of Shandong and Jiangsu in rural China. Household status is used as a way to capture three specific indicators, namely, the amount of domestic labor, gender division of domestic tasks, and gender division of household decision-making influence. These indicators go beyond welfare and its conventional indicators of income, resources, and commodities, and our approach is consistent with the measurement of capabilities, as discussed in the feminist capabilities literature.

The main finding reflects that women have lower household status than men based upon the indicators of their greater total work burden (by nine hours per week), greater domestic work burden (by 7.5 hours per week), greater responsibility for domestic tasks, and lower influence over household decisions compared to men.

In terms of the determinants of women's household status, first, market work time is not a statistically significant determinant of domestic labor time. Women are unable to substitute market work time for domestic labor time, which may occur, as suggested by the in-depth interviews, because women view domestic labor as their duty. Second, the wage rate is a statistically significant determinant of domestic labor time, and thus, we conclude that market work that generates visible financial resources does enable women to reduce their domestic labor time. Third, women's relative household income contribution is a statistically significant determinant of the gendered division of labor of domestic tasks. Fourth, evidence supporting the hypothesis that market work positively impacts women's household decision-making control is mixed. While regression results for the sample of women do not support this hypothesis, results based on the sample of men indicate that increases in men's relative household income contributes to male decision-making control within the household. The finding that men's relative income contribution is an important determinant of the amount of male control over household decisions, suggests that women's earnings are therefore important to their decision-making control within the household. Hence, the findings from the male sub-sample offers some evidence of what would happen to women if they were denied access to waged employment.

The mixed results relating to the hypothesis that market work and its corresponding income positively affects household decision-making influence necessitates further exploring the nature and determinants of bargaining through more qualitative analysis of bargaining, which may in turn suggest fruitful lines of quantitative analysis.

These results indicate that increased market work opportunities for women can contribute to improvements in women's household status but, like previous researchers, we conclude that this relationship must be qualified. First, when looking at the role market work plays in determining of household status, access to waged employment does not alone enable women to reduce their domestic labor time and to shift the gender division of domestic tasks, since we find that women were unable to substitute market work hours for domestic hours. It is not the provision of labor time to the market that matters, rather, it is women's financial contribution to the household (relative to their spouses'), which is determined by wages and the gender wage gap that directly affects domestic labor time and the gender division of domestic tasks. Even though women were unable to substitute market work for domestic labor, as men could, the in-depth interview results indicate that women do value their waged jobs. Second, access to waged employment, while important, cannot be assumed to improve all dimensions of women's household status, given the mixed evidence on the relationship between relative household income and household decision-making influence. Women's wages had an impact on the amount of domestic labor and gender division of domestic labor but did not directly affect the third indicator of household status – decision-making control in the household – in the regression for female respondents.

Should employment opportunities for women increase with China's membership in the WTO, improvements in women's household status will also depend upon the wages and the gender wage gap experienced in this new employment. Thus, the government should implement and monitor labor programs not only to promote gender equity in hiring in order to ensure access to employment; further, given the currently lower opportunities for women to receive training, be promoted, and participate in enterprise decision-making programs to promote gender equity within organizations are also important. Apart from programs to ensure equitable access to employment at all levels, promotion of wage equity is critical for reducing the gender wage gap and enabling women to contribute more equally with men to the household. Finally, programs to encourage equal sharing of domestic responsibilities and care between men and women may help change the norms about who should provide the domestic labor, although the lack of change in the gender division of labor during the Mao period cautions against such a program having success if implemented alone.

Fiona MacPhail, University of Northern British Columbia, Economics,
3333 University Way, Prince George, British Columbia V2N 4Z9, Canada
e-mail: macphail@unbc.ca

Xiao-yuan Dong, University of Winnipeg, Economics,
515 Portage Avenue, Winnipeg, Manitoba R3B 2E9, Canada
e-mail: x.dong@uwinnipeg.ca

ACKNOWLEDGMENTS

The authors would like to thank Paul Bowles, four anonymous reviewers, Günseli Berik, Gale Summerfield, Junjie Chen, James Hughes, Nancy Folbre, and the participants at the Gender, China, and the WTO Workshop held at Rice University for their very helpful comments on a previous version of the paper. This research is part of the University of British Columbia Centre for Chinese Research Project on Rural Change in the People's Republic of China and was carried out with aid of a grant from the International Development Research Centre, Ottawa, Canada.

NOTES

[1] The term welfare has been used by economists to refer to outcomes in bargaining models and neoclassical models more generally, as indicated in paragraph one and the quote used.

[2] Since 1978, real per capita income has quadrupled (Shujie Yao 2002: 354); however, the dramatic rise in absolute income has been accompanied by an enormous increase in inequality making income distribution in China one of the most unequal in the world (Azizur Khan and Carl Riskin 2001; Gene H. Chang 2002). For information on market reforms, see for example, Barry Naughton (1995), Joseph Fewsmith (1997), Sarah Cook, Shujie Yao, and Juzhong Zhuang (2000).

[3] While TVEs can be found in most sectors of the economy, the majority are in the industrial sector, producing light consumer goods (Michelle S. Mood 1997: 134) and using labor-intensive production methods. In terms of the export orientation of TVEs, in 1992, TVEs produced 25.5 percent of China's total exports (calculated from People's Republic of China 1993: 148 and People's Republic of China 1996: 580).

[4] While the TVE sector offers wage employment opportunities, considerable industrial and occupational segregation by gender exists, with women more likely to be involved as production workers and in light industries. Bohong Liu (2000) for example, reports that only 8 percent of women are employed in occupations requiring "skill" and not physical labor.

[5] For details of the process of privatization, see Samuel P. S. Ho, Paul Bowles, and Xiao-yuan Dong (2003).

[6] For the impact of the WTO accession on manufacturing employment in China, see Aimin Chen (2002), Rong (2002), and Kym Anderson, Jikun Huang, and Elena Ianchovichina (2004: Table 2).

[7] Wang Xiancai, Deputy Secretary-General of the Committee of the Chinese People's Political Consultative Conference, Jiangxi Provincial Committee, has been reported as advocating the return of married women to the home in order to care for children (*Beijing Review* 2001).

[8] While bargaining models postulate that individual household members may have common and separate interests, they vary as to the proposed mechanism underlying the allocation of resources. The models can be categorized into one of two groups depending upon the mechanism assumed for how resources are allocated. In the earlier cooperative models, resources are allocated in accordance with individuals' relative threat points or fall-back positions (Marilyn Manser and Murray Brown 1980; Marjorie McElroy 1990). The later non-cooperative models, take more account of gender roles and how individuals respond to each other's contributions (Shelley Lundberg and Robert A. Pollak 1993; John Hoddinott and Lawrence Haddad 1995; Zhiqi Chen and Frances Woolley 2001).

[9] For more on patriarchy in China, see Elisabeth Croll (1983), Judith Stacey (1983), Margery Wolf (1985), Xiaoxian Gao (1994), and Delia Davin (1995).

[10] Robeyns (2003) offers a method for selecting capabilities to analyze gender inequality and proposes a set for discussion purposes, as opposed to a list useful for all purposes.

[11] Jacka (1997) further notes that women recognize the value of their own domestic labor in the household (see, also, Wolf [1985: 138]; Sam Wai Kam Yu and Ruby Chui Man Chau [1997]).

[12] Despite dramatic changes in women's paid labor since the 1950s, there has been little change in the sexual division of labor in the home, and women remain responsible for domestic tasks (Croll 1983; Wolf 1985: 211; Jacka 1997: 103).

[13] A study by W. Xia (1989), cited by Nailin Bu and Carol A. McKeen (2000), reports that female workers spent an average of 3.7 hours per day on housework in contrast to 2.2 hours per day for male workers. The actual reported amounts of time depends upon the categories of tasks considered and how simultaneous tasks, such as cooking and childcare, are aggregated.

[14] Although, studies in industrialized countries suggest that the availability of appliances has changed the norms of domestic labor more than reducing the time commitments.

[15] The data collected for this paper are part of a larger project on the impact of TVE privatization, which is a collaborative endeavor of Chinese and Canadian researchers. While the two groups discussed the fieldwork methodologies, the actual surveying and in-depth interviews reported upon here were conducted by the researchers from Shandong University and the Jiangsu Academy for Social Sciences. This was partly due to a policy implemented in 1998 by the Chinese government which prohibited foreign researchers undertaking primary research. All personal information that would allow the identification of any person described in the article has been removed.

[16] We selected the forty-five enterprises from a list of about fifty enterprises presented to us by the local governments.

[17] The remaining respondents are workers who have no spouse, i.e., single, widowed, or divorced.

[18] As a result of this more limited variation in income among respondents, the estimates of income effects on domestic labor may have larger standard errors and lower t-ratios.

[19] We examine the intrahousehold allocation of time and decisions only among workers who are married, and thus, the contributions and positions of unmarried or widowed individuals who work in the TVE sector are not part of this study.

[20] In our sample, the income from family members other than husband and wife only account for 7.4 percent of the total household income, indicating that most of the elder parents living with their adult children in the sample are economically dependent on their children for support.

[21] The "condition" referred to includes the items in Table 2. The Chinese word for "status" is *diwei*.

[22] On a daily basis, this converts to 3.2 hours for women and 2.1 hours for men. These estimates of time spent on domestic tasks are comparable to studies reported in the literature (see discussion earlier in the paper and endnote 13). However, these estimates do not provide the level of detail and accuracy associated with estimates derived from time-use diaries. See Suzanne M. Bianchi, Melissa A. Milkie, Liana C. Sayer, and John P. Robinson (2000) for analyses of the impact of different data collection methods on time-use estimates in the US context. Bianchi et al. (2000) note, however, that the ratios of married women's to men's housework time are similar for data collected from time-use diaries compared to surveys using one question on housework.

[23] We thank James Hughes for pointing out this possibility.

[24] The predicted value of the wage is obtained from a regression model that assumes wage as a function of years of schooling, experience and its squared term, and two location dummy variables.

[25] The predicted value of market work hours is obtained from a reduced form regression for weekly work hours in which the independent variables are years of schooling, experience and experience squared, age, number of children, spouse's income, and dummy variables for living with parents or parents-in-law, locality, and working in an enterprise that is profitable or could improve its financial performance by laying-off 10 percent of the existing workers. The two dummy variables for enterprise characteristics are introduced as proxy variables for demand for labor, which are statistically significant in the reduced form regression. The statistical significance indicates that the variables are correlated with market hours and hence are valid instruments for this variable. The determinants of predicted wages such as years of schooling, experience, and experience squared are included in the reduced form regression for weekly work hours because the wage rate is an explanatory variable for allocation of time among market work, domestic labor, and leisure. The inclusion of the determinants of the wage variable does not appear to cause a serious multi-collinearity problem as the correlation coefficient of predicted wages and predicted market hours is small (0.09 for the combined sample, 0.24 for the male sample, and 0.3 for the female sample).

[26] The presence of children and living with parents or parents-in-law are measured by dummy variables which take the value 1 if the worker has children and lives with his/her parents or parents-in-law. We assume that the pattern of time allocation of an extended family is not substantively different from that of a non-extended family. To test the plausibility of this assumption, we estimated the domestic hours determination equation separately for workers in each type of family structure and found that the two sets of estimates are not qualitatively different from each other. Due to the small sample size, we are unable to further explore the difference between the two types of household structures in this paper.

[27] Note this point estimate of elasticity is calculated at the mean values of about fifty-five work hours and fifteen hours of domestic labor per week. Numerically, it means that if a male worker worked a half hour more, he would spend about seventeen minutes less

on domestic tasks. The value of the elasticity declines as the number of hours spent on market work increases.

[28] Bianchi et al. find that for the US households the presence of children under 12 increases wives' housework time by more than three times their husbands' (2000: 215).

[29] Although these variables are statistically significant, based on the regression evidence, we are unable to assess the quantitative impact of a given change in these two variables on the gender division of labor.

[30] There are gender differences in the perceptions because this 21.2 percent is considerably greater than the 6.9 percent of women who view decisions about major purchases being made by spouse or parents/in-laws (option 0) and mostly spouse in consultation with self (option 1). Since the men and women in this sample do have partners outside of the sample it is not necessary that the views should align themselves.

[31] We cannot evaluate whether this lower significance arises from differences in the variation of the data in the two samples arising from sample selection or the weaker economic importance collectively of the independent variables.

REFERENCES

Agarwal, Bina. 1997. "'Bargaining' and Gender Relations: Within and Beyond the Household." *Feminist Economics* 3(1): 1–51.

Alderman, Harold, Pierre-Andre Chiappori, Lawrence Haddad, John Hoddinott, and Ravi Kanbur. 1995. "Unitary Versus Collective Models of the Household: Is It Time to Shift the Burden of Proof?" *World Bank Research Observer* 10(1): 1–19.

Anderson, Kym, Jikun Huang, and Elena Ianchovichina. 2004. "Will China's WTO Accession Worsen Farm Household Incomes." *China Economic Review* 15(4): 443–56.

Aslanbeigui, Nahid, Steven Pressman, and Gale Summerfield. 1994. *Women in the Age of Economic Transformation: Gender Impact of Reforms in Post-Socialist and Developing Countries.* London and New York: Routledge.

Bao, Xinyan. 2002. "More Women Wear the Pants." *China Daily,* September 10.

Beijing Review. 2001. "Women's Choice: Home or Work?" April 25: 24–6.

Benería, Lourdes. 1995. "Toward a Greater Integration of Gender in Economics." *World Development* 23(11): 1839–50.

Bianchi, Suzanne M., Melissa A. Milkie, Liana C. Sayer, and John P. Robinson. 2000. "Is Anyone Doing the Housework? Trends in the Gender Division of Labor." *Social Forces* 79(1): 191–228.

Bu, Nailin and Carol A. McKeen. 2000. "Work and Family Expectations of the Future Managers and Professionals of Canada and China." *Journal of Managerial Psychology* 15(8): 771–94.

Chang, Gene H. 2002. "The Cause and Cure of China's Widening Income Disparity." *China Economic Review* 13(4): 335–40.

Chen, Aimin. 2002. "The Structure of Chinese Industry and the Impact from China's WTO Entry." *Comparative Economic Studies* 44(1): 72–98.

Chen, Zhiqi and Frances Woolley. 2001. "A Cournot–Nash Model of Family Decision Making." *Economic Journal* 111(474): 722–48.

Cook, Sarah, Shujie Yao, and Juzhong Zhuang, eds. 2000. *The Chinese Economy Under Transition.* Hampshire and London: MacMillan Press and New York: St Martin's Press.

Croll, Elisabeth. 1983. *Chinese Women Since Mao.* London: Zed Books.

Davin, Delia. 1995. "Women, Work and Property in the Chinese Peasant Household of the 1980s," in Diane Elson, ed. *Male Bias in the Development Process*, 2nd. ed., pp. 29–50. Manchester, UK: Manchester University Press.

Dong, Xiao-yuan, Fiona MacPhail, Paul Bowles, and Samuel P. S. Ho. 2004. "Gender Segmentation at Work in China's Privatized Rural Industry: Some Evidence from Shandong and Jiangsu." *World Development* 32(6): 979–98.

Dong, Xiao-yuan, Jiangchun Yang, Fenglian Du, and Sai Ding. 2006. "Women's Employment and Public-Sector Restructuring: The Case of Urban China," in Grace O. Lee and Malcolm Warner, eds. *Unemployment in China: Economy, Human Resources and Labour Markets*, pp. 87–109. London and New York: Routledge.

Elson, Diane. 1995. "Gender Awareness in Modeling Structural Adjustment." *World Development* 23(11): 1851–68.

——. 1999. "Labor Markets as Gendered Institutions: Equality, Efficiency and Empowerment Issues." *World Development* 27(3): 611–27.

Elson, Diane and Ruth Pearson. 1981. "'Nimble Fingers Make Cheap Workers': An Analysis of Women's Employment in Third World Export Manufacturing." *Feminist Review* 7: 87–108.

Fewsmith, Joseph. 1997. "Plan Versus Market: China's Socialist Market Economy," in Christopher Hudson, ed. *The China Handbook*, pp. 97–108. Chicago: Fitzroy Dearborn Publishers.

Floro, Maria S. 1995. "Economic Restructuring, Gender and the Allocation of Time." *World Development* 23(11): 1913–29.

Gao, Xiaoxian. 1994. "China's Modernization and Changes in the Social Status of Rural Women," in Christina K. Gilmartin, Gail Hershatter, Lisa Rofel, and Tyrene White, eds. *Engendering China*, pp. 80–100. Cambridge, MA: Harvard University Press.

Greene, William H. 2003. *Econometric Analysis,* 5th ed. Upper Saddle River, NJ: Prentice Hall.

Gronau, Reuben. 1986. "Home Production – A Survey," in Orley Ashenfelter and Richard Layard, eds. *Handbook of Labour Economics*, vol. 1, pp. 273–302. Amsterdam: Elsevier Science Publishers BV.

Ho, Samuel P. S., Paul Bowles, and Xiao-yuan Dong. 2003. "'Letting Go of the Small': An Analysis of the Privatization of Rural Enterprises in Jiangsu and Shandong." *Journal of Development Studies* 39(4): 1–26.

Hoddinott, John and Lawrence Haddad. 1995. "Does Female Income Share Influence Household Expenditures?" *Oxford Bulletin of Economics and Statistics* 57(1): 77–96.

International Labour Organization (ILO). 2004. "An Employment Agenda for China". Background Paper for the China Employment Forum. http://www.ilo.org/public/english/chinaforum/download/original.pdf (accessed April 2007).

Iversen, Vegard. 2003. "Intra-Household Inequality: A Challenge for the Capability Approach?" *Feminist Economics* 9(2/3): 93–116.

Jacka, Tamara. 1997. *Women's Work in Rural China.* Cambridge: Cambridge University Press.

Joekes, Susan. 1999. A Gender-Analytical Perspective on Trade and Sustainable Development. Paper presented at the UNCTAD Expert Workshop on Trade, Sustainable Development and Gender, Geneva, Switzerland. http://www.unctad.org/en/docs/poedm_m78.en.pdf (accessed April 2007)

Kandiyoti, Deniz. 1998. "Gender, Power and Contestation," in Cecile Jackson and Ruth Pearson, eds. *Feminist Visions of Development*, pp. 135–51. London and New York: Routledge.

Khan, Azizur and Carl Riskin. 2001. *Inequality and Poverty in China in the Age of Globalisation.* Oxford: Oxford University Press.

Koggel, Christine. 2003. "Globalization and Women's Paid Work: Expanding Freedom?" *Feminist Economics* 9(2/3): 163–84.

Lardy, Nicholas R. 2002. *Integrating China into the Global Economy*. Washington, DC: Brookings Institution Press.

Liu, Bohong. 2000. "Chinese Women's Employment." *Chinese Education and Society* 33(2): 73–94.

Lundberg, Shelly and Robert A. Pollak. 1993. "Separate Sphere Bargaining and the Marriage Market." *Journal of Political Economy* 101(6): 988–1010.

Manser, Marilyn and Murray Brown. 1980. "Marriage and Household Decision-Making: A Bargaining Analysis." *International Economic Review* 21(1): 31–44.

Maurer-Fazio, Margaret and James Hughes. 2002. "The Effects of Market Liberalization on the Relative Earnings of Chinese Women." *Journal of Comparative Economics* 30(4): 709–31.

Maurer-Fazio, Margaret, Thomas Rawski, and Wei Zhang. 1999. "Inequality in the Rewards for Holding Up Half the Sky: Gender Wage Gaps in China's Urban Labour Market, 1984–94." *China Journal* (41): 55–88.

McElroy, Marjorie. 1990. "The Empirical Content of Nash-Bargained Household Behavior." *The Journal of Human Resources* 25(4): 559–83.

Mood, Michelle S. 1997. "The Impact and Prospects of Rural Enterprise," in Christopher Hudson, ed. *The China Handbook*, pp. 122–36. Chicago: Fitzroy Dearborn Publishers.

Naughton, Barry. 1995. *Growing Out of the Plan: Chinese Economic Reform, 1978–1993*. Cambridge: Cambridge University Press.

Nussbaum, Martha. 2003. "Capabilities as Fundamental Entitlements: Sen and Social Justice." *Feminist Economics* 9 (2/3): 33–60.

People's Republic of China. 1993. *Township and Village Enterprises Statistical Yearbook*. Beijing: Agricultural Press.

———. 1996. *China Statistical Yearbook*. Beijing: China Statistical Publishing House.

Robeyns, Ingrid. 2003. "Sen's Capability Approach and Gender Inequality: Selecting Relevant Capabilities." *Feminist Economics* 9(2/3): 61–92.

Rong, Mo. 2002. "Some Effects of China's Joining the WTO on Employment, and Certain Policy Proposals in Response to the Problem." *The Chinese Economy* 34(5): 3–19.

Sen, Amartya. 1985. *Commodities and Capabilities*. Amsterdam: North-Holland.

Song, Lina. 2000. "In Search of Gender Bias in Household Resource Allocation in Rural China." *Chinese Economy* 33(4): 69–95.

Stacey, Judith. 1983. *Patriarchy and Socialist Revolution in China*. Berkeley: University of California Press.

Summerfield, Gale. 1994. "Economic Reform and the Employment of Chinese Women." *Journal of Economic Issues* 28(3): 715–32.

Thomas, Duncan. 1990. "Intra-household Resource Allocation." *The Journal of Human Resources* 24(4): 634–64.

United Nations Development Programme (UNDP). 1999a. *Human Development Report 1999*. New York and Oxford: Oxford University Press.

———. 1999b. *The China Human Development Report 1999*. Beijing: China Financial & Economic Publishing House.

———. 2003. *China's Accession to WTO: Challenges for Women in the Agricultural and Industrial Sectors. Overall Report*. New York: UNDP. http://www.undp.org.cn/downloads/gender/GenderWTOAg-en.pdf (accessed April 2007).

Whitehead, Ann. 1984. "'I'm Hungry, Mum': The Politics of Domestic Budgeting," in Kate Young, Carol Woklowitz, and Roslyn McCullagh, eds. *Of Marriage and the Market: Women's Subordination Internationally and Its Lessons*, pp. 93–116. London: Routledge & Kegan Paul.

Wolf, Margery. 1985. *Revolution Postponed*. Palo Alto, CA: Stanford University Press.

Yao, Shujie. 2002. "China's Rural Economy in the First Decade of the 21st Century: Problems and Growth Constraints." *China Economic Review* 13(4): 354–60.

Yu, Sam Wai Kam and Ruby Chui Man Chau. 1997. "The Sexual Division of Care in Mainland China and Hong Kong." *International Journal of Urban and Regional Research* 21(4): 608–19.

Zhang, Linxiu, Alan de Brauw, and Scott Rozelle. 2004. "China's Rural Labor Market Development and its Gender Implications." *China Economic Review* 15: 230–47.

Zhang, Weiguo. 2002. "Changing Nature of Family Relations in a Hebei Village in China." *Journal of Contemporary Asia* 32(2): 147–70.

GENDER DYNAMICS AND REDUNDANCY IN URBAN CHINA

Jieyu Liu

INTRODUCTION

State enterprises were once the main livelihood for urban workers in China, providing lifetime employment, housing, and welfare. However, with the market reforms of the 1980s–90s, many enterprises faced painful choices of mergers, closures, or bankruptcy, and millions of workers were thrown out of their work units, *danwei.*[1] Since market reforms began, women have been especially hard hit: though women are a minority (about 40 percent) of the workforce, females have comprised a majority (about 60 percent) of laid-off workers (Gale Summerfield 1994; Zhang Qiujian 1999; Shufeng Song 2003), and these female workers have become an "urban underclass" (Wang Zheng 2000: 66). When China formally joined the World Trade Organization (WTO) in December 2001, the state media hailed this as a chance to boost prosperity, but some researchers postulated that it would worsen the situation of urban redundant workers and widen the income gap between men and women (Dorothy J. Solinger 2003; United Nations Development Programme [UNDP] et al. 2003).

Drawing upon fieldwork in Nanjing in 2003, this paper focuses on older women's experiences of working life and redundancy and the gendered consequences of the dismantling of state enterprises. Here, "redundancy" refers to any situation in which workers lost their jobs for reasons beyond their control, which includes instances in which workers' ties to their workplace continue. The variety of forms of redundancy in China reflects the transitional nature of its labor market institutions, as they evolve from guaranteed lifetime employment toward insecure labor contracts. As part of the social welfare system under socialism, state enterprises hired too many employees, but market reforms guided by the principle of efficiency have made these workers redundant. Such reforms are still evolving, gaining further momentum after China's entry to the WTO, and they continue to generate redundancy.

Studies of the economic reform period, even those drawing attention to women's greater vulnerability to redundancy, have focused on the macro-structural features of this process. By contrast, adopting a qualitative model, my research proposes to add a fresh perspective to the study of social change, shifting employment patterns, and the status of women in China. Based on life-history interviews, I examine the micro-processes under-pinning the outcome of economic restructuring, and through a gender-based analysis, I show how and why these working women were rendered vulnerable during the economic transformations.

This trend is undermined by Chinese policy-makers and scholars' tendency to emphasize economic reform as a rejection, by design, of everything Mao represented and as a break with the past. However, I question this disjuncture: rather than analyzing gender discrimination as something introduced by economic restructuring,[2] I explore the conti-nuities of gender inequalities represented in the life histories of redundant women workers. In particular, I identify the links between women's prior employment status (more limited skills, limited social connections, and household responsibilities) and their likelihood of becoming redundant, their prospects for re-employment, and the types of jobs they get. I show that women's unequal working experiences and social disadvantages in the pre-reform era shaped their greater vulnerability to redundancy during economic restructuring. This link is particularly evident in the experiences of older, redundant women workers from the Cultural Revolution generation, called the "unlucky generation" in China for having experi-enced famine in the 1950s, the Cultural Revolution in the 1960s–70s, the one-child policy after 1979, and redundancies from the late 1980s. For these women, redundancy was yet one more sacrifice demanded of their cohort in particular for the development of China, and these women are unlikely to gain any benefit from whatever advantages accrue from China's economic integration into the global economy.

Finally, research on redundancy found a positive relationship between the nature of social connections and success in the job search but has not focused on women through the lens of gender. By examining the lives of older women workers and highlighting their use of social connections in seeking reemployment, I also add a gendered perspective to existing studies of social connections and prospects for reemployment in China.

GENDER, GLOBALIZATION, AND ECONOMIC RESTRUCTURING IN CHINA

Since the 1980s, accelerated globalization has affected national economies and many aspects of social, political, and cultural life (Lourdes Benería 2003) and has led to the intensification of social inequalities and the marginalization of the poor and other groups (Diane Elson and Nilüfer Çağatay 2000). Parallel to this process of globalization and trade liberalization, labor market deregulation has resulted in the profound reorganization of production and changes in employment conditions. In particular, employment instability has sharply increased, and unemployment affects more workers (Benería 2003). How women are affected in this process is varied and context-specific.

Feminist economists have put forth two main arguments for analyzing the gendered impact of economic restructuring. Focusing on employment changes during a short-term recession, Jane Humphries (1988) tested the segmentation, buffer, and substitution hypotheses, suggesting that women workers' experiences varied according to specific industries, occupations, and types of enterprises. According to the segmentation hypothesis, employment in manufacturing is more susceptible to layoffs, whereas services are relatively insulated from cyclical variation in output and employment. Thus, women's concentration in services may shield them from redundancy (Humphries 1988). The buffer hypothesis suggests that women are especially vulnerable to cyclical unemployment and are shed disproportionately in the downswing and recruited intensively in the upswing (Humphries 1988). The substitution hypothesis indicates that recession opens up new opportunities for women workers and substitutes them for men within workforces (Humphries 1988). In contrast, Elson and Çağatay suggest that women are more likely to suffer the most under neoliberal economic restructuring as a result of three biases in macroeconomic policies: deflationary bias resulting from government budget cuts, male breadwinner bias in wage employment, and commodification bias.[3] As a result of these biases women are more vulnerable to losing their jobs than men and usually have worse access than men to social safety nets (Elson and Çağatay 2000).

Studies of other countries have shown how women lost out during economic restructuring (Lourdes Benería and Shelley Feldman 1992; Benería 2003). Helen I. Safa and Peggy Antrobus (1992) showed that, during the economic crisis in the Caribbean (Jamaica and Dominican Republic), structural adjustment policies forced families to take on a greater share of the cost of survival as a result of cutbacks in social services, which in turn increased the burden on women, demonstrating the effects of the commodification bias identified by Elson and Çağatay (2000). Meanwhile, Safa and Antrobus (1992) found that export manufacturing showed a preference for women workers because they were cheaper to employ and had greater patience for the tedious assembly line work, consistent with Humphries's substitution hypothesis (1988). Gender stratification also occurred in East Germany where women's labor power was devalued and they were increasingly excluded from work, showing the male breadwinner bias (Elizabeth C. Rudd 2000). In the Czech Republic, Anna Pollert (2003) found that women particularly suffered in light industries, such as textiles, as a result of trade deregulation and competition, supporting Humphries's buffer hypothesis (1988). In Nicaragua, Nan Wiegersma's research (1994) suggested that women over the age of 35 had the greatest difficulty finding jobs due to the closing down or privatization of garment and textile factories, showing an age differentiation in women's employment. Pollert also found that transition in five Central and Eastern European countries caused a recession and the ensuing increase in unemployment, poverty, and inequality was "both a class and a gendered process" (2003: 350).

Research on China's economic reforms also suggests that the cost of restructuring has fallen upon women disproportionately (Summerfield 1994). In China, redundancies occur in the context of economic restructuring rather than a short-term recession. Adapting Humphries's buffer and segmentation hypotheses (1988) to a longer process of relative decline in manufacturing and the rise in services with economic liberalization suggests that while women are disproportionately laid off from state manufacturing enterprises, their concentration in the growing service sectors may protect them from losing jobs in future downturns. In addition, in the course of restructuring, some factories are replacing male workers with young migrant women to cut down on costs (Fan Zhai and Zhi Wang 2002), which lends support to Humphries's substitution hypothesis. The increasing importance of services in China is likely to favor some young women (Wang 2000). Women workers in state enterprises, however, are adversely affected by the three biases of China's economic restructuring. In the early 1990s, the tight fiscal and monetary policies adopted by the government exacerbated the reduction in state subsidies and further worsened the financial situation of state enterprises. The traditional breadwinner ideology – "men dominate the outside, women dominate the inside" – has hardly changed despite the socialist rhetoric of women's liberation; even in the late 1990s, employers often argued that women workers should be laid off because they could still depend financially on their husbands. The budget cuts that were part of China's overall reforms and obligation to the WTO resulted in the dismantling of welfare provision in the *danwei*. Employees, enterprises, and the state were all required to contribute to the social fund for pension and medical care, and employees had to purchase services that were previously free of charge. This all took place in the context of a booming economy that offered many other opportunities. One of the advantages of looking at China is that it demonstrates that similar gender biases occur in layoffs in an economy where reforms have had rapid success in high growth rates in contrast to those where reforms have resulted in recession or have been deflationary.

Recent studies found that many redundant urban workers in their 40s and 50s formed the same cohort of people whose education was ruined by the Cultural Revolution.[4] Scholars argue that the generation caught up in the Cultural Revolution was the hardest hit by the economic restructuring because of their cohort-specific experiences (Li Peiling, Zhang Yi, and Zhao Yandong 2000; Eva P. W. Hung and Stephen W. K. Chiu 2003). As Hung and Chiu put it, their life course had been shaped by a series of state policies "in a largely detrimental and often unintended way" (2003: 207), and they felt that the state had betrayed them for the second time. For instance, many of them lost their educational opportunities as a result of the Cultural Revolution. Although they share hardships with other redundant workers, this generation feels particularly bitter because the reform era has emphasized educational qualifications and competence that they lack.

While the literature draws our attention to this generation's experience, no study has investigated these workers' accounts of their life histories. Beyond highlighting cohort specificity, the literature pays little attention to why women workers disproportionately lost out in the economic reforms. Some scholars highlight Chinese men's predicament (Li, Zhang, and Zhao 2000), arguing that, because of their traditional breadwinner role, redundancy was psychologically detrimental to men since their masculine pride was challenged by the loss of their jobs. Some male Chinese scholars even called on women workers to return home in order to relieve the unemployment problem (Sun Liping 1994; Lin Songle 1995). In contrast, I attempt to highlight the micro-processes brought out by the life narratives of older women redundant workers to consider the gendered conse-quences of China's economic restructuring. By examining the social disadvantages these women experienced, I show the continuities of gender inequalities over their lifetimes. I identify the effects of age, gender, and social hierarchy, drawing attention, in particular, to the experiences of older and less-educated women. By examining their life after redundancy,

I also bring out new empirical evidence on gendered social networks in the job search.

State enterprises and labor market deregulation

In 1978, the Chinese government adopted an "opening-up" policy in hopes of achieving economic development after the misery of the Cultural Revolution. Among major developments was the promotion of different types of enterprise ownership. Before the reforms, state-owned enterprises were the major employers and providers of essential goods and services though a small number of collectively owned enterprises played a supplementary role (Louis Putterman and Xiao-yuan Dong [2000]; see Table 1 below). State enterprises, the *danwei* (work units), were more than economic entities: they guaranteed lifetime employment and were also residential and welfare communities providing workers with services such as housing and healthcare, in addition to wages and retirement pensions. There were three types of *danwei*: profit-making enterprises producing material commodities, nonprofit institutions providing non-material services, and administrative institutions (Bian Yanjie 1994).[5] As the reforms unfolded after 1986, the state-run, production-oriented enterprises faced serious competition from non-state enterprises because they still employed a substantial number of employees and bore the burden of welfare provision. Their economic performance began to deteriorate rapidly in the

Table 1 Employment in urban China, 1952–2002

	State-owned			Collectively owned			Other ownership		
	Total		No. of	Total		No. of	Total		No. of
Year	No.	%	women	No.	%	women	No.	%	women
1952	15.8	98.8	–	0.2	1.2	–	–	–	–
1965	37.4	75.3	–	12.3	24.7	–	–	–	–
1970	47.9	77.1	–	14.2	22.9	–	–	–	–
1978	74.5	78.4	21.3	20.5	21.6	10.2	–	–	–
1980	80.2	76.7	24.7	24.3	23.3	12.3	–	–	–
1985	89.9	72.8	29.1	33.2	26.9	15.7	0.4	0.3	0.2
1990	103.5	73.6	35.4	35.5	25.2	16.7	1.6	1.2	0.8
1995	109.6	73.5	39.6	30.8	20.6	13.7	8.8	5.9	4.2
2000	78.8	69.9	29.5	14.5	12.9	6.1	19.4	17.2	8.5
2002	69.2	65.6	26.2	10.7	10.1	4.4	25.6	24.3	10.9

Note: Number is shown in millions. The dashes for women between 1952–80 mean that information was not gathered.
Source: Compiled from *China Labour Statistical Yearbook* (National Bureau of Statistics and Ministry of Labor and Social Security 1998) and the *China Statistical Yearbook* (National Bureau of Statistics 1999, 2002, 2003).

late 1980s. In the early 1990s, the tight fiscal and monetary policies adopted by the government further reduced state subsidies and worsened their financial situation. When the leadership determined to accelerate China's assimilation into the world economy, the restructuring of state enterprises became inevitable because as part of its pursuit of WTO membership China had to commit to remove trade barriers and reduce state subsidies, thereby leaving state enterprises subject to heightened market competition.

The enterprise reforms in the 1980s mainly consisted of reorganization in order to enhance enterprises' efficiency. In 1986, the State Council introduced a labor contract system that put all new recruits on fixed-term (but renewable) contracts alongside an existing permanent labor force (Tan Shen 1993). The peak period of "optimal labor reorganization" was 1986–8. In this period, the State Council required that employers use assessments and examinations to identify workers with the best skills and transfer them to the most important posts. The total number of posts was reduced so some workers with poor skills or no skills became surplus labor. As a result, these workers were asked to stay home with reduced wages in order for enterprises to lower production costs (Ting Gong 2002). However, the state still subsidized urban enterprises so the number of people affected was small. But the profits of state-run enterprises continued to decline; by 1992, two-thirds were operating in the red (Gong 2002).

In 1992, at its Fourteenth Plenary Congress, the Communist Party formally decided to establish a socialist market economy, and, by endorsing layoffs or *xiagang* (literally "leaving the post"), aimed at enabling state-run enterprises to compete more efficiently with non-state ones. But the scale of redundancy was relatively small since China adopted a gradual approach to restructuring; merger rather than bankruptcy was the solution for loss-making firms. From 1994 onward, the government started a policy of restructuring small and medium state enterprises while protecting larger enterprises: bankruptcies, mergers, or leases applied to small and medium firms, but big firms were reorganized in strategic sectors (Ching Kwan Lee 2005). In 1995, the Labor Law formally required state enterprises to put all employees on contract, thereby ending the lifetime employment system that dominated the Maoist era. At its Fifteenth Plenary Congress in 1997, the Party confirmed the decision to reform state-run enterprises by reducing employees and moving forward with aggressive restructuring. As a result, many unprofitable enterprises were shut down, and state enterprises were required to shift to modern forms of corporate governance (John Giles, Albert Park, and Fang Cai 2006). Progress in reforming China's state enterprises was a litmus test for assessing the Chinese leadership's willingness to seek membership in the WTO. The November 1999 agreement between Chinese and US authorities on terms for China's WTO accession enforced a Chinese commitment to expose state enterprises to more fundamental market discipline and reform. China's

2001 accession to the WTO further accelerated the state enterprise reforms. The *Agreement on Subsidies and Countervailing Measures* (SCM) under WTO membership required China to substantially reduce subsidies to the state enterprise sector (Claustre Bajona and Tianshu Chu 2004). Consequently, bankruptcies and complete privatization took place in many state enterprises, and more state workers became vulnerable to unemployment.

State enterprise reforms pushed by China's integration into the world economy produced massive numbers of jobless workers. In the 1990s, the official discourse used two terms to denote urban citizens without jobs. According to the National Bureau of Statistics (1999: 179), "unemployed" refers to an urban citizen who has no job but desires to be employed and has been registered at the local employment service agencies to apply for a job. Accordingly, unemployed persons include those young people who could not find jobs after graduation. The second term, *xiagang*, was the official term referring to workers who lost their jobs but still retained ties to their former enterprises. However, as I show below, beyond this official recognition of just two categories of jobless workers, state enterprises adopted a variety of measures to get rid of their employees. So I use redundancy to include any scenario in which urban workers lost their jobs because of restructuring – including, but not limited to, the situation of *xiagang* – but excluding urban youth who failed to find jobs after college. Redundancy measures have taken various forms, represented by numerous terms used nationally and regionally, but most redundant workers worked in industrial enterprises. Below is a list of forms of redundancy in chronological order (according to when they came into being).

(1) *Extended maternity leave.* This practice extended the statutory maternity leave period of fifty-six days indefinitely. This measure specifically aimed at making women redundant from the late 1980s and early 1990s.

(2) *Internal or in-house retirees (neitui).* Beginning in 1992, older redundant workers who would reach their legal retirement age within five to ten years retain a connection with their enterprise and receive a proportion of their former wage (depending on the industry and financial situation of the enterprise).[6] However, they receive no bonus or wage increase until they became eligible for a state pension.

(3) *Laid-off workers (xiagang).* This includes (a) those who are called in on an as needed basis – *daigang* (literally "waiting for post"); (b) unpaid leave of workers who are no longer working in the enterprise but still remain affiliated with their enterprises, referred to by various names such as *tingxin liuzhi* ("stopping pay but preserving positions") and *liangbuzhao* (literally "neither party looks

for the other") (Dorothy J. Solinger 2001: 680); and (c) workers who entered a re-employment service center in 1998–2001,[7] if they failed to find work within the period, they could be registered as "unemployed" and become entitled to state unemployment benefits for two years. Laid-off workers in categories (a) and (c) are supposed to receive the basic livelihood allowance, but this varies according to the profitability of individual enterprises. This practice has been common since the mid-1990s.

(4) *Bought-out workers* (*mai duan gong ling*). These workers are paid a lump sum (which varies by industry and enterprise), at which point they cease to have any formal connection with their *danwei* and have to settle their own pension arrangements (Hung and Chiu 2003). This is a recent practice, having been in effect only since 1997; "buy-outs" (along with internal retirees) are officially excluded from *xiagang* (laid-off) and thus, omitted from official layoff statistics.

In 1997 official statistics showed a steady rise in the numbers of registered unemployed workers but a much sharper increase in the numbers of laid-off workers (*xiagang*), whose ties to their former workplaces were not completely severed (Table 2). However, the state statistics do not include

Table 2 Official statistics of unemployed and laid-off workers (*xiagang*) in urban China 1992–2002 (in millions)

Year	Registered unemployed workers		Laid-off workers	
	Total	*Women*	*Total*	*Women*
1992	3.6	–	c. 2.5	–
1993	4.2	–	3.0	–
1994	4.7	–	3.6	–
1995	5.1	–	5.6	–
1996	5.5	–	8.9	–
1997	5.7	–	13.2	–
1998	5.7	3.0	c. 8.9	–
1999	5.8	2.5	c. 9.0	–
2000	6.0	3.2	9.1	–
2001	6.8	3.0	7.4	3.2
2002	7.7	3.2	6.2	2.8

Note: The c that precedes some of these numbers indicates that the figure is an estimate. The dashes for women here mean that statistics were not gathered in these years. The two categories (registered unemployed workers and *xiagang* workers) are mutually exclusive, and one becomes registered unemployed after their *xiagang* status ends (and also after one's status in any of the other redundancy categories ends).
Source: Data derived from Zhang (1999: 86, Table 18) and *China Labor Statistics Yearbook* (National Bureau of Statistics and Ministry of Labor and Social Security 2000, 2003).

workers from the other three redundant categories shown above, so the number of redundant workers has always been a controversial issue (see Solinger 2001). Even within the reported category of laid-off workers (*xiagang*), there are still inconsistencies. For example, the State Statistical Bureau gave the number of laid-off workers at the end of 1997 as 12 million in its online report but 14.35 million in the *China Labour Statistical Yearbook* (cited in Yang Guang 1999: 12). These totals also differ from the official figures reported in Table 2 derived from Zhang (1999: 86, Table 18). Researchers outside China were not able to clarify such inconsistencies, but they "uniformly agree that official statistics...are far from the mark and are decidedly too low" (Solinger 2001: 672).

Three major causes for this massive redundancy have been posited (Edward X. Gu 1999; Song 2003). First, the "institutional unemployment" was generated by China's transformation from a socialist planned economy to a market economy (Gu 1999). In the planned economy, China attempted to maximize urban employment so state enterprises absorbed more laborers than they needed, which resulted in "hidden unemployment" (Gu 1999). In the market economy, unemployment had to be made open in order to reduce the financial burden and to enhance the efficiency of state enterprises.

Second, China has experienced structural changes and unemployment since the 1980s (Song 2003). Song documents the decline of employment shares in agricultural and manufacturing sectors and suggests that with economic structural changes people lost their jobs in one sector and had to find jobs in new rising sectors such as services. However, as I show in this paper, many redundant workers – older women, in particular – lost their jobs from inefficient enterprises without any prospect of being rehired in the growing sectors.

Third, domestic enterprises suffered from the growing competition of imports resulting from integration into the global economy (Zhai and Wang 2002; Solinger 2003). Well before its formal accession to the WTO, China had to take concrete steps to demonstrate its commitment to reducing or eliminating subsidies to state-owned enterprises and trade barriers. For example, China lowered its tariffs on imported foreign goods beginning in the late 1980s in preparation for joining the General Agreement on Trade and Tariffs (Dorothy J. Solinger 2006). In December 1995, China decided to cut tariffs by a further 30 percent in order to gain US support for its WTO application. In the face of strong competition from imports and the direct influence of the global market, traditional textiles and the clothing industry were adversely affected in the late 1990s, which resulted in closures and mergers with many workers losing their jobs (Solinger 2003).

Because of the upsurge in joblessness, the state government adopted various measures. For example, re-employment service centers were set up as part of the Re-employment Project launched in 1995 and included various active labor market policies to provide job-replacement and job-training with cooperative efforts from enterprises and governments at different levels (Edward X. Gu 2000). Officially, "three guarantees" were promised to counter urban poverty: a basic livelihood allowance issued to workers who were qualified as "laid-off";[8] unemployment insurance to those deemed "unemployed," including those whose firms had disappeared completely either by bankruptcy or merger; and a minimum cost of living guarantee set by local governments for urban residents whose income fell below that standard (Dorothy J. Solinger 2002). However, due to financial difficulty, some enterprises could not afford to pay their share to the social fund, and scholars pointed out the ineffectiveness of these programs and called for an installation of a genuine social security system in China (Sarah Cook 2002; Solinger 2002, 2003). In 2004 responsibility for supporting newly laid-off workers was legally transferred from the *danwei* to the state (Information Office of the State Council of the People's Republic of China 2004). Therefore, local governments become the key actors in implementing national policies. Lee (2005) suggests that this resulted in uneven protection for workers, depending on the economic structure of the province and the integrity and competence of local officials.

Men and women were positioned differently in relation to these market transformations, and various Chinese studies have shown that women were disproportionately affected. A 1987 survey by the national trade union in eleven provinces found that women accounted for 64 percent of "excess workers" (which is another term used by the employers for redundant workers) in 660 enterprises (Tamara Jacka 1990). In the early round of redundancies, many excess workers were transferred to the auxiliary or service sectors of their *danwei* (Jacka 1990; Meng Xianfan 1995). However, beginning in 1992, women were heavily hit by extended maternity leave and internal retirement policies (Tan 1993). Extended maternity leave, in particular, was a common means of making women redundant in the late 1980s and early 1990s. Women received a basic wage during the statutory leave period but, as an example of the male breadwinner bias, were unpaid or partially paid in the extended period, which made them dependent on their husbands. The ownership of rights in employment is constructed around a full-time, life-long participation in the workforce and excludes women whose participation does not typically fit this norm. In 1993, a seven-province survey carried out by the national trade union found that women made up 60 percent of workers who lost their jobs (Meng 1995). Despite the paucity of gender data in official statistics (Table 2), recent studies have found that being female, being middle-aged, having a low educational level, and working in the manufacturing sectors increased the chance of losing one's job (Li Qiang, Hu Junsheng, and Hong Dayong 2001; Peter Saunders and

Xiaoyuan Shang 2001; Simon Appleton, John Knight, Lina Song, and Qingjie Xia 2002; Xiao-yuan Dong and Louis Putterman 2002), and it is generally accepted that nearly 60 percent of *xiagang* workers in the late 1990s were women (Yang 1999; Wu Zhaohua 2001). This macro picture has thus borne out the conclusion of Elson and Çağatay (2000) that women are more likely to be the losers during economic liberalization. Although there is an expectation that China's membership in the WTO will increase women's employment by re-boosting textiles and clothing sectors, whether redundant women workers will benefit is uncertain.

GENDER INEQUALITIES IN THE WORKPLACE

Redundant women workers in Nanjing: context and method of study

Most studies have recognized that the Cultural Revolution generation was the hardest hit by economic restructuring, but they have provided at best only a limited gender analysis (Richard H. Price and Fang Liluo 2002; Hung and Chiu 2003). Hence, I took a gendered and historically located approach to investigate female redundancy and, instead of using quantitative methods, collected life histories of older women workers in Nanjing in 2003 to investigate the factors that had shaped their lives and to explore their understandings of the processes and events in which they had been involved. Because of the sensitivity of the topic and the difficulty of gaining access to workers through official channels, I resorted to informal networking and snowballing strategies to recruit participants (Jieyu Liu 2006). I interviewed twenty-seven redundant women workers, five women who had survived or witnessed the economic restructuring but were not made redundant, and one official, and I organized a focus group with another three redundant women workers. Their ages ranged from 37 to 59 years; twenty of the redundant workers were of the Cultural Revolution generation; all were or had been married; and almost half had spent over twenty years in their *danwei*.[9] The industries in which they formerly worked roughly corresponded with Nanjing's industrial structure.

Nanjing is an important industrial base in East China with petrochemicals, electronics, and car manufacturing as its mainstay industries, and machine manufacturing, textiles, and metallurgy as its local feature industries. It contributes about one percent of the national gross industrial production (Liu Houjun, Zeng Xiangdong, and Zhang Erzheng 2002). The large-scale layoffs occurred mostly in Central-West China, old industrial base areas, and areas with relatively rapid market development (Zhang 1999; Xiao-yuan Dong 2003). Located near Shanghai, Nanjing has experienced the market development that has subjected traditional industries more directly to the dynamics of global economic demands.

According to previous surveys, women workers in Nanjing experienced redundancy types similar to their national counterparts. They were asked to leave their posts mainly through internal retirement, *daigang* ("waiting for the post"), or extended maternity leave (Wang Xiuzhi 1993). In 1997, women over 35 accounted for 71 percent of redundant female workers in Nanjing (Zhu Qinghong 1999). Nanjing is the capital of Jiangsu province, which is known for its strong textile industries that employ many women workers. Because most redundant women workers come from the machinery and textiles industries nationwide (Zhang 1999), my case study has wider relevance for the situation of redundant women workers in China.

Gender segregation at work

Research has postulated that a link exists between the disproportionate female redundancy in the current reform era and gender inequalities in the socialist planned economy (e.g., Wang 2000; Ping Ping 2002), and my study of economic and non-economic factors in the workplace supports this argument. Women respondents were disadvantaged by gendered working practices and cultural assumptions and were also subjected to greater surveillance of their behavior at and outside work than men. The *danwei* system perpetuated gender inequality despite the socialist rhetoric of equality.

During the pre-reform era, the Chinese labor market was characterized by horizontal and vertical segregation,[10] and my interviews demonstrated that both dimensions of segregation were present in the Chinese workplace. Horizontal segregation at the industrial and workplace levels was based on assumptions of "natural" differences between women and men, manifested through the division of work into "heavy" and "light" industry. This pattern continued as state enterprise reforms evolved. According to the 1990 census, women comprised 70 percent of workers in light industries (leather-making, textiles, and clothing) but less than 20 percent in heavy industries (construction and metal processing) (Liu Dezhong and Niu Bianxiu 2000). All of my informants who had worked in light industries reported that there were far more women in their factories, whereas those who had worked in heavy industries reported the opposite. Mother Murong (aged 40), who had worked in a lamp-making factory reported, "Most women were assemblers. Men often work downstairs because it was really heavy work and required physical strength – such as punching." Although the underlying assumption was that women's "weak" physique was best suited to "light" work, without a clear definition of "heavy" or "light" the judgment of work allocation was arbitrary. Men were more often allocated to work associated with "skills," and in light industries, where most women worked, men were also more connected with technical knowledge. Mother Xiu (aged 47) had been working in the technical sector of a wool-knitting factory where men "designed the pattern, that is, the flower or animal image on the clothes. We were responsible for knitting the clothes... They [men] were mainly drawing patterns because women were worse at drawing anyway." In commercial sectors such as retailing, Mother Jun, reported that few men worked as shop assistants: "People say if men stand behind counters, they would become shorter."[11] These examples bear out Anne Philips and Barbara Taylor's conclusion that "Skill definitions are saturated with sexual bias. The work of women is often deemed inferior simply because it is women who do it" (1980: 79).

As for vertical segregation, although women and men were entitled to equal chances of promotion under the Chinese Constitution, in reality men were always prioritized for upward mobility (Zheng Xiaoying 1995). Similar to the national pattern reported by the Research Institute of All-China Women's Federation, Department of Social Science and Technology Statistics, and the State Statistical Bureau (1998: 434), my interviewees were mostly placed lower in the *danwei* hierarchy and, as workers, institutionally segregated from higher-ranked cadres, the superiors or supervisors usually associated with the Communist Party. Mid-level cadres at or beyond the section and workshop level were mostly men; the few women who became mid-level cadres mostly held symbolic posts with little real power. Admission into the Party was carried out at the workplace (Bian 1994). My interviewees talked about membership as an economic resource, similar to other awards and chances of promotion, and said that most members were men. A few women had tried to join, mostly without success.[12]

Job segregation by sex in capitalist economies is the major source of wage inequalities between men and women (Heidi Hartmann 1976). By contrast, and consistent with China's socialist rhetoric of promoting gender equality, before the large-scale reform, gender earnings inequality was relatively low, with female wages placed around 80 percent of male earnings (Martin K. Whyte 1984). However, studies based on national representative data (1988–94) found that although overt wage discrimination for men and women performing similar work was constrained, the main source of wage inequality was the concentration of women workers in low-paying sectors of China's economy (Margaret Maurer-Fazio, Thomas G. Rawski, and Wei Zhang 1999). In my study, most interviewees recalled the state principle of "equal pay for equal work" (*tong gong tong chou*), but they were aware of the difference between wages in different sectors – "light" industries, such as textiles, found much lower pay than "heavy" industries, such as machinery. So sex and "strength" acted as the criteria of work remuneration. As the economic reforms moved forward, the gap in earnings between women and men seemed to increase. Maurer-Fazio, Rawski, and Zhang (1999) found that the ratio of women's wages to men's declined every year from 1988 to 1994. They also found that foreign-owned and private enterprises – the newly developed types of ownership in the reform – held the largest gender wage gap. Xiao-yuan Dong, Jianchun Yang, Fenglian Du, and Sai Ding (2005) found that between 1995 and 2003 the gender wage gap for both state and non-state firms combined rose from 15.6 to 23.0 percent and that women faced greater degrees of wage discrimination in the post-restructuring period. One of the long-term consequences is that women collect less unemployment benefit and pension income than men.

Women's limited social connections (*guanxi*)

Before the reforms, women's poor representation among Communist Party members and the cadres with real power largely excluded them from power and denied access to resources in the work unit. As I highlight, workplace inequalities, in turn, limited women's use of social connections, or *guanxi*, and contributed to gender inequalities in re-employment prospects.

In China in the 1980s and 1990s, there was an increase in reliance on connections to get promoted or to get a good job. "[C]onnections (*guanxi*), not ability, were the major way to get promoted, get a good job, assignment, and so forth" (Andrew G. Walder 1986: 176). Some scholars have equated *guanxi* to "social capital" in western society (see Nan Lin 2001).[13] Bian found that the purpose of using connections was "to find someone who has the power or influence to break through the bureaucratic control of opportunities" (1994: 98). My interviewees' accounts suggest that as women cultivated connections with men in order to realize a particular goal, this also contributed to reinforcing their subordination.

The final object of *guanxi* could be reached directly or indirectly through intermediaries (Bian 1994). My interviewees mainly used three channels. First, women could capitalize on the connections of their natal family members, mostly through their father. If a woman failed to be born with a silver spoon in her mouth, her second chance for access to powerful connections was marriage. Lisa Rofel (1999) notes in her ethnographic study of a silk factory that women usually married up; my interviewees also reported this: "At that time, many women in the shop wanted to marry some powerful man. As soon as you married him, he would have the say to transfer you away from the shop floor" (Mother Jing, aged 50). Third, a woman who had established a good relationship with her immediate leader as a result of good *biaoxian* (literally "performance"),[14] might be able to translate it into connections. However, the power of connections accessed this way was limited, subject to change, and likely to wane if the leader was transferred out of the *danwei*. Furthermore, surveillance of women's social relationships and sexuality constrained this mode of finding connections. Women had to be able to withstand gossip about using their "immoral" behavior to gain favors. Those who became leaders were similarly rumored to have slept with male leaders and were described as "able women, unlike ordinary women" by my interviewees. By asking the women with whom they mainly socialized during the Spring Festival, I found that the friends of women cadres were mostly leaders while workers associated with other workers; the differential scope and power of their social networks had implications for their chances of finding re-employment (see the section entitled "Life post-redundancy" later in this paper). My findings accord with Mayfair Mei-Hui Yang's (1994) conclusion that working-class women are likely to be more circumscribed than men in their daily lives to small circles of acquaintances on the job and at home and that women cadres and intellectuals are more involved in connections with more powerful individuals than workers.

After accessing *guanxi*, what was it used for? Apart from using *guanxi* to find their first job, women interviewees reported some more specific applications. Unlike their male counterparts who used connections for upward mobility (Bian 1994), when women workers changed jobs, many of them took new jobs at the same wage level and some were even transferred to menial or degrading jobs. Their ultimate goals were mainly to avoid doing shift work and to cope with the demands of both work and family duties more smoothly. Mother Tang (aged 46), for example, transferred to a factory where her father-in-law was chief secretary of the Party committee: "In 1986, I had no choice but to ask to be transferred to work here. It was purely because my daughter would go to school soon and no one else was available to look after her."

In sum, women were allocated to the *danwei* by the state and provided with work; but their work was a job rather than a career, they had very restricted access to power and resources due to horizontal and vertical segregation, suffered various forms of gendered discrimination, and were disadvantaged in their work development. As a result, women's unequal working experiences and imputed or actual lack of "skills" before the economic reforms shaped their greater vulnerability to redundancy in economic restructuring.

EXPERIENCES AND PERCEPTIONS OF REDUNDANCY

Experiences of redundancy

Beginning in 1986 women faced difficulties securing jobs. But their hardship increased as economic reforms advanced, causing the scale of redundancy to worsen and the terms under which workers were made redundant to change over time, offering the workers less protection and amounting to varied practices and treatment between *danwei*. Twenty-seven interviewees were made redundant (eighteen were internally retired,[15] six laid off, and three bought out, see Table 3); two had also previously experienced a one-year period of extended maternity leave on three-quarters pay. Of the rest, one was selected to be laid off at the age of 42 but managed to stay on, three had retired in due time, one (a former factory leader) had resigned to start her own company, and one was a Women's Federation officer. Their remuneration varied considerably, depending on the type of *danwei* and industry, the financial state of the individual enterprise, and mode of redundancy (Table 3). One common thing among respondents was that they all were stripped of the bonuses attached to the basic wage,[16] even as the basic wage stagnated and bonuses became a key part of workers' income during the reforms. Bonuses also formed a key part of wage disparity for those who were made redundant because they were deprived of any bonuses even when they were kept on the state enterprise's payroll.

Monthly payments given to internal retirees varied widely across different industries (¥135 – ¥650), whereas the remuneration for laid-off workers was fairly similar (¥190 – ¥300). As shown in Table 3, with a few exceptions the remuneration for internal retirees was actually well below the average monthly income of Nanjing citizens: these women were mostly paid between ¥135 and ¥650, which represented about 10 percent to 47 percent of the average monthly income for 2002.[17] In particular, textile internal retirees who retired in the early 1990s found ten years later that they received only about one-tenth of the average monthly income. With the exception of the chemical industry, buy-outs were treated fairly equally: women who worked in machine manufacturing and "light" industries, including textile and clothing reported that buy-outs received from ¥400 to ¥650 per year of service in a lump sum payment that is not directly comparable with the remuneration for the other two forms of redundancy. In Nanjing, as one of the "three guarantees," a minimum living standard allowance of ¥248 per month, was issued to workers whose income was less than this amount, but none of the women interviewed had applied for this benefit. They commented that they would not make a fuss by going through the complicated application which involved regular checking up on their income by issuing officers who would talk with their neighbors. This program was also ineffective among laid-off workers in the cities of Guangzhou and Wuhan (Joe C. B. Leung and Hilda S. W. Wong 1999; Solinger 2002).

Rising healthcare costs worsened the financial situation of the women I interviewed. Redundant workers were supposed to receive partial reimbursement of medical expenses from their former *danwei* but because many enterprises ran at a loss or were near closure, this was often unavailable. The medical security reform that could help healthcare costs started in 2001 in Nanjing but the number of enterprises included (forty-six) was still small (Gu Zhaonong 2000). Mother Li commented that

Table 3 Financial remuneration received by women according to types of work unit and industry, forms of redundancy, and year of redundancy

Type of work unit	Industry	Internal retirement			Laid-off			Buy-out			Total
		N	Monthly wage (yuan)	Year	N	Monthly wage (yuan)	Year	N	Amount per year of service^a (yuan)	Year	
Nonprofit units (*shiye*)		2	1,200	1996 1997							3
Profit-making units (*qiye*)	Textiles	1 1	1,800 160 1	2003 1992 135	1993			1	400	1998	4
	Machine manufacturing	1 1	200 200 600	1994 1992 2002	1 1^b	350 190	1996 1999				4
	Other "light" industries	1 1^c	300 400 2,000	1993 2001 2003	1	0 350	1995 1997				5
	Chemicals	1 1	800 900	1998 2000	1	400	2001	2	2,500	2001 2002	5
	Electronics	1 1 1	600 400 600								3
	Commerce	1 1	400 650	1997 2000	1	190	1998				3
Total		18			6			3			27

Notes: ^{a}The lump sum, one-time payment for buy-outs is calculated by multiplying the amount per year of service by years of service. The remuneration for buy-outs is not directly comparable to the payments for other forms of redundancy. ^{b}This woman was laid off as "*liangbuzhao*" ("neither party looks for each other"). ^{c}This woman's factory was among the top ten profit-making enterprises in Nanjing.

140

a few of her former colleagues had committed suicide rather than go to the hospital when they found out that they had a very serious illness. Hence, the most common wish among my interviewees was not to fall ill.

Redundant workers were stratified depending upon the nature of their *danwei*, specific industries, finances of individual enterprise, and their prior working conditions (Table 3). Zhang (1999: 89) found in a three-year national investigation that the vast majority (86.5 percent) came from the profit-making enterprises, 13.2 percent from the nonprofit institutions, and 0.3 percent from the administrative institutions. Similarly, I found that those from the profit-making enterprises were the hardest hit. Most interviewees had previously worked in profit-making enterprises and did poorly compared to those who were from nonprofit institutions. Those formerly in nonprofit institutions received the most lucrative benefits; and none of the redundant interviewees worked in administrative institutions (Table 3). The difference between workers and cadres continued after redundancy. Six of the twenty-seven women interviewed were cadres, but only one was a mid-level cadre and had managed to enter the pension scheme as a retiree. Because women faced difficulties in being promoted to mid-level cadres prior to reforms, their chances of being made redundant increased. Similarly, Zhao Yandong found that 7 percent of 621 laid-off workers in Wuhan had once been cadres and only 2 percent of them were mid-level cadres (2001: 22). In a survey of four cities Li, Zhang, and Zhao (2000) also found that workers were far more likely to be made redundant than mid-level cadres.

Finally, divisions existed among enterprises depending on the industrial sector. The textile factories in Nanjing were among the first enterprises in the city to be heavily hit. As Solinger put it, "among textile workers, supposedly members of a winning industrial sector, millions of mill hands have already been let go with the international destruction of over 9 million out-of-date spindles by the end of 1999" (2003: 78–9). Most of the factories in which my interviewees had worked had been closed. Ten of the twenty-seven interviewees were made redundant by factory closures. Textile workers also suffered the greatest financial loss; they were made redundant earlier as internal retirees, received the lowest remuneration, and benefited least from the social protection schemes that were installed several years after they had lost their jobs. By contrast, chemical industries were relatively profitable in Nanjing; although several factories were required to merge together at the call of the state enterprises reforms, redundant chemical workers were much better remunerated (Table 3). An interesting practice was found in commerce, a heavily feminized sector where women accounted for over 80 percent of workers in the 1990s. Consistent with the segmentation hypothesis, the sector might afford women workers relative protection as it is relatively insulated from cyclical variation in output and employment (Humphries 1988). Indeed, in 1992 the Nanjing

Women's Federation praised this sector for having a large number of female workers but no redundancies. By the end of the 1990s, however, the commerce sector introduced a redundancy scheme that targeted older workers (mostly women).

Perceptions of redundancy

How did the women perceive this big event in their lives? Here, I have followed Hung and Chiu (2003) and divided them into birth cohorts. Cohort 1 consisted of three women born between 1944–7; Cohort 2, the Cultural Revolution generation, eighteen women born between 1948–57; and Cohort 3, six women born between 1958–66. Like Hung and Chiu before me, I discovered that Cohort 2 women interpreted redundancy in generational terms. My respondents echoed Hung and Chiu's finding that "*xiagang* workers from this lost generation were acutely aware of how their misfortunes were linked to their cohort-specific experiences" (2003: 211). As Mother Zheng (aged 51) put it, "Our generation is totally wasted." Similarly, Mother Li (aged 54) commented:

> The life of our generation was really tough. When we were schoolchildren, everything was messed up by the Cultural Revolution. We learned nothing at all. Then when we were allocated a job at the work unit, how were we to know that the factory would run down in twenty years time? Our generation is so unlucky!

Despite their grievances, Cohort 2 took redundancy as a matter of course: "our whole generation is unlucky" and commonly reported sentiments similar to Hung and Chiu's interviewees who said that they were "just in time to run into all these (*gan shang le*)" and were a generation "full of misfortunes" (2003: 232). The oldest cohort, Cohort 1, who were near formal retirement age and had not suffered in the same way from the Cultural Revolution, interpreted their redundancy more at a societal level, accepting it as an inevitable concomitant of the economic reforms, as a change of era, "a social trend that is beyond control of ordinary people"(Mother Ye, aged 56). Women in the youngest cohort,[18] Cohort 3, however, interpreted this event more on an individual level, directing their anger at the factories. Mother Bi (aged 40) said, "Like us, ...who would take pity on you? The society wouldn't pay attention to you. The factory already kicked you out. You had to go find a way on your own."

However, all the women pointed out that the mismanagement of former factory leaders should be blamed for the poor performance of the enterprises, a view that Gu (1999) also found. They reported that their factory-level leaders did not suffer like ordinary workers: they were transferred to other factories or government sectors. Thus, while making sense of their redundancy in their own terms, the different cohorts were well aware of the inequalities and unfairness in the market reform, which they accepted as another social event in their lives that they could do little about.[19]

LIFE POST-REDUNDANCY

Being made redundant deprived these women of the welfare services of the *danwei*. Fortunately, they were the beneficiaries of support from their families, though most of that was limited to non-material forms. They also received emotional support from other women who had been made redundant, some of whom were friends from their former workplaces and others, mainly neighbors in their husband's *danwei*,[20] with whom they had become acquainted as a result of their common experience of redundancy. Such companionship did not alter their circumstances, but it helped ease the loss deriving from unemployment.[21] Analysis of the process and outcome of women's searches for re-employment showed that only one had entered the re-employment service center; the rest had drawn on their own resources which, particularly for the poor and unskilled women workers, were their social contacts (other women) and those of their husbands and relatives.

Social capital or *guanxi* is vital to the process of finding work (Li, Hu, and Hong 2001; Zhao Yandong 2002). A survey of laid-off workers (*xiagang*) from four cities in 1997 found that connections had positive effects upon the chances of getting re-employed (Li, Zhang, and Zhao 2000: 96–7). Here, I draw upon concepts from Zhao's (2001, 2002) survey-based study of the social capital of 621 laid-off workers in Wuhan and confine my discussion to social capital at a micro level. He found that generally "laid-off workers have a smaller amount of possessed social capital than the population in general" (Zhao 2002: 567) and that laid-off workers in Wuhan mainly used informal methods and got substantial help (influence) from their contacts to find new employment. However, he paid little attention to the gender dimension and also focused only on the individual's connections. I found that women might draw upon their husband's connections, and unlike Zhao's informants, seldom had a direct connection with the person who played the most important role in finding jobs.

Possessed social capital

Zhao explored the effects of "possessed social capital" and "the social capital actually used in re-employment" (2002: 556). To measure possessed social capital, I asked twenty-four redundant workers (excluding three from the focus group and including the eighteen women from the Cultural Revolution cohort) questions similar to Zhao's: "to how many relatives, friends, and acquaintances did you 'pay a new year's call' [*bainian*] during

143

the Spring Festival?'' and "what were those people's jobs or *danwei*?'' I then assessed the network size (number of members), network density (proportion of relatives among members), and embedded network resources (such as occupations of members) of these women. Their network size (average number: eleven; range five to fifteen) was smaller than the average network size (twenty-one) in Zhao's sample (2002: 562) and that of Chinese urban citizens in general (thirty-one) (Bian Yanjie and Li Yu 2001 in Zhao 2002: 563). Most contacts were relatives and friends, and their network density (73 percent) was much higher than that of Zhao's informants (49.44 percent) or of citizens in general (28.36 percent) (Zhao 2002: 563). The women in my study possessed poorer connections in comparison with the respondents to similar studies (for example, Li, Zhang, and Zhao 2000; Zhao 2002),[22] which also reflect their limited connections in the *danwei*. Most had relatives who were manual workers, some of whom were also redundant. Their friends were former colleagues and/or neighbors from their own or their husbands' *danwei* or from school days and were also mostly manual workers. By contrast, one woman mid-level cadre and one professional possessed richer connections, since most of their contacts were professional people and leaders. Although their network size and network density differed little from those of the other women, I suggest that their embedded network resources produced their better jobs.

Social capital actually used in re-employment

By asking respondents about the methods they used to find jobs, the kinds of resources they gained from their personal network, and the character-istics of the contact whom they considered "played the most important role,'' I examined how they actually used connections in finding their new jobs. Most (seventeen) found their first job by informal methods. Only one found her first job through a formal method by reading newspaper advertisements; six went for self-employment, of whom four became street vendors; and two did some piecework at home. Table 4 shows the characteristics of the most important contact involved in introducing the first job in relation to type of work.

I found three types of connections and the types of jobs they led to. First, there is a difference between women using their own social connections and their husband's social connections in finding a job. Women who sought jobs through their husband's connections, with whom they hardly had any relationship, were more likely to be full-time and well paid. This distinction explains why women workers tend to marry up to cadres or professionals who possess richer and wider social connections (Rofel 1999). Women can draw on their husband's social connections; their husbands may also independently use their social contacts to find work for their wives.

Table 4 The characteristics of the core contact in first job search by informal methods (seventeen)

Contact	Status of contact	Sex of contact	Type of job found	N of women
Husband's friend or colleague	Managerial/ professional	Male	Various full-time jobs (shop assistant, accountant, etc.).	5
Former workmate	Manual	Female	Cleaning, cooking, caring, selling (part-time)	6
Former work contact	Professional administrative	Male	Accountant (full-time) Consultant (full-time)	2
Relative	Professional; manual	Female Male	Selling insurance (part-time) Cooking (part-time)	2
Schoolmate	Professional	Male	Accountancy (full-time)	1
Neighbor	Manual	Female	Cleaning (part-time)	1

Thus, as Xu Yanli and Tan Lin (2002) argue, marriage is a certain form of social capital for Chinese women.

Second, there is a relationship between the work status of contacts (manual or non-manual) and the types of jobs they led to. Eight women had contacts who were only manual workers with no post or rank, consistent with Zhao's (2002) findings. Those jobs introduced by manual-worker contacts were mostly cleaning, baby-sitting, and cooking meals for families or companies. This also supports Jin Yihong's (2000) suggestion that laid-off women workers comprised a substantial group within the irregular labor market; most women in her national study were employed in vending, laundry services, or baby-sitting. By contrast, in my study, the mid-level cadre and one professional found full-time and stable jobs through the introduction of their social contacts, who were themselves professionals. My data indicate that the higher the rank of the contact, the better the jobs that could be obtained; hence, the power of contacts directly affected the quality of accessible jobs. Here I want to highlight that interviewees' prior social status was closely related to the work status of their contacts. Manual workers were mostly associated with manual workers while mid-level cadres and professionals had more chances to be acquainted with professional and managerial staff. For example, the cadre and the professional's prior status advantage was maintained in the job search: Mother Zhou, the director of her former factory's trade union, was asked by the municipal trade union leader whom she already knew to work for them as a full-time consultant after she retired. Mother Fei, a senior accountant in her former company, was working full-time for a private trade company to which she had been introduced by her neighbor, the director of an accounting agency. Their newly introduced jobs also offered the potential of gaining additional high quality social connections from which they might benefit in the future. But women manual workers with poor social connections were trapped in a vicious circle of low-paid, unskilled, part-time work providing only further poor social connections. Former cadres were able to maintain their social positions, but the workers were vulnerable to downward mobility.

Third, the gender of the social contacts also affected the types of jobs they led to. Women's social networks were mostly made up of women, consonant with gender segregation in the workplace, as is shown in other studies (e.g., Irina Tartakovskaya and Sarah Ashwin 2004). However, the gender-specific network did them no favors. Their lower position in the labor market affected the connections they could make for their contacts. As Table 4 shows, jobs secured through women contacts were like the irregular kinds of work mentioned by Jin (2000). By contrast, the job connections made through male contacts were more likely to be full-time. Based on a 1998 survey in eighteen Chinese cities, Lin found that men held a substantial advantage over women in respect to social capital (2001: 109). Hence, due to poorer social capital held by women, gender discrimination had been reproduced in job searches because of these gender-specific networks.

Constraints

Gendered networking in job searches is not the only mechanism limiting the scope of jobs available for women and reproducing sex segregation in the labor market (Tartakovskaya and Ashwin 2004); indeed, my inter-viewees described other hindrances to finding work. Familial demands created hurdles because being redundant reinforced women's domestic roles.[23] They not only had to look after their own family, but they were also regarded as an unpaid reserve labor force by the wider family circle, which justified demands being made of them by their own and their husband's kin, even to the extent of obliging them to give up a hard-won job. Age also seemed to limit the types of work open to them, though women near 40 years old sometimes found their way around discriminatory practices. For example, after Mother Ding was first laid off at 36, she became a product promoter in a department store, but a few years later, because of a crisis, all promoters over 40 were fired. Through a friend's introduction, she interviewed to be a saleswoman for another product; she dressed up and looked smart and energetic, so the manager thought she was only in her 30s and accepted her. The expansion of service sectors in the economic restructuring was once praised for absorbing a large proportion of women workers. Such jobs increasingly require the deployment of "feminine" charms and skills, and newly coined terms such as "youth occupations" refer to the physical attractiveness they require. As Mother Ding found, younger faces are more likely to benefit from the booming service industries.

No matter how many constraints they faced or what social connections they might draw upon, most of my interviewees found some form of work, albeit mostly lower paid and part-time jobs, which exposed them to unpleasant and unregulated conditions.[24] No one who worked in the private sector had a formal contract. Pay for part-time workers was not legally regulated: women who worked varied hours each day received the same amount of money at the end of the month. As Mother Dai (aged 54) put it, "You are just a temporary worker, whoever will take you seriously? ... Also there are so many people out there looking for jobs, aren't there? ...Now you don't have a say. You must give up everything [face, dignity, etc.] ... Otherwise, you just stay at home eating porridge." Those who became self-employed were no better off; according to state measures encouraging re-employment, laid-off workers were entitled to be tax-exempt or pay lower taxes, but none of the four who tried street vending benefited because they did not bother to apply as they thought the application procedure would be too complicated. By contrast, the few who had acquired non-manual positions made positive comments such as learning from the new job or being away from the control and surveillance in their former *danwei*, which suggests that redundancy could create an opportunity for women's personal development. However, the extent to which they became empowered depended on a combination of factors such as financial resources, possession of rich social connections, and professional skills. The few who were empowered by new opportunities were far outnumbered by those disempowered through redundancy. Most perceived the experience of redundancy as another unpleasant sacrifice they had made for the development of the nation:[25]

> Our generation has run into everything in our life. When we should receive education, we didn't have the chance, only graduated from primary school. When we started work only at 15, we worked in three-shift rotations, destroying our health. When you tried to study something, the three-shift rotation prevented you from it. Later when you could devote yourself at 40, the factory went down and you were laid off. Now you want to work, but nobody wants you. I feel our whole life is miserable enough. (Mother Jing, aged 50)

CONCLUSION

I have focused on the experiences of working life and redundancy recounted in life history interviews with women workers in Nanjing and outlined the gendered consequences of China's economic restructuring and the accompanying social transformations. My study shows that women bore the cost of economic restructuring disproportionately, which is consistent with feminist literature on gender and globalization. However, Chinese women's experiences are differentiated by age, gender, and social hierarchy as also exemplified in other post-socialist societies (for example, Pollert 2003). In particular, I drew attention to the experiences of a group of older and less-educated women, many of whom comprise the Cultural Revolution cohort, and show that these women perceived redundancy as another sacrifice for the development of China. Despite the state's rhetoric of gender equality and the major efforts made to implement it, in reality, women workers still experienced gender inequalities in the pre-reform era. Since the 1990s, when the reforms began to take place on a large scale, women have been thrown out into the marketplace, and they no longer have even the state rhetoric to protect their interests. Their prior lower social position has been reproduced in the process of finding work due to their poor connections.

After China's entry into the WTO, the state enterprise reforms accelerated. Due to further budget cuts committed by China to the WTO, many state enterprises carried out even larger-scale employee cutbacks. By the end of 2004, it was estimated that the number of unemployed state sector workers was as high as 60 million (Solinger 2006). At the time of my interviews in 2003, some women workers who themselves had been made redundant over the previous ten years also expressed deep concerns about their husband's job security as privatizations were ongoing in various state enterprises.

In spite of the massive redundancy and increasing urban poverty, the WTO is still hailed by some scholars and the Chinese media for its power to generate more jobs. The textile and clothing industries, in particular, are expected to benefit through the removal of export quotas and the expiration of the Multi-Fiber Agreement (Elena Ianchovichina and Will Martin 2004).[26] However, Solinger suggests that millions of textile factory workers had already been let go by the end of 1999 due to their factories' inefficiency in the face of fierce international competition. The textile industry in Nanjing had been heavily hit by 1998. Recent studies show that the new opportunities offered in the rebuilding of textiles do not necessarily secure posts for those who have and will be dismissed from the plants (Dorothy J. Solinger 2005).

Similarly, although the officer in the Women's Federation I talked to revealed that the textile industry was revitalizing in the city, I was told by other interviewees that joint ventures or private owners took over previous state textile factories and demanded the release of large numbers of former employees. When recruiting employees, they hired young migrant women workers at lower labor costs (see also Zhai and Wang 2002; Dong 2003). By contrast, older redundant women workers, who are disadvantaged in gaining skills and faced with age and sex discrimination, have mostly been confined to lower paid and unpleasant jobs. Moreover, as a result of increasing redundancy and rural–urban migration, there is growing competition from male redundant workers and migrant women workers (Dong et al. 2005). Flemming Christiansen (2001) concluded that in the short term the situation of the pensioners and the urban unemployed with low skill levels would most definitely worsen. I would add that older, less educated women workers, many of whom were from the "unlucky generation," are unlikely to gain any benefit from whatever advantages accrue from China's economic integration into the global economy.

In light of these results, more comprehensive anti-discrimination policies and their implementation are urgently called for. Government regulations to redress the gender bias of the reform process are essential to improve Chinese women's lives. For example, age discrimination should be incorporated into labor law and employers who do not comply should face serious penalties. Although the state has long advocated gender equality and has made discrimination related to sex illegal, policy-makers should seriously focus on putting rhetoric into action. In the face of growing job insecurity, the social security system should be fully in place and widely implemented. Given that many of the redundant workers came from the Cultural Revolution cohort whose life course had been affected by changing state policies, the state should take sole responsibility to fully recognize and compensate these workers who have endured a lifetime of sacrifices and suffering.

Jieyu Liu, Centre for Chinese Business and Development,
14–20 Cromer Terrace, University of Leeds,
Leeds LS2 9JT, United Kingdom,
e-mail: j.y.liu@leeds.ac.uk

ACKNOWLEDGMENTS

I am grateful to Günseli Berik, Gale Summerfield, and Xiao-yuan Dong who offered invaluable advice at every stage of this paper. I would like to thank Diana Strassmann and all the staff at the *Feminist Economics* editorial office for their warm support and assistance. I would also like to thank the anonymous reviewers and all the participants in the "Gender, China, and the WTO" workshop for their comments and criticism. Finally thanks to Anne Akeroyd who commented on the earlier draft of this article.

NOTES

[1] The work unit was the basic unit of social organization in urban China between 1950 and the early 1990s. For the vast majority of urban residents, it was not only the source of lifetime employment and material benefits, but it was also the institution through which the urban population was housed, organized, and regulated.

[2] In this paper, I use "economic restructuring" to refer to China's transformation from a socialist to a capitalist economy.

[3] The commodification bias is the shift from state-based provision of goods and services to purchase of services on the market by those who can afford them (Elson and Çağatay 2000: 1354–5).

[4] During the Cultural Revolution, class struggle took precedence in every aspect of social life. Large numbers of urban students were sent down to the countryside to learn from the peasants; students who stayed in the city were involved in various political campaigns rather than receiving a more conventional education.

[5] The three types of enterprises are *qiye danwei*, *shiye danwei*, and *xingzheng danwei*, respectively.

[6] The state retirement age for women is 50 for workers and 55 for cadres (*ganbu*), who are workplace superiors, but it is 60 for both male workers and cadres. Within the category of cadre, there are several hierarchical levels.

[7] These centers acted as the trustee for laid-off workers. The first opened in Shanghai in mid-1996 and was extended to other cities in 1998, but many firms could not finance their centers and many workers were unwilling to enter them (Edward X. Gu 2000). In 2001 the nationwide operation ended. In Nanjing, there was a "Double Ten" policy – workers who had worked continuously for ten years and had less than ten years until formal retirement could remain as *xiagang* (officially laid off) and then upgrade into internal retirement when they reached the set age (Nanjing Government 1999). Otherwise, they would have had to enter the center or choose to be "buy-outs." (One interviewee in this study met the requirements but others commented that because it was a one-off policy they did not "catch" this benefit). The National Textile Union negotiated a regulation that allowed some single-skilled textile workers, who had worked for twenty years and were within ten years of retirement, to be eligible for early retirement and thereby enter the state pension system (Zhang Zuowei 1998).

[8] This was a transitional policy during 1998–2001 and is now being phased out. Laid-off workers instead become eligible for the other two guarantees.

[9] Interviews averaged two hours; the longest was four hours. I have used pseudonyms here prefixed by "Mother" because I also interviewed their daughters.

[10] Horizontal segregation is where women and men take different types of work and vertical segregation is where women are situated in the lower ranking occupations (Catherine Hakim 1979).

[11] "Becoming shorter" is a metaphor implying that men's status would be reduced. However, it also suggests that women's work carries less prestige.

[12] Bian Yanjie, John R. Logan, and Xiaoling Shu (2000: 118, Table 7.1) showed that the number of male party members was always higher than that of female members.

[13] Social capital refers to "the accessible resources embedded in the social structure or social networks that will bring benefits to their owners (Bourdieu 1986; Coleman 1990; Lin 1999)" (Zhao Yandong 2002: 555).

[14] *Biaoxian* implies "actual work performance in addition to one's political thought, work attitude, virtue, morality, and other subjective qualities" (Walder 1986: 133).

[15] Among this group, two were given early retirement enabling them to enter the state pension scheme, one benefited from the one-off policy towards textile workers, and another was a cadre who managed to get early retirement.

[16] A bonus system was introduced as part of the state enterprise reform to increase workers' motivation at work. Bonuses are calculated according to workers' work performance, the importance of their posts and the profits of each enterprise.

[17] In Nanjing in 2002, the average monthly income was ¥1,257 in profit-making enterprises, ¥1,551 in nonprofit institutions, and ¥2,023 in administrative institutions (Nanjing Statistical Bureau 2003: 33).

[18] As my sample mainly consisted of women workers from the Cultural Revolution cohort, the conclusion about perceptions of the other two cohorts is tentative and requires further confirmation from bigger sample studies.

[19] Hung and Chiu's study, which includes both men and women, found similar generational understandings (2003). However, literature also suggests that redundant workers have started labor protests (Elizabeth J. Perry and Mark Selden 2000). My talk with officers on the street committee revealed that employers were more likely to lay off women workers, as they would not make a fuss, unlike their male counterparts. Two informants' husbands were told they were to be made redundant but they went and argued with their leaders and succeeded in keeping themselves on. Street committees are the grassroots units in the state social control and welfare system; they are connected to the street office of the municipal government and local police. They are also responsible for issuing the unemployment insurance and the minimum living allowances.

[20] Both spouses often worked in different *danwei* but mostly lived in the husband's *danwei*.

[21] Existing studies found that male workers experienced a loss of face after being made redundant (Li, Zhang, and Zhao 2000). My informants seldom expressed this feeling, but when they mentioned their husbands who had been made redundant, they all mentioned that being redundant was emotionally tough for men as they were traditionally the "breadwinners."

[22] I have no data about the social capital possessed by men, but Lin (2001), who analyzed a 1998 survey in seventeen Chinese cities, found women citizens had lower social capital than men in general.

[23] Being made redundant pushed women into full-time domesticity (see also Dong et al. 2005). However, it has not been documented that redundant male workers experienced this; indeed, my informants reported that when their husbands were made redundant, they still did nothing to help in domestic work.

[24] Based on survey data collected in four cities (Shengyang, Qingdao, Changsha, and Chengdu), Li, Zhang, and Zhao (2000: 97) found that a man is 1.94 times more likely to find new work than women.

[25] The state rhetoric justified redundancy as an inevitable consequence of China's inexorable transition to a market economy. The old generation had to be sacrificed because they had few qualifications and skills. Women workers in particular were called upon to return home to open up more job opportunities for men.

[26] Godfrey Yeung and Vincent Mok (2004) argue that whether the reduction of Chinese import tariffs and export quotas would benefit the industry still depends upon the size and ownership types of firms. Hence, the textiles and clothing industries are not necessarily the winners because of China's entry into WTO, as the state media would have us believe.

REFERENCES

Appleton, Simon, John Knight, Lina Song, and Qingjie Xia. 2002. "Labour Retrenchment in China: Determinants and Consequences." *China Economic Review* 13(2/3): 252–75.

Bajona, Claustre and Tianshu Chu. 2004. China's WTO Accession and Its Effects on State-Owned Enterprises. Working Paper Economics Series 70, East–West Center, Hawaii.

Benería, Lourdes. 2003. *Gender, Development, and Globalization: Economics as if All People Mattered*. New York and London: Routledge.

Benería, Lourdes and Shelley Feldman, eds. 1992. *Unequal Burden: Economic Crises, Persistent Poverty, and Women's Work*. Boulder, CO: Westview Press.

Bian Yanjie. 1994. *Work and Inequality in Urban China*. Albany: State University of New York.

Bian Yanjie and Li Yu. 2001. "Zhongguo chengshi jiating de shehui wangluo ziben [Social Network Capital in Chinese Urban Families]." *Tsinghua Sociological Review* 2: 1–18.

Bian Yanjie, John R. Logan, and Xiaoling Shu. 2000. "Wage and Job Inequalities in the Working Careers of Men and Women in Tianjin," in Barbara Entwisle and Gail E. Henderson, eds. *Re-drawing Boundaries: Gender, Households, and Work in China*, pp. 111–33. Berkeley: University of California Press.

Christiansen, Flemming. 2001. Will WTO Accession Threaten China's Social Stability? Paper presented at the Fourth ECAN Annual Conference on China's WTO Accession: National and International Perspectives, Berlin.

Cook, Sarah. 2002. "From Rice Bowl to Safety Net: Insecurity and Social Protection during China's Transition." *Development Policy Review* 20(5): 615–35.

Dong, Xiao-yuan. 2003. "China's Urban Labour Market Adjustment: A Literature Review." East Asia Human Development Sector Unit, World Bank.

Dong, Xiao-yuan and Louis Putterman. 2002. "China's State-Owned Enterprises in the First Reform Decade: An Analysis of a Declining Monopsony." *Economics of Planning* 35(2): 109–39.

Dong, Xiao-yuan, Jianchun Yang, Fenglian Du, and Sai Ding. 2005. "Women's Employment and Public-Sector Restructuring: The Case of Urban China," in Grace Lee and Malcolm Warner, eds. *Unemployment in China: Economy, Resources, and Labour Markets*, pp. 87–107. London and New York: Routledge.

Elson, Diane and Nilüfer Çağatay. 2000. "The Social Content of Macroeconomic Policies." *World Development* 28(7): 1347–64.

Giles, John, Albert Park, and Fang Cai. 2006. "How Has Economic Restructuring Affected China's Urban Workers?" *The China Quarterly* 185: 61–95.

Gong, Ting. 2002. "Women's Unemployment, Re-employment, and Self-Employment in China's Economic Restructuring," in Esther Ngan-Ling Chow, ed. *Transforming Gender and Development in East Asia*, pp. 125–39. New York and London: Routledge.

Gu, Edward X. 1999. "From Permanent Employment to Massive Layoffs: The Political Economy of 'Transitional Unemployment' in Urban China (1993–8)." *Economy and Society* 28(2): 281–99.

——. 2000. "Massive Layoffs and the Transformation of Employment Relations in Urban China." *Labour, Capital and Society* 33(1): 46–74.

Gu Zhaonong. 2000. "Nanjing jiben yiliao baoxian zhidu gaige fang'an chutai [The Issue of Medical Insurance Reform Schedules in Nanjing]." *People's Newspaper*, December 18.

Hakim, Catherine. 1979. Occupational Segregation. Research Paper 9, Department of Employment, London.

Hartmann, Heidi. 1976. "Capitalism, Patriarchy and Job Segregation by Sex." *Signs* 1(3): 137–68.

Humphries, Jane. 1988. "Women's Employment in Restructuring America: The Changing Experience of Women in Three Recessions," in Jill Rubery, ed. *Women and Recession*, pp. 20–47. London and New York: Routledge and Kegan Paul.

Hung, Eva P. W. and Stephan W. K. Chiu. 2003. "The Lost Generation: Life Course Dynamics and *Xiagang* in China." *Modern China* 29(2): 204–36.

Ianchovichina, Elena and Will Martin. 2004. "Impacts of China's Accession to the World Trade Organization." *The World Bank Economic Review* 18(1): 3–27.

Information Office of the State Council of the People's Republic of China. 2004. "China's Social Security and Its Policy." http://www.china.org.cn/e-white/20040907/index.htm (accessed September 2004).

Jacka, Tamara. 1990. "Back to the Wok: Women and Employment in Chinese Industry in the 1980s." *The Australian Journal of Chinese Affairs* 24: 1–23.

Jin Yihong. 2000. "Feizhenggui laodongli shichang de xingcheng he funü jiuye [The Formation of Irregular Labor Market and Women's Employment]." *Journal of Women's Studies* 3: 16–8.

Lee, Ching Kwan. 2005. Livelihood Struggles and Market Reform: (Un)marking Chinese Labour after State Socialism. Occasional Paper 2, United Nations Research Institute for Social Development.

Leung, Joe C. B. and Hilda S. W. Wong. 1999. "The Emergence of a Community-Based Social Assistance Programme in Urban China." *Social Policy and Administration* 33(1): 39–54.

Li Peiling, Zhang Yi, and Zhao Yandong. 2000. *Jiuye yu zhidu bianqian: liangge teshu qunti de qiuzhi guocheng* [Employment and Institutional Change: Job Searches of Two Special Groups]. Hangzhou, China: Zhengjiang People's Publishing House.

Li Qiang, Hu Junsheng, and Hong Dayong. 2001. *Shiye xiagang wenti duibi yanjiu* [A Comparative Study between Unemployment and Layoff]. Beijing: Tsinghua University Press.

Lin, Nan. 2001. *Social Capital: A Theory of Social Structure and Action*. Cambridge: Cambridge University Press.

Lin Songle. 1995. "Guanyu xinbie jiaose de jici zhenglun [The Several Debates of Gender Roles]." *Sociology Studies* 1: 106–8.

Liu Dezhong and Niu Bianxiu. 2000. "Zhongguo de hangye xingbiegeli yu nüxing jiuye [Chinese Occupational Segregation and Women's Employment]." *Journal of Women's Studies* 4: 18–20.

Liu Houjun, Zeng Xiangdong, and Zhang Erzheng. 2002. *Nanjing chengshi zonghe jingzhenli yanjiu* [The Study of Comprehensive Competitive Capacity of Nanjing City]. Nanjing: South-Eastern China University Press.

Liu, Jieyu. 2006. "Researching Chinese Women's Lives: 'Insider' Research and Life History Interviewing." *Oral History* 34(1): 42–52.

Maurer-Fazio, Margaret, Thomas G. Rawski, and Wei Zhang. 1999. "Inequality in the Rewards for Holding up Half the Sky: Gender Wage Gaps in China's Urban Labour Market, 1988–94." *The China Journal* 41: 55–88.

Meng Xianfan. 1995. *Zhongguo gaige dachaozhong de nüxin* [Chinese Women in the Reforms]. Beijing: China Social Sciences Publishing House.

Nanjing Government. 1999. "Shizhengfu guanyu zhixing 'nanjing shi chengzhen qiye zhigong yanglao baoxie shishi yijian' de buchong tongzhi [The Supplementary Document on the Implementation of 'Carrying out Social Security Reform among Urban Workers']." http://www.njqh.gov.cn/articleinfo.php?infoid=913 (accessed August 2004).

Nanjing Statistical Bureau, comp. 2003. *Nanjing Statistical Yearbook 2003*. Beijing: China Statistical Press.

National Bureau of Statistics, comp. 1999. *China Statistical Yearbook 1999*. Beijing: China Statistical Press.

———. 2002. *China Statistical Yearbook 2002*. Beijing: China Statistical Press.

———. 2003. *China Statistical Yearbook 2003*. Beijing: China Statistical Press.

National Bureau of Statistics and Ministry of Labour and Social Security, comp. 1998. *China Labour Statistical Yearbook 1998.* Beijing: China Statistical Press.

——. 2000. *China Labour Statistical Yearbook 2000.* Beijing: China Statistical Press.

——. 2003. *China Labour Statistical Yearbook 2003.* Beijing: China Statistical Press.

Perry, Elizabeth J. and Mark Selden, eds. 2000. *Chinese Society: Change, Conflict and Resistance,* 1st ed. London and New York: Routledge.

Philips, Anne and Barbara Taylor. 1980. "Sex and Skill: Notes towards a Feminist Economics." *Feminist Review* 6: 79–88.

Ping, Ping. 2002. "State Women Workers in Chinese Economic Reform: The Transformation of Management Control and Firm Dependence," in Esther Ngan-ling Chow, ed. *Transforming Gender and Development in East Asia,* pp. 141–64. New York and London: Routledge.

Pollert, Anna. 2003. "Women, Work and Equal Opportunities in Post-Communist Transition." *Work, Employment and Society* 17(2): 331–57.

Price, Richard H. and Fang Liluo. 2002. "Unemployed Chinese Workers: the Survivors, the Worried Young and the Discouraged Old." *Journal of Human Resource Management* 13(3): 416–30.

Putterman, Louis and Xiao-yuan Dong. 2000. "China's State-Owned Enterprises: Their Role, Job Creation, and Efficiency in Long-Term Perspective." *Modern China* 26(4): 403–47.

Research Institute of All-China Women's Federation, Department of Social Science and Technology Statistics, and State Statistical Bureau, comp. 1998. *Zhongguo xiebie tongji ziliao 1990–1995* [Gender Statistics in China 1990–5]. Beijing: China Statistical Publishing House.

Rofel, Lisa. 1999. *Other Modernities: Gendered Yearnings in China after Socialism.* Berkeley: University of California Press.

Rudd, Elizabeth C. 2000. "Reconceptualizing Gender in Post-Socialist Transformations." *Gender and Society* 14(4): 517–39.

Safa, Helen I. and Peggy Antrobus. 1992. "Women and the Economic Crisis in the Caribbean," in Lourdes Benería and Shelley Feldman, eds. *Unequal Burden: Economic Crises, Persistent Poverty, and Women's Work,* pp. 49–82. Boulder, CO: Westview Press.

Saunders, Peter and Xiaoyuan Shang. 2001. "Social Security Reform in China's Transition to a Market Economy." *Social Policy and Administration* 35(3): 274–89.

Solinger, Dorothy J. 2001. "Why We Cannot Count the 'Unemployed.'" *China Quarterly* 167: 671–88.

——. 2002. "Labour Market Reform and the Plight of the Laid-Off Proletariat." *China Quarterly* 170: 304–26.

——. 2003. "Chinese Urban Jobs and the WTO." *China Journal* 49: 61–87.

——. 2005. WTO and China's Workers. Paper presented at Monash University.

——. 2006. "The Creation of a New Underclass in China and its Implications." *Environment and Urbanization* 18(1): 177–93.

Song, Shufeng. 2003. "Policy Issues of China's Urban Unemployment." *Contemporary Economic Policy* 21(2): 258–69.

Summerfield, Gale. 1994. "Economic Reform and the Employment of Chinese Women." *Journal of Economic Issues* 28(3): 715–32.

Sun Liping. 1994. "Chongjian xingbie jiaose guanxi [Re-establishing Gender Roles]." *Sociology Studies* 6: 65–8.

Tan Shen. 1993. "Social Transformation and Women's Employment in China," in Center for Women's Studies, Tianjin Normal University, ed. *Chinese Women and Development: Status, Health and Employment: Collection of Essays from Summer School of Tianjin Normal University 1993,* pp. 337–71. Zhengzhou, China: Henan People's Publishing House.

Tartakovskaya, Irina and Sarah Ashwin. 2004. Who Benefits from Networks? Paper presented at the Employment Research Unit 19th Annual Conference, Cardiff.

United Nations Development Programme (UNDP), United Nations Development Fund for Women (UNDFW), Chinese National Development and Reform Commission (CNDFC), and China International Center for Economic and Technical Exchange (CICETE). 2003. *China's Accession to WTO: Challenges for Women in the Agricultural and Industrial Sectors.* New York: UNDP.

Walder, Andrew G. 1986. *Communist Neo-Traditionalism: Work and Authority in Chinese Industry.* Berkeley: University of California Press.

Wang Xiuzhi. 1993. "Nanjing funü jiuye qingku yu jianjie [The Situation and Insights on Women's Employment in Nanjing]," in Hu Shangjin, Peng Yanru, and Wang Yuanhui, eds. *Investigation into Women's Social Status in Jiangsu,* pp. 174–82. Beijing: Chinese Women's Publishing House.

Wang Zheng. 2000. "Gender, Employment and Women's Resistance," in Elizabeth J. Perry and Mark Selden, eds. *Chinese Society: Change, Conflict and Resistance,* 1st ed, pp. 62–82. London and New York: Routledge.

Wiegersma, Nan. 1994. "State Policy and the Restructuring of Women's Industries in Nicaragua," in Nahid Aslanbeigui, Steven Pressman, and Gale Summerfield, eds. *Women in the Age of Economic Transformation,* pp. 192–205. London and New York: Routledge.

Whyte, Martin K. 1984. "Sexual Inequality Under Socialism: The Chinese Case in Perspective," in James L. Watson, ed. *Class and Social Stratification in Post-Revolution China,* pp. 198–283. Cambridge: Cambridge University Press.

Wu Zhaohua. 2001. "Zhongguo jingji zhuanxing qi: nüxing mianling de tiaozhan yu duiche [Challenges and Strategies to Chinese Women during China's Economic Transformations]," in Li Qiufang, Qu Wen, Li Jingzhi, and Zhu Li, eds. *Women's Development in Half of the Century,* pp. 172–80. Beijing: Contemporary China Press.

Xu Yanli and Tan Lin. 2002. "Lun xiebiehua de shijian peizhi yu nüxing zhiye fazhan [On Gendered Time Allocation and Women's Career Development]." *Journal of China Women's College* 14(6): 1–7.

Yang Guang. 1999. Facing Unemployment: Urban Layoffs and the Way Out in Post-Reform China (1993–99): An Empirical and Theoretical Analysis. Working Paper Series 30, Institute of Social Studies, The Hague.

Yang, Mayfair Mei-Hui. 1994. *Gifts, Favors and Banquets: The Art of Social Relationships in China.* Ithaca, NY: Cornell University Press.

Yeung, Godfrey and Vincent Mok. 2004. "Does WTO Accession Matter for the Chinese Textile and Clothing Industry?" *Cambridge Journal of Economics* 28(6): 937–54.

Zhai, Fan and Zhi Wang. 2002. "WTO Accession, Rural Labour Migration and Urban Unemployment in China." *Urban Studies* 39(12): 2199–217.

Zhang Qiujian. 1999. Zhongguo hehui zhuanxingqi nügong jiuye bianqian [Changes in Women's Employment during China's Social Transformations]. PhD dissertation, China's People's University, Beijing.

Zhang Zuowei. 1998. *Geige de dileizhen* [The Minefield of Reforms: Layoff and Unemployment]. Zhuhai, China: Zhuhai Publishing House.

Zhao Yandong. 2001. Shehui ziben, renli ziben yu xiagang zhigong de zai jiuye [Social Capital, Human Capital and Reemployment of Laid-Off Workers]. PhD dissertation, Chinese Academy of Social Sciences.

———. 2002. "Measuring the Social Capital of Laid-Off Chinese Workers." *Current Sociology* 50(4): 555–71.

Zheng Xiaoying, ed. 1995. *Zhongguo nüxing renkou wenti yu fazhan* [Chinese Female Population Problems and Development]. Beijing: Beijing University Press.

155

Zhu Qinghong. 1999. "Fazhan shequ fuwuye, wei xiagang nügong zai jiuye kaipi xingmenlu [Developing Service Industry in the Community in order to Make New Breakthroughs in the Re-employment of Laid-Off Women Workers]," in Women's Federation of Nanjing, ed. *Collection of the Sixth Excellent Studies 1997–8 of Women's Federation of Nanjing*, pp. 1–7. Nanjing: Women's Federation of Nanjing.

An Ocean Formed from One Hundred Rivers: The Effects of Ethnicity, Gender, Marriage, and Location on Labor Force Participation in Urban China

Margaret Maurer-Fazio, James Hughes, and Dandan Zhang

INTRODUCTION

Women's labor force participation is influenced by a variety of economic, demographic, and cultural factors that have attracted the attention of both neoclassical and feminist economists. In addition to easily quantifiable influences such as wages, education, and the number and ages of children, gendered norms and expectations greatly influence women's labor force participation. Women's status in both the household and society at large and expectations about gendered household roles exert considerable influence on women's willingness and ability to participate in market work.

We are particularly interested in exploring the effects of gender norms in China's multiethnic society where social roles and expectations have changed rapidly during the transition from socialism to a more market-driven economy. We expect these influences to vary considerably by ethnic group.

In urban China's pre-reform labor system where the state guaranteed workers a job and expected individuals to work, women appeared to internalize the ideology and rhetoric that participation in paid labor would dramatically improve their status.[1] Even so, China's female labor force participation rates, 72.5 percent in 1990, were very high in international perspective – exceeding those of its Asian neighbors, other developing countries, and socialist nations (Table 1). Some women may have participated in the labor force not of their own free choice but rather because they dared not resist the implementation of policies and ideologies that purported to liberate women by means of participation in paid labor.[2] Although minority women in China have long suffered (along with their Han sisters) as a result of traditional attitudes and opinions that regard men as important and women as unimportant,[3] they have also benefited from the post-1949 government policies establishing women's rights and protecting women's status.

China's economic reforms and increased openness widened the range of women's opportunities for paid employment as the economic structure shifted away from capital-intensive heavy industry towards labor-intensive light industry and commercial services. However, the transition also created new obstacles for women's labor force participation. The state's retreat from its commitment to socialist ideology and the enforcement of workplace protections for women coincided with a reemergence of traditional patriarchal values (Elisabeth Croll 1995; Barbara Entwisle and Gail E. Henderson 2000). This combination of factors put pressure on women to leave the labor force and return to more subordinate roles. Increased workplace discipline also made it more difficult for working women to cope with household responsibilities, thereby raising the costs of labor force participation, particularly for married women.

Moreover, reform-era decentralization of enterprise decision-making not only allowed managers much more leeway to determine the composition of their workforces and to reward productivity, it also allowed managers more freedom to engage in discriminatory practices. Recent empirical work reveals that over the first two decades of China's reform, gender wage gaps increased (Margaret Maurer-Fazio, Thomas Rawski, and Wei Zhang 1999; James W. Hughes and Margaret Maurer-Fazio 2002; Margaret Maurer-Fazio and James W. Hughes 2002), although the extent to which these increases are attributable to discrimination remains controversial.

Table 1 Labor force participation: International comparisons (in percentages)

	1987–91	1997–2000
Brazil		
Male	85.8	81.9
Female	43.2	54.4
China		
Male	84.7	83.0
Female	72.5	70.6
Czech Republic		
Male	72.9	69.6
Female	60.8	51.6
France		
Male	64.4	62.2
Female	44.5	47.4
Japan		
Male	77.2	76.4
Female	50.1	49.3
Korea		
Male	73.3	74.0
Female	46.5	48.3
Pakistan		
Male	84.9	82.5
Female	11.3	15.3
Poland		
Male	74.3	64.1
Female	57.0	49.7
Russian Federation		
Male	77.4	67.1
Female	61.0	51.8
US		
Male	72.7	74.7
Female	55.5	60.2

Sources: All countries except China: International Labour Office (ILO) *Year Book of Labour Statistics* (Various years). ILO data selected to be as close as possible in date to the 1990 and 2000 Chinese censuses. For China, authors' calculations are based on the 1 percent and 0.095 percent micro-samples of the 1990 and 2000 population censuses of China.

China's urban labor markets underwent dramatic changes in the late 1990s as a result of the pervasive restructuring of the economy – changes engendered, at least in part, by anticipation of WTO membership (Sarah Cook and Margaret Maurer-Fazio 1999; Xin Meng 2000; Nicholas R. Lardy 2002; John Knight and Lina Song 2005). Market forces intruded on the state's system of labor allocation. Concerns about the inefficiency of state-owned enterprises led to massive layoffs; by the end of 1999, over twenty-five million workers had been laid off (National Bureau of Statistics and Ministry of Labor and Social Security 2000). Most of the job losses occurred in the state sector where employment levels peaked in 1995 at 109.6 million and then fell dramatically to 78.8 million by 2000 (National Bureau of

Statistics and Ministry of Labor and Social Security 2004: 23, Table 1-14). Women were disproportionately laid off (Simon Appleton, John Knight, Lina Song, and Qingjie Xia 2002; Margaret Maurer-Fazio 2006; Jieyu Liu 2007, in this volume) and experienced more difficulty finding reemployment in the private sector. Many women became so discouraged that they left the labor force altogether, as evidenced by the sharp decline in their rates of labor force participation (Margaret Maurer-Fazio, James W. Hughes, and Dandan Zhang 2005; John Giles, Albert Park, and Fang Cai 2006).

While a good deal of research has focused on the gender implications of public-sector downsizing, to date little is known about the consequences of recent labor market dislocations on China's ethnic minority populations. What we do know is that during the 1980s, the gap in occupational attainment between the Han majority and China's ethnic minorities increased (Emily Hannum and Yu Xie 1998). We also know that the gap in per capita rural income between the Han and the ethnic minorities increased quite substantially and rapidly between the late 1980s and the mid-1990s, largely due to the concentration of minorities in poor regions (Bjorn Gustafsson and Shi Li 2003).

In this paper, we focus on gender and ethnicity-differentiated labor force participation rates and on the changes in these rates over the period from 1990 to 2000. By examining the differences and changes in labor force participation rates by gender and ethnicity, we seek to infer the effects of labor market dislocations on differing segments of China's urban work force. We are particularly interested in whether the potential differences in majority and minority experiences of these labor market dislocations mirror the differences in the experiences of men and women. In the following analysis, we first use descriptive statistics to determine whether women and minorities bore a disproportionate share of the costs (in the form of sharper declines in labor force participation and sharper increases in unemployment rates) of the restructuring of state-owned enterprises. We also employ probit analysis to explore whether any observed female or minority disadvantages were due to managers' prejudices in hiring and firing decisions.

CHINA'S ETHNIC NATIONALITIES

We use the term ethnic minority here to refer to the fifty-five national minorities that, along with the Han majority, make up the fifty-six ethnic groups officially recognized by the Chinese central government.[4] Chinese policies towards ethnic minorities stem in part from a legacy inherited from dynastic leaders, in part from an ethnic identification project built on Stalinist principles and implemented in the early years of the People's Republic, and in part from an array of adaptations to specific local situations. Although the Chinese constitution prohibits discrimination against China's ethnic minorities, they are often classified on a continuum from primitive (*luohou*) to advanced (*fada*) on the basis of particular economic and social practices (Susan Blum 2001: 18). Many Han view themselves as more advanced than most minorities and believe that minorities need help in modernizing or – as Stevan Harrell (1995) puts it – the Han are involved in a "civilizing" project. Harrell also points out the potential parallel between the construction of the concept of women (*funu*) as a category in the communist ideology of sexual equality and the construction of the concept of minorities (*shaoshuminzu*) in the communist ideology of ethnic equality (1995: 12). In Chinese society, women and minorities are both portrayed as subordinate (Harrell 1995; Dru Gladney 2004).

According to the 2000 population census, there were 106.43 million ethnic minority people in China, constituting 8.47 percent of the Chinese population. Since the 1960s, China's ethnic minority population has increased both in absolute number and as a share of the total population (Table 2). A change in government policy in the mid-1980s increased the

Table 2 Population of China's major ethnic groups[a] in five censuses

Nationality	1953	1964	1982	1990	2000
Total	577,856,141	691,220,104	1,003,913,927	1,130,510,638	1,242,612,226
Bai	567,119	706,623	1,132,224	1,598,052	1,858,063
Bouyei	1,237,714	1,348,055	2,119,345	2,548,294	2,971,460
Dai	478,966	535,389	839,496	1,025,402	1,158,989
Dong	712,802	836,123	1,426,400	2,508,624	2,960,293
Han	542,824,056	651,296,368	936,674,944	1,039,187,548	1,137,386,112
Hani	481,220	628,727	1,058,806	1,254,800	1,439,673
Hui	3,530,498	4,473,147	7,228,398	8,612,001	9,816,805
Kazak	509,375	491,637	907,546	1,110,758	1,250,458
Korean	1,111,275	1,339,569	1,765,204	1,923,361	1,923,842
Li	360,950	438,813	887,107	1,112,498	1,247,814
Manchu	2,399,228	2,695,675	4,304,981	9,846,776	10,682,262
Miao	2,490,874	2,782,088	5,021,175	7,383,622	8,940,116
Mongolian	1,451,035	1,965,766	3,411,367	4,802,407	5,813,947
Tibetan	2,753,081	2,501,174	3,847,875	4,593,072	5,416,021
Tujia	0	524,755	2,836,814	5,725,049	8,028,133
Uygur	3,610,462	3,996,311	5,963,491	7,207,024	8,399,393
Yao	665,933	857,265	1,411,967	2,137,033	2,637,421
Yi	3,227,750	3,380,960	5,453,564	6,578,524	7,762,272
Zhuang	6,864,585	8,386,140	13,383,086	15,555,820	16,178,811
All others	2,579,218	2,035,519	4,240,137	5,799,973	6,740,341
Minority % of total population	6.06	5.78	6.70	8.08	8.47

Note: [a]All ethnic groups with population greater than 1 million in 2000.
Source: NBS and SEAC (2003: 2–3, Table 1-1).

161

benefits of minority identification,[5] providing an incentive for individuals to reclaim ethnic minority status.[6] Excluded from these benefits, some of the Han oppose minority benefits as unfair, not unlike majority opposition to affirmative action policies in the United States. The Han, like whites in the US, typically occupy positions of economic, political, and cultural dominance (Blum 2001: 57).

Much of China's total land area (63.9 percent), particularly the politically sensitive border regions in northwestern, southwestern, and northeastern China, is designated as autonomous ethnic minority regions (State Ethnic Affairs Committee [SEAC] 2003: 545), and many of China's minority people (75 percent) reside in these specially designated areas (Information Office of the State Council of the People's Republic of China 1999: 15). Published economic statistical data on China's minority peoples is almost always presented by autonomous region rather than by ethnic group.[7] This makes it difficult to shed light on questions about the economic well-being of China's minority peoples since the Han often comprise a significant proportion of the population in autonomous regions.[8]

Overall economic indicators show a rising standard of living in ethnic minority regions. Colin Mackerras (2003: 56–76) examines numerous indicators of the standard of living in China's minority areas, including measure of rural income, wages, healthcare provision, infrastructure development, and industrial development, concluding that since 1990 minorities have radically improved their standard of living. However, these improvements have not kept pace with developments in the national economy. China's minorities dwell predominately in western China (Table 3), a region that includes China's poorest provinces and lags far behind the eastern seaboard provinces in terms of income and economic development.

Gustafsson and Li (2003) directly assess the differences in rural income between the Han majority and ethnic minorities using household survey data of nineteen provinces in 1988 and 1995. They find that the earlier period's per capita income gap of 19.2 percent grew to 35.9 percent in the latter period. Their decomposition of the observed income differential into differences due to endowments and treatment reveals that the vast majority of the differential is due to differences in endowments, particularly location. They find minority incomes to be lower than Han incomes, largely because minorities are clustered in provinces with low per capita GDP and tend to dwell in mountainous areas as well as areas officially designated as poor.

Hannum and Xie (1998) employ data on individuals from two Chinese population censuses to compare the effects of market reform on the occupational attainment of Xinjiang's (mainly Turkic) minorities to the Han's. Between the 1982 and 1990 censuses, they find that the ethnic gap in occupational attainment between the Han and the minorities widened.

Table 3 Distribution of China's minority population across provinces as of 2000 population census

Province	Total population	Han population	Minority population	Minority population as % of prov. pop.	% of national minority pop.
Total	1,242,612,226	1,137,386,112	104,490,735	8.41	100.00
Anhui	58,999,948	58,602,112	397,712	0.67	0.38
Beijing	13,569,194	12,983,696	585,381	4.31	0.56
Chongqing	30,512,763	28,539,156	1,973,448	6.47	1.89
Fujian	34,097,947	33,514,147	582,822	1.71	0.56
Gansu	25,124,282	22,925,063	2,199,180	8.75	2.10
Guangdong	85,225,007	83,955,870	1,266,186	1.49	1.21
Guangxi	43,854,538	27,024,974	16,827,705	38.37	16.10
Guizhou	35,247,695	21,911,687	12,625,500	35.82	12.08
Hainan	7,559,035	6,245,329	1,313,521	17.38	1.26
Hebei	66,684,419	63,781,603	2,902,669	4.35	2.78
Heilongjiang	36,237,576	34,465,039	1,772,411	4.89	1.70
Henan	91,236,854	90,093,286	1,143,375	1.25	1.09
Hubei	59,508,870	56,911,968	2,596,839	4.36	2.49
Hunan	63,274,173	56,863,479	6,410,512	10.13	6.14
Inner Mongolia	23,323,347	18,465,586	4,857,633	20.83	4.65
Jiangsu	73,043,577	72,783,674	258,489	0.35	0.25
Jiangxi	40,397,598	40,271,881	125,356	0.31	0.12
Jilin	26,802,191	24,348,815	2,453,212	9.15	2.35
Liaoning	41,824,412	35,105,991	6,718,332	16.06	6.43
Ningxia	5,486,393	3,590,563	1,895,830	34.56	1.81
Qinghai	4,822,963	2,606,050	2,216,888	45.97	2.12
Shaanxi	35,365,072	35,188,651	176,385	0.50	0.17
Shandong	89,971,789	89,339,046	632,591	0.70	0.61
Shanghai	16,407,734	16,303,862	103,639	0.63	0.10
Shanxi	32,471,242	32,368,083	103,018	0.32	0.10
Sichuan	82,348,296	78,229,697	4,118,424	5.00	3.94
Tianjin	9,848,731	9,581,775	266,918	2.71	0.26
Tibet	2,616,329	158,570	2,453,942	93.79	2.35
Xinjiang	18,459,511	7,489,919	10,969,425	59.42	10.50
Yunnan	42,360,089	28,201,274	14,151,343	33.41	13.54
Zhejiang	45,930,651	45,535,266	392,049	0.85	0.38

Source: NBS and SEAC (2003: 4–27, Table 1-2).

Hannum and Xie attribute the rising gap to an increasing disparity in educational attainment between the Han and the minorities as well as a strengthening of the relationship between educational attainment and higher-status occupations.

The papers of Gustafsson and Li and Hannum and Xie suggest that minorities are not faring well in China's transition – both income and occupational attainment gaps have widened. The former paper posits that geography is a very important contributing factor in explaining differences between majority and minority incomes. The latter suggests important ethnic differences in labor market outcomes, even after carefully controlling for location. Building on these previous efforts, this project employs more recent and extensive data to examine the effects of ethnicity, gender, marital status, and on labor market outcomes.

In the following analysis, we concentrate on four important minority groups chosen to vary considerably in terms of socioeconomic conditions, degree of integration with the Han, geographic concentration, and location – the Hui, Koreans, Uygurs, and Zhuang. We focus on the Hui because of their unusual degree of integration with the Han, geographic dispersion, and Muslim faith. The Hui speak and write Chinese. Hui people reside in most provinces. In many parts of central and eastern China they may constitute the only ethnic group that their Han neighbors are likely to encounter. The most salient feature (and some would argue the only feature) that distinguishes Hui from Han is religion. We focus on Koreans because of their principal residence in northeastern China and atypically high levels of education and urbanization. Most of the Koreans in China are descendents of immigrants who entered China in the nineteenth century (Mackerras 2003: 185). We focus on the Uygurs because of their tight geographic concentration, location in a politically sensitive area, low degree of urbanization, Muslim faith, and residence in northwestern China. Uygurs are of Turkic origin and speak a Turkic language that has its own script. There is a great deal of tension between the Uygurs and the Han Chinese; in particular, the Chinese leadership is quite concerned about potential Uygur separatist tendencies. Finally, we focus on the Zhuang, China's largest ethnic minority because of their numerical importance and primary residence in southwestern China. They are well integrated with the Han. The Zhuang have their own language, but many speak Chinese and resist efforts to provide Zhuang-language education for their children (Katherine Palmer Kaup 2000).

RESEARCH STRATEGY

This paper adds to the thin literature on ethnicity in China's economic transition by examining the changes in the labor force participation of ethnic minorities in reform-era urban labor markets. We overcome some of the data scarcity problems caused by the statistical focus on region rather than ethnicity by employing newly available individual data from the 1990 and 2000 population censuses of China. We use descriptive statistics to assess whether the costs of labor restructuring in state-owned enterprises in the late 1990s fell disproportionately upon women and ethnic minorities in the forms of sharper declines in labor force participation and larger increases in unemployment rates. We compare the labor force participation patterns of the Hui, Koreans, Uyghur, and Zhuang to each other and to the majority Han population, examining differences in labor force participation rates between minority and Han men and women and tracking changes in these rates over time.

We then use probit analysis to explore whether any observed minority disadvantage can be attributed to managerial prejudice in firing/hiring decisions. If managers indulge prejudices against women and minorities by refusing to hire them or laying them off disproportionately, women and minorities might become "discouraged workers" and withdraw from the labor force at greater rates than men and ethnic Han. Economic reforms increased managers' ability to discriminate by decentralizing decision making to firms. However, the reforms also increased managers' stake in the cost effectiveness of firms and thus reduced their incentives to discriminate. Reforms thus set in motion opposing forces; managers were freer to indulge discriminatory preferences in hiring and lay off decisions, yet they were also accountable for any adverse performance consequences of such discrimination. The net effect of these opposing forces is ambiguous. The multivariate regression analysis enables us to sort out the various influences. For example, if the human capital characteristics of the majority Han population were substantially better than those of an ethnic minority in a particular area, managers may rationally favor Han workers over less qualified minorities. While simple descriptive statistics might suggest greater discrimination in the reform period, multivariate analysis that controls for basic human capital characteristics helps us better distinguish between managers' possible discrimination and their rational preferences for better qualified workers. In effect, we employ ethnicity variables as proxies for discrimination. In this sense, we interpret a convergence of ethnic minority and Han majority labor force participation rates over time as consistent with a decline in discrimination and a divergence in these rates as consistent with an increase in discrimination. This is, of course, a very loose definition of discrimination; we attribute the disadvantages that cannot be explained by worker qualifications to discrimination. In this residual sense, a finding of a statistically significant marginal effect of gender and/or ethnicity would be consistent with discrimination.

We also use probit analysis to explore whether some of the observed gender differentials can be attributed to the resurgence of traditional attitudes towards women's roles in the home and in society. For this purpose, we track changes in the effect of marriage on labor force participation over time. A finding that marriage has an increasingly negative effect on labor force participation would be consistent with a reemergence of traditional gender norms in China. We also compare the patterns of labor force participation between ethnic groups of different religions. In addition, we geographically stratify our data to address the relative importance of ethnicity and geography in explaining outcomes. Specifically, we want to explore whether any observed minority disadvantage is due to ethnicity per se or due to living in an economically depressed region.[9]

Although our probit regressions based on national samples include controls for location, we find it useful to account for the geographic concentration of a particular ethnic minority by subdividing the data on the basis of geographic region. For example, if we find (as we do) in the 2000 national sample that ethnic Koreans have much lower labor force participation rates in urban areas than the Han, the question still remains as to whether these lower rates are due to discriminatory treatment of Koreans, differences in Korean and Han attitudes to paid work, or to the fact that the vast majority of China's Koreans live in China's rustbelt, the three northeastern provinces of Jilin, Liaoning, and Heilongjiang.

To isolate the effects of regional economic conditions on minority labor force participation, we split our data into sub-samples of one or more provinces according to areas of principal residence for each of the minority groups in our study. For example, to compare the labor force participation of Koreans to that of other ethnic groups living in the same region, we limit our sample to the data for Jilin, Liaoning, and Heilongjiang. To address the same question for the Zhuang, we use data for Guangxi, Guangdong, and Yunnan, the provinces where a large majority of Zhuang reside. Xinjiang is the sole province of principal residence for the Uygurs. Although the Hui are recognized as residing in nineteen of China's provinces, we restrict our sample to the eight provinces with the largest Hui populations – Ningxia, Gansu, Henan, Xinjiang, Qinghai, Yunnan, Hebei, and Shangdong.[10]

DATA

Our analysis is based on a one percent micro-data sample of the 1990 population census and a 0.095 percent micro-data sample of the 2000 population census for China.[11] Since we focus on labor issues, we restrict our samples to include only those aged 15 and above. Ethnicity is reported directly on the census questionnaires. In our analyses, we control for each of the nineteen ethnic groups with populations exceeding one million in 2000. We aggregate all others into a residual group.

Individuals are considered to be in the labor force if they reported having a job on the day of the census, or if they were unemployed and looking for work at that time. The census questionnaires do not distinguish between part- and full-time employment.[12]

We restrict our analyses to individuals living in urban areas and identify individuals in the 1990 census sample as urban on the basis of an administrative location code. The first two digits of this code indicate province, the third and fourth digits indicate region, and the fifth and sixth digits indicate whether the location is considered as an urban district or county. We classify the individuals dwelling in counties as rural and those in districts as urban. This procedure yields a figure of 25.25 percent urban for the entire population in 1990.[13] The data released in the 0.095 percent sample of the 2000 census contain only the first four digits of the administrative code, precluding use of the same categorization scheme. In any event, the 2000 census sample directly reports individuals as residing in city, town, or rural areas. We aggregate those in cities and towns into an urban category constituting 36.9 percent of the population.[14]

We aggregate some of the educational attainment categories. We group illiterate and semi-literate together, aggregate all types of senior middle schools into one category, and combine all types of post-secondary education into one category.

DESCRIPTIVE RESULTS

Table 4 reveals an extremely sharp drop in the overall labor force participation rates of the urban Chinese population between the 1990 and 2000 population censuses. Urban women's participation rates declined by 11.2 percentage points to 57.7 percent and urban men's by 7.9 percentage points to 74.0 percent. We know that women were laid off disproportionately (Giles, Park, and Cai 2006; Maurer-Fazio 2006) and expect this factor to contribute to a gender imbalance in the discouraged worker effect and labor force exit. The relatively large decline in Chinese women's labor force participation is mirrored in European post-socialist economies.[15]

Table 4 Urban women and men's labor force participation rates by ethnic group aged 15 and above, 1990 and 2000

	Women			*Men*		
	1990	*2000*	*Change 1990–2000*	*1990*	*2000*	*Change 1990–2000*
Ethnic group						
Total population	68.91	57.71	11.20	81.92	74.00	7.92
Han	68.88	57.79	11.09	81.98	74.16	7.82
Total ethnic minority population	69.44	55.97	13.47	80.66	70.47	10.19
Hui	69.44	51.65	17.79	79.88	71.48	8.40
Korean	66.11	48.15	17.96	81.29	63.37	17.92
Uygur	60.64	50.73	9.91	80.99	60.82	20.17
Zhuang	78.25	65.45	12.80	83.34	77.67	5.67

Sources: 1 percent micro-sample of the 1990 population census of China and 0.095 percent micro-sample of the 2000 population census of China.

In Table 4, we see that urban minority women decreased their labor force participation rates by 13.5 percentage points to 55.97 percent, a decrease exceeding Han women's 11.1 percentage points and both Han and minority men's decreases of 7.8 and 10.2 percentage points, respectively. These simple descriptive statistics support the notion that minority women may be doubly disadvantaged; their participation rates have declined more and have come to rest at lower levels than those of Han men and women and minority men.[16]

The changes in participation rates of the aggregate urban population and aggregate urban minority population discussed above mask substantial variation in both the levels and changes in participation rates of specific minorities. The overall participation rates of Zhuang women significantly exceeded those of the Han and other minorities in both 1990 and 2000. Uygur women started out the period with rates of participation that were substantially lower than those of other women but experienced a relatively muted decline over the decade. Uygur men, by contrast, experienced a decline in participation rates over the period of a remarkable 20 percentage points. The labor force participation rates of Hui women and

Table 5 Job status and unemployment rates by sex, 1990 and 2000 (in percentages)

	With higher education[a]		Illiterate[b]		With high-status job[c]		Unemployed[d]	
	1990	2000	1990	2000	1990	2000	1990	2000
				Urban male				
Ethnicity								
Han	25.50	37.01	8.16	3.17	15.03	14.74	1.92	7.45
Hui	21.33	33.01	13.20	5.35	12.44	14.04	3.60	8.45
Korean	37.87	53.77	3.15	0.50	18.19	17.73	2.39	18.79
Uygur	24.95	34.61	14.62	5.66	15.55	14.75	3.27	11.52
Zhuang	16.61	34.55	8.16	1.24	6.46	12.23	2.13	6.11
				Urban female				
Ethnicity								
Han	19.70	29.41	22.63	11.15	14.29	16.91	2.30	9.15
Hui	18.65	30.83	27.10	14.14	13.79	19.27	3.05	12.18
Korean	29.81	43.47	11.76	6.31	17.47	22.03	2.43	11.89
Uygur	21.94	34.20	20.70	9.03	18.20	24.01	3.81	10.64
Zhuang	8.85	22.83	26.43	7.95	2.83	11.92	1.32	5.18

Notes: [a]percentage of urban population aged 15 and above that completed schooling above junior/middle school.
[b]percentage of urban population aged 15 and above that is not in school and is illiterate or semi-literate.
[c]percentage of the urban labor force that is in professional, technical, and administrative jobs.
[d]percentage of the urban population aged 15 and above reporting as "waiting for work" in 1990 and "unemployed" in 2000.
Source: 1 percent micro-sample of the 1990 population censuses of China and 0.095 percent micro-sample of the 2000 population census of China.

both Korean men and women fell precipitously over the decade. The extent of the decline in Korean labor force participation is surprising given that Koreans' educational levels far exceed those of any other ethnic group. However, the vast majority of Koreans live in the northeast, an area hit hard by the decline of inefficient state-run enterprises. We next explore possible explanations for these differences using multivariate analysis.

PROBIT RESULTS

For ease of exposition, the results of our probit models are presented in the tables below as marginal changes in the probability of labor force participation rather than probit regression coefficients.[17] Table 6 presents the means and proportions of the variables underlying our analysis of nationwide data. Table 7 presents the results of probit regressions controlling marital status, educational level,[18] age,[19] ethnicity, and location using nationwide data. Ethnicity is represented here by eighteen binary variables that indicate membership in one of China's largest ethnic minority groups, plus a nineteenth variable indicating membership in one of the smaller remaining ethnic minorities. Since we use the majority Han as the omitted category, all results for ethnicity should be interpreted as relative to the Han. The base case, for purposes of comparison, is an unmarried individual of Han ethnicity with middle school education residing in Jiangsu Province.

Our probit analysis of the nationwide data (Table 7) reveals a remarkable reversal of marriage's effect on women's participation in the labor force between 1990 and 2000. In 1990, married women were almost 9 percent more likely to be in the labor force than unmarried women. By 2000, married women were 1 percent less likely to be in the labor force than their unmarried counterparts. The change in the effect of marriage on participation for men was just the opposite; that is, the effect of marriage on men's labor force participation increased over time. Marriage increased the likelihood of participation by 10 percentage points in 1990 and by 13.5 percentage points in 2000.

Table 7 reveals that in 1990, after controlling for marital status, education, age, ethnicity, and province, the women of each of the four ethnic groups at the center of our analysis had participation rates that were higher than Han women's. The rates of the Zhuang, Korean, Uygur, and Hui women's participation exceeded that of Han women by 10.6, 8.3, 3.4, and 3.0 percent, respectively. By 2000, the situation changed quite noticeably; Hui and Uygur women's participation rates had become lower than that of Han women by 5.5 and 7.3 percent, respectively. Korean women's rate became indistinguishable from that of Han women. Zhuang women's rate remained greater than that of Han women but the differential was reduced by half.

Table 6 Descriptive statistics for urban residents, national samples

	1990		2000	
	Male	*Female*	*Male*	*Female*
Labor force participation rates	0.82	0.69	0.74	0.58
Age and marital status				
Married	0.67	0.70	0.71	0.71
Mean age	36.56	37.07	38.43	38.71
Education level				
Illiterate	7.7%	21.1%	2.5%	9.1%
Primary school	26.1%	25.8%	14.3%	17.0%
Junior middle school	38.3%	31.2%	28.3%	27.3%
Senior middle school	20.2%	17.9%	38.4%	35.1%
Post-secondary	7.7%	3.9%	16.5%	11.5%
Nationality (share)				
Han	97.6%	97.7%	97.9%	97.9%
Hui	1.1%	1.2%	1.0%	1.0%
Korean	0.2%	0.3%	0.3%	0.3%
Uygur	0.4%	0.4%	0.4%	0.3%
Zhuang	0.4%	0.4%	0.5%	0.5%
Bai	0.1%	0.2%	0.1%	0.0%
Bouyi	0.1%	0.1%	0.1%	0.1%
Dai	<0.1%	0.0%	0.0%	0.0%
Dong	0.1%	0.0%	0.1%	0.0%
Hani	<0.1%	0.0%	0.0%	0.0%
Kazak	0.0%	0.0%	0.0%	0.0%
Li	0.0%	0.0%	0.0%	0.0%
Manchu	0.8%	0.7%	0.8%	0.8%
Miao	0.2%	0.2%	0.2%	0.2%
Mongolian	0.3%	0.4%	0.3%	0.3%
Tibetan	<0.1%	<0.1%	0.1%	0.1%
Tujia	0.4%	0.4%	0.2%	0.2%
Yao	0.0%	0.0%	0.0%	0.0%
Yi	0.2%	0.2%	0.1%	0.1%
Other nationalities	0.2%	0.1%	0.1%	0.1%
Provinces				
Anhui	4.9%	4.9%	2.8%	2.8%
Beijing	2.4%	2.5%	3.6%	3.4%
Chongqing	a	a	2.2%	2.2%
Fujian	2.7%	2.8%	2.5%	2.5%
Gansu	2.0%	2.1%	1.4%	1.3%
Guangdong	4.9%	4.5%	10.0%	10.3%
Guangxi	2.1%	2.2%	2.1%	2.0%
Guizhou	1.8%	1.8%	1.4%	1.4%
Hainan	0.1%	0.1%	0.5%	0.5%
Hebei	3.8%	3.9%	4.0%	4.0%
Heilongjiang	5.8%	6.1%	4.3%	4.4%
Henan	3.7%	3.6%	4.6%	4.7%
Hubei	6.9%	7.2%	5.4%	5.3%
Hunan	7.4%	7.2%	3.5%	3.4%
Inner Mongolia	2.7%	2.9%	1.9%	2.0%

(*continued*)

Table 6 (continued)

	1990		2000	
	Male	Female	Male	Female
Jiangsu	3.8%	4.0%	6.4%	6.6%
Jiangxi	4.2%	4.2%	1.8%	1.8%
Jilin	3.1%	3.3%	3.2%	3.2%
Liaoning	5.8%	6.1%	6.7%	6.7%
Ningxi	0.2%	0.3%	0.4%	0.4%
Qinghai	0.3%	0.4%	0.3%	0.3%
Shaanxi	2.7%	2.8%	2.3%	2.3%
Shandong	6.2%	6.3%	7.5%	7.9%
Shanghai	4.3%	2.8%	4.8%	4.5%
Shanxi	2.6%	2.7%	2.4%	2.4%
Sichuan	6.2%	6.3%	4.2%	4.1%
Tianjin	2.7%	2.5%	1.9%	1.9%
Tibet	<0.1%	<0.1%	0.1%	0.1%
Xinjiang	1.7%	1.7%	1.7%	1.5%
Yunnan	1.7%	1.8%	1.6%	1.5%
Zhejiang	3.1%	3.3%	4.7%	4.6%
Number of observations	247,992	230,290	114,885	113,976

Notes: [a]Prior to 1997, Chongqing was part of Sichuan Province.

Sources: 20 percent random sample of the 1 percent micro-sample of the population census of China for 1990 and 0.095 percent micro-sample of the population census of China 2000.

After controlling for marital status, education, age, ethnicity, and province, only Uygur men started the period with a participation rate that exceeded the Han (by 4.5 percent). The participation rates of Zhuang and Korean men were not significantly different from the Han. Hui men's rate was 3.3 percent lower. By 2000, both Uygur and Korean men's rates were approximately 7.5 percent lower than the Han's. The Hui differential changed little over the decade, and the Zhuang's rates remained statistically indistinguishable from the Han's.

We next test whether the above differences in labor force participation rates by ethnic group are robust with respect to location. To do this, we subdivide our data into four geographic regions representing the regions of principal residence of the Hui, Koreans, Uygurs, and Zhuang, and then run probit regressions on each subset that control for the same variables (marital status, educational attainment, age, ethnicity, and province). In our first sub-sample comprised of individuals residing in areas that are home to the Hui, we continue to observe that Hui men's participation rate is lower than the Han men's in 1990 (Table 8). This differential disappears over the subsequent decade, and by 2000, Hui men's participation rates become indistinguishable from the Han's. In the sub-sample of Hui areas, the difference in the participation rates of Hui women from 1990 to 2000 is quite remarkable. They start the

Table 7 Probability of labor force participation, marginal changes by human capital, sex, ethnicity, and province for urban dwellers, aged 15 and older

	1990		2000	
	Women	*Men*	*Women*	*Men*
Human capital and sex				
Married	0.089***	0.104***	−0.018***	0.135***
Illiterate	−0.097***	0.024***	0.056***	0.155***
Primary school	−0.058***	0.003	−0.056***	0.089***
Senior middle	0.006	−0.071***	−0.007*	0.090***
Post-secondary	−0.147***	−0.223***	0.058***	−0.029***
Age	0.076***	0.048***	0.091***	0.078***
Age squared	−0.001***	−0.001***	−0.001***	−0.001***
Net effect of age	0.002	−0.025	0.014	0.001
Ethnicity				
Hui	0.030***	−0.033***	−0.055***	−0.039***
Korean	0.083***	−0.011	−0.029	−0.075***
Uygur	0.034*	0.045***	−0.073**	−0.076***
Zhuang	0.106***	0.004	0.057**	0.019
Bai	0.065**	−0.096***	0.103	0.050
Bouyi	0.017	0.028	0.107*	0.147***
Dai	−0.267	–	0.063	0.123
Dong	−0.143**	0.026	−0.008	−0.056
Hani	−0.174	–	0.124	−0.208*
Kazak	−0.042	0.061*	−0.081	−0.099
Li	−0.056	−0.037	0.075	−0.022
Manchu	−0.043***	0.008	−0.028	−0.013
Miao	0.153***	0.014	0.100**	−0.019
Mongolian	0.036**	0.013	0.019	0.000
Tibetan	–	–	−0.115	−0.304***
Tujia	0.092***	0.009	−0.011	0.036
Yao	−0.195*	−0.194***	0.050	0.034
Yi	0.154***	0.012	0.091*	−0.024
Other nationalities	−0.162***	−0.019	−0.053	0.040
Province				
Anhui	0.034***	0.016***	−0.057***	−0.021**
Beijing	−0.056***	0.000	0.014	−0.030***
Chongqing	–	–	−0.080***	−0.013
Fujian	−0.264***	0.005	−0.033***	0.026**
Guangdong	−0.087***	−0.036***	0.030***	0.061***
Guangxi	0.057***	0.015***	−0.042***	−0.025*
Gansu	−0.055***	−0.036***	−0.080***	−0.035**
Guizhou	0.071***	−0.002	−0.116***	−0.038***
Hebei	−0.073***	0.005	−0.083***	−0.056***
Hubei	0.059***	0.008**	−0.057***	−0.037***
Heilongjiang	−0.293***	−0.039***	−0.217***	−0.114***
Henan	−0.028***	0.008	−0.043***	−0.026***
Hunan	−0.038***	0.006	−0.065***	−0.061***
Hainan	−0.075*	0.013	−0.003	−0.027
Jilin	−0.190***	−0.005	−0.180***	−0.127***
Jiangxi	−0.013	0.013***	−0.134***	−0.044***

(*continued*)

172

Table 7 (continued)

	1990		2000	
	Women	*Men*	*Women*	*Men*
Liaoning	−0.110***	−0.025***	−0.103***	−0.057***
Neimongol	−0.210***	−0.025***	−0.177***	−0.056***
Ningxi	−0.202***	−0.012	−0.056**	0.029
Qinghai	−0.153***	−0.023*	−0.180***	−0.056**
Shaanxi	−0.137***	−0.005	−0.127***	−0.067***
Shandong	0.048***	0.004	−0.034***	−0.001
Shanghai	−0.072***	0.024***	−0.087***	−0.032***
Shanxi	−0.184***	0.008	−0.173***	−0.052***
Sichuan	0.060***	−0.003	−0.038***	−0.037***
Tianjin	−0.145***	−0.002	−0.160***	−0.060***
Tibet	−	−	0.021	0.037
Xinjiang	−0.227***	−0.076***	−0.129***	−0.059***
Yunnan	0.072***	0.02***	−0.075***	−0.007
Zhejiang	−0.017*	0.054***	−0.012	0.055***
Number of obs.	230,290	247,992	113,976	114,885
Obs. P	0.688	0.818	0.577	0.740
Pred. P	0.680	0.900	0.506	0.790
Log likelihood	−94,129	−70,739	−57,613	−39,039
LR Chi^2 (degrees of freedom)	97,668 (53)	94,038 (51)	40,057 (56)	53,598 (56)
Psuedo R^2	0.342	0.399	0.258	0.407

Notes: *indicates statistical significance at the 10 percent level; **indicates statistical significance at the 5 percent level; ***indicates statistical significance at the 1 percent level. Entries represent the change in the probability that an individual is in the labor force when the binary variable toggles from zero to one, evaluated at the sample mean. "Net effect of age" is the combined marginal effect of the age and age-squared variables, evaluated at the sample mean. Base case consists of single Han residents of Jiangsu with junior middle school educations.

decade with a participation rate 8.5 percentage points higher than Han women and end the period with a participation rate 8.0 percentage points lower, a drop of 16 percentage points vis-à-vis Han women. Since urban Hui women have virtually the same age distribution and the proclivity to marry as the general population of urban women in both 1990 and 2000, neither of these factors can be used to explain the differences or decline in their participation rates.[20]

When we restrict the sample to the three provinces of northeastern China, the differences between Korean and Han men's participation rates are more pronounced (Table 9). That is, the deficit in Korean men's participation rates grows from 1.8 percentage points in 1990 to 9.5 percentage points in 2000. However, Korean women's labor force participation patterns are more similar to Han women of the Northeast (their neighbors) than to Han women nationwide. By 2000, Korean women's participation rates in the Northeast are indistinguishable from Han women's. The differential in the participation rates of Korean and

Table 8 Probability of labor force participation, marginal changes by human capital, sex, ethnicity, and province for Hui relative to others in Ningxia, Gansu, Xinjiang, Hebei, Henan, Qinghai, Shandong, and Yunnan provinces (urban dwellers, aged 15 and older)

	1990		2000	
	Women	*Men*	*Women*	*Men*
Human capital and sex				
Married	0.130***	0.114***	0.009	0.139***
Illiterate	-0.041***	0.032***	0.018	0.163***
Primary school	-0.017***	-0.006***	-0.052***	0.103***
Senior middle school	-0.033***	-0.088***	0.012	0.105***
Post-secondary	-0.085***	-0.217***	0.092***	-0.004
Age	0.065***	0.047***	0.099***	0.079***
Age squared	-0.001***	-0.001***	-0.001***	-0.001***
Net effect of age	-0.006	0.003	-0.007	-0.001
Ethnicity				
Hui	0.085***	-0.029***	-0.080***	-0.008
Korean	0.177*	0.044	-0.079	-0.050
Uygur	0.014	0.05***	-0.071	-0.081***
Zhuang	-0.148**	-0.064	-0.255*	-0.289*
Bai	0.087***	-0.055***	0.161**	0.079
Bouyi		-0.051		
Dai	-0.197	-0.093	0.115	0.118
Dong	-0.661***	-0.196*		-0.485
Hani	-0.085***		0.130	-0.104
Kazak	-0.035	0.037**	-0.090	-0.069
Li				-0.430
Manchu	-0.021	-0.016	-0.085	-0.008
Miao	0.163***	0.006	0.051	0.173*
Mongolian	0.128***	0.046***	0.006	-0.023
Tibetan	-0.186*	-0.599***	-0.049	-0.259**
Tujia	-0.123	0.049		-0.387
Yao	-0.370	0.031		
Yi	0.133***	0.045***	0.109*	-0.003
Other nationalities	-0.047*	-0.243***	-0.107	-0.021
Province				
Gansu	0.111***	-0.016**	-0.030	-0.062**
Hebei	0.102***	0.022***	-0.034	-0.081***
Henan	0.141***	0.021***	0.010	-0.050*
Qinghai	0.060***	0.010	-0.137***	-0.089**
Shandong	0.197***	0.017***	0.020	-0.025
Xinjiang	-0.006	-0.051***	-0.082***	-0.086***
Yunnan	0.198***	0.027***	-0.022	-0.035
Number of obs.	230,164	244,005	24,693	24,652
Obs. P	0.710	0.817	0.588	0.743
Pred. P	0.717	0.897	0.522	0.800
Log likelihood	$-92,792$	$-72,099$	$-12,252$	$-8,349$

(*continued*)

174

Table 8 (continued)

	1990		2000	
	Women	*Men*	*Women*	*Men*
LR Chi^2 (degrees of freedom)	91,687 (31)	87,740 (31)	8,953 (28)	11,408 (31)
Psuedo R^2	0.331	0.378	0.268	0.406

Notes: *indicates statistical significance at the 10 percent level; **indicates statistical significance at the 5 percent level; ***indicates statistical significance at the 1 percent level. Entries represent the change in the probability that an individual is in the labor force when the binary variable toggles from zero to one, evaluated at the sample mean. "Net effect of age" is the combined marginal effect of the age and age-squared variables, evaluated at the sample mean. Base case consists of single Han residents of Jiangsu with junior middle school educations.
Sources: 1 percent micro-sample of the 1990 population censuses of China and 0.095 percent micro-sample of the 2000 population census of China.

Han women in 1990 is halved to four percentage points when we limit our sample to the Northeast.

The Uygur population is tightly concentrated in Xinjiang. Comparing the participation rates of Han and minorities in Xinjiang in 2000, only Uygur men have a distinctly lower participation rate than the Han (Table 10). In 1990, Uygur men had a 10.1 percentage point higher participation rate than that of their Han neighbors (fellow Xinjiang residents). By 2000, this rate fell to 9.9 percentage points lower, a 20 percentage point decline relative to the Han in just ten years. At the start of the decade, the participation rates of Uygur women were 5 percentage points higher than those of neighboring Han women but became statistically indistinguishable by 2000.[21]

The Zhuang reside primarily in China's Southwest. Limiting our sample to this region mutes the significantly higher participation rate of Zhuang women seen in the 1990 national sample. In the Southwest, Zhuang women's participation rates remain higher than those of the Han in 1990. However, the size of the differential is reduced to 6 percentage points (Table 11). The labor force participation rates of Zhuang men and women become statistically indistinguishable from those of the neighboring Han by 2000.

In sum, when we split our data geographically by regions of principal residence for each of the four studied ethnic groups and control for age, marital status, education, and location we find that in 1990 ethnic minority men and women were more likely, rather than less likely, to be in the labor force than their Han neighbors. By 2000 the participation rates of the Korean, Uygur, and Zhuang women declined and converged with those of their female Han neighbors. Hui women's participation, however, declined precipitously and strongly diverged from that of their female Han neighbors. Over the decade, Hui and Zhuang men's participation rates

175

Table 9 Probability of labor force participation, marginal changes by human capital, sex, ethnicity, and province for Koreans relative to others in Jilin, Liaoning, and Heilongjiang provinces (urban dwellers, aged 15 and older)

	1990		2000	
	Women	*Men*	*Women*	*Men*
Human capital and sex				
Married	0.004	0.135***	−0.043***	0.173***
Illiterate	−0.332***	−0.019***	−0.148***	0.026
Primary school	−0.177***	−0.008***	−0.157***	0.055***
Senior middle school	0.068***	−0.060***	−0.082***	0.046***
Post-secondary	0.082***	−0.042***	0.086***	−0.035***
Age	0.100***	0.051***	0.104***	0.091***
Age squared	−0.001***	−0.001***	−0.001***	−0.001***
Net effect of age	−0.006	0.001	−0.014	−0.007
Ethnicity				
Hui	−0.021	−0.023**	0.007	−0.089**
Korean	0.040***	−0.018***	−0.016	−0.095***
Zhuang	0.158	−0.122		
Dai		−0.137		
Dong		−0.251*		
Manchu	−0.092***	0.019***	−0.002	−0.003
Miao	0.104			
Mongol	−0.071***	−0.008	0.014	−0.080
Tibetan				
Tujia	−0.152	0.049		−0.061
Yi	−0.494**			
Other nationalities	−0.122***	0.023	−0.049	0.274***
Province				
Heilongjiang	−0.119***	−0.033***	−0.038***	0.017
Liaoning	0.066***	−0.022***	0.082***	0.072***
Number of obs.	177,446	181,616	16,223	16,202
Obs. P	0.624	0.811	0.511	0.703
Pred. P	0.559	0.885	0.387	0.721
Log likelihood	−77,232	−51,703	−8,160	−5,885
LR Chi^2 (degrees of freedom)	80,566 (18)	72,584 (18)	6,161 (14)	7,928 (15)
Psuedo R^2	0.343	0.412	0.274	0.403

Notes: *indicates statistical significance at the 10 percent level; **indicates statistical significance at the 5 percent level; ***indicates statistical significance at the 1 percent level. Entries represent the change in the probability that an individual is in the labor force when the binary variable toggles from zero to one, evaluated at the sample mean. "Net effect of age" is the combined marginal effect of the age and age-squared variables, evaluated at the sample mean. Base case consists of single Han residents of Jiangsu with junior middle school educations.
Sources: 1 percent micro-sample of the 1990 Population Censuses of China and 0.095 percent micro-sample of the 2000 Population Census of China.

converged with those of their Han neighbors while Korean and Uygur men's rates fell markedly and diverged strongly from those of the Han. The participation rates of Uygur men, like those of Hui women, declined precipitously.

Table 10 Probability of labor force participation, marginal changes by human capital, sex, ethnicity, and province for Uygurs relative to others in Xinjiang province (urban dwellers, aged 15 and older)

	1990		2000	
	Women	*Men*	*Women*	*Men*
Human capital and sex				
Married	0.088***	0.089***	−0.050	0.149***
Illiterate	−0.250***	−0.041***	−0.253***	0.097
Primary school	−0.145***	−0.025***	−0.169***	0.067
Senior middle school	0.042***	−0.043***	−0.101***	0.082***
Post-secondary	0.126***	0.005	0.256***	0.061
Age	0.115***	0.077***	0.132***	0.093***
Age squared	−0.002	−0.001***	−0.002***	−0.001***
Net effect of age	0.003	0.006	−0.008	−0.002
Ethnicity				
Hui	−0.034*	0.000	0.033	−0.008
Uygur	0.050***	0.101***	−0.053	−0.099***
Zhuang	−0.174	0.091		
Bai				
Dong				
Hani				
Kazak	−0.107***	0.059***	−0.116	−0.149
Manchu	0.145	0.021	0.412	0.122
Miao	−0.189	0.030		
Mongol	−0.048	−0.015	−0.021	0.201
Tibetan	0.134			
Tujia	−0.203*	0.041		
Yi				
Other nationalities	−0.140***	0.068**	−0.087	0.174
Province				
Xinjiang				
Number of obs.	20,034	20,795	1,740	1,914
Obs. P	0.616	0.769	0.550	0.712
Pred. P	0.578	0.841	0.450	0.751
Log likelihood	−9,437	−6,819	−792	−660
LR Chi^2 (degrees of freedom)	7,809 (17)	8,831 (16)	812 (13)	977 (13)
Psuedo R^2	0.293	0.393	0.339	0.425

Notes: *indicates statistical significance at the 10 percent level; **indicates statistical significance at the 5 percent level; ***indicates statistical significance at the 1 percent level. Entries represent the change in the probability that an individual is in the labor force when the binary variable toggles from zero to one, evaluated at the sample mean. "Net effect of age" is the combined marginal effect of the age and age-squared variables, evaluated at the sample mean. Base case consists of single Han residents of Jiangsu with junior middle school educations.
Sources: 1 percent micro-sample of the 1990 population censuses of China and 0.095 percent micro-sample of the 2000 population census of China.

SUMMARY AND CONCLUSIONS

We began our analysis of recent Chinese population census data with a series of questions in mind. Did economic liberalization affect the labor

Table 11 Probability of labor force participation, marginal changes by human capital, sex, ethnicity, and province for Zhuang relative to others in Guangxi, Guangdong, and Yunnan provinces (urban dwellers aged 15 and older)

	1990		2000	
	Women	*Men*	*Women*	*Men*
Human capital and sex				
Married	0.091***	0.091***	−0.140***	0.022**
Illiterate	0.037***	0.036***	0.073***	0.075***
Primary school	0.030***	0.014***	0.010	0.072***
Senior middle	−0.015***	−0.065***	0.075***	0.099
Post-secondary	−0.316***	−0.430***	0.018	−0.014***
Age	0.074***	0.061***	0.075***	0.067***
Age squared	−0.001***	−0.001***	−0.001***	−0.001***
Net effect of age	−0.004	0.006	−0.002	0.004
Ethnicity				
Hui	−0.044	−0.044**	−0.055	−0.111**
Korean	0.135		−0.225	0.004
Zhuang	0.060***	0.021***	0.038	0.025
Bai	0.076***	−0.065***	0.137*	0.056
Bouyi	−0.098	−0.271		
Dai	−0.147	−0.161	0.106	0.092
Dong	0.059	−0.199*	0.155	
Hani	−0.152		0.115	−0.024
Kazak				
Li		−0.228	−0.297	
Manchu	−0.043	0.019	−0.100	−0.440***
Miao	0.139***	0.037	0.113	0.143**
Mongol	0.007	−0.071	0.188	−0.001
Tibetan	−0.056	−0.058		
Tujia	−0.055	0.078	0.040	0.131**
Yao	−0.035	0.017	0.036	0.095*
Yi	0.125***	0.051***	0.099*	0.004
Other nationalities	−0.021	−0.134***	−0.114	0.027
Province				
Guangdong	−0.117***	−0.031***	0.055***	0.079***
Yunnan	0.013**	0.001	−0.027	0.020***
Number of obs.	97,243	109,131	15,756	15,595
Obs. P	0.702	0.784	0.649	0.797
Pred. P	0.707	0.888	0.612	0.854
Log likelihood	−38,258	−31,258	−7,944	−4,720
LR Chi^2 (degrees of freedom)	41,883 (25)	51,447 (24)	4,528 (24)	6,281 (22)
Psuedo R^2	0.354	0.451	0.222	0.400

Notes: *indicates statistical significance at the 10 percent level; **indicates statistical significance at the 5 percent level; ***indicates statistical significance at the 1 percent level. Entries represent the change in the probability that an individual is in the labor force when the binary variable toggles from zero to one, evaluated at the sample mean. "Net effect of age" is the combined marginal effect of the age and age-squared variables, evaluated at the sample mean. Base case consists of single Han residents of Jiangsu with junior middle school educations.
Sources: 1 percent micro-sample of the 1990 population censuses of China and 0.095 percent micro-sample of the 2000 population census of China.

force participation of men and women differentially? How did China's ethnic minority groups fare in the transition process? Were minorities particularly disadvantaged in the restructuring of the Chinese economy? Should observed differences in the economic status of China's minorities be attributed to differential, discriminatory treatment of ethnic minority people or to artifacts of local economic conditions?

Previous research (Hannum and Xie 1998; Gustafsson and Li 2003) suggested that minorities did not fare well in China's transition; both income and occupational attainment gaps between ethnic minorities and the Han had widened. In the descriptive part of our analysis presented above, we find that minority women experienced steeper declines in labor force participation and had lower rates of participation than either minority men or Han men and women. It thus appears, at first glance, that the burden of reform-induced restructuring fell disproportionately on minority women. However, the story becomes increasingly nuanced and complicated when we focus on specific minority groups. When we apply multivariate analysis and control for location by splitting our data into the minority groups' areas of principal residence, we continue to find that minority women experienced steeper declines in their labor force participation rates over the decade than Han women but not necessarily steeper declines than men of the same or other ethnic groups. For three of the four minority groups under study, women's participation rates converged with and became indistinguishable from those of Han women. By 2000, only Hui women were found to have significantly lower participation rates than Han women. Given the high degree of assimilation of the Hui into Han society, it is difficult to attribute this finding to discrimination; we expect this to be a robust cultural or religious difference that surfaced with the relaxation of state control over individuals' lives. While Zhuang and Hui men's rates of participation converged with those of their Han neighbors, Uygur and Korean men were particularly disadvantaged by the labor market dislocations of the 1990s. Uygur men's participation rates fell by a dramatic 20 percentage points over this period relative to those of their Xinjiang Han neighbors, while Korean men's rates fell 9 percentage points more than those of their rustbelt Han neighbors. The drop in Uygur male labor force participation rates is consistent with discriminatory hiring and layoff practices, especially in light of the relatively robust urban economy in Xinjiang of the late 1990s.

Previous research (Hughes and Maurer-Fazio 2002) found a pronounced marriage penalty in terms of gender wage gaps and suggested that Chinese women bear primary responsibility for household chores which was a contributing factor. We also find evidence that many married women left the labor force in order to turn to home production. In our national probit regression (Table 7) and in each of our geographically restricted probits (Tables 8–11), by 2000 we find that marriage significantly lowered women's and raised men's labor force participation when age, education, ethnicity, and location are controlled. This pattern is consistent with a return to more traditional expectations about gendered household roles and an exit of married women from paid labor to home production.

Finally, probit results from our geographically restricted samples indicate that location does matter, at least in some cases. In the descriptive analysis, we observe that, in absolute terms, most ethnic groups experienced larger declines in labor force participation rates than the Han. In the geographically restricted samples, the differences in rates of participation between the Han and a number of our gender-differentiated ethnic groups become statistically indistinguishable. For other groups, particularly Uygur and Korean men and Hui women, marked differences emerge.

Our analysis suggests that men and women of particular minority groups have been disproportionately affected by reductions in urban sector employment and have exited the labor force more rapidly than Han men. The rapid decrease of approximately seven million urban formal-sector jobs per year, in the years preceding WTO entry (1995–2001), has slowed to losses of approximately 1.5 million jobs per year in the post-accession period (National Bureau of Statistics and Ministry of Labor and Social Security 2004: 23, Table 1-14). The adjustment process thus shows signs of abating. We expect the labor market dislocations of the post-WTO-accession period to be less severe than those of the years just prior to accession.

In this paper, we focus specifically on the intersection of gender and ethnicity in labor force participation. In future endeavors, we plan to deepen this analysis by incorporating women's fertility and other demographic factors. We also plan to broaden the scope of our analysis to compare the well-being of China's twenty largest ethnic groups in terms of educational attainment, occupational attainment, and unemployment.

Margaret Maurer-Fazio, Bates College, Economics,
120 Lane Hall, 2 Andrews Road, Lewiston, ME 04240, USA
e-mail: mmaurer@bates.edu

James Hughes, Bates College, Economics,
120 Lane Hall, 2 Andrews Road, Lewiston, ME 04240, USA
e-mail: jhughes@bates.edu

Dandan Zhang, Australian National University, Division of Economics,
Rm7113, Coombs Building, ANU, Canberra, ACT 0200, Canberra, Australia
e-mail: dandan.zhang@anu.edu.au

ACKNOWLEDGMENTS

The authors thank the anonymous referees; the volume editors: Xiao-yuan Dong, Gale Summerfield, and Günseli Berik; the volume's workshop discussants: Joyce Jacobsen and Janet Kohlhase; and the other participants in the Workshop on China, Gender, and the World Trade Organization, held March 31–April 2, 2006 at Rice University, for their insightful comments and assistance. We have received, and wish to acknowledge, diligent and able research assistance from our students on the larger project which underlies this paper: Vaibhav Bajpai, Daniel Barsky, Michelle Ladonne, Oi Yen Lam, Joanna Mak, Hwei Ling Ng, Lucia Tiererova, and Catherine Yu. Anna Purtell's undergraduate thesis inspired us to start this line of research. We thank Shuhui Yang for his thoughtful and colorful contribution to the title of this paper.

NOTES

[1] Karyn Loscocco and Christine Bose (1998) report that women exhibited a strong sense of entitlement to a good job in the early post-Mao period.

[2] Marianne A. Ferber (1994) argues that in the Czech case, communist ideology and policies pushed Czech women into the labor force while ignoring their roles in the household, a form of "forced emancipation." With the fall of communism, some women chose to return to more traditional roles in the home. In a similar fashion, communist ideology pushed Chinese women into the labor force. The consequences of defying Maoist policies were draconian, so few challenged these policies.

[3] Colin Mackerras reports this attitude to be strongest in the ethnic groups that adhere most strongly to the tenets of Confucianism and Islam (2003: 144).

[4] The Chinese government initially used the primary characteristics of common territory, language, economy, and culture to identify its national minority groups. It currently allows group members to claim minority status based on ancestry (Christopher J. Smith 2000: 273–8).

[5] The government's preferential policies toward ethnic minorities include an exemption from, or easing of, the restrictions of the government's family planning program, as well as preferential treatment in school admissions, hiring, and promotion; the financing and taxation of businesses; and the provision of infrastructure (Barry Sautman 1998: 86). The extent to which minorities actually benefit from these policies is a key issue. Bruce Gilley (2001) reports that in Xinjiang the benefits of the central government's western development campaign accrue in large part to the area's Han population and that Han firms simply do not hire Uygur workers.

[6] Matthew Hoddie (1998) reports that twenty-four million more people identified themselves as ethnic minorities in the 1990 population census than in the 1982 census. He claims that fertility trends were such that an increase of only ten million was expected. Note the extreme increases in Manchu and Tujia populations between the 1982 and 1990 censuses in Table 2.

[7] See for example *China's Ethnic Statistical Yearbook* (State Ethnic Affairs Committee [SEAC], Department of Economic Development and National Bureau of Statistics of China [NBS], PRC Department of Integrated Statistics 2000), *China's Yearbook of Ethnic Works* (SEAC 2003), and the *China Statistical Yearbooks* (NBS 2005). Katherine Palmer

Kaup (2000: 149) suggests that the income inequalities between ethnic groups are so pronounced that if published, they would become a very contentious issue.

[8] For example, in 2002 the minority population of the Inner Mongolian Autonomous Region constituted only 20.9 percent of its total population. Comparable figures for Guangxi Zhuang and the Ningxia Hui Autonomous Regions are 38.4 percent and 35.4 percent, respectively. Tibet and Xinjiang Uygur Autonomous Regions are notable exceptions, with the minority populations constituting 96.7 and 60.1 percent of their respective populations (NBS and SEAC 2003: 564, Tables 2–8).

[9] We also tested the importance of regional macroeconomic variables such as per capita income and foreign direct investment in explaining differences in labor force participation. We found such variables to have little explanatory power in our regressions. Since their presence did not alter our main results, we have therefore excluded these variables from the regressions presented here.

[10] We included each province that was home to more than 5 percent of the Hui population. Taken together, these eight provinces are home to 74.1 percent of the total Hui population.

[11] The 1990 sample was obtained from the Data User Services of China Population Information and Research Center.

[12] The 1990 census does not report individuals as unemployed but rather as "waiting for work." We equate those classified as "waiting for work" as seeking employment and thus part of the labor force.

[13] This is slightly below 26.41 percent urban reported in official statistics (State Statistical Bureau, Department of Population and Employment 1998: 352, Tables 4–6).

[14] A great deal of urbanization occurred between the 1990 and 2000 censuses. Since the data do not allow us to use a consistent method of classifying individuals as urban or rural, some of our results may be affected. We do not have any further information that would allow us to predict systematic bias in our results. However, this figure compares well to the official statistics reporting that 36.22 percent of the population is urban in 2000 (NBS and SEAC 2003: 4, 28, 52).

[15] Anna Pollert (2005) reports similar declines in women's participation rates in a study of ten central and eastern European countries. She attributes part of the decline to women moving from formal to informal employment.

[16] The sharp decline in overall participation rates coincides with marked increases in unemployment. This suggests that the restructuring of the economy may be one of the most important factors in explaining labor force exit. Table 5 reveals that urban unemployment rates rose rapidly over the 1990–2000 period for Han and minority women and men alike. The decline in labor force participation and increase in unemployment exist despite increases in education levels and decreases in illiteracy rates. Table 5 also reveals that the percentage of urban men and women whose education levels surpass the government-mandated junior/middle school level has risen steadily for Han and minority women and men and that declines in illiteracy are widespread.

Table 5 reveals an unanticipated result in terms of occupational attainment. In the percentage of high-status jobs held, women have gained relative to men, and minority women relative to Han women. This result seems surprising given the disproportionate reductions in minority women's labor force participation and disproportionate increases in their unemployment. This apparent gain is probably a selection effect; the burden of layoffs fell disproportionately on the least powerful, which are women with few skills (Giles, Park, and Cai 2006; Maurer-Fazio 2006). Those who managed to avoid layoff are thus more likely to be higher skilled and to hold higher-status jobs.

[17] For binary variables, the table entries represent the discrete change in probability, as the binary independent variable is toggled from zero to one. For continuous variables

such as age, the table entries are the change in the probability of labor force participation resulting from a one-unit change in the independent variable. Age is entered into our probit regressions in quadratic form. The marginal effect of age reported in our tables combines the effect of the base and the squared term. All probabilities are calculated at the sample mean.

[18] The effects of education on the probability of labor force participation are both interesting and puzzling. In the 1990 data, the largest and most puzzling educational effect was that female and male post-secondary graduates, the most highly educated people, were, respectively, 15 and 22 percent less likely to be in the labor force than middle school graduates. Such relatively low labor force participation rates for college graduates is contrary to basic human capital theory, which predicts higher labor force participation to recoup the investment in additional education. We wonder if this result for post-secondary graduates indicates a residual effect of the Cultural Revolution's repression of the educated. By 2000, this anomalous result reversed for women and shrank considerably for men.

[19] Age has a positive effect on participation rates for both men and women. The marginal effect of age increases from 1990 to 2000. Maurer-Fazio, Hughes, and Zhang (2005) have shown that Chinese women (both urban and rural) of prime child-bearing age, between 23 and 35, do not reduce their labor force participation rates. In both the 1990 and 2000 population censuses, women in this age group had higher participation rates than women of any other age cohort.

[20] Of the urban population aged 15 and older, the mean age of Hui and Han women varies by less than 0.2 years, and the proclivity to marry varies by less than 1 percent.

[21] In the data for the national urban population aged 15 and older, the mean age of Uygurs is 2 years younger than that of the general population in 1990 and 5.5 years younger in 2000. Likewise, in 1990, Uygurs were 5.4 percent less likely than the general Chinese population to be married and 11.8 percent less likely in 2000.

REFERENCES

Appleton, Simon, John Knight, Lina Song, and Qingjie Xia. 2002. "Labour Retrenchment in China: Determinants and Consequences." *China Economic Review* 13(2/3): 252–75.

Blum, Susan. 2001. *Portraits of "Primitives": Ordering Human Kinds in the Chinese Nation.* Lanham, MD: Roman and Littlefield Publishers.

Cook, Sarah and Margaret Maurer-Fazio, eds. 1999. *The Workers' State Meets the Market: Labour in China's Transition.* London: Frank Cass.

Croll, Elisabeth. 1995. *Changing Identities of Chinese Women: Rhetoric, Experience, and Self-Perception in Twentieth-Century China.* Atlantic Highlands, NJ: Zed Books.

Entwisle, Barbara and Gail E. Henderson, eds. 2000. *Re-drawing Boundaries: Work, Households, and Gender in China.* Berkeley: University of California Press.

Ferber, Marianne A. 1994. "Czech Women in Transition." *Monthly Labor Review* 117(11): 32–6.

Giles, John, Albert Park, and Fang Cai. 2006. "How Has Economic Restructuring Affected China's Urban Workers?" *The China Quarterly* 185(March): 65–91.

Gilley, Bruce. 2001. "Uighurs Need Not Apply." *Far Eastern Economic Review* 23 (August): 9.

Gladney, Dru. 2004. *Dislocating China: Muslims, Minorities, and Other Subaltern Subjects.* Chicago: University of Chicago Press.

Gustafsson, Bjorn and Shi Li. 2003. "The Ethnic Minority–Majority Income Gap in Rural China During Transition." *Economic Development and Cultural Change* 51(4): 805–22.

Hannum, Emily and Yu Xie. 1998. "Ethnic Stratification in Northwest China: Occupational Differences between Han Chinese and National Minorities in Xinjiang, 1982–1990." *Demography* 35(3): 323–33.

Harrell, Stevan. 1995. "Introduction: Civilizing Projects and the Reaction to Them," in Stevan Harrell, ed. *Cultural Encounters on China's Ethnic Frontiers*, pp. 3–36. Seattle: University of Washington Press.

Hoddie, Matthew. 1998. "Ethnic Identity Change in the People's Republic of China: An Explanation Using Data from the 1982 and 1990 Census Enumerations," in William Safran, ed. *Nationalism and Ethnoregional Identities in China*, pp. 119–41. London: Frank Cass.

Hughes, James W. and Margaret Maurer-Fazio. 2002. "The Effects of Marital Status, Education, and Occupation on the Female/Male Wage Gap in China." *Pacific Economic Review* 7(1): 137–56.

Information Office of the State Council of the People's Republic of China. 1999. *National Minorities Policy and Its Practice in China*. Beijing: Information Office of the State Council of the People's Republic of China.

International Labour Office (ILO). Various years. *Year Book of Labour Statistics*. Geneva: International Labour Office.

Knight, John and Lina Song. 2005. *Towards a Labour Market in China*. Oxford: Oxford University Press.

Lardy, Nicholas R. 2002. *Integrating China into the Global Economy*. Washington, DC: Brookings Institution Press.

Liu, Jieyu. 2007. "Gender Dynamics and Redundancy in Urban China." *Feminist Economics* 13(3/4): 125–58.

Loscocco, Karyn and Christine Bose. 1998. "Gender and Job Satisfaction in Urban China: The Early Post-Mao Period." *Social Science Quarterly* 79(1): 91–109.

Mackerras, Colin. 2003. *China's Ethnic Minorities and Globalization*. London and New York: Routledge Curzon.

Maurer-Fazio, Margaret. 2006. "In Books One Finds a House of Gold: The Role of Education in Labor Market Outcomes in Urban China." *The Journal of Contemporary China* 15(47): 215–31.

Maurer-Fazio, Margaret and James W. Hughes. 2002. "The Effects of Institutional Change on the Relative Earnings of Chinese Women." *The Journal of Comparative Economics* 30(4): 709–31.

Maurer-Fazio, Margaret, James W. Hughes, and Dandan Zhang. 2005. Economic Reform and Changing Patterns of Labor Force Participation in Urban and Rural China. Working Paper 787, William Davidson Institute Working Paper Series, University of Michigan.

Maurer-Fazio, Margaret, Thomas Rawski, and Wei Zhang. 1999. "Inequality in the Rewards for Holding Up Half the Sky: Gender Wage Gaps in China's Urban Labour Market, 1988–94." *The China Journal* 41: 55–88.

Meng, Xin. 2000. *Labour Market Reform in China*. Cambridge: Cambridge University Press.

National Bureau of Statistics China (NBS). 2005. *China Statistical Yearbook*. Beijing: China Statistics Press.

National Bureau of Statistics and Ministry of Labor and Social Security, comp. 2000. *Zhongguo laodong tongji nianjian 2000* [China Labor Statistical Yearbook 2000]. Beijing: Zhongguo tongji chubanshe.

—— . 2004. *Zhongguo laodong tongji nianjian 2004* [China Labor Statistical Yearbook 2004]. Beijing: Zhongguo tongji chubanshe.

National Bureau of Statistics, PRC Department of Population, Social Science, and Technology Statistics and State Ethnic Affairs Commission, Department of Economic Development (NBS and SEAC). 2003. *The Tabulation on Nationalities of 2000 Population Census of China*, vol. 1. Beijing: Ethnic Publishing House.

Palmer Kaup, Katherine. 2000. *Creating the Zhuang: Ethnic Politics in China*. Boulder, CO: Lynne Rienner Press.

Pollert, Anna. 2005. "Gender, Transformation and Employment in Central Eastern Europe." *European Journal of Industrial Relations* 11(2): 213–30.

Sautman, Barry. 1998. "Preferential Policies for Ethnic Minorities in China: the Case of Xinjiang," in William Safran, ed. *Nationalism and Ethnoregional Identities in China*, pp. 86–118. London: Frank Cass.

Smith, Christopher J. 2000. *China in the Post-Utopian Age*. Boulder, CO: Westview Press.

State Ethnic Affairs Committee (SEAC). 2003. *China's Yearbook of Ethnic Works 2003*. Beijing: Ethnic Publishing House.

———, Department of Economic Development, and National Bureau of Statistics, PRC, Department of Integrated Statistics. 2000. *China's Ethnic Statistical Yearbook, 2000*. Beijing: Ethnic Publishing House.

State Statistical Bureau, Department of Population and Employment. 1998. *China Population Statistics Yearbook 1998*. Beijing: China Statistical Publishers.

GENDER EQUITY IN TRANSITIONAL CHINA'S HEALTHCARE POLICY REFORMS

Lanyan Chen and Hilary Standing

INTRODUCTION

An August 2005 study by the Development Research Center of the State Council in China pronounced that China's healthcare system reforms that began with liberalization in the 1980s, have been largely unsuccessful and have led to "a decline in both the fairness of services and the efficiency of investment in the sector" (Sen Gong and Yanfeng Ge 2005: 23–4; Wenyi Zhu 2005: 25–6). That study points out that the increasing market orientation of the system has unacceptably driven up costs of healthcare for most individuals and that the low level of coverage of medical insurance schemes has increased vulnerability to medical poverty by leaving many people, especially in China's rural areas, uninsured. This theme is echoed in analyses of the impact of China's transition to a market economy on its healthcare system over the last decade (Xing-yuan Gu, Gerald Bloom,

Shenglan Tang, and Henry Lucas 1995; Gerald Bloom and Xing-yuan Gu 1997; David Blumenthal and William Hsiao 2005).

International health research has paid increasing attention to the impact of gender inequality in access to healthcare and in health outcomes, particularly in interaction with other social markers such as poverty, age, and ethnicity.[1] This paper examines the impact of China's healthcare reforms on gender equity in health in the context of rapid social and economic transformation. It explores the ways in which economic reform policies may have contributed to actual or potential gender inequities in health and healthcare delivery and draws out policy implications for the provision of a more gender-equitable healthcare system. The analysis is based on secondary data, both from official sources and from research studies of a mainly qualitative nature. Some of the analysis is therefore speculative and conclusions are necessarily tentative as data are limited and sex disaggregated data are particularly lacking.

We particularly look at three areas where economic liberalization and associated reforms and changes in the health sector may have generated inequities or where inequities may emerge: the impact of reforms on the provision of basic services – such as reproductive healthcare – that adversely affected women in particular; the changes in health financing which have driven up costs and resulted in disparities in healthcare access and outcomes by gender; and the ongoing demographic transition to an increasingly aging society in which women face a greater burden of informal care provision compared to men.

Since China's accession to the World Trade Organization, moreover, the government has lifted its protection of the domestic markets in medical services and insurance, which has contributed to rising healthcare costs. Better drugs and new equipment are imported and expensive, and greater reliance on these imports puts health services beyond the means of the poor. With the opening of the market, more foreign companies are entering the industry by operating clinics, hospitals, and insurance companies that provide services at higher costs. In remote rural areas there are fewer choices because local healthcare facilities are increasingly underfunded and under-resourced and preventive healthcare and care for mothers and children are particularly neglected (Joan Kaufman 2005).

In recognition of the problems generated by the reform process, China has sought to shift its policy and engage in new experiments in healthcare provision since the late 1990s. Using a combination of state- and employer-based mechanisms, it has been moving toward provision of universal entitlements in health and social security (Jun Gao, Juncheng Qian, Shenglan Tang, Bo Eriksson, and Erik Blass 2002; White Papers of the Government of China 2004, 2005). These include urban and rural social insurance and schemes to assist the poorest with major illness costs. Different models are being piloted, including the BMI (Basic Medical

Insurance for urban employees) scheme, which was introduced in urban areas in 1998 and combines social pooling with personal accounts, and the revival of the CMS (cooperative medical care system), which began operating in rural areas in 2002 and is financed by joint contributions of individuals and local governments (White Paper of the Government of China 2004). The effectiveness of this process will also depend on taking into consideration gendered healthcare needs, particularly in access to sexual and reproductive health and preventive health services, management of health insurance and social security, and appropriate services to meet the changing health needs of women and men resulting from demographic and epidemiological transition. As important is enabling citizens to have a voice in policy and implementation; rural women, in particular, have less voice in both formal and informal institutions of Chinese society (Lanyan Chen 2000: 243–4). They may not be able to benefit from these policy changes unless they are included in how these are formulated and implemented and can voice their concerns and needs.

CONCEPTUAL FRAMEWORK

The connections between gender, health, and equity have received increasing attention since the early 1990s. A growing body of research has highlighted both biological and social aspects of gender inequities in health (Gita Sen, Asha George, and Piroska Ostlin 2002: 1–33). This research has informed and been informed by strong rights-based advocacy for women's health through the 1994 International Conference on Population and Development in Cairo, the 1995 International Women's Conference in Beijing, and leading international conventions framed within human rights law. These have placed responsibilities on state parties to create suitable conditions for the exercise of rights to attain health as a complete state of physical, mental, and social well-being.[2] Specifically, "women's right to health," particularly reproductive health, has become the responsibility of the state (Kaufman 2005). China is a signatory to these conventions and conference declarations, which means that there is a national apparatus for monitoring adherence, providing national advocates with an important avenue of accountability.

Research on gender and health makes a distinction between equality and equity. Formal equality, in the sense of treating males and females equally will not necessarily produce equity in health. This is because both biology and social relations create specific gendered needs. These needs derive from particular health conditions, from culturally constructed biases, from inequalities in access to treatment and care, and from structural factors such as biases in formal entitlements to health resources and insurance schemes. In order to ensure gender equitable health outcomes, policymakers and healthcare providers must address both the needs rooted in biological differences between men and women and the social inequalities in needs, access, and utilization.

In this body of research, two broad perspectives on thinking about gender and health equity can be distinguished (Hilary Standing 1997). A *women's health perspective* highlights the specific health needs of women and girls as a consequence of biological and social differences. This perspective has provided a strong advocacy framework for focused healthcare interventions to address women's needs and protect their right to health. It is useful for examining the extent to which healthcare reform policies meet the specific health needs of women. A women's health perspective is relevant to China, where reforms have particularly compromised the availability and accessibility of services to meet women's reproductive healthcare needs. A *gender relations perspective* emphasizes the broader role of gender relations in the production of health inequities in outcomes, access, and utilization of services. It therefore also encompasses power relations and ideologies rooted in gender, including the gender impact on men's health. This perspective is extremely useful in examining gender and health inequities in China, as it provides an understanding of the gendered nature of vulnerabilities, including health impacts, during social and economic transitions. Vulnerabilities can occur through the loss of employment, property, and family resources; through the loss of entitlements, such as pensions, social security, and health insurance; and through social exclusion from the structures and institutions that provide opportunity and voice in society.[3] Understanding these losses in relation to social markers of gender, age, and poverty enables recognition of the changing dynamics of vulnerability and provides pointers towards dealing with them through broader public policy responses. We apply both the women's health perspective and the gender relations perspective in examining the gendered impact of healthcare reforms in China.

HEALTHCARE SYSTEMS REFORMS IN CHINA

After the founding of the People's Republic, Chinese officials implemented plans to provide comprehensive basic healthcare in both rural and urban areas. In 1952, they set up a public healthcare scheme financed by the central government that covered civil servants, soldiers, and social sector employees and a labor insurance scheme financed by employers that covered workers in productive and sales units. These programs provided healthcare coverage to almost every urban resident. In rural areas in the 1950s, the government developed a social safety net based on cooperative principles, including a collective old-age support system and a cooperative medical scheme (CMS). By the late 1970s, over 90 percent of the villages had set up a CMS financed by a collective fund that supported one or two village "barefoot doctors" and provided rudimentary medical equipment.[4]

This healthcare system ensured access to preventive health services, health education outreach, and primary care, and at relatively low cost to the economy. In the thirty years from 1950 to 1980, total expenditures on healthcare annually were less than 3 percent of Chinese GDP, in an economy that was much smaller than at present (Zhu 2005: 25).

As the 2005 *Human Development Report* (United Nations Development Programme [UNDP] 2005) notes, this healthcare system – though favoring urban areas – effectively improved the overall health of both rural and urban residents in China. Over this period, China made substantial gains in health indicators. The number of Mother and Child Health Clinics rose from nine in 1,949 to 2,610 in 1980 (Research Institute of All-China Women's Federation and State Statistical Bureau 1998: 159). Life expectancy increased from 35 in 1949 to 68 in 1978; infant mortality declined from 200 per thousand in 1949 to 34 per thousand in 1978 (Keqing Rao and Yuanli Liu 2004: 35–6; Zhu 2005: 32); and the maternal mortality rate (MMR) was steadily reduced from 1,500 per 100,000 in 1949 to 76 per 100,000 in 1978 (Marge Koblinsky 2001).

In the late 1970s, as China began its transition to a socialist market economy, key policy decisions were taken that considerably affected the structure and financing of the healthcare system. Fiscal decentralization transferred most of the responsibility for health financing to provincial and local levels (Tony Saich and Joan Kaufman 2005). Combined with the decline of the commune system, fiscal decentralization starved the healthcare system of funds and contributed to the collapse of the CMS in rural areas by the early 1980s, which seriously affected the rural poor. In urban areas, from the late 1980s onward, pressure for cost-saving measures deterred state enterprises and urban collectives from fulfilling workplace-based healthcare obligations (Jun Gao, Shenglan Tang, Rachel Tolhurst, and Rao Keqing 2001). The privatization of many small and medium-sized state-owned enterprises in the 1990s created large numbers of redundant workers, many of whom joined the ever-growing informal workforce of migrants and fell out of labor insurance coverage (see Rachel Tolhurst, Qian Xu, Hilary Standing, and Shenglan Tang [2001] and Jieyu Liu [2007], in this volume).

Between the late 1970s and the late 1990s, central government transfers for health expenditures fell by half and have continued to fall since then (Kaufman 2005). Although total government spending on health increased, the government share of health spending went down from 36.4 percent of the total health expenditure in 1980 to 15.3 percent in 2003; the share covered by individuals increased from 23.2 percent in 1980 to 60.2 percent in 2003 while health expenditures by social organizations covered the remaining share (Rao and Liu 2004: 36–7). This reduction had three major impacts. First, it brought about a de facto privatization of the system as facilities turned to the sale of drugs and other health commodities to finance their operations and pay doctors' salaries. Prices were regulated for routine services and treatments, so facilities had to increase revenue through promoting the use of high-technology services and selling expensive drugs. This change in financing greatly increased the cost to users; between 1978 and 2002, personal health expenditure rose forty-fold (Blumenthal and Hsiao 2005).

Second, the reduction of central government fiscal transfers greatly exacerbated the inequalities between rich and poor areas (particularly the wealthy, highly urbanized eastern parts of the country and the predominantly rural, impoverished areas of western China) in terms of availability of affordable healthcare. Eighty percent of government spending on health is now concentrated in large cities, with thirty percent of that allocated to major hospitals of these cities, used especially for purchasing high priced equipment (Zhu 2005: 25). The former barefoot doctors and local level rural facilities were no longer adequately compensated for their services (Bloom and Gu 1997; Blumenthal and Hsiao 2005). Barefoot doctors thus became private, village-level providers or switched to other work. While better-off areas have been able to raise local funds to finance services, poor areas have struggled to do so, leaving township level health services largely to finance themselves through user fees.

Third, underfunding has resulted in a decline in the availability and quality of preventive care, particularly reproductive healthcare, in rural and inland areas (Shiyong Kang 2003; Keqing Rao, Hu Guoqing, Hu Linlin, Xin Ying, and Qian Juncheng 2004; Kaufman 2005). The one-child policy also diverted funds and attention away from providing general reproductive care. The family planning programs competed for local funds that would have gone to general care, and women could not receive general reproductive healthcare when they visited the family planning clinics (Kaufman 2005).[5] Since budgets are inadequate for the upgrading, supervising, and quality control of local health worker skills, the quality of care has deteriorated in some rural areas, even as patients face costly healthcare.

The sharp rise in medical costs in the 1990s came at a time when there was a major fall in health insurance coverage as a result of state sector reforms, industrial restructuring, and rural–urban migration. The share of urban residents lacking health insurance coverage jumped from 27.3 percent in 1993 to 44.1 percent in 1998 and stood at 44.8 percent in 2003.[6] As Table 1 shows, the Ministry of Health found that of the 49,698 total urban population surveyed in 2003, 30.4 percent had access to urban workers' insurance (BMI), 8.6 percent had publicly funded healthcare, and an additional 16.2 percent were covered by commercial medical insurance and insurance for catastrophic diseases. Thus, only about 55 percent of the urban population that worked for the public sector or foreign joint ventures had medical insurance that was adequate to enjoy the growing choices of care and services.

Table 1 Health insurance coverage by sex in urban areas in 2003

	Total group (%)	Male (%)	Female (%)	Sample (number)
Type of coverage				
Urban worker's insurance	30.4	52.4	47.6	15,023
Publicly funded healthcare	8.6	53.8	46.2	4,247
Other social security	10.7	47.9	52.1	5,300
Commercial insurance	5.5	49	51	2,723
Covered total	55.2			27,578
Uncovered total	44.8	46	54	22,120
Total	100			
Total sample (number)				49,698

Note: The Urban Workers' Insurance operates on social pooling with individual accounts and was implemented as a result of the 1998 healthcare reform efforts. The publicly funded healthcare continues from before the reforms covering civil servants, soldiers, and those who are employed in public sectors. The third category includes those who have one of the above types of insurance and still purchase commercial health insurance. The fourth type of insurance can be purchased by anyone and covers mostly those who are outside the coverage of the first two. A commonly purchased commercial insurance is one that covers the high costs of catastrophic diseases.
Source: Ministry of Health (2004a: 93).

The Ministry of Health's Third National Health Services Survey in 2003 indicated that there has been a general decline in hospital visits due to the high prices of healthcare services and the lack of health insurance. According to the Ministry of Health (2004a: 13), the annual increase of per capita income between 1998 and 2003 was 8.9 percent in urban areas and 2.5 percent in rural areas. Annual expenditure on healthcare, however, had gone up at a rate of 13.5 percent for the urban population and 11.8 percent for the rural population. In 2003, a visit to the hospital cost 219 yuan on average in urban areas and 91 yuan in rural areas. Compared to the 1998 rates, this was an increase of 85 percent and 103 percent, respectively, in nominal terms. On average, a person paid 7,606 yuan per year for hospitalization in urban areas and 2,649 yuan in rural areas, up by 88 percent and 73 percent from 1998. Table 2 shows that higher percentages of low-income groups – such as farmers, unemployed/home workers, and retired people – did not seek medical service while sick due largely to economic difficulty.

HEALTHCARE REFORMS SINCE THE LATE 1990s

In the late 1990s, the Chinese government launched a set of health-care reforms to try to tackle the problems of underfunding, lack of preventive services, and the impact of the loss of insurance-based entitlements in both urban and rural areas.[7] Reform policies have focused particularly on rehabilitating the CMS in rural areas and on the

Table 2 Rate of sickness in the two weeks prior to the survey (2003) and non-use of care due to economic difficulty among selected occupations and ages

2003 survey	Total	Manager	Technical	Office staff	Worker	Farmer	Retired	Unemployed & home worker
Sample (number)	135,595[a]	4,522	4,055	8,423	3,894	73,644	5,967	11,290
Total group (%)	100[b]	3.33	2.99	6.21	2.87	54.31	4.4	8.33
Male (%)	48.5	61.7	62.4	53.9	59.5	46.8	40.9	41.6
Female (%)	51.5	38.3	37.6	46.1	40.5	53.2	59.1	58.4
15–24 age (%)	19.53	5.57	11.86	13.43	6.88	13.74	0.32	13.84
25–34 age (%)	20.35	24.68	31.59	32.65	25.71	21.93	0.12	21.35
35–44 age (%)	23.63	33.48	28.95	31.69	33.9	25.57	1.64	28.11
45–54 age (%)	23.03	28.02	21.68	18.78	28.89	25.15	33.5	23.84
55–64 age (%)	13.46	8.25	5.92	3.45	4.62	13.61	64.42	12.85
Sick in the two weeks prior to the survey (%)	13.57[c]	9.51	8.80	8.63	10.81	14.96	26.63	13.54
But did not seek care (%)	13.97[d]	9.53	12.32	8.53	11.88	15.39	9.31	14.52
Sick but not hospitalized (%)	41.61[e]	12.99	20.17	25.22	52.29	42.10	48.15	56.92
Due to economic difficulty (%)		36.84	33.33	32.69	34.62	76.31	55.00	77.27

Notes: Farmers accounted for over half of the sample size. Among seven occupational groups, women were the majority in the last three low-income groups: farmers, retired, and unemployed and home workers. Farmers also have a higher rate of sickness in the two weeks previous to the survey (second only to the retired) and had one of the highest rates of non-use of care in those two weeks even though they were sick, due primarily to economic difficulty at 76.31 percent (second only to the unemployed).
[a] This total sample size includes two other groups of population: students (10,054) and other (13,746).
[b] This total percentage also includes students (amounting to 7.41 percent) and other (10.14 percent).
[c] This percentage includes the people of the total surveyed population who reported an illness or injury within the two weeks period prior to the survey. Most self-reported illnesses related to chronic non-communicable diseases including hypertension and diseases of the circulatory, respiratory, and digestive systems.
[d] This percentage includes the surveyed population reporting illnesses or injuries within the two week period prior to the survey who did not seek any treatment. Farmers and unemployed and home workers, of whom women are the majority, had the highest rates of not seeking care.
[e] This percentage indicates the rates of people failing to be hospitalized despite being referred by a doctor among those who reported illness in the two weeks previous to the survey. This rate rises significantly from the first four higher-income groups to the three lower-income groups, in which women are a majority.
Source: Ministry of Health (2004a: 109–10).

establishment of a more unified social insurance in urban areas, through the BMI.

In 1997 the government produced a policy statement on rural healthcare reforms focused on reestablishing the CMS. Under this scheme, the central and local governments provide the equivalent of US$2.50 per annum for each household to the CMS fund and each household contributes US$1.25. In all, these cooperative healthcare reforms to restore the CMS have had very limited success so far, although there are ongoing efforts to increase both population coverage and conditions that are covered (Hao Yu, Henry Lucas, Xing-yuan Gu, and Baogang Shu 1998; William Hsiao 2004; Office of the World Health Organization Representative 2004). Concern among government departments over the financial burden of implementing CMS for the government and farmers has hampered its application. By 2003 the CMS was reestablished in less than 10 percent of rural areas (Rao and Liu 2004: 412). The low level of funding means that only in-patient care is covered, leaving preventive healthcare needs, including sexual and reproductive health needs, without coverage. Moreover, these schemes do not cover most of the millions of rural migrants who have traveled to urban areas in search of employment and who face the prospect of paying out of pocket for more costly medical care in the city rather than in their native localities.[8]

In 2003, the National Health Services Survey polled a survey population of 143,991 from the countryside and found that 9.5 percent had cooperative healthcare and an additional 9.2 percent had either social security or commercial insurance (Ministry of Health 2004a: 93). Thus, over 80 percent of the rural population had no medical insurance. In order to fill this gap, the government has been developing medical financial assistance (MFA) schemes in rural (and more recently urban) areas to provide a medical safety net for the poor. This concept began in 1998 as a World Bank funded project in seventy-one of the poorest counties in western China and aimed to cover the poorest 5 percent of households for basic services, including maternity services (Zhenzhong Zhang 2003: 19). However, if this program is to cover all the poor, it will need to be greatly expanded (Xingzhu Liu and Yunni Yi 2004).

In urban areas, the government launched the basic medical insurance schemes in 1998. The BMI combines social pooling with personal accounts and sets limits on maximum insurance payouts. The employee's premium and 30 percent of the employer's premium go into the employee's personal insurance account, used mainly for out-patient services; the other 70 percent of the employer's contribution goes into the social pool, used mainly for hospitalization (White Papers of the Government of China 2004). Recent evidence indicates limited expansion of coverage. According to Kang (2003: 182–5), half of the forty cities that first instituted the medical insurance reforms have at least 60 percent of enterprises participating in the BMI schemes. Fourteen cities have less than 50 percent of the enterprises participating. While employees pay one or two percent of their salaries into their personal accounts, the rates at which employers pay premiums into the fund vary much more. There are twenty-six cities where employers pay above 10 percent of the employee's salary and fourteen cities where employers pay less than 10 percent. The highest rate is 13.5 percent in Ningpo, Zhejiang and the lowest rate is 7 percent in Tongchuan, Shaanxi. Enterprises that used to be under the protection of the labor insurance system that existed in the pre-reform period generally have a higher rate of participation in the new insurance programs. Employees in individually owned companies and joint ventures, especially in the service sectors (including hotels and restaurants), are unlikely to have a chance to pay into their personal accounts as their employers refuse to join the new insurance programs (Ling Xu 2004).

The groups that are most liable to loss or absence of health entitlements are laid-off workers and pensioners, those working on short contracts or for employers providing little formal coverage, and migrants who do not qualify for urban benefits. Women are represented disproportionately in most of these categories. It is likely that medical poverty and declining health indicators will constitute an increasing risk for these groups unless alternative forms of provision of care can be developed to reach them.

As Liu and Yi (2004) note, health reforms have tended to be reactive and concerned with ameliorating the negative impacts of market reform on healthcare. Healthcare reform efforts have yet to reach their goal of providing affordable quality care for all Chinese. Facilities continue to be underfinanced and thus continue to raise money from prescribing expensive (and often medically unnecessary) drugs and services. The reforms have not yet separated the provision of essential medical services from the distribution of drugs that would deter the profit-seeking behavior of some healthcare institutions.

GENDER AND HEALTH IMPACTS IN TRANSITIONAL CHINA

After 1949, China achieved far-reaching improvements in the status of women. This was due in considerable measure to women's positions, both economically and ideologically, as productive workers in the planned economy. Women also enjoyed high levels of employment protection, including maternity and other health benefits provided by their employers, and experienced improvements in basic indicators of well-being, as indicated in the previous section.

China's transition from a planned economy to a market-based economy has brought about tremendous changes to the labor market, which have important health impacts differentiated by gender. These impacts interact with trends associated with China's WTO accession resulting in new vulnerabilities, including in health.[9] In the following sections, we focus particularly on the effects of reforms on the capacity of the health sector to meet women's health needs and on how economic transformation, particularly of labor markets, changes gender relations in ways that can produce health inequities.

Gendered access and utilization of healthcare

The high cost of health services particularly affects rural populations in China. While the vast majority of rural residents are uninsured (approximately 80 percent), there is no gender disparity among the uninsured (49.6 percent of the uninsured are female). The lack of insurance, however, may impact women more heavily because of maternity care, family care, and security issues. About half of the insured rural residents are covered by the CMS program and the rest by social security or commercial insurance. While almost equal numbers of men and women are covered by the CMS program (49.9 percent of those covered are women) and by commercial insurance (46.6 percent are women), there is gender disparity among those with social security coverage (37.9 percent are women) (Ministry of Health 2004a: 93). A tiny proportion of the elderly are covered under the CMS and there is discrepancy between women and men: among men over 65 only 2 percent had access to CMS while the figure among women over 65 was even lower at 0.5 percent (Jun Gao 2004).

Gao's analysis of health services use by the elderly (over 65) taken from three National Health Service Surveys (1993, 1998, 2003) found that financial difficulty is the main reason for the non-use of inpatient services in both urban and rural areas (2004). While the use rates of services are higher among the elderly compared with non-elderly, the rates of non-use – meaning cases in which the individual does not take up needed treatment – are also higher, particularly for women. Among urban men over 65, non-use was 59 percent and among urban women over 65 it was 69 percent. In rural areas, the figures were 80 percent for men and 83 percent for women.

Gender inequities in access to basic services are closely linked to socioeconomic inequalities. Surveys indicate that the strongest predictors of inequity of access are being female and living in a rural area of a poor province (Fang Jing 2004; Kaufman 2005). Research over the last decade by Jing and Kaufman has provided a detailed analysis of the way changes in health financing noted above have significantly worsened women's access to basic preventive and curative reproductive (non-contraceptive) health services in the poorest western provinces of China. The key factors are the high cost of healthcare and the collapse of preventive services in an increasingly privatized health sector. Xiuhua Jiang (2006: 92) shows that the number of publicly funded reproductive health clinics for women has declined from 3,179 in 1995 to 2,998 in 2004. Many enterprises, especially private firms, have abolished the practice of providing regular reproductive health examinations for women employees. As a result, the rate of reproductive health examinations for women dropped and stayed at 38 or 39 percent over the past ten years (Jiang 2006: 93). More disturbingly, the proportion of women among those diagnosed with HIV/AIDS increased sharply from 15.3 percent in 1998 to 32.3 percent in 2004 (Jiang 2006: 86).

Basic indicators on healthcare and health outcomes reveal the rural/urban disparity: In 2003, 96.4 percent of urban women versus 85.6 percent of rural women (but only 63.2 percent in the poor rural areas) had visited a doctor during pregnancy (Ministry of Health 2004a: 75). In 2002, urban and rural maternal mortality rates were 54 and 72 per 100,000, respectively, and under-five child mortality was 14 per 1,000 in urban areas and 39 per 1,000 in rural areas. MMR figures for rural areas, especially in the western and interior provinces, are less reliable and there is a high rate of underreporting or missing data. It has been suggested that rural MMR could be double or even three to five times higher than the national rates (Bohong Liu 2005: 48–9).[10]

Low-income women are less likely to seek help from skilled staff in births. Table 3 shows the distribution of coverage of births by skilled attendants and place of birth by household income quintiles for 2002 (World Health Organization [WHO] 2002). Women in the poorest quintile were only two-thirds as likely to be attended by a healthcare professional and half as likely to deliver in a public facility as women in the highest quintiles. Almost half of the women in the two lowest quintiles delivered at home, as compared to almost no women in the highest two quintiles.[11]

Gender inequities in healthcare access are also rooted in traditional gender values that persist. According to Xiuhua Jiang (2003: 375–7), the 2000 Survey on the Status of Chinese Women shows that the majority of the women were reluctant to seek a doctor's help when they had gynecological problems (see Table 4). Jiang notes that although 80 percent of women in the poor provinces she studied – Xinjiang, Guizhou, Guangxi, Sichuan, Gansu, Shaanxi, Inner Mongolia, and Hebei – reported that they suffered from gynecological problems such as infections, many of them did not think they were sick. She speculates that this is partly because most women in poor rural areas put up with such problems, regarding them as part of women's lot, if they did not get in the way of daily activities. If a woman admits that she is affected in this way, her identity as a woman would be in question: she would label herself as a woman who cannot perform her role as a wife and who is no longer a caregiver but a care receiver. Women, often make do without the medical care they need and suffer serious consequences.[12] Poor healthcare systems and health information reinforce this attitude. Due to the decline in public health in China's transition process, women (as well as men) do not have the awareness about how to pursue safer sexual and reproductive lives.[13]

197

Table 3 Birth delivery care by income strata

| | Women aged 18–49 | Delivery care | | | | Place of delivery | | | | | | | |
		Need	Coverage	SE	Unknown	Public health facility	SE	Private health facility	SE	Home	SE	Unknown
Urban	366	18.2	87.9	4.8	11.6	72.9	5.2	8.9	3.8	0.5	0.5	17.7
Rural	930	20.7	84.6	2.9	13.2	74.7	7.9	2.4	1.6	9.7	6.4	13.1
Q1 (poorest)	174	12.3	66.7	11.5	25.6	46.4	11.1	9.4	7.7	18.6	5.6	25.6
Q2	218	22.4	90.9	4.8	16.7	45.8	18.6	10.0	5.9	27.5	15.5	16.7
Q3	200	18.3	84.4	5.1	13.3	77.7	6.7	6.8	6.6	2.2	2.2	13.3
Q4	341	24.7	91.0	3.1	0.2	91.3	0.0	0.0	0.0	0.0	0.0	0.7
Q5 (richest)	261	19.3	89.0	4.0	10.3	82.1	6.3	0.0	0.0	0.7	0.7	17.3
Total (average)	1,296	20.0	85.4	2.6	12.8	74.2	6.0	4.1	1.6	7.4	4.9	14.3

Notes: SE = standard error of percent of birth delivery care indicators covered.

Total = number of female respondents of reproductive age (18–49 years old).

"Need" refers to the percentage of the sample who required delivery care for a live birth in the last five years.

"Coverage" refers to the percent of those who needed delivery care who indicated having received assistance with birth delivery from a health care professional (doctor, nurse or midwife) during their last birth.

Source: Adapted from WHO (2002: Table 5.04 Birth Delivery Care).

Table 4 Action taken by women for their gynecological problems (in percentages)

	National	*Urban*	*Rural*
Seek doctor's help	28.7	32.5	27.7
Buy medicine	42.5	42.2	42.5
Endure or refuse	26.7	22.5	27.8
Other	2.2	2.8	2.0

Note: Based on the Second Survey on the Status of Chinese Women in 2000, sample size 48,192.
Source: Jiang (2003: 376).

There is also substantial evidence that values and practices favoring boys and discriminating against girls have reemerged in the era of the one-child policy (for example, see Therese Hesketh and Weiming Zhu 2005). Weakened healthcare services, especially in the countryside, high costs, and long distances to a care facility make it more likely that neglect and discrimination towards girls who are in need of care will occur (Shuzhuo Li and Chuzhu Zhu 1996; Judith Banister 2002). A study of a county in Shaanxi province (Shuzhuo Li and Chuzhu Zhu 2001: 154–62) found differences in treatment between girls and boys by parents, relatives, and other villagers. When a son is sick, parents are more likely to seek medical care without regard to costs or circumstances. When a daughter is sick, parents are more likely to consider the cost and wait for a more convenient time, hoping that the girl will get better herself. In two clinics in the same county from June to December 1997, doctors studied thirty-one cases of deaths (sixteen male and fifteen female) of children aged 0–5. Based on their interviews with the parents, they found that it took seventy-one hours on average for parents to first seek medical care for their daughters compared to twenty-five hours for boys. Parents were more ready to give up treatment for their daughters than sons when it was doubtful that they could be saved. Such evidence suggests that changing parents' attitude towards daughters is necessary to improve girls' lives. At the same time, the provision of affordable quality care would improve the likelihood that parents would seek care.

Labor market restructuring

Studies suggest that labor market restructuring in China has a different impact on access to healthcare for women and men at different ages and income levels.[14] Higher levels of unemployment and informal employment among women, for instance, affect their capacity to build up social security entitlements such as health insurance, creating both social and economic vulnerability if they become sick or require maternity or preventive care (Rachel Tolhurst, Hilary Standing, and Qian Xu 2004). Besides labor market restructuring, changes in household size and composition and gender ideologies concerning roles and expected behaviors also shape the health impacts of social and economic transitions (Monica Das Gupta, Sunhwa Lee, Patricia Uberoi, Danning Wang, Lihong Wang, and Xiaodan Zhang 2000). Gender has a cumulative impact on the capacity of women to build assets or entitlements in their own right, for instance, through the pursuit of full-time or lifetime careers in the segmented labor market. Age is significant in the sequence of paid and unpaid activity over a person's lifetime. This sequence again affects type of employment and entitlements, such as health insurance, that they can accrue at different stages in the life cycle. Individuals who have not been able to fulfill an uninterrupted cycle of paid, stable employment are less likely to experience security when they leave their employed life behind. Illness, the risk of which rises with age, can increase insecurity where assets and entitlements are not sufficient to manage the costs. The educational levels and work histories of women and men reflect the major transitions that have occurred or are occurring over people's lifetimes and introduce a historical understanding of how assets and entitlements are determined (Lisa Rofel 1999). They also play a role in differentiating longer-term security and the entitlements of women and men with consequences for their health needs and access to healthcare.

Urban women are more likely to be uninsured and have lower rates of coverage with the main publicly funded schemes compared to men since relatively fewer women than men are employed in the public sector (NBS 2004: 43). Many who were dropped from coverage were laid off from state owned enterprises and these were disproportionately women, which suggests that the fall in coverage has been greater for women than for men. This gender difference in coverage for urban residents forms a contrast to those in rural areas, discussed earlier, where the gender difference was mainly among the elderly.

The urban health insurance reforms in 1998 were designed to reverse the fall of coverage, but the measures have struggled to meet their goals and have inadvertently contributed to gender disparity in coverage. This is because social security schemes (including health insurance) for urban workers were still based on workplace entitlements, leaving laid-off and self-employed individuals uncovered. Tolhurst, Standing, and Xu (2004) conclude from their study of urban health reforms that there is little evidence at present of systematic or direct gender bias in the operation of insurance schemes. Differences in coverage likely reflect differences in the proportion of women in employment. They note that in the past women had mostly gained access informally to subsidized healthcare through their husband's workplace, but this is increasingly difficult as most employers are trying to keep down or reduce their healthcare costs. Also, women are disproportionately represented in the categories of informal workforce and home workers.

Healthcare challenges in China

The challenges facing healthcare in China in the first decades of the twenty-first century remain serious, especially considering that by 2020 China is expected to have 65 percent of its population living in cities. As Rao, Guoqing, Linlin, Ying, and Juncheng (2004: 3–4) estimate, by 2020 demands for healthcare will increase by 120 percent and 64 percent in urban and rural areas, respectively. The population of people over 60 years old will reach 170 million, bringing about a 55 percent increase of elderly patients between 2000 and 2020. These patients are more likely to have non-communicable diseases like heart disease, diabetes, and cancer. Many in the current elderly population – and women, in particular – are uninsured and live in the countryside. In the coming years, this growing population will still be unable to afford care other than relying on their children or local support networks unless initiatives are taken to address their needs.

The rising care burden on families poses another challenge in the ongoing demographic transition to an increasingly aging society. Due to the effect of the one-child policy on family demographics and the labor burdens of urban households, growing numbers of married couples will have sole responsibility for four parents and one child. As longevity increases and the one-child family comes of age, the household-based informal care economy faces greater pressure (Cynthia N. Milwertz 1997; Anqi Xu 2006). Women are likely to face greater responsibility than men to care for the elderly at home. As a result, more women may leave the workforce to provide home care or have shorter or more intermittent paid work careers, affecting their own capacity to build independent entitlements to healthcare and retirement benefits. There is also the potential for an overload of care work on family care systems for those who experience long-term dependency of the elderly, particularly in the case of the chronically sick and those with disabilities.

The unpaid informal care sector is an understudied area and information is very limited. Some information is available from time-use surveys such as the Survey on the Status of Women in Shanghai (2000), which shows the time spent on housework among Shanghai residents. According to an analysis of the data from this survey, women generally spend more hours than men on unpaid housework at home and that difference has increased between 1990 and 2000 (Jianmin Lu 2003: 320–1). While these data suggest rising unpaid care work of women at home, further studies are urgently needed to examine the healthcare needs at home, their consequences for women, and the emerging responses to these changes. Such changes would include a recognition of the unpaid care work within social security systems, the provision of more private and public elder and childcare facilities, and an increasing market in private care workers.

More systematic data collection is needed to discern the gendered health consequences of labor restructuring. There is some sex disaggregated information from surveys to enable the mapping of changes in both men's and women's health with respect to specific diseases (although child health data are not disaggregated), but more information, including of a qualitative nature, is needed on trends in service use and treatment patterns by gender and on gender-specific behaviors that affect health outcomes. For instance, recent survey data indicate both the enormous importance of growth in tobacco and alcohol consumption and its overwhelmingly gendered nature. The WHO shows that 46 percent of men reported themselves to be regular daily smokers as compared to less than 2 percent of women, and the highest rates are in the poorest quintile (2002: section 4.1). Men also have much higher rates of alcohol intake, although this is spread more evenly across the quintiles. The picture in relation to mental health is the reverse, with women self-reporting much higher rates of diagnosis or treatment (WHO 2002).

Within a broader rights framework, in recent years women's organizations in China have actively campaigned for greater public action against violations of women's human rights, particularly their reproductive and sexual rights. Gender issues such as domestic violence, sex trafficking and sexual abuse have increasingly attracted the government's and the public's attention and have entered the realm of community organizing. For example, women's campaign efforts intensified in China in 1999 with the support of UNIFEM as women's organizations, small and large, came together and spoke against domestic violence in a unified voice to the media and the government. Organized public meetings among women's organizations, other mass organizations, and government agencies, as well as the media on this issue, have raised enough awareness among some men and policy-makers. In April 2001, domestic violence as a crime was finally written into the Marriage Law, after which women in many provinces across the country have increased community-organized efforts in speaking out about their experiences with violence at home and resorting to legal redress.

Lesley Doyal (2002) notes the way in which global restructuring has opened up space for women to engage in health politics through workplace and community activism at both national and international levels. Increasingly, campaigns – including those on workplace health hazards affecting women in highly sex-segregated industries (Sally Theobald 1999) – have crossed local and national boundaries, linking activists to broader human rights movements and legal channels of redress.

CONCLUSION: GENDER EQUITY IN HEALTH IN THE CONTEXT OF RAPID TRANSITION

In this paper we have examined major trends in the transformation of China's healthcare system and its gender-differentiated health impacts in the context of China's reform process. We have argued for the need to pay attention to the implications of China's transition and healthcare reforms for women's health needs and for gender relations impacts that may produce health inequities. We have suggested that changes in the labor market and in the relations of social reproduction at the household level are creating new vulnerabilities for women. China's economic reforms have made access to healthcare more costly and forced cuts in basic, preventive health services, including reproductive care. Poor, rural, older women emerge as especially vulnerable in terms of health status and access to services. These women are in a very different situation from young, educated urban women who are benefiting more from the changing labor market and are more likely to have access to healthcare through their employment. It is possible that inequities between young women and men may also increase if attention is not paid to potential biases as social security systems are reformed.

In addressing actual or likely gender inequities, we suggest there are three priority areas that need attention from Chinese policy-makers and monitoring efforts by researchers and activists. The first is the need for more systematic monitoring of health impacts and trends from a gender perspective to inform public health policy. The second area for policy attention is to strengthen rural medical facilities and train staff to meet the basic healthcare needs of rural populations, giving greater attention to reproductive health needs beyond those of contraception. It is also urgent to increase insurance coverage. It is encouraging that the government study with which we began this paper recommends increasing public funding on health. Its proposal is for the government to underwrite universal coverage for an essential services package that incorporates a list of medicines and basic healthcare services. Any universal coverage must also include sexual and reproductive health services appropriate to the changing needs of rural and urban women and men, as well as a guaranteed right to maternity and other reproductive healthcare for all women, including migrants. The third issue for urgent study is any potential gender biases in eldercare and more comprehensive social security systems. Women need to be able to build up and maintain entitlements to benefits such as health insurance in a transformed labor market and in a context where they may have enhanced responsibilities as caregivers.

As China's economy continues its rapid opening up, helped by the WTO accession process, this space for active engagement and rights-based advocacy can be expected to increase. Such advocacy will hopefully encourage the national and local governments to consider the gendered needs of those rendered vulnerable by social and economic changes in their policies, especially in access to sexual and reproductive health and primary and preventive services. It will also empower Chinese women to design their own community health plans, including health saving schemes and insurance packages, and demand the integration of these plans into the government reform agenda for cooperative health insurance and social security (Fang Jing 2000). Only with women's equitable participation in the healthcare reform process will appropriate services be devised to meet the changing health needs of women and men resulting from the multiple transitions taking place in China.

Lanyan Chen, Tianjin Normal University of China,
Gender and Social Development Studies,
509, Administration Building, Main Campus,
Xiqing District, Tianjin, China 300384
e-mail: lanyanc@hotmail.com

Hilary Standing, Institute of Development Studies,
University of Sussex, Falmer, Brighton BN1 9RE, UK
e-mail: H.Standing@ids.ac.uk

ACKNOWLEDGMENTS

We are grateful to two anonymous readers and the guest editors for helping the paper reach its final version. We also thank Joyce P. Jacobsen, Denise Hare, and Marion Jones for their valuable comments. Lanyan Chen is grateful to Peter Forster, Xianghong Cheng, Hongwei Yang, and Ling Xu for their help with research. Hilary Standing would like to thank Joan Kaufman for generously sharing her insights on health in China over the last few years.

NOTES

[1] For summaries of this research, see Hilary Standing (1997), World Health Organization (1998), Gita Sen, Asha George, and Piroska Ostlin (2002), and Aifang Shao and Xiaoying Zheng (2003).

[2] For instance, the General Comment in 2000 of the Committee on Economic, Social and Cultural Rights stated: "[W]here essential health services are not reasonably available, accessible and acceptable, states are in violation of individuals' right to the highest attainable standard of health protected by the Covenant on Economic, Social and Cultural Rights" (Rebecca J. Cook 2003: 64–5). According to Cook, accessibility of services has four overlapping dimensions: there is no discrimination in services, which are accessible to all; health facilities and services must be within safe physical reach for all members of the population; health services must be affordable to all;

and all persons have the right to seek, receive, and impart information and ideas concerning health issues (2003: 63).

3 For discussions of this understanding of vulnerability, see Bloom and Gu (1997) and Rachel Tolhurst, Hilary Standing, and Qian Xu (2004).

4 "Barefoot doctors" was the term used for minimally trained rural healthcare workers who provided basic medical services on the communes from the mid-1960s until the reforms (Kaufman 2005: 114). See Kaufman (2005) for more on China's health policies for rural areas during Mao's era.

5 In the early 1980s, family planning, which was better funded, was relocated from the Ministry of Health to its own national administrative unit, now called the National Population and Family Planning Commission. The separation of family planning from the Ministry of Health has increased the funding for family planning but reduced the funds available for maternal and children health services (Kaufman 2005).

6 These statistics that draw from national surveys were reported by Ling Xu (2004). These figures do not include migrant workers as they do not hold urban residential registration and are excluded from policies providing benefits to urban residents.

7 The government started further healthcare reforms in 1997 by adopting initiatives entitled "Decisions on Healthcare Reform and Development" and by issuing a proposal by the Ministry of Health to "Develop and Improve Rural Cooperative Healthcare" in 1997, "Decision on the Establishment of Basic Medical Insurance for Urban Employees" in March 1998, and the "Guidelines on the Management Reforms of Drugs and Healthcare Services in Cities and Towns" in 2000 (Rao et al. 2004; Rao and Liu 2004).

8 While rural migrants to urban areas are supposed to get healthcare coverage where they are registered, most do not return to their home villages for routine coverage or to obtain care when ill. Since they are usually not covered by health insurance in the city, they have to pay the higher urban rates out of pocket. Some rural villages provide partial coverage for migrants in urban areas by paying the amount that would have been covered if the migrant had been treated in the rural area. According to the Chinese Experts Panel (2000–3: 81), a township in Hubei pays for medical expenses according to a sliding scale. For those who work in other areas, any medical costs below 1,000 yuan were self-financed and only 30 percent of the costs that exceed 1,000 yuan were compensated, with a cap of 1,200 yuan per incident. For local residents, however, 50 percent of medical costs that are below 500 yuan and 60 percent of costs that exceed 500 yuan were covered. This arrangement is by no means representative but a case study of good practice. Many rural migrant workers have no medical coverage from their home villages.

9 Lesley Doyal (2002) notes that globalization changes the distribution of income and poverty within and across nation states, creating both winners and losers. Gender is often a key attribute of the changes in income distribution and poverty. Ill health is frequently closely linked with rising poverty. For instance, young women may benefit from the rise in new, better paid employment opportunities but are often disproportionately exposed to new occupational health hazards because of their preponderance in the lightly regulated export industries. (Also see International Labour Office [2004] and Vivienne Wee [2004]).

10 In 2002, under-five mortality was 39.6 per thousand in the countryside, twice as high as that of the urban rate at 14.6 (Ministry of Health 2004b: 159). Maternal mortality in less developed western provinces, such as Tibet and Xinjiang (at 327.27 and 169.16 per hundred thousand), was much higher than the national average of 50.2 in 2001 (National Bureau of Statistics 2004: 75; Liu 2005: 49).

11 Acknowledging the higher MMR in poor rural areas, the Chinese government has given high visibility to reducing it. Provincial governors are now required to hold local

official agents to account and to publish their MMR regularly. Pressure from Beijing, combined with improved referral systems and a move to increased facilities-based deliveries are having an impact in some of the poorest areas (Jiang 2006).

[12] Jiang (2003: 378) told the story of a man in Yilong, Sichuan, who complained about his wife having a vaginal infection for over twenty years that affected her movement and sex life. Both the man and his wife did not think to go and see a doctor. In another case, a Beijing TV series about China's poverty eradication efforts (sponsored by UNDP and UNIFEM) captured the story of a woman whom the crew met in Guizhou and who died from neglect of long term health problems. These are not isolated cases, as Jing (2004) notes, women of reproductive age in rural areas suffer high levels of untreated morbidity.

[13] A recent study by the Alan Guttmacher Institute (2003), conducted among men aged 15–54 in forty-five countries, found that the failure to provide information and care services to men is jeopardizing efforts to fight sexually transmitted diseases, including HIV/AIDS, and reduce unwanted pregnancy. The results of a study in Guangdong sponsored by UNIFEM and UNICEF show that men's sexual attitude and behavior are products of men's dominant position and reasons for concern in the prevention of AIDS (Qiuxiua Long and Jiaming Zhu 2003).

[14] As Monica Das Gupta, Sunhwa Lee, Patricia Uberoi, Danning Wang, Lihong Wang, and Xiaodan Zhang (2000) point out, the increasing gender wage gap has already adversely affected women's status and bargaining power within the family. Urban China may be witnessing a return to more traditional views of women's role in society and in the division of labor within the family (Cynthia N. Milwertz 1997; Björn Gustafsson and Shi Li 2000). Any restructuring of family dependency will have implications for women's capacity to accrue entitlements if they are based on employment status.

REFERENCES

Alan Guttmacher Institute. 2003. "In Their Own Right: Addressing the Sexual and Reproductive Health Needs of Men Worldwide." http://www.guttmacher.org/presentations/itor_slides_US.html (accessed March 2007).

Banister, Judith. 2002. "The Dearth of Girls in China Today: Origins, Geography, and Comparative Perspective." Paper prepared for the UNFPA China Office.

Bloom, Gerald and Xing-yuan Gu. 1997. "Health Sector Reform: Lessons from China." *Social Science and Medicine* 45(3): 351–60.

Blumenthal, David and William Hsiao. 2005. "Privatization and Its Discontents – The Evolving Chinese Healthcare System." Health Policy Reports. *New England Journal of Medicine* 353(11): 1165–70.

Chen, Lanyan. 2000. "Women and Informal Work in China: Reflections on Two Poverty Alleviation Pilot Projects." *Canadian Journal of Development Studies* 21(2): 233–53.

Chinese Experts Panel. 2000–3. *Rural Cooperative Medical System (RCMS): Best Practice Study in China* [in Chinese]. Beijing: UNDP, WHO, and the Ministry of Health of China.

Cook, Rebecca J. 2003. "Human Rights Relating to Women's Reproductive Health: Implications for Health Sector Reform," in *Experts' Perspectives on Globalization, Health Sector Reform, Gender, and Reproductive Health*. New York: Ford Foundation. www.fordfound.org/publications/recent_articles/docs/globalization/thinkpieces.pdf (accessed April 2007).

Das Gupta, Monica, Sunhwa Lee, Patricia Uberoi, Danning Wang, Lihong Wang, and Xiaodan Zhang. 2000. State Policies and Women's Autonomy in China, the Republic of Korea, and India 1950–2000: Lessons from Contrasting Experiences. Policy Research Report on Gender and Development Working Paper Series 16, World Bank.

Doyal, Lesley. 2002. "Putting Gender into Health and Globalisation Debates: New Perspectives and Old Challenges." *Third World Quarterly* 23(2): 233–50.

Gao, Jun. 2004. Aging and Health Care. Powerpoint presentation at the Senior Level Seminar on National Health Services Survey of China, Center for Health Statistics and Information, Beijing.

Gao, Jun, Juncheng Qian, Shenglan Tang, Bo Eriksson, and Erik Blass. 2002. "Health Equity in Transition from Planned to Market Economy in China." *Health Policy and Planning* 17(Suppl. 1): 20–9.

Gao, Jun, Shenglan Tang, Rachel Tolhurst, and Rao Keqing. 2001. "Changing Access to Health Services in Urban China: Implications for Equity." *Health Policy and Planning* 16(3): 302–12.

Ge, Yanfeng. 2005. "Reflections on Chinese Healthcare System Reforms" [in Chinese]. *Xinhua Wenzhai* 16: 21–3.

Gong, Sen and Yanfeng Ge. 2005. "Recognizing the Issues in Building the Urban Healthcare Insurance System" [in Chinese]. *Xinhua Wenzhai* 16: 21–4.

Gu, Xing-yuan, Gerald Bloom, Shenglan Tang, and Henry Lucas. 1995. Financing Health Services in Poor Rural China: A Strategy for Health Sector Reform. IDS Working Paper 17, Institute of Development Studies, Brighton, UK.

Gustafsson, Björn and Shi Li. 2000. "Economic Transformation and the Gender Earnings Gap in Urban China." *Journal of Population Economics* 13(2): 305–29.

Hesketh, Therese and Weiming Zhu. 2005. "The Effect of China's One-Child Family Policy After 25 Years." *The New England Journal of Medicine* 353(11): 1171–6.

Hsiao, William. 2004. "Disparity in Health: The Underbelly of China's Economic Development." *Harvard China Review* 5(1): 64–70.

International Labour Office (ILO). 2004. *A Fair Globalization: World Commission on the Social Dimension of Globalization.* Geneva: ILO.

Jiang, Xiuhua. 2003. "Study of Health Status of Rural Women and Their Use of Healthcare Services," in Jiang Yongping, ed. *Chinese Women's Social Status at the Turn of the Century* [in Chinese]. Beijing: Contemporary China Publishing House.

———. 2006. "Chinese Women's Health Status," in Tan Lin, ed. *Report on Gender Equality and Women's Development in China (1995–2005)*, pp. 80–98. Beijing: Social Sciences Academic Press.

Jing, Fang. 2000. "Participation: A Way to Better Health Outcomes?" *IDS Bulletin* 31(1): 37–42.

———. 2004. "Health Sector Reform and Reproductive Health Services in Poor Rural China." *Health Policy and Planning* 19(Suppl. 1): 40–9.

Kang, Shiyong, ed. 2003. *Social Security Administration* [in Chinese], 2nd ed. Beijing: The Publishing House of the Chinese Labor and Social Security.

Kaufman, Joan. 2005. "China: The Intersections Between Poverty, Health Inequity, Reproductive Health, and HIV/AIDS." *Development* 48(4): 113–9.

Koblinsky, Marge. 2001. *Reducing Maternal Mortality: Learning from Bolivia, China, Egypt, Honduras, Indonesia, Jamaica and Zimbabwe.* Washington, DC: World Bank.

Li, Shuzhuo and Chuzhu Zhu. 1996. "Analysis of Sex Ratio at Birth in China and Girls' Living Conditions" [in Chinese]. *Renkou yu Jingji* [Population and Economics] 94(1): 13–8.

———. 2001. *Research and Community Practice on Gender Difference in Child Survival in China* [in Chinese]. Beijing: China Population Publishing House.

Liu, Bohong. 2005. "The Impact of Globalization on Women's Health in China," in Cordia Chu, ed. *Reproduction Health Promotion in China: From Needs Assessment to Policy Development* [in Chinese], pp. 37–64. Beijing: China Social Sciences Publishing House.

Liu, Jieyu. 2007. "Gender Dynamics and Redundancy in Urban China." *Feminist Economics* 13(3/4): 125–58.

Liu, Peilong, ed. 2002. *WTO and Health in China: Collection of the Workshop Documents* [in Chinese]. Beijing: Publishing House of People's Health.

Liu, Xingzhu and Yunni Yi. 2004. The Health Sector in China: Policy and Institutional Review. Background paper prepared for the World Bank China Rural Health Study 2004, the World Bank, Beijing.

Long, Qiuxiua and Jiaming Zhu. 2003. *The Reflection of Red Ribbon* [in Chinese]. Guangzhou: Guangdong Science and Technology Press.

Lu, Jianmin. 2003. "The Status of Women's Family Conditions in Shanghai and the Factors that Influence Them," in Jiang Yongping, ed. *Chinese Women's Social Status at the Turn of the Century* [in Chinese]. Beijing: Contemporary China Publishing House.

Milwertz, Cynthia N. 1997. *Accepting Population Control: Urban Chinese Women and the One-Child Family Policy.* Richmond, UK: Curzon Press.

Ministry of Health. 2004a. *An Analysis Report of National Health Services Survey in 2003* [in Chinese]. Beijing: Center for Health Statistics and Information.

———. 2004b. *China Health Statistical Yearbook.* Beijing: Xiehe Medical University Press.

National Bureau of Statistics (NBS), Department of Population, Social Science, and Technology. 2004. *Women and Men in China: Facts and Figures 2004.* Beijing: China Statistics Press.

Office of the World Health Organization Representative. 2004. *Implementing the New Co-operative Medical Schemes in Rapidly Changing China: Issues and Options.* Beijing: Office of the World Health Organization Representative. http://www.wpro.who.int/NR/rdonlyres/68DA93DB-9D5C-4637-9EB8-C3CBC89C9A9F/0/rcms_en.pdf (accessed April 2007).

Rao, Keqing, Hu Guoqing, Hu Linlin, Xin Ying, and Qian Juncheng. 2004. "Issues and Development of Urban Healthcare System Reforms in China," in the Committee of Compilers and Editors, eds. *Research on Health Reform Issues in China, 2003* [in Chinese]. Beijing: Center for Health Statistics and Information, Ministry of Health.

Rao, Keqing and Yuanli Liu. 2004. "A Study of Rural Healthcare System and Related Policy Issues in China," in the Committee of Compilers and Editors, eds. *Research on Health Reform Issues in China, 2003* [in Chinese]. Beijing: Center for Health Statistics and Information, Ministry of Health.

Research Institute of All-China Women's Federation and State Statistical Bureau. 1998. *Gender Statistics in China (1990–5)* [in Chinese]. Beijing: China Statistical Publishing House.

Rofel, Lisa. 1999. *Other Modernities: Gendered Yearning in China after Socialism.* Berkeley: University of California Press.

Saich, Tony and Joan Kaufman. 2005. "Financial Reform, Poverty, and the Impact on Reproductive Health Provision: Evidence from Three Rural Townships," in Yasheng Huang, Tony Saich, and Edward Steinfeld, eds. *Financial Sector Reform in China*, pp. 178–203. Cambridge, MA: Harvard University Asia Center Publications.

Sen, Gita, Asha George, and Piroska Ostlin, eds. 2002. *Engendering International Health: The Change of Equity.* Cambridge, MA: MIT Press.

Shao, Aifang and Xiaoying Zheng. 2003. "A Study of Health Status of Chinese Women and Their Self-Rated Conditions," in Jiang Yongping, ed. *Chinese Women's Social Status at the Turn of the Century* [in Chinese]. Beijing: Contemporary China Publishing House.

Standing, Hilary. 1997. "Gender and Equity in Health Sector Reform Programmes: A Review of Current Issues." *Health Policy and Planning* 12(1): 1–18.

Theobald, Sally. 1999. "Community Responses to the Electronics Industry in Thailand." *Development* 42(4): 126–9.

Tolhurst, Rachel, Hilary Standing, and Qian Xu. 2004. "Gendered Impacts and Implications of Health Sector Reform in the Context of Multiple Transitions in Urban China," in Gerald Bloom and Shenglan Tang, eds. *Health Care Transition in Urban China*, pp. 127–42. Aldershot, UK: Ashgate.

Tolhurst, Rachel, Qian Xu, Hilary Standing, and Shenglan Tang. 2001. "Access to Health Care in the Context of Economic Liberalisation in Urban China: A Gender Analysis." Draft Report to the Ford Foundation, Beijing.

United Nations Development Programme (UNDP). 2005. *China Human Development Report*. Beijing: China Translation & Publishing Corporation.

Wee, Vivienne. 2004. "The Gendered Impacts of Globalization on Women's Health." *The Journal of Comparative Asian Development* 3(2): 183–207.

White Papers of the Government of China. 2004. "China's Social Security and Its Policy." http://www.china.org.cn/e-white/20040907/index.htm (accessed April 2007).

White Papers of the Government of China. 2005. "Gender Equality and Women's Development in China." http://www.china.org.cn/e-white/20050824/index.htm (accessed April 2007).

World Health Organization (WHO). 1998. Gender and Health. Technical Paper WHO/FRH/WHD/98.16, World Health Organization.

———. 2002. *World Health Survey 2002. Report on China*. Geneva: World Health Organization. http://www.who.int/healthinfo/survey/whschn-china.pdf (accessed May 2007).

Xu, Anqi. 2006. "Chinese Women's Family Life," in Tan Lin, ed. *Green Book on Women: Report on Gender Equality and Women Development in China (1995–2005)* [in Chinese], pp. 65–79. Beijing: Social Sciences Academic Press.

Xu, Ling. 2004. Health Insurance Coverage in China. Paper presented at the Senior Level Seminar on National Health Services Survey of China, Center for Health Statistics and Information, Beijing.

Yu, Hao, Henry Lucas, Xing-yuan Gu, and Baogang Shu. 1998. Financing Health Care in Poor Rural Counties in China: Experience from a Township-Based Co-operative Medical Scheme. IDS Working Paper 66, Institute of Development Studies, Brighton, UK.

Zhang, Zhenzhong. 2003. "Study of Healthcare Assistance to the Rural Poor in China," in Chinese Expert Panel, eds. *Rural Cooperative Medical System: Best Practice Study in China* [in Chinese]. Beijing: Sponsored by UNDP, WHO, and Ministry of Health.

Zhu, Wenyi. 2005. "Big Monopolizing Hospitals." *Shenghuo Zhoukan* [Life Weekly] 349(31): 25–6.

FOREIGN DIRECT INVESTMENT AND GENDERED WAGES IN URBAN CHINA

Elissa Braunstein and Mark Brenner

INTRODUCTION

Many economists and policy-makers treat foreign direct investment (FDI) as a premier agent of economic growth in developing countries. Especially since the financial crises of the late 1990s, when short-term capital flows proved to be unreliable and destabilizing, governments have courted FDI as the international capital flow of choice.[1] In addition to directly raising investment and consequent growth, FDI is often lauded for expanding employment opportunities, introducing technological and managerial know-how, and providing valuable access to highly competitive export markets. As a result, for many developing economies, FDI has become one of the most sought-after commodities in the global marketplace. Even so, the empirical evidence for a causal connection between FDI and growth, to say nothing of broad development, is actually quite weak – certainly not enough to support the types of subsidies that many developing country governments have begun to offer multinational investors (Gordon H. Hanson 2005). Yet for all of the uncertainty over whether FDI in fact helps industrializing countries, we know even less about its effects from a gender perspective. In this study, we investigate China, the largest recipient of FDI in the developing world – indeed, one of the largest in the world. By assessing the effect of FDI on gender-based wages in urban China, we shed light on one of the key social and developmental impacts of both globalization and FDI.

Looking at FDI in China through a gendered lens extends the feminist literature on women and globalization. The rising rate of women's employment worldwide is linked with changing patterns of international production, as the growth among industrializing countries in labor-intensive, export-oriented assembly and manufacturing has been associated with a feminization of the manufacturing labor force (Guy Standing 1989, 1999; Nilüfer Çağatay and Sule Ozler 1995). A similar feminizing effect has resulted from export-oriented FDI (that is, foreign investment seeking export production platforms). Where export-oriented FDI inflows have been sizeable – primarily in East and Southeast Asia and in parts of Latin America and the Caribbean – the share of female employees in export-oriented industry is also large (Susan Joekes and Ann Weston 1994). However, export-oriented FDI's impact on wages is distinct from trade because it combines the dynamics of trade and investment. Although FDI is associated with the same systematic segregation of women and men into different industries that we see in most export-oriented firms regardless of ownership, export-oriented FDI is more globally mobile than domestic (locally sourced) investment so workers in foreign-invested firms have less bargaining power vis-à-vis capital to raise wages. When capital is more mobile in industries that primarily employ women, the bargaining effect will put downward pressure on the gender-wage ratio (female wages as a proportion of male wages) (Stephanie Seguino 2000b). Moreover, regardless of its link with trade, if foreign investment in female-dominated industries is less capital intensive than foreign investment in male-dominated industries, changes in FDI will have gender-specific effects on wages.

The Chinese context for evaluating these wage dynamics is complex. By world standards, the gender-wage ratio in urban China is high, albeit declining – 83.2 percent in 1995 versus 82.8 percent in 2002 according to this study. China's course of economic reform and liberalization is associated with this decline. Microeconomic studies in China show that the greater the share of private ownership in a firm, the lower its gender-wage ratio (Margaret Maurer-Fazio, Thomas G. Rawski, and Wei Zhang 1999; Bjorn Gustafsson and Shi Li 2000; Pak-Wai Liu, Xin Meng, and Junsen Zhang 2000; Margaret Maurer-Fazio and James Hughes 2002). We do not know, however, whether working for a foreign-invested firm plays a role in these changes, or to what extent, if any, the presence of foreign investment in developing economies brings wider structural changes to labor markets that affect economy-wide wages.

Addressing these questions, this study evaluates the impact of foreign investment on urban women's and men's wages by combining province-level macro-data with household survey data for eleven Chinese provinces in 1995 and 2002. By comparing outcomes in the two years, we are able to link changes in the structure of foreign investment with changes in gender-based wages. Our results show that foreign investment has a positive impact on the wages of women and men in China, both for those who work directly for foreign-invested enterprises and for those working in provinces with higher levels of FDI. However, the gender-based wage advantage of this relationship reverses between the two years. In 1995, women get a higher wage premium than men in provinces with higher levels of FDI as a proportion of investment, with the opposite being true in 2002. We conclude that these results stem from the segregation of Chinese women and men into different industries, a segregation that interacts with the changing structure of FDI to illustrate how wage dynamics differ by gender.

A key innovation of this study is that it combines macroeconomic and microeconomic data, which allows us to evaluate the impact of FDI much more broadly than just for the particular firms and workers linked directly with foreign investors. FDI can have considerable structural effects on economies, as the literature on FDI and growth makes clear.[2] By combining province-level macro-data with household survey data, we are able to look at the overall effects of FDI on gendered wages while controlling for the types of individual characteristics that might otherwise weaken a purely macroeconomic approach.[3]

FDI AND GENDER-BASED WAGE INEQUALITY

Most of the empirical research on FDI and wage inequality is gender-blind. Two notable exceptions come from the feminist literature on globalization. In a macroeconomic study of South Korea and Taiwan, Seguino (2000b) finds a positive correlation between total FDI (inward plus outward FDI) and the gender-wage gap in Taiwan but no similar relationship in Korea. Seguino explains that this is partly due to differences in each country's FDI, as FDI in Korea is more capital intensive and related to more male-dominated industries than in Taiwan. She also notes that Korean firms in female-dominated industries faced strict controls on physical capital mobility and responded to increasing female wages by raising productivity and by moving into niche markets where quality matters (Seguino 2000b: 457). In an industry-level study of export-led growth and gender-wage inequality in Taiwan, Günseli Berik (2000) included a measure of outward FDI in her analyses of women's and men's wages and the gender-wage ratio (female to male wage ratio). She finds that a higher proportion of outward FDI as a share of GDP is negatively correlated with all three wage measures, though none are statistically significant (Berik 2000: 16).

Two studies from the gender-blind literature on FDI and wages back up these results from the feminist literature. In a study of FDI and wages in developing and developed countries, Eva A. Paus and Michael Robinson (1998) find a structural shift in the relationship between FDI and wages beginning in the late 1980s, when what had been a positive correlation between FDI and wages disappears. They suggest that increasing global capital mobility is the likely culprit. Another study on China, the Philippines, Singapore, and Thailand found evidence that FDI contributed to an increase in the responsiveness of labor demand to wage increases (Ozay Mehmet and Akbar Tavakoli 2003). The authors proffer this as evidence of a race-to-the-bottom dynamic – that the ease with which foreign investors could move production when labor costs increase dampened the rise in wages within these countries. These studies attest to the importance of the footloose nature of foreign direct investment in determining wages, a dynamic that may also have gender-specific effects.

Another important basis for the link between FDI and gender-based wage inequality involves industrial upgrading and gendered job markets. When upgrading differs by industry, the effect on wages will differ by gender. Berik's (2000) study of Taiwan mentioned above shows that increasing capital intensity has a positive effect on both female and male wages but benefits men more than women. In a study of the Mexican maquiladora industry, Elizabeth Fussell (2000) argues that technological upgrading spurred employers to look for more skilled, male laborers, as women were perceived as largely unprepared for such employment. Similar gender reversals in export-oriented employment, following industrial upgrades, have occurred in India, Ireland, and Singapore (Diane Elson 1996; Susan Joekes 1999; Jayati Ghosh 2001). If FDI in male- and female-dominated industries is associated with different levels of capital intensity, then changing rates of foreign investment inflows will be correlated with changes in gendered wages.

THE INSTITUTIONAL CONTEXT

The changing structure of FDI in China[4]

Although we use only two years of data in the study, 1995 and 2002, they represent two distinctive periods in China's economic reforms and FDI policies. Between the late 1970s and the late 1990s, FDI was a key feature of China's "Open Door Policy" – a carefully staged opening to the global economy. These policies utilized FDI to simultaneously develop an export-led and import substitution growth strategy by implementing a combination of constraints and incentives to guide FDI, including preferential income tax policies, exemption from trade duties, reduced fees for land use, and export and local content requirements (Chunlai Chen 1996; Yasheng Huang 1998).

China's FDI strategy; its high-skill, low-cost labor force; the increasing costs of production in other export manufacturers in East Asia; combined with China's cultural connections to overseas Chinese resulted in an FDI stock largely owned by East Asian Newly Industrializing Economies (NIEs, which include Hong Kong, Singapore, South Korea, and Taiwan). This is illustrated by Table 1, which shows FDI stocks by source country between 1983 and 2002. NIEs account for 61 percent of FDI stock in China during this period.[5] Although industry-level data on foreign-invested enterprises (FIEs) by source country is difficult to come by, individual studies show that industrialized country investors are geared towards larger, more capital- or technology-intensive ventures and are also more likely to target China's domestic market (Chunlai Chen 1997; John Henley, Colin Kirkpatrick, and Georgina Wilde 1999; Bohm Park and Keun Lee 2003; Peter Buckley and Chen Meng 2005). In contrast, a number of studies indicate that FDI sourced from NIEs tends to be concentrated in smaller, labor-intensive export-oriented manufacturing firms (Chen 1997; World Bank 1997; Park and Lee 2003; Buckley and Meng 2005).

Beginning in the late 1990s, the NIEs lost FDI stock share due to increasing investments from industrialized countries, especially Western Europe and the United States.[6] The share of FDI stocks from all industrialized countries (Europe, Japan, the US, Canada, Australia, and New Zealand) increased from 21.5 percent in 1983–95 to 29.5 percent in 2000–2. This increase parallels the turn towards accession to the WTO by

Table 1 Accumulated FDI stock in China by source countries, 1983–2002 (2002 US$)

	1983–95		1996–99		2000–02		1983–02	
	Billion US$	Percent	Billion US$	Percent	Billion US$	Percent	Billion US$	Percent
NIEs	93.1	72.6	104.9	61.7	68.8	49.0	266.8	60.8
Hong Kong	75.5	58.9	75.4	44.3	50.2	35.7	201.1	45.8
Taiwan	11.4	8.9	12.2	7.1	9.3	6.6	32.9	7.5
Singapore	3.9	3.0	10.8	6.4	6.7	4.7	21.4	4.9
South Korea	2.3	1.8	6.5	3.8	2.7	1.9	11.5	2.6
Japan	9.6	7.5	14.2	8.4	11.5	8.2	35.3	8.0
Europe	6.1	4.7	16.4	9.7	13.3	9.5	35.8	8.2
USA	10.0	7.8	14.7	8.6	14.3	10.2	38.9	8.9
Other	5.0	3.9	14.8	8.7	25.1	17.9	44.9	10.2
Total	128.2	100	170.1	100	140.6	100	438.9	100

Sources: Authors' calculations based on data drawn from Chen (1997: Table 1) and *China Statistical Yearbook* (National Bureau of Statistics China [NBS] various years).

the Chinese leadership in the late 1990s. In early 1999 Chinese authorities agreed to undertake the opening of China's domestic market necessitated by WTO accession (Nicholas R. Lardy 2002: 19). The shift would initiate and lock in a number of domestic market reforms that were relevant for foreign investors, among them guaranteed domestic market access for a wide set of industries protected by China's pre-WTO regime.

Once again, though we do not have FDI data disaggregated by source country and industry, individual studies show that industrialized country investors are geared towards larger, more capital- or technology-intensive ventures, and are also more likely to target China's domestic market (Chen 1997; Henley, Kirkpatrick, and Wilde 1999; Park and Lee 2003; Buckley and Meng 2005). One way to gauge these differences is by looking at relative labor productivity by ownership type, as illustrated in Table 2.[7]

The first column gives the national total, beginning with an index of 100 in 1998. All of the other indices are relative to the 1998 national total, so for instance, in 2002 labor productivity in state-owned enterprises was 210 or 2.1 times the 1998 national total. Enterprises receiving funds from Hong Kong, Macao, and Taiwan (HKMT) are recorded separately from other FIEs, which is helpful because we can treat that column as a reasonable proxy for investment from the East Asian NIEs (in all other cases in this article, HKMT investment is included with foreign investment). In order of productivity for the entire period, FIEs lead, followed by enterprises with funds from HKMT, then state-owned enterprises, and finally collectives (although state-owned enterprises outstrip HKMT enterprises in 2002). The difference between HKMT enterprises and FIEs is stark and indicates a real structural difference between the two types of foreign enterprises, which reflects others' findings about the relative labor intensity of investment from the East Asian NIEs. As the share of non-NIE investment grows, we would expect an increase in labor productivity in the foreign-

Table 2 Labor productivity indices by enterprise ownership (National 1998 index = 100)

	National total	State-owned enterprises	Collectives	Enterprises with funds from Hong Kong, Macao, & Taiwan	Foreign-invested enterprises
1998	100	93	91	141	206
1999	119	114	101	157	252
2000	146	147	114	185	287
2001	166	175	124	189	314
2002	191	210	139	199	338

Notes: All indices are relative to 1998 national total. The subcategories are not a full representation of all ownership types.
Source: Authors' calculations based on Tables 13–21 of the *China Statistical Yearbook* (NBS 2003: 508).

invested sector that is consistent with increasing capital or technological intensity.

In sum, we argue that the increasing share of industrialized economies in China's inward FDI reflects a new period in its FDI regime. Prior to deciding on WTO accession, China's FDI strategy focused on export orientation and import substitution, with the result that FIEs were largely labor-intensive, export-oriented firms linked with the East Asian NIEs. After China committed to opening domestic markets in preparation for WTO accession, the share of larger, more capital-intensive, and domestically oriented FIEs grew.[8]

Gender in the Chinese labor market

The issues of liberalization, foreign investment, and gender in China are complicated by the highly segmented nature of Chinese labor markets. Enterprise ownership is a key determinant of wage structure in China. State-owned enterprises (SOEs) have historically offered the best pay and benefits to China's urban workforce. During the course of liberalization, collective enterprises have become increasingly important sources of employment. These locally and collectively owned firms are typically smaller and more labor-intensive than SOEs, with fewer non-wage benefits. Joint ventures, which have foreign and/or private investors, have also emerged during this process, with FIEs falling into this category. When we compare wages across enterprises, we find they tend to be the highest for both women and men in joint enterprises, followed by SOEs, and finally collectives (Gustafsson and Li 2000; Maurer-Fazio and Hughes 2002). As mentioned in the introductory section, female-to-male wage ratios vary according to ownership. The lowest gender-wage ratios have been found in private firms and the highest in SOEs. On a continuum of ownership structures, joint ventures and private firms occupy one extreme, with SOEs at the other and collectives in the center.

While we would expect women working for FIEs to make higher wages than their counterparts in other sectors, we would also expect these women to experience greater gender-wage inequality compared to those in other types of firms. Our own data reflect this result: in 1995 women working in state firms made 76.9 percent of what female FIE workers earned; the figure for women working in collective firms was 67 percent. By 2002 these ratios converged somewhat but maintained the ownership/wage hierarchy: female state-sector workers earned 83.7 percent of female FIE wages, with women in the collective sector earning 69.4 percent. Gender-wage inequality is also higher in foreign-owned firms in our data, though it is the highest of all ownership forms only in the 2002 data. The female-to-male wage ratio for SOEs, collectives, and FIEs, respectively, was 88.8 percent, 80.7 percent, and 87.2 percent in 1995 and 84.8 percent, 82.2 percent, and 73.0 percent in 2002.

Industrial segregation by gender is also common in China, and scholars argue it is a much more important factor in gender-wage inequality than occupational segregation (Maurer-Fazio, Rawski, and Zhang 1999; James Hughes and Margaret Maurer-Fazio 2002; Cindy C. Fan 2003). To a great extent, women in urban China are paid less because they are crowded into low-paying industries.

Women are also segregated within the foreign-invested sector. It is difficult to get industrial-level data disaggregated by gender, much less by ownership structure. But multiple studies show that, as in other areas of the developing world, the export-oriented, labor-intensive industries that are destinations for FDI in China also have high proportions of female employees (Sally Baden and Susan Joekes 1993; Gale Summerfield 1995; Fan 2003; Delia Davin 2004). These export-oriented enterprises may have workforces that are up to eighty percent women (Shen Tan 2000). Many of these women are rural–urban migrants, members of China's "floating population" of 100 million people who seek work in urban areas without the benefit of permanent resident status. Investigating this type of employment is one way to gauge the changing impact of foreign investment on gender inequality in China, but the quasi-legal status of this migration and the consequent paucity of nationally representative time-series data make such a task difficult.

In this study, we are interested in answering more general questions: How have increasing inflows of foreign investment affected wages by gender in urban China? How has the changing structure of foreign investment affected gendered labor markets overall, over and above the immediate effects that FIEs have on their workers' wages? Exploring gender inequality from these perspectives enables us to capture the externalities of the relationship between globalization and gender that reach beyond the microeconomic level.

THE STUDY

Theoretical approach

We use a reduced form model of wage determination to assess the role of foreign investment in women's and men's wages. The basic model is summarized by equation:

$$\ln w_{ij} = \alpha + X_{ij}\beta + Z_j\delta + \varepsilon_{ij} \quad i = 1, \ldots, N; \quad j = province \quad (1)$$

with the dependent variable being the natural log of wages of person i in province j.

Separate models are posited for women and men using a vector of individual-level variables (X_{ij}), a vector of province-level variables (Z_j), and an error term (ε_{ij}). In terms of the individual-level variables, the model is based on a standard Mincerian human capital model of wage determination that includes controls for human capital, occupation, and industry. Because we are interested in investigating the impact of working for a foreign-owned firm, enterprise ownership structure is also included in the individual-level variables.

The province-level macro variables include a set of controls that also affect wages at the microeconomic level in China: economic growth, total investment, the size of the state sector (as a proxy for the extent of privatization), international trade, and foreign investment. It is important to note that by including the province-level trade and foreign investment variables, we capture the wage effects of working in provinces with higher levels of trade and FDI, independent of whether an individual is directly linked to the global sector through their own paid work. We hypothesize that globalization structurally impacts labor markets in ways beyond individual characteristics of workers.

Since we focus on FDI, it is important to explain the nature of macroeconomic pathways from a gender-aware perspective. The key determinant of different outcomes for women and men in this context is the gendered segregation of labor markets – that gender tends to be highly correlated with skill set, industry, and occupation (Richard Anker 1998). To the extent that FDI adds to (rather than crowds out) domestic investment, foreign investment in female-dominated industries will raise labor demand and female wages. In addition, foreign-invested enterprises in developing economies generally possess higher technology and are larger in scale than domestically owned firms (Robert Lipsey and Fredrik Sjoholm 2005: 24). If these effects "spill over" into the rest of an industry, either directly via technological diffusion into domestically owned firms or indirectly by putting upward pressure on wages for women in foreign-invested industries, the result may also increase wages for women across the economy.

The technological effect might also work the other way, however. A rise in the capital intensity of foreign-invested firms creates more demand for skilled workers in local markets, which is likely to benefit men more than women because women are segregated in lower skill and less capital-intensive sectors. Research in developing economies done at the industry-level indicates that foreign investors pay higher wages but that skilled workers receive most of the benefits (Robert C. Feenstra and Gordon H. Hanson 1997; Dirk Willem te Velde 2003). To the extent women are concentrated in less-skilled jobs, these results suggest that employment segregation is a key aspect of the relationship between FDI and wages. Feminists and others point out that another source of downward pressure on female wages is the global mobility of foreign investment, which potentially dampens wage demands via credible threats to relocate (the bargaining effect). If foreign investment in female-dominated industries is more footloose than others types of investment, the bargaining effect will pull down female wages.

Controlling for international trade is important for studying these effects, as FDI and trade are closely linked in China (in 2002, FIEs were responsible for 52.2 percent of China's export value and 54.3 percent of its import value). Since we are interested in the independent impact of FDI, including trade thus isolates the macroeconomic pathways of FDI, labor markets, and gender.

Data

In order to examine the differential impact of FDI on women's and men's wages in urban China, we draw on nationally representative household income and expenditure surveys for 1995 and 2002. The surveys were designed and overseen by scholars at the Institute of Economics within the Chinese Academy of Social Sciences (CASS) and provide the only publicly available, nationally representative household data from mainland China in the reform era.[9] Households in the CASS sample are drawn from the Chinese State Statistical Bureau's (SSB) annual income and expenditure survey, and SSB enumerators were contracted to administer the CASS questionnaires. In both years the CASS urban survey covers eleven provinces: Beijing, Shanxi, Liaoning, Jiangsu, Anhui, Henan, Hubei, Guangdong, Sichuan, Yunan, and Gansu. The 1995 data contain a total of 6,931 households and 21,694 individuals, while the 2002 data contain 6,835 households and a total of 20,632 individuals.

Because the CASS surveys are drawn from the SSB's parent sample, they inherit many of its features, including several problems discussed in Shaohua Chen and Martin Ravallion (1996). Perhaps the most striking of these for our purposes is that the SSB sample frame is constructed on the basis of households' residence of record. The so-called floating migrants are not enumerated in either their village of origin or their current place of residence, so our study is based for the most part on permanent urban residents.[10] This is a regrettable limitation of the study. Finally, it bears note that the CASS surveys also follow the SSB's method for sample selection, using a procedure known as the "equidistant selection method" (*duichen dengju chouyang fangshi*), which roughly corresponds to systematic sampling.[11]

We supplement these household survey data with province-level macroeconomic data drawn from the *China Statistical Yearbook* (various years) compiled by the National Bureau of Statistics of China (formerly the State Statistical Bureau).[12]

Estimation methodology

Beginning with the individual-level variables, the dependent variable – the average monthly wage – is the annual total of wages, bonuses, and overtime pay divided by twelve. The first set of independent variables includes level of educational attainment, age, and age-squared, which together capture the accumulated skills and experience of each respondent. The specific levels of education identified in our survey data include college or above, upper middle school to professional school, lower middle school, and elementary school.[13] Along with these human capital variables, we include two individual-level demographic variables as dummy variables, specifically ethnic minority status (equivalent to ethnicities other than Han Chinese) and Communist Party membership. Prior research has shown that both are important determinants of wages, as ethnic minorities in China suffer disadvantages in the labor market while Communist Party membership carries substantial material rewards (e.g., Bjorn Gustafsson and Shi Li 2003; Linda Yueh 2004).

At the individual level we also control for occupation (whether they are high-level managers); economic sector (whether they work in manufacturing); and workplace ownership (whether they work in a state-owned enterprise, foreign-invested firm, or the private sector – all of which are relative to working in the locally owned collective sector).[14] Adding occupational and industry controls is a common practice in wage equation estimation, and these controls have proven to be important determinants of wages in both advanced industrial and transition economies (Alan B. Krueger and Lawrence H. Summers 1988; Jan Svejnar 1999). Controlling for these variables in a discrimination study can have mixed results, however. If women are sorted into particular occupations, industries, or firms because of their gender, extended human capital models may understate the impact of gender on wages.[15] Presenting different wage equations for women and men enables us to assess gender differences in these variables.

The next set of independent variables includes macroeconomic measures at the provincial level. Most important is our measure of FDI, which is defined as the three-year moving average of the ratio of FDI to total investment at the provincial level. The three-year average smoothes out short-term volatility in foreign investment flows. The moving average is taken over the years (n), $(n-1)$, and $(n-2)$. Provincial controls (all of which are taken as three-year moving averages unless otherwise noted) for total investment and trade are measured as shares of GDP.

The size of the state sector is measured by the share of state-owned enterprise (SOE) output in gross industrial output. In the context of China's gradual transition from a centrally planned to a market economy, and the concomitant processes of breaking up the central government's monopoly in urban industry and easing the entry of non-state firms, the SOE variable reflects the macroeconomic impact of the changing balance between state and non-state sectors and the increasing reach of the private sector. For urban workers at least, this shift is critical. At the beginning of the reform period in 1980, state-owned firms employed more than three-quarters of urban workers. Fifteen years later the proportion had declined to 59 percent, and by 2002 the share of SOEs in urban employment dropped to 30 percent. Part of this decline stemmed from layoffs in the state sector. Between 1995 and 2002, employment in the state sector declined by more than one-third. Since the risk of being laid-off or furloughed from SOEs is higher for women than for men (Simon Appleton, John Knight, Lina Song, and Qingjie Xia 2002), we would expect there to be gender differences in the impact of the SOE variable on wages.

To control for the impact of a province's longer-term economic dynamism, we also include an eight-year measure of cumulative real GDP growth.[16] We assume here that wages are related to longer-term economic growth in distinct ways from short-term (or cyclical) fluctuations in macroeconomic variables. Including a variable for the longer-term growth dynamics also helps control for the tendency of foreign investors to be attracted to places with high levels of economic growth.[17]

In terms of the econometrics, we have made a few adjustments: To control for the sample selection issues associated with estimating a female wage equation, we employ the commonly used Heckman selection correction technique. We estimate the selection equation and wage equation jointly using maximum-likelihood methods, utilizing marital status and number of children younger than ten years old as independent predictors of a woman's selection into the labor market.

A second econometric issue we must address is that independent variables are measured at differing levels of aggregation. As the econometrics literature has widely recognized, combining variables grouped at high and low levels of aggregation introduces the potential for serious downward bias when estimating regression coefficient standard errors, the so-called "Moulton effect" (Brent R. Moulton 1990). We take this problem into account by estimating standard errors clustered on provinces, the usual method for addressing such problems. We also correct standard errors for heteroskedasticity using the Huber-White "sandwich" method for both the male and female wage equations.

Where appropriate, we test for coefficient equality between male and female wage equations using a cross-model Hausman specification test. This test is based on combining estimation results of the two equations into a single parameter vector and simultaneous variance-covariance matrix, which enables us to apply a generalized Hausman specification test for differences between cross-model parameters. We also test the specific cross-equation restriction that the coefficient for FDI is equal for men and women. In all cases we are able to reject the hypothesis of coefficient equality with 99 percent confidence.

Results

Table 3 contains the means for our dependent and independent variables. Several gender-specific differences within these data are worth noting. First, as mentioned in the introduction, the wage ratio (female/male wages) declined slightly between 1995 and 2002 – from 83.2 to 82.8 percent. In 1995 women's educational attainment at the highest reported level (college or above) was roughly half of men's – 5.3 percent of the sample versus 10.8 percent. By 2002 this gap had closed considerably, with 37.9 percent of men reporting college or above versus 33 percent for women. A substantially greater share of women reported membership in the Communist Party in 2002 vis-à-vis 1995 (23.2 percent versus 15.2 percent). Approximately 36 percent of men reported Party membership in both years.

With regard to occupation, industry, and workplace ownership, several things also stand out. First, women report a much lower concentration in the state sector than men in both years, although somewhat surprisingly a greater percentage of both men and women report working in a state-owned enterprise in 2002 versus 1995 despite an overall decline in state-sector employment between those years. This seemingly anomalous trend emerges because our 1995 sample includes a lower proportion of workers in the state sector than was the case in the general population and should be kept in mind as a limitation of the 1995 urban CASS data. A much smaller proportion of our sample worked in manufacturing in 2002 than did in 1995, consistent with the increasing diversification of the Chinese economy more generally. A final noteworthy feature of our data is the rapid rise in private sector employment. In 1995 less than 0.1 percent of both men and women reported working in privately owned workplaces, a figure rising to nearly four percent of survey respondents by 2002. Although the proportion of women and men who worked in a FIE doubled between 1995 and 2002, the overall percentages are still quite low – 2.2 percent for women respondents and 2.6 percent for men.[18] According to national data, FIE workers made up 3.1 percent of all urban workers in 2002 (NBS 2003: 126–7). Since FIE workers are a smaller proportion of the CASS sample relative to the overall urban population, statistically significant results on FIE ownership are a strong finding.

Looking at the province-level variables, we note that despite the increase in absolute terms in FDI between 1995 and 2002, its mean share of total investment has declined, from 15.5 percent in 1995 to 12.4 percent in 2002. Trade averages about 44 percent of GDP in both years. Investment as a share of GDP increased slightly, though there is less inter-provincial variability in 2002 than in 1995. Due to changes in data collection methods between the two years, the data on state enterprise output as a proportion of gross industrial output cannot be compared. In 1995 gross industrial output includes all enterprises but in 2002 it includes only enterprises that

Table 3 Sample means and standard deviations for women and men (in percent unless otherwise indicated)

	1995		2002	
	Women	*Men*	*Women*	*Men*
Individual-level variables				
Female wage/male wage	83.2		82.8	
Monthly wage (2002 yuan)	429.6	516.2	898.6	1085.5
	(255.4)	(297.8)	(643.8)	(687.7)
College or above	5.3	10.8	33.0	37.9
	(22.4)	(31.0)	(47.0)	(48.5)
Upper middle school to	56.4	56.9	45.4	37.0
professional school	(49.6)	(49.5)	(50.0)	(48.3)
Lower middle school	32.1	27.9	19.5	22.7
	(46.7)	(44.9)	(40.0)	(41.9)
Elementary school	5.6	4.3	1.9	2.3
	(22.9)	(20.2)	(13.6)	(14.9)
Age (years)	37.3	40.1	39.0	42.0
	(8.9)	(10.3)	(8.3)	(9.2)
Age squared (years)	1,472.7	1,712.6	1,586.9	1,847.0
	(669.0)	(834.5)	(644.9)	(760.9)
Ethnic minority	4.3	4.2	4.1	3.9
	(20.3)	(20.0)	(20.0)	(19.4)
Communist Party member	15.2	34.2	23.2	38.2
	(35.9)	(47.4)	(42.2)	(48.6)
Work in state-owned enterprise	22.9	30.8	30.4	37.6
	(42.0)	(46.2)	(46.0)	(48.5)
Work for private sector firm	0.1	0.1	4.3	3.9
	(3.7)	(3.1)	(20.3)	(19.5)
Work for foreign-invested firm	1.2	1.3	2.2	2.6
	(11.0)	(11.2)	(14.7)	(15.9)
High-level manager	29.1	39.2	30.5	38.7
	(45.4)	(48.8)	(46.1)	(48.7)
Manufacturing	39.6	41.4	25.4	28.4
	(48.9)	(49.3)	(43.5)	(45.1)
Observations (number)	5,716	6,332	3,858	4,872
Province-level variables				
Total investment as a share of GDP	32.8		34.5	
	(10.1)		(7.8)	
SOE output as a share of gross	41.8		53.7	
industrial output	(16.4)		(18.0)	
Cumulative GDP growth	57.7		66.0	
	(14.5)		(7.8)	
FDI as a share of total investment	15.5		12.4	
	(20.9)		(22.9)	
Trade as a share of GDP	43.9		43.9	
	(109.9)		(113.8)	
Observations (number)	11		11	

Source: Individual variables are authors' calculations based on CASS data for 1995 and 2002 for all working adults (15 years or older). Province-level variables are authors' calculations based on the *China Statistical Yearbook* (NBS various years). Standard deviations are reported in parentheses below sample means.

exceed a designated size. Therefore the base is structurally lower in 2002 than in 1995 and the mean ratio consequently higher despite a secular decline in the relative size of the state sector. We ran the regressions using state sector output as a proportion of GDP with little difference in the results, and we hence use the gross industrial output measure because it made more intuitive sense in thinking about the relevance of the state sector to urban wages. Lastly, the mean of provincial cumulative real GDP growth increased between the two years, from about 58 to 66 percent, though there is some provincial convergence in that the 2002 data show less inter-provincial variability in growth rates than the 1995 figures.

Turning to our regression results, Table 4 presents estimates for 1995 and 2002. Although a number of interesting patterns emerge, our main interest is in FDI, and we will therefore focus our discussion on the enterprise ownership and FDI results. For both the individual- and macro-level variables the results are as expected, though we obtained some gender and year differences that would be worth exploring in a later study.

Starting with enterprise ownership variables, and looking first at the results for 1995, we find that relative to the collective sector, working in either a state-owned enterprise or foreign-owned firm has a sizeable positive effect on wages for both men and women. In both SOEs and FIEs, this effect is larger for women than for men, though the premium for working in a FIE is much higher for both sexes, and only the gender difference in the SOE coefficient is statistically significant. These gender differences in working for a SOE are also economically significant. The wage premium that female state sector workers receive relative to their male counterparts amounts to nearly one-third of the 1995 gender difference in overall mean wages. We do not get a statistically significant effect of private workplace ownership, most likely due to the extremely small number of respondents falling into this category in 1995. Turning to 2002, some interesting differences arise. Relative to working in a collectively owned firm, the wage premium associated with working in a SOE has disappeared for both women and men. The relative wage penalty for working in a domestic private enterprise is now larger and statistically significant for women, due in part to the increased number of workers in this category in 2002. Female private sector workers make about ten percent less than their collective sector counterparts, a substantial difference. Working in a FIE continues to carry with it a wage premium, although unlike in 1995 there is a statistically significant difference in the gender-based advantage of that premium. Men receive a 0.15 percentage point higher boost than women for FIE employment – an economically significant premium that is the equivalent of three-quarters of the mean gender wage difference.

With regard to our macroeconomic measure of FDI as a proportion of investment, working in a province with higher levels of FDI is positively correlated with wages for both men and women in 1995 and 2002. The

Table 4 FDI and the determinants of female and male wages in urban China

	1995		2002	
	Women	Men	Women	Men
College or above	1.248***	2.312***	1.925***	2.230***
	(0.100)	(0.351)	(0.264)	(0.559)
Upper middle school to	1.114***	2.204***	1.667***	2.036***
professional school	(0.093)	(0.354)	(0.259)	(0.558)
Lower middle school	0.938***	2.095***	1.424***	1.879***
	(0.105)	(0.362)	(0.266)	(0.559)
Elementary school	0.702***	1.965***	1.396***	1.801***
	(0.105)	(0.398)	(0.287)	(0.551)
Age	0.167***	0.127***	0.159***	0.134***
	(0.011)	(0.013)	(0.014)	(0.011)
Age squared	-0.002***	-0.001***	-0.002***	-0.001***
	(0.000)	(0.000)	(0.000)	(0.000)
Ethnic minority	-0.094***	-0.079	0.170***	0.018
	(0.036)	(0.049)	(0.061)	(0.048)
Communist Party member	0.112***	0.073***	0.109***	0.064***
	(0.021)	(0.019)	(0.030)	(0.017)
Work in state-owned enterprise	0.271***	0.212***	0.026	0.008
	(0.040)	(0.037)	(0.036)	(0.016)
Work for private sector firm	0.328	-0.091	-0.100**	-0.112
	(0.303)	(0.188)	(0.048)	(0.087)
Work for foreign-owned firm	0.431***	0.382***	0.200***	0.318***
	(0.061)	(0.085)	(0.060)	(0.071)
High-level manager	0.197***	0.097***	0.296***	0.164***
	(0.020)	(0.018)	(0.031)	(0.020)
Manufacturing	-0.029*	0.002	-0.050**	-0.141***
	(0.015)	(0.014)	(0.023)	(0.029)
Investment as a share of GDP	1.294***	1.107***	0.397	0.755*
	(0.138)	(0.112)	(0.591)	(0.389)
SOE output as a share of	0.785***	0.445*	0.826**	0.940**
industrial output	(0.197)	(0.218)	(0.344)	(0.328)
Cumulative GDP growth	0.845***	0.610***	1.083***	1.010*
	(0.157)	(0.125)	(0.374)	(0.483)
FDI as a share of total investment	2.409***	1.286***	1.019	1.963***
	(0.376)	(0.402)	(0.685)	(0.565)
Trade as a share of GDP	-0.165***	0.027	0.499***	0.356***
	(0.056)	(0.044)	(0.130)	(0.074)
R-squared	0.320	0.321	0.288	0.281
Test of Equality on FDI coefficient between women and men				
F-statistic	31.75***		21.43***	

Notes: Robust standard errors in parentheses. * significant at 10 percent; ** significant at 5 percent; *** significant at 1 percent.
Source: Authors' calculations.

effect is larger for women than for men in 1995; however, the gender advantage shifts in 2002 (and the difference, as demonstrated by the reported F-tests in Table 4, is statistically significant). Quantitatively, a 10 percent increase of FDI as a proportion of investment in 1995 raises female wages by 3.7 percent and male wages by 2.0 percent. A 10 percent increase in 2002 raises female wages by 1.3 percent and male wages by 2.4 percent. Are these amounts economically significant? Consider that the FDI as a proportion of investment mean actually declined 20 percent between 1995 and 2002, implying a 2.6 percent decline in female wages and a 4.8 percent decline in male wages at the mean. If FDI as a proportion of investment had instead remained constant, the female-to-male wage ratio would have declined to 81.0 (as opposed to 82.8).

Thus, even after accounting for the wage premiums women and men receive from working for FIEs directly, we find there are still strong, positive effects from working in provinces with higher proportions of FDI in investment. A similar dynamic exists for the state sector. While controlling for the wage premium of working in a SOE, we find both women and men receive wage premiums for working in provinces with relatively large state sectors. From 1995 to 2002, the gender advantage of this premium shifts in a way similar to that associated with working in provinces with high rates of FDI. Thus, the payoff for men increases from less than women (in 1995) to more (in 2002), albeit this result may partly reflect the wage patterns in larger SOEs in 2002 (recall that the 2002 provincial SOE measure includes only enterprises larger than a certain size).

Looking to trade, in 1995 trade as a proportion of GDP is negatively correlated with female wages, a result consistent with trade-related employment offering relatively low-wage opportunities. It could also be that provinces with high levels of trade attract more female rural–urban migrants, labor force participants who, despite labor-market segregation by household registration status, are still crowded into sectors that have labor supply effects in non-migrant urban labor markets. Even so, this negative correlation is quantitatively much smaller than any other macroeconomic effect in our model. In contrast, the correlation between trade and wages for both men and women turns strongly positive in 2002. Explaining this shift would be pure speculation, and gives us fodder for future work, but it is interesting that both women and men receive this benefit.

Robustness

To test the robustness of these results, we also constructed a set of three simultaneous equations, which we estimated using seemingly unrelated regression estimation as in Berik (2000). Berik uses industry-level data to first calculate the determinants of male and female wages by industry separately and then a gender-wage ratio by industry derived from these two equations. To apply this method to our data, we calculated city-wide averages by sex for all of the individual-level variables in the model (using the sixty-nine cities in the 1995 data and seventy-seven cities in the 2002

226

data). Then we ran the city average of female log wages on the female-only averages for the individual characteristics as well as the macro variables, doing the same for men. Lastly, we regressed the gender-wage ratio as a function of the combined averages for men and women together by city. The results at the city-level broadly mirror the results of our individual-level regression results, and the sign and statistical significance of the FDI variable on women's and men's wages follow the patterns we found using individual-level regressions.[19] That is, a higher proportion of FDI in total investment raises the female-to-male wage ratio in 1995 (although the amount is not statistically significant) and considerably lowers the gender-wage ratio in 2002. We use this methodology only as a test because we do not have city-level data on any of the variables; all our data is taken either at the individual or province level. This creates a particular problem in terms of the provincial variables, as province-level macroeconomic indicators are weak proxies for city-level observations.

Reverse causality

The causal direction between FDI and wages may also run in the other direction: low wages may in fact attract foreign investors. Stephanie Seguino (2000a) argues that gender-based wage inequality stimulated growth in semi-industrialized countries via its positive effects on exports and investment. Women, crowded into export sectors, earn lower wages – increasing global competitiveness, consequent investment and access to technology, and ultimately growth. Her study does not differentiate between FDI and other forms of domestic investment, but it does suggest that the causality can indeed run from wages to investment.

In terms of our model, accounting for potential reverse causality necessitates using an instrumental variable (IV) approach, as others have done in studies of FDI (for example, Eric Neumayer and Indra De Soysa [2005], who ultimately reject the IV specification). The challenge is to find a good instrument, a variable correlated with FDI as a proportion of investment but not with wages. Demographic instruments such as population size are inappropriate since we use FDI as a proportion of investment. For instance, population size may serve as an instrument in that it is positively correlated with FDI levels but not with wages. However, our variable is FDI as a proportion of investment, and there is no a priori relationship between this proportional measure and FDI level instruments such as population size. Other potential instruments with regional variations are also likely to be correlated with wages (e.g., infrastructure or geography[20]). Using weak instruments introduces biases of their own that will render the resulting estimates worse than OLS (John Bound, David Jaeger, and Regina Baker 1995). In light of the unavailability of suitable IVs for IV estimation, we elected to use OLS.

In terms of the possible impact of reverse causation on our results, after controlling for worker productivity, we would expect the correlation between wages and FDI to be negative. That is, lower wages would draw in more foreign investment, ceteris paribus. If this is indeed the case, the estimates of the positive impact of FDI on wages represent a lower bound. Still, we do not know if or how this effect would alter male and female wages differently. One could argue that any negative relationship between wages and FDI would be higher for women than for men, as women are more likely to be employed in industries and firms that are highly cost sensitive and internationally mobile. This is a question that requires further study.

CONCLUDING REMARKS

The relationship between FDI and gendered wages in urban China shifted between 1995 and 2002. While women received a bigger boost in their wages relative to men from working in provinces with a higher proportion of FDI as a share of investment in 1995, men gained the relative advantage in 2002 (both when they worked directly for FIEs and when they were employed in provinces with higher levels of FDI). We argue that these results reflect the shift of foreign-invested enterprises to higher productivity and more domestically oriented production. Because women and men are segregated into different types of industries, however, with women more likely to be employed in low-skilled, export-oriented production and men in higher productivity and domestically targeted industries, the changing composition of FDI is associated with increasing inequality of female to male wages. In terms of the pathways between FDI and wages discussed at the beginning of this article, the econometric study does not enable us to specify the precise nature and relative contributions of these different pathways. But we can say that FDI in male-dominated industries is likely to be more capital-intensive and less internationally mobile than FDI in female-dominated industries. As a consequence, men receive higher relative wages. Still, these shifts have occurred in a context of positive absolute effects of FDI on wages for both women and men, effects that seem to spill over into the rest of the economy in the sense of having impacts on workers not directly employed by a foreign-invested enterprise.

Although this study looks at only two years over a relatively short time span, it marks two very different points in China's course of market liberalization. China's WTO accession in 2001, and the domestic policy changes that led up to it in the late 1990s, represent a major turning point in Chinese economic development. As Liqun Jin (China's Vice Minister of Finance) said in an address at the World Bank in 2002, China's accession is a "wrecking ball...the destructive force that smashes whatever is left in the edifice of the more or less closed economy'' (2). It therefore seems reasonable to consider the differences between 1995 and 2002 as indicative of future developments. China is likely to remain a popular destination for FDI and the shift towards higher productivity and domestically oriented production is likely to continue. If women and men continue to be segregated into differently structured and rewarded industries, then higher levels of FDI may widen the gender differences in wage gains. If China continues to expand its light industrial exports – the types of industries that traditionally employ women – then the resulting trade-related labor demand effects may somewhat attenuate this trend. Unless China makes public policy efforts to counter gender segregation in its urban labor markets, the structure of continuing trends in FDI, trade, and employment will bestow fewer wage benefits on women relative to men.

Elissa Braunstein, Department of Economics, Colorado State University,
Fort Collins, Colorado, 80523 USA
e-mail: Elissa.Braunstein@colostate.edu

Mark Brenner, Labor Notes
104 Montgomery St., New York, NY 11225, USA
e-mail: Mark@labornotes.org

ACKNOWLEDGMENTS

We are in great debt to the editors of this volume, as well as to our anonymous reviewers, for their help in improving this paper. All remaining mistakes are, of course, our own.

NOTES

[1] An investment is considered FDI when the investor acquires some proportion of direct ownership of an enterprise in a country other than the one in which she has citizenship. Countries differ as to what minimum proportion of ownership qualifies an investment as FDI, but a common standard is a 10 percent or greater share of ownership. As such, FDI is seen as a longer-term type of investment than portfolio investment because the former denotes a direct involvement in production that is not as easy to divest as the selling of stock.

[2] For a survey of developing country studies, see Luiz R. de Mello (1997) and Gordon H. Hanson (2001).

[3] There is one other study that uses a similar combination of micro- and macro-data to assess the impact of global integration on gendered labor market outcomes, Cem Başlevent and Özlem Onaran (2004).

[4] Unless otherwise indicated, all statistics discussed in this article are based on authors' calculations of data drawn from the *China Statistical Yearbook* (NBS various years).

[5] With about 45 percent of FDI stocks during the period, Hong Kong has long been the main source of FDI in China, partly because of its role as an entrepôt for other

229

countries. It is also the main thoroughfare for round-tripping, whereby Chinese domestic investment gets funneled through Hong Kong and back into China in order to take advantage of the privileges afforded to foreign investors. Estimates of round-tripping range between 15 and 25 percent of Hong Kong investment, a substantial amount (Peter Harrold and Rajiv Lall 1993; Shang-Jin Wei 2000; Yasheng Huang 2003).

[6] The sharp increase in the "other" category, which ranges from 3.9 percent of FDI stock prior to 1995 to 17.9 percent of FDI stock between 2000 and 2002, is due to increased inflows from tax-haven countries. A large percentage of these inflows are thought to be linked to round-tripping, and so the decline in NIEs' dominance could be partly due to a diversion of Chinese capital outflows from Hong Kong to other tax haven countries. These countries include the British Virgin Islands, the Cayman Islands, and Samoa.

[7] Table 2 does not present all ownership types, but the ownership types listed represent more than 80 percent of industrial output in China in 2002.

[8] Other factors also contributed to increasing productivity and capital intensity across all types of firms. For instance, high savings rates and increasing wages may have changed the relative costs of labor versus capital and led to greater capital intensity as well.

[9] The 2002 data are not yet publicly available. The 1995 data are available through the Inter-University Consortium for Political and Social Research (ICPSR), holding number 3012. See Carl Riskin, Zhao Renwei, and Li Shi (2001) for more details. A similar survey was also conducted for 1988 and is available through the ICPSR, holding number 9836. See Keith Griffin and Zhao Renwei (1993) for more details.

[10] Although the 2002 CASS data contain a separate survey of rural–urban migrants, these data contain no information on individual wage earnings and therefore cannot be combined with the 2002 urban survey data to examine gender-based wage inequality.

[11] See Marc Eichen and Zhang Ming (1993) for a complete discussion of the sample selection methods used in the 1988 survey data (which were also followed in 1995 and 2002). Briefly, the "equidistant selection method" is applied to the selection of counties within the province, as well as villages within the county and households within the village. The unit to be selected is ranked, usually by per capita income, and selection is made at fixed intervals after a random start. Generally for counties with a population over 450,000, eighty households are selected, and for those under 450,000, sixty are chosen. Since ten households are usually surveyed in each village, these figures imply that eight or six villages are surveyed, depending on whether the county population is more or less than 450,000. See Chen and Ravallion (1996) for more details.

[12] In 1997 Chongqing, which had been a part of Sichuan province, was given province-level status in a manner similar to other large metropolitan areas like Beijing and Shanghai. To make the two survey years comparable, we combine data on Chongqing and Sichuan in 2002 to make it equivalent to Sichuan in 1995.

[13] We omit educational levels of less than elementary school or illiterate, so the coefficients on the education variables are returns relative to these omitted categories.

[14] The regressions were also run using more extensive categories for ownership (seven instead of four), occupation (eight instead of one), and sector (twelve instead of one). The results were essentially the same and are available upon request. In terms of industry, it is important to note that the vast majority of FDI is highly concentrated, with the manufacturing sector receiving over 70 percent of all inward FDI in 2002.

[15] This could also be argued of our human capital variables.

[16] In deciding what length of time to use to represent cumulative growth, we wanted the time horizon to be short enough to capture only the dynamics of the reform period but long enough to span shorter cyclical changes. We tried time periods varying between five and ten years with little difference in our results. Eight years was chosen as a midpoint.

[17] In addition to growth, we also ran the regressions with province-level per capita GDP to test whether the FDI variable picked up effects associated with higher income levels. GDP per capita was not statistically significant and adding this variable actually increased the statistical significance of FDI with little effect on parameter magnitude.

[18] We also checked for correlation between our individual-level variables, as ethnic/minority workers or Communist Party members may also have higher levels of human capital owing to their relative social positions. Most of these two-way correlations register coefficients well below 0.05. The same is true of correlations between the individual- and province-level variables.

[19] These results are available from the authors upon request.

[20] Geography has been closely linked with the extent of economic reform in China: the level and pace of liberalization was both more extensive and rapid in the coastal than in the inland regions because government policy designated coastal regions for outward-oriented liberalization. We do include a control for economic reforms in our study – the relative size of the state sector.

REFERENCES

Anker, Richard. 1998. *Gender and Jobs: Sex Segregation of Occupations in the World.* Geneva: International Labour Organization.

Appleton, Simon, John Knight, Lina Song, and Qingjie Xia. 2002. "Labor Retrenchment in China Determinants and Consequences." *China Economic Review* 13: 252–75.

Baden, Sally and Susan Joekes. 1993. Gender Issues in the Development of the Special Economic Zones and Open Areas in the People's Republic of China. Paper presented at Fudan University Seminar Women's Participation in Economic Development, Shanghai, People's Republic of China.

Başlevent, Cem and Özlem Onaran. 2004. "The Effect of Export-Oriented Growth on Female Labor Market Outcomes in Turkey." *World Development* 32(8): 1375–93.

Berik, Günseli. 2000. "Mature Export-Led Growth and Gender Wage Inequality in Taiwan." *Feminist Economics* 6(3): 1–26.

Bound, John, David Jaeger, and Regina Baker. 1995. "Problems with Instrumental Variables Estimation When the Correlation between Instruments and the Endogenous Explanatory Variables Is Weak." *Journal of the American Statistical Association* 90(430): 443–50.

Buckley, Peter and Chen Meng. 2005. "The Strategy of Foreign-Invested Manufacturing Enterprises in China: Export-Oriented and Market-Oriented FDI Revisited." *Journal of Chinese Economic and Business Studies* 3(2): 111–31.

Çağatay, Nilüfer and Sule Ozler. 1995. "Feminization of the Labor Force: The Effects of Long-Term Development and Structural Adjustment." *World Development* 23(11): 1883–93.

Chen, Chunlai. 1996. Recent Developments in Foreign Direct Investment in China. Chinese Economy Research Unit Working Paper 96/3, University of Adelaide.

——. 1997. Comparison of Investment Behaviour of Source Countries in China. Chinese Economics Research Centre Working Paper 97/14, University of Adelaide.

Chen, Shaohua and Martin Ravallion. 1996. "Data in Transition: Assessing Rural Living Standards in Southern China." *China Economic Review* 7(1): 23–56.

Davin, Delia. 2004. "The Impact of Export-Oriented Manufacturing on the Welfare Entitlements of Chinese Women Workers," in Shahra Razavi, Ruth Pearson, and Caroline Danloy, eds. *Globalization, Export-Oriented Employment and Social Policy: Gendered Connections*. Geneva: UNRISD and Palgrave MacMillan.

Eichen, Marc and Zhang Ming. 1993. "Annex: The 1988 Household Sample Survey – Data Description and Availability," in Keith Griffin and Zhao Renwei, eds. *The Distribution of Income in China*, pp. 331–46. London: Macmillan.

Elson, Diane. 1996. "Appraising Recent Developments in the World Market for Nimble Fingers," in Amrita Chhachhi and Renee Pittin, eds. *Confronting State, Capital and Patriarchy: Women Organising in the Process of Industrialization*, pp. 35–55. New York: St. Martin's Press.

Fan, Cindy C. 2003. "Rural–Urban Migration and Gender Division of Labor in Transitional China." *International Journal of Urban and Regional Research* 27(1): 24–47.

Feenstra, Robert C. and Gordon H. Hanson. 1997. "Foreign Direct Investment and Relative Wages: Evidence from Mexico's Maquiladoras." *Journal of International Economics* 42(3–4): 371–93.

Fussell, Elizabeth. 2000. "Making Labor Flexible: The Recomposition of Tijuana's Maquiladora Female Labor Force." *Feminist Economics* 6(3): 59–79.

Ghosh, Jayati. 2001. Globalisation, Export-Oriented Employment for Women and Social Policy: A Case Study of India. Paper prepared for UNRISD project on Globalization, Export-Oriented Employment for Women and Social Policy.

Griffin, Keith and Zhao Renwei. 1993. *The Distribution of Income in China*. London: Macmillan.

Gustafsson, Bjorn and Shi Li. 2000. "Economic Transformation and the Gender Earnings Gap in Urban China." *Journal of Population Economics* 13: 305–29.

———. 2003. "The Ethnic Minority-Majority Income Gap in Rural China during Transition." *Economic Development and Cultural Change* 51(4): 805–22.

Hanson, Gordon H. 2001. Should Countries Promote Foreign Direct Investment? United Nations Conference on Trade and Development G-24 Discussion Paper Series 9.

———. 2005. "Comment," in Theodore Moran, Edward Graham, and Magnus Blomstrom, eds. *Does Foreign Direct Investment Promote Development?* pp. 175–78. Washington, DC: Institute for International Economics.

Harrold, Peter and Rajiv Lall. 1993. China Reform and Development in 1992–93. World Bank Discussion Paper 215, The World Bank.

Henley, John, Colin Kirkpatrick, and Georgina Wilde. 1999. "Foreign Direct Investment in China: Recent Trends and Current Policy Issues." *The World Economy* 22(2): 223–43.

Huang, Yasheng. 1998. *FDI in China: An Asian Perspective*. Singapore: The Institute of Southeast Asian Studies.

———. 2003. *Selling China: Foreign Direct Investment during the Reform Era*. Cambridge: Cambridge University Press.

Hughes, James and Margaret Maurer-Fazio. 2002. "Effects of Marriage, Education and Occupation on the Female/Male Wage Gap in China." *Pacific Economic Review* 7(1): 137–56.

Jin, Liqun. 2002. China: One Year Into the WTO Process. Paper presented at World Bank, Washington, DC.

Joekes, Susan. 1999. "A Gender-Analytical Perspective on Trade and Sustainable Development," in *Trade, Sustainable Development and Gender*, pp. 33–59. New York and Geneva: UNCTAD.

Joekes, Susan and Ann Weston. 1994. *Women and the New Trade Agenda*. New York: UNIFEM.

Krueger, Alan B. and Lawrence H. Summers. 1988. "Efficiency Wages and the Inter-Industry Wage Structure." *Econometrica* 56(2): 259–93.

Lardy, Nicholos R. 2002. *Integrating China into the Global Economy*. Washington, DC: Brookings Institution Press.

Lipsey, Robert and Fredrik Sjoholm. 2005. "The Impact of Inward FDI on Host Countries: Why Such Different Answers?" in Theodore Moran, Edward Graham, and Magnus Blomstrom, eds. *Does Foreign Direct Investment Promote Development?* pp. 23–43. Washington, DC: Institute for International Economics.

Liu, Pak-Wai, Xin Meng, and Junsen Zhang. 2000. "Sectoral Gender Wage Differentials and Discrimination in the Transitional Chinese Economy." *Journal of Population Economics* 13: 331–52.

Maurer-Fazio, Margaret and James Hughes. 2002. "The Effects of Market Liberalization on the Relative Earnings of Chinese Women." *Journal of Comparative Economics* 30(4): 709–31.

Maurer-Fazio, Margaret, Thomas G. Rawski, and Wei Zhang. 1999. "Inequality in the Rewards for Holding up Half the Sky: Gender Wage Gaps in China's Urban Labour Market, 1988–1994." *The China Journal* 41: 55–88.

Mehmet, Ozay and Akbar Tavakoli. 2003. "Does Foreign Direct Investment Cause a Race to the Bottom?" *Journal of the Asia Pacific Economy* 8(2): 133–56.

de Mello, Luiz R. 1997. "FDI in Developing Countries and Growth: A Selective Survey." *Journal of Development Studies* 34(1): 1–34.

Moulton, Brent R. 1990. "An Illustration of a Pitfall in Estimating the Effects of Aggregate Variables on Micro Units." *Review of Economics and Statistics* 72(2): 334–8.

Neumayer, Eric and Indra De Soysa. 2005. "Trade Openness, Foreign Direct Investment and Child Labor." *World Development* 33(1): 43–63.

National Bureau of Statistics of China (NBS). Various years. *China Statistical Yearbook*. Beijing: China Statistics Press.

Park, Bohm and Keun Lee. 2003. "Comparative Analysis of Foreign Direct Investment in China." *Journal of the Asia Pacific Economy* 8(1): 57–84.

Paus, Eva A. and Michael Robinson. 1998. Globalization and Labour: The Impact of Direct Foreign Investment on Real Wage Developments, 1968–1993. Paper presented at the XXI International Congress of the Latin American Studies Association, Chicago.

Riskin, Carl, Zhao Renwei, and Li Shi. 2001. *China's Retreat from Equality: Distribution and Economic Transition*. Armonk, NY: M. E. Sharpe.

Seguino, Stephanie. 2000a. "Accounting for Gender in Asian Economic Growth." *Feminist Economics* 6(3): 27–58.

———. 2000b. "The Effects of Structural Change and Economic Liberalization on Gender Wage Differentials in South Korea and Taiwan." *Cambridge Journal of Economics* 24(4): 437–59.

Standing, Guy. 1989. "Global Feminization through Flexible Labor." *World Development* 17(7): 1077–96.

———. 1999. "Global Feminization through Flexible Labor: A Theme Revisited." *World Development* 27(3): 583–602.

Svejnar, Jan. 1999. "Labor Markets in the Transitional Central and East European Economies," in Orley Ashenfelter and David Card, eds. *Handbook of Labor Economics*, vol. 3B, pp. 2810–57. Amsterdam: North Hollans/Elsevier.

Summerfield, Gale. 1995. "The Shadow Price of Labour in Export Processing Zones: A Discussion of the Social Value of Employing Women in Export Processing in Mexico and China." *Review of Political Economy* 7(1): 28–42.

Tan, Shen. 2000. "The Relationship between Foreign Enterprises, Local Governments, and Women Migrant Workers in the Pearl River Delta," in Loraine A. West and Yaohui Zhao, eds. *Rural Labor Flows in China*, pp. 292–309. Berkeley: University of California Institute of East Asian Studies.

te Velde, Dirk Willem. 2003. "FDI and Income Inequality in Latin America." London: Overseas Development Institute. http://72.14.253.104/search?q=cache:Kt8giDv86JgJ :www.odi.org.uk/IEDG/Meetings/FDI_feb2003/fdi_la_dwtv.pdf+FDI+and+Income+ Inequality+in+Latin+America&hl=en&gl=us&ct=clnk&cd=1 (accessed December 2005).

Wei, Shang-Jin. 2000. "Why Does China Attract So Little Foreign Direct Investment?" in Takatoshi Ito and Anne O. Krueger, eds. *The Role of Foreign Direct Investment in East Asian Economic Development*, pp. 239–61. Chicago and London: University of Chicago Press.

World Bank. 1997. *China Engaged: Integration with the Global Economy*. Washington, DC: The World Bank.

Yueh, Linda. 2004. "Wage Reforms in China during the 1990s." *Asian Economic Journal* 18(2): 149–64.

GENDERING THE DORMITORY LABOR SYSTEM: PRODUCTION, REPRODUCTION, AND MIGRANT LABOR IN SOUTH CHINA

Pun Ngai

INTRODUCTION

This paper discusses the dormitory labor system, a Chinese labor system through which the international division of labor shapes the lives of women migrant workers. We understand this dormitory labor system as a gendered form of labor use that fuels global production in newly industrialized regions, especially in South China. Since the establishment of four Special Economic Zones (SEZs) in South China in the late 1970s, the new export-oriented industrialized regions, dominated by foreign-invested companies, have relied on the use of migrant laborers, mostly women, who work in the factories and live in the factory dormitories. All companies that employ migrant workers – irrespective of the company's industrial sector and whether it is domestic or foreign-invested – provide accommodation to these workers. By combining work and residence, production and daily reproduction are hence reconfigured for the sake of global capital use, with daily reproduction of labor almost entirely controlled by foreign-invested or privately owned companies.

China's dormitory labor system is not a new arrangement under capitalism; the provision of dormitories for workers has a long history both in Western and Eastern contexts of industrialization (Gail Hershatter 1986; Chris Smith 2003; Chris Smith and Pun Ngai 2006). However, the Chinese dormitory labor system is unique in that dormitories, located on the factory compound or close by, are available to all workers and industries. This widespread availability of factory dormitories facilitates the Chinese labor system's reliance on short-tenure migrant labor. The state still plays a substantial role in shaping Chinese labor markets, regulating labor mobility from rural to urban industrial areas, and providing housing to migrant workers. In most of the newly industrialized towns, the Chinese state provides the dormitories for the factory owners to rent, but some firms build their own dormitories. Housing provision is not for families, so factory owners are not interested in the reproduction of the next generation of laborers. Instead, they focus on maximizing the utilization of temporary, migrant, and contract labor by controlling the daily reproduction of their labor power.

The state does not permit the migrant working class to stay in the city, unless the workers have employment to support their temporary residence. Dormitories not only facilitate the temporary attachment of laborers to companies and the massive circulation of labor, but they also constrain labor mobility since laborers need these attachments to remain in the city. Through the employer's integration of working and living spaces and the state's regulation of migration, wage increases are suppressed and the workday is lengthened. This creates a hybrid, transient workforce that circulates between the factory and countryside and is dominated by employers' control over housing and state controls over residency permits.

Among the waves of internal migrant workers arriving in the industrial cities over the past two decades, young women have been among the first to be picked up by the new export-oriented industries. Young women constitute a high proportion of the factory workers, making up over 70 percent of the total workforce in the garment, toy, and electronics industries (Ching Kwan Lee 1998; Pun Ngai 2005a). Their gender, in addition to their youth and rural migrant status, is an integral part of China's export-led industrialization facilitating production for the world market. This gendered process of proletarianization echoes the feminization of labor use and the growth of new factory-towns under the export-led industrialization model prevalent in Latin America and Asia since the 1960s (Diane Elson and Ruth Pearson 1981; June Nash and

Maria P. Fernández-Kelly 1983; Aihwa Ong 1987; Frederic Deyo 1989; Dorinne Kondo 1990; Lee 1998; Leslie Sklair 2001).

This article draws from a 2003–4 case study of an electronics factory in Shenzhen, Guangdong, in South China to provide a detailed discussion of the operation of the dormitory labor system underlying the booming export-oriented industrial production of China that has been further boosted by its accession into the World Trade Organization. The paper also looks at dormitories as sites of control and resistance and shows how the dormitory labor system simultaneously provides workers with opportunities to resist management practices and achieve some victories in improving working conditions. But, ultimately, the temporary nature of the employment contracts and the workers' disempowered status as temporary urban residents limits their ability to fundamentally challenge the conditions of work and dormitory living.

SITUATING WOMEN IN THE DORMITORY LABOR SYSTEM

China is already well known as a "world factory," attracting transnational corporations (TNCs) from all over the world, especially from Hong Kong, Taiwan, Japan, the US, and Western Europe. Guangdong Province in southern coastal China is an industrial hub for global production. Clothing, textiles, and electronics are the major industries involved in export processing work in China, as in other developing countries. Guangdong is the largest production base for these exports, creating labor-intensive jobs for workers, particularly for women migrant workers in major cities such as Shenzhen, Dongguan, Foshan, Zhongshan, and Guangzhou. The economy of Guangdong grew an average of more than 14 percent per year during the 1990s. In 2006, Guangdong attracted US$14.5 billion in foreign direct investment (FDI), approximately one-fourth of the country's total and a seventeen percent increase from the previous year. Its total trade amounted to US$520 billion, about one-third of the country's total (*China Daily* 2007).

This rapid expansion of export-oriented production was associated with a sharp rise in jobs with private, foreign-owned, and joint-venture enterprises that now dot the coastal cities of China. Since the late 1970s, decollectivization of agriculture has generated a massive labor surplus in rural areas. At the same time, the central government has facilitated an unprecedented surge in internal rural-to-urban migration by partially loosening the restrictions of *hukou*, the household registration system.[1] These changes and the opportunities in the cities have resulted in massive waves of rural–urban migrants, forming a new working class of internal rural migrant laborers (the *dagong* class) in contemporary China (Pun 2005a). Until the early 1990s, the consensus was that the number of floaters was about 70 million nationwide.[2] The Fifth National Population Census of China in 2000 estimated that there were over 120 million internal migrant workers in cities, while other estimates ranged from 100 to 200 million persons (William Lavely 2001: 3; Arianne M. Gaetano and Tamara Jacka 2004; Zai Liang and Ma Zhongdong 2004).[3] In the early 2000s, women constituted a considerable proportion of the rural migrant population, estimated to be around 40 percent of migrants nationally and 60 percent (or 6 million) in the Guangdong region (Ye Zhang 2002).

TNCs and their subcontractors recruit millions of rural migrants to work in China's export-processing industries. In the late 1970s, the development of the SEZs along the southeastern coast was one of the first major economic reforms of the period. Within a few years, similar zones were set up in other parts of China, called export-oriented industrial zones or technology development zones. These zones, similar to export-processing zones in other developing economies, harnessed young workers, particularly unmarried women, who are often the lowest paid and most compliant laborers (see Lee 1998; Pun Ngai 1999, 2005a; Gaetano and Jacka 2004).

These women migrant workers are often called *dagongmei*, a new gendered labor identity produced during the emergence of private and transnational capital in post-socialist China. *Dagongmei* embraces multiple meanings and denotes a new kind of labor relationship fundamentally different from Mao's period. *Dagong* means "working for the boss" or "selling labor," connoting commodification and a capitalist exchange of labor for wages (Pun 2005a). In post-socialist China, labor, especially the alienated (wage) labor that was supposedly emancipated by the Chinese Revolution, is once again sold to the capitalists, and this time under the auspices of the state. Unlike the Maoist working-class *gongren*, "worker," which carried the highest status in the socialist rhetoric of Mao's day, *dagong* signifies a lesser identity – that of a hired hand – in a context shaped by the rise of market factors in labor relations and hierarchy. Both terms – *gongren* and *dagong* – are gender neutral and used for both women and men. The new term, *dagongmei*, however, is specific for young women. *Mei* means younger sister. It denotes not only gender, but also marital status – *mei* is unmarried and young and thus often of a lower status (Pun 2005a).[4]

Why have so many women left their rural homes in search of city-based waged labor? Any rigorous response to this question must unfold along two related levels of analysis. The first level of analysis is structural: owing to the deep rural–urban divide, rural authorities have submitted to the central government's direction and have, thus, agreed to inter-provincial labor cooperation and program initiatives to maximize urban economic growth (Dorothy J. Solinger 1999: 94). Since late 1991, the bordering provinces of Hunan and Guangxi have systematically exported their peasant labor to Guangdong. In exchange, these provinces benefited from remittances sent back by rural migrant workers. This is also the case of the populous, impoverished Sichuan province, which is a considerable distance from Guangdong. Increasing competition in the global market for agricultural products and the resulting adverse price effects due to WTO accession have added to the pressure for out-migration (see Denise Hare, Li Yang, and Daniel Englander [2007] and Junjie Chen and Gale Summerfield [2007] in this volume). As a result, provincial labor policies assure a continuous replenishment of internal migrant laborers to the global-production powerbases in the coastal cities of South China. State initiatives support the labor needs of industry and facilitate labor supply flow to the global production sites. The government's labor-management offices usually screen young, female applicants from inland provinces and arrange for transportation to send rural women directly to the coastal factory sites in return for earning management fees on a per capita basis from the company (Ching Kwan Lee 2007).

The second level of analysis examines the individual and familial level, at which rural people contend with low prices for agricultural products in the post-WTO accession era and limited educational and village-employment opportunities – indeed, these last two challenges are particularly acute for females. Many young rural women have no choice but to begin migrating as *dagongmei* in their late teens. Some rural women also aspire to escape arranged marriages, familial conflicts, and patriarchal oppression. Still others want to widen their horizons and experience modern life and cosmopolitan consumption in cities (Lee 1998; Pun 2005a). In sum, personal decisions in out-migration are heavily mediated and strongly affected by both sociocultural factors and economic concerns.

However, the state usually identifies rural migrants as temporary residents who work in the city and lack a formal urban *hukou*. Although enforcement of the old *hukou* system has relaxed since the late 1990s, the restrictions on welfare benefits, housing, and education of children are still mostly in place and contribute to the exploitative mechanisms of labor appropriation in the cities. This newly forming working class is typically denied permanent roots and legal identities in the city. The *hukou* system and its labor controls construct the ambiguous identity of rural migrant labor while simultaneously deepening and obscuring the economy's exploitation of this huge population. Hence, this subtle and multi-faceted marginalization of a vast swath of the rural labor supply has created a contested, if not a deformed, citizenship that has disadvantaged Chinese migrant workers attempting to transform themselves into urban workers.

Dislocated in the cities, migrant labor is distinguished by its transient nature. China's overall economy, while needing the labor of the rural population, does not need the city-based survival of that population beyond the daily reproduction of the migrant worker. A worker, especially a female worker, will usually spend three to five years as a wage laborer in an industrial city before getting married. Most women have to return to their rural homes to marry because it is difficult to find a partner in the city. Rural communities have long exercised – and have long been expected to exercise – the extended planning of life-cycle activities such as marriage, procreation, and family. Although the costs of daily reproduction of the individual workers are partially borne by the factory while the workers are employed, reproduction of the next generation of labor is left to the rural villages. The cost of reproducing the labor force includes the costs of bearing, rearing, and educating children; healthcare; and eldercare. These activities benefit industrial development in urban areas, and their cost is only partially offset by remittances. As more and more segments of the population have entered the labor force as migrant workers, the dormitory labor system that facilitates this process has become an essential component of the changes in post-socialist China.

FORMATION OF THE CHINESE DORMITORY LABOR SYSTEM

Since the early 1980s, China has refashioned an old form of labor use into a hybrid form of work-residence that aids in the daily reproduction of labor and embodies labor control and resistance. While in the past domestic industries in urban and rural areas and township and village enterprises commonly provided dormitory accommodations for workers from other localities, their provision by factories that produce for the global market is a recent phenomenon. As millions of migrant workers pour into industrial towns and cities, the provision of dormitories has become a necessity for these enterprises.

Factory dormitories were introduced in China in the early twentieth century on a limited scale. In a study of cotton and silk workers in Tianjin from 1900 to the 1940s, Hershatter (1986: 165–6) describes how foreign-owned companies began to introduce dorms to lower costs through the feminization and use of migrant workers. Workers, however, were not willing to stay in company-provided dormitories if they had the choice of living with their relatives or co-villagers in nearby residential areas. As Hershatter points out:

> Had they been able to, the Tianjin millowners would have made the factory a closed environment, serviced by company institutions and secured by company guards. But workers voted with their feet, resisting the attempt to turn housing into a "tool of discipline." (1986: 165)

Dormitories therefore became the preserve of single, migrant women workers, those without family or local connections, and workers were prevented from leaving and locked in at night (Hershatter 1986). A similar study by Emily Honig (1986) of female cotton workers in Shanghai in the 1930s also notes that the contractors hired thugs to guard the dormitories and accompany women workers, even on their holidays and days off, and that women had to share beds and endure sexual abuse from contractors, overcrowding, and poor sanitation.

The prominent labor institution from the socialist period was the *danwei* system. Unlike the pre-Revolution dormitory system, the *danwei* system conferred greater status upon an individual worker. In this system, the state-owned enterprises provided accommodations to workers and their families as a matter of workers' rights.[5] The system was both an economic and social institution set up to provide a long-term commitment to the employees, some of them even providing kindergarten and primary school, medical clinics, and common canteens to the workers and their family members staying in the housing unit.

The decline of the *danwei* system in the 1990s left an institutional vacuum that allowed a remodeled dormitory labor system to develop in the new export-processing zones. The dormitory labor system is hence the hybrid outgrowth of China's global integration combined with the legacies of state socialism. What is striking about today's China is that due to a combination of state controls (the lingering *hukou* system), extensive provision of factory dorms, and shortages of independent accommodation, the dormitory labor system is pervasive. The new *dagong* subjects are not from the local or urban area where workplaces are based, but come as inter-provincial migrants for a temporary sojourn in a factory.

In this reconfigured system, workers' mobility is shaped by two conditions: peasant-workers' "freedom" to sell their labor to global and private capital that is allowed in post-socialist China, and state laws on population and the remaining limits on mobility through the *hukou* system. These laws attempt to restrain workers' freedom of mobility in order to meet the demands of transnational capital as well as China's urban development. This double social conditioning is basically a paradoxical process: the freedom of the rural migrants to work in the industrial urban areas is checked by social constraints preventing their permanent settlement in the cities.

On finishing their labor contracts, which usually last one to two years, the workers must return to their place of birth or find another temporary employment contract (Andrew Walder 1986; Lee 1998; Solinger 1999; Pun 2005a), again to be confined in the dormitory labor system. Factory dormitories thus attract migrant workers for the short term, and accommodation is not the means for cultivating a long-term or protracted relationship between the individual firm and the individual worker, which is the rationale for accommodation in some other paternalistic factory forms elsewhere (Saskia Sassen 1988; Perry 1996).

Under the dormitory labor system, management within foreign-invested or privately owned companies has exceptional control over the workforce. With no access to a home space independent of the enterprise, time spent moving from living space to the shop floor is eliminated and working days are extended to suit production needs. This permits a flexible utilization of labor time and means employers can respond to product demand more readily than in situations where workers' time is regulated by the state or the workers themselves. If, as Karl Marx noted, the "length of the working day fluctuated within boundaries that are physical and social'" (quoted in David Harvey 2001: 108), then employers within this dormitory labor form have the power to extend the length of the workday close to its physical limits. Compared to the "normal" separation between work and home that factory arrangements usually entail, the dormitory labor system exerts greater breadth of control into the working and non-working day of laborers. This contrasts with accommodation arrangements of the pre-reform period, which were not used to prolong working hours.

Dormitories in China's foreign-invested manufacturing plants are communal multi-story buildings that house several hundred workers. Rooms are shared, with typically between eight and twenty workers per room. Washing facilities and toilet facilities are communal and are located between rooms, floors, or whole units, such that the living space is intensely collective, with no area, except that area within the closed curtains of a worker's bunk, available for limited privacy. Women and men are highly segregated in order to control sexual behaviors even though the living conditions of both genders are quite similar. Separated from family, home, and rural life, these women workers concentrate in workspaces and submit to a process of homogenization and individuation since they are taken as "individual workers" by the management, untied from communal bonds, and responsible for their own behavior. And insofar as their connection to the firm is short-term and contractual, more factors contribute to the alienation of workers than simply their separation from ownership of the product or their lack of production skills. The dormitory labor system alienates workers from their pasts and replaces a customary rural setting with factories dominated by unfamiliar others, languages, foods, production methods, and products. The dormitory life makes workers vulnerable to exploitation by employers due to the constraints of the *hukou* system, and the temporary nature of employment dampens workers' interest to fight for better pay and better working conditions.

However, the dormitory is not only a means of labor control and discipline but also provides benefits to employees and even to society. It helps reduce the costs of travel and living expenses, facilitates savings and remittances, and provides a relatively protected environment for young, vulnerable women workers. The isolation of the individual worker is also mitigated to some extent by factories' reliance on kinship and ethnic ties in recruitment and utilization of the migrant labor.

The dormitory labor system operates according to the following strategies of control and domination:

1. The lengthening of the workday results in compression of a "work-life."
2. Employers' divide and rule tactics rely on workers' kinship and ethnic allegiances nourished in the dormitories to extract greater productivity per hour of work and discipline from workers.
3. The system leads to a suppression of wage-increase demands because the rapid circulation of temporary labor makes it more difficult for workers to demand wage increases.
4. Easy access to labor power during the workday facilitates a labor system for just-in-time production and quick-delivery order and distribution systems, increasing profits for the company.
5. Control of the daily reproduction of labor power rests with the factory since accommodation, food, travel, social, and leisure pursuits all occur within a production unit.
6. Employers have direct control over the labor process by relying on a system of labor discipline that imposes penalties on workers not only in the workplace, but also in the dormitory, such as mandating times they may enter or leave the dormitory.
7. The gender hierarchy almost completely overlaps with the supervisory labor-production worker hierarchy, with 80 percent of the production workers being women and factory directors, managers, and most of the foremen being males.
8. State policies that restrict labor mobility and a lack of genuine implementation of labor laws and regulations over the dormitory labor system affect the overall labor process and increase profits for the company.

These characteristics of China's dormitory production systems have undermined any pro-labor policies proposed by the central government. In recent years, the central government has introduced new regulations concerning, for example, minimum wage and working hours. The stated goal underlying these regulations is a unified legal framework for the protection of all workers against exploitation and inhumane treatment. On May 28, 1993, the Standing Committee of the Shenzhen People's Congress passed *The Regulations on Labor Conditions in the Shenzhen Special Economic Zone* in order to institutionalize the labor recruitment system and govern labor relations at both the enterprise and city levels.[6] The notable feature of these regulations is the important labor protection they offer, including minimum wage, working hours, and social insurance for internal migrant workers throughout the city. However, in the course of these government-initiated labor reforms, at least two deficiencies have surfaced. First, labor policies and labor regulations are at best unevenly implemented at the local level. Second, state and collective workers have been hit hard by economic restructuring, leading to the loss of jobs with labor protections (see Jieyu

Liu [2007], in this volume), which further exposes the official lip service paid to labor. Concurrently, as private and foreign capital flows to coastal cities and industrialized zones, competitiveness among TNC factory suppliers and local enterprises has spurred each to try lowering the cost of their just-in-time production while trying to raise the quality of their products. This trend has become especially pronounced since China's accession to the WTO. As a result, employers have become more resistant to enforcing labor regulations and have sought to squeeze more labor out of workers for a given level of labor costs, both of which have been made possible by the dormitory labor system.

A CASE STUDY OF THE DORMITORY LABOR SYSTEM

This section presents a detailed case study of China Elton Electronics (a pseudonym), a joint-venture company owned by a Hong Kong corporation and located in the Shenzhen SEZ. Fieldwork in this factory was conducted in 2003–4 and involved interviews with the factory managers and thirty workers.[7]

Established in 1991, the company was controlled by a Hong Kong director and a few dozen Hong Kong managers, and another hundred Chinese mainland supervisory staff members were in charge of daily management and the operation of production. The company quickly built up a workforce of more than 4,500 workers, which was the size of the company during my fieldwork in 2003. Most workers were migrants from other parts of China, and approximately 70 percent were women. With production orders from mainly Japanese and Korean brand buyers such as Sony and Samsung, China Elton produced high-tech electronic devices such as mobile phones, MP3 players, voice speakers, and other consumer electronic goods. China Elton had a position at the high end of the global production chain; it had three subcontractors, one in the Shanghai region and another two outside the Shenzhen SEZ in the Pearl River Delta, that provided parts such as LD screens or other electronic components to China Elton. The company also subcontracted final processing and packaging jobs to other small local producers located in small towns in Guangdong and Jiangxi. China Elton achieved lower costs of production through subcontracting upstream production and packaging operations, since land and labor were cheaper and more easily available for the local subcontractors in inland China.

According to its upper management, from its inception, China Elton aspired to build the most advanced and modern enterprise in Shenzhen, outshining the thousands of other plants in the same sector. To attract its huge investment of RMB 30 million (US$3.7 million) in the early 1990s, the local government granted China Elton privileges on land resources, facilities, and telecommunications; flexible practices on import/export of raw materials and products; tax exemption; and other incentives. The company was able to survive in severe global competition by introducing modern management models and a modern factory space conducive to high productivity. The managers were proud of building what they perceived to be a new "factory empire" in China, something physically grand and magnificent. Located in the most expensive part of the Shenzhen SEZ, initially the factory consisted of two three-story buildings housing the production facilities, machines, raw materials, and final products, with an attached administrative block for general management, meetings, and research and design purposes. In addition, there were dormitories that housed the male and female workers separately.

The workers migrated from villages or towns all over the country, including Guangdong, Guangxi, Hunan, Huibei, Sichuan, Jiangxi, Anhui, and Guizhou. In 2003, approximately 70 percent of the workers were women, and most were between 20 and 26 years of age, with the youngest being 17 and the oldest 42. At the time, China Elton employed most workers for about two to three years. The production workers were paid on an hourly rate averaging about RMB 3.3 (US$0.40) per hour for regularly scheduled hours and RMB 4.2 (US$0.50) for overtime, and they were paid an average monthly wage of between RMB 900–1,000 (US$110–124), which includes overtime work. These were typical earnings for production workers in Shenzhen in 2003, but substantially higher than what the mainly rural workers could earn in farming or off-farm work in their local areas. However, the overtime rate was below that stipulated by law, which is supposed to be 150 percent the regular rate in evenings and 200 percent on weekends.[8]

The working day involved ten to twelve hours per day – eight hours at regular pay (RMB 3.3 per hour) and two to four hours at overtime pay (RMB 4.2), six days per week. This means that the regular workweek at China Elton was between sixty and seventy-two hours, far exceeding the legal workweek in China. The Chinese Labor Law, which went into effect on January 1, 1995, stipulates that a five-day workweek should not exceed forty hours and that overtime work must be limited to a maximum of thirty-six hours per month. At China Elton, except for public holidays, it was difficult to get time off even for illness. The supervisory, technical, managerial, and office staff were paid on monthly rates, with an average salary of RMB 1,500–2,000 (US$185–247).

Physical space and working conditions in China Elton were better than in other electronics factories, especially those located outside the Shenzhen SEZ, but also better than the conditions in the region's garment factories that employ large numbers of women workers.[9] Nonetheless, many women respondents complained that they were not treated well and that as dagongmei they shared the common fate of having less power and resources to fight unfavorable working conditions. They complained about long work hours and working conditions in general, but as long as they were paid regularly and compensated for overtime – even though the overtime rate was below the legal requirement – workers would not resist. Another common complaint was that it was difficult to quit because the factory kept two months of workers' salaries as a deposit, which the workers would forfeit if they left the workplace without formal approval. Yet getting formal approval to leave was difficult: China Elton had a quota for job resignations, and every month the workers hoping to resign exceeded that number, which meant many workers had to wait three to six months to get approval.

And there were also few protections for workers on the job. There were no workplace codes of conduct in China Elton.[10] As was the case in most factories, there weren't any government agencies to enforce China's labor laws at China Elton. The Labor Bureau would take some action to investigate only if there were serious violations of the law and they received many complaints from workers.

China Elton invested a further RMB 10 million to build new dormitories in 1995 in order to upgrade the company image with visiting clients and because the living conditions of workers had become part of the international labor monitoring system (Pun Ngai 2005b). Empire-like, the dormitory compound stood like a housing estate in 2003, with four buildings for workers and one building for managers. These five buildings were enclosed by a long wall and a giant iron gate. There was a small side door that was open twenty-four hours and watched over by security guards. Inside the compound, there were two open areas for workers' recreational activities such as playing badminton and basketball, and there were a few tables and several dozen chairs at another corner where workers could chat and eat. A shop adjacent to two huge dining halls was crowded with workers in the evening, most of whom were watching TV programs. The dining halls could each seat one thousand workers. Workers had to pay RMB 50 each month for accommodation and RMB 3 for each meal. Even though the workers consider this to be a reasonable cost for basic living expenses, the workers had no other choice even if they would like to live or eat outside the factory compound. There was also a clinic and a reading room located on the ground floor of the managers' building that the workers could use.

A hierarchy of accommodation existed that reflected the segmentation of labor force according to status and gender. There were huge differences in the provisions for the predominantly male Hong Kong managers, Mainland Chinese managerial staff, and technical and clerical staff and the remaining, predominantly female, production workers. The managers' building was divided into three-bedroom flats, with a dining room, kitchen, toilet, and bathroom. These flats were well furnished with TV sets, refrigerators, air conditioners, and cooking and bathing facilities. The male director and each of the male Hong Kong managers were provided with their own flats, while between three and six Mainland assistant managers, foremen and technicians, and general staff shared a flat. The dormitory for the workers was a hospital-like structure composed of similar-sized rooms, with a shared toilet in each room, and a common room for hot water provision on each floor. Each dormitory room housed eight to twelve production workers, with men and women living in separate areas. Living and sanitary conditions were generally poor. The workers were not provided with their own storage space for their clothes and personal belongings, which they had to hang over their beds. Fans were installed, but many of them were out of order and never repaired. Spatial differences and hierarchies were built into the workplace and crystallized through the labor process and dormitory provisions and hence nurtured workers' consciousness of class and gender differences in the workplace.

Given the sheer size of the China Elton workforce, the management relied on meticulous controls over the dormitory life of the women workers. There were more than twenty regulations relating to sleeping, eating, bathing, and leaving the dormitory compound, each with associated punishments. The major regulations were as follows:

Dormitory Regulations
1. Dormitory conditions shall be kept clean and sanitary. A room found dirty will be fined RMB 10.
2. Spitting will incur a fine of RMB 10 if seen in the dormitory compound.
3. No noise is allowed after midnight. Everybody has to keep quiet once they enter the dormitory rooms. Those caught being noisy after midnight will be penalized.
4. No argument or fighting is allowed. Those found fighting in the compound will be dismissed at once.
5. Dormitory facilities shall be protected. Anyone who has caused malicious damage will be penalized and dismissed.
6. Stealing dormitory property or residents' property will result in dismissal.
7. No visitors are allowed to stay overnight. If overnight visitors are caught, a fine of RMB 100 will be imposed.
8. Except for night-shift work or in times of emergency, nobody is allowed to enter or leave the compound after 12 a.m.
9. Identity cards have to be carried at all times in the compound. If lost, the person will be charged RMB 20.
10. No cooking or eating is allowed in the rooms. Secretly cooking will mean a penalty of RMB 20.
11. Nobody is allowed to independently change his or her bunk. If they do so, a penalty of RMB 50 will be incurred.

The company expected these strict disciplinary rules, which were posted throughout the dormitory buildings, to cultivate a better quality workforce with more, in their terms, "civilized" attitudes and a good work ethic because only those who were able to put up with the strict discipline of the dormitory and, by implication the workplace discipline, were able to retain their jobs. Two Facilities Managers, responsible for managing accommodation and food provisions, justified the dormitory discipline in the following terms:

> We provide regular inspections in workers' dormitories, and we have no choice but to keep discipline as strict as possible; otherwise, how could we control 4,000 workers?

> We won't allow workers to wander around in the street at midnight. For male workers, it will be too easy for them to create trouble, [and they would have] no spirit to work in the daytime. For female workers, it is unsafe for them to be outside the dormitory compound at midnight. They need protection.

"Protection" was often used to rationalize control and punishment of women. The paternalistic concern over the female workers' private time implied prolonged management control in a way not possible where there is a separation between home and work. Dormitory techniques of power were central to the extraction of labor from workers. The entire ethic of the dormitory system was not just to impose severe discipline and punishment but also to create a discourse on self-discipline, which was often emphasized at the workplace. Self-management of dormitory rooms was expected so that the workers could learn how to behave themselves as proper, in the management's language, "modern" workers. This dormitory system exemplified what Michel Foucault (1977) described as internalized surveillance, deploying a series of disciplinary rules as well as subtle surveillance and meticulous self-supervision of everyday lives. In short, creating a well-trained, disciplined female workforce directed to the maximization of output is what I call "the political technology" of the dormitory labor system.

THE DORMITORY AS A SITE FOR STRUGGLE

Despite its systemic and near-total domination of laborers' lives, the Chinese dormitory labor system also opens up space for struggle and resistance. In female dorms, workers manipulate their dormitory space for their own uses. Overcrowding and intensive human interaction might cause conflicts among workers, but being together – sharing a "common fate" – also closely nests their working lives. Intensive contact allows women workers to share information on promotion, skills, wages, and strategies for job hopping. In the face of management abuses, the women also share grievances with each other and sometimes come up with acts of defiance or even collective action. The dormitory constitutes a gendered place, one that generates emotional links and sisterhood among female workers, thus meriting careful analysis. In the dormitories, the women workers – already aligned along gender lines – further cluster themselves along kinship and ethnic lines that link to widespread networks outside the workplace setting. These kinship and ethnic networks benefit industrial capital by strengthening the recruitment, training, and disciplining of the labor force. For example, every kin and ethnic group has "big" sisters to take care of their members. These big sisters usually have more skills or experience working in the factory and help train their kin and ethnic groups in order to help them adjust to factory life as quickly as possible. Management also uses ethnic and kinship networks to intensify labor by organizing women workers along kinship and *tongxiang* (co-villagers) networks. For example, workers from Hunan or Sichuan group themselves in the production line as well as in the dormitory. This facilitates management's control over workers by using divide and rule tactics. The senior management picks certain kin or *tongxiang* groups as model groups and rewards them in order to fuel competition among workers. The basis of competition is a quota that each production line has to secure. At the end of each day, the volume of the product made in the line is written on the board to promote future competition among production lines on the shop floor. The production line that exceeds the quota is rewarded with a one-time bonus that is calculated on a weekly basis.

However, these same networks also facilitate migration flows, job searches, and the circulation of work information and strengthen workers' capacity to cope with factory life and the hardships of the city (Pun 2005a). Employers' reliance on these networks to enhance the training of workers, upgrade workers' skills, and accelerate workers' acceptance of factory life translates into a mechanism that simultaneously gives rise to workers' exploration of collective force. Contrary to the view that a collective workers' spirit stems solely from class-based factors, this same spirit among China's mostly female migrant workers reveals the powerful influence of kinship, ethnicity, and gender (Honig 1986; Elizabeth Perry 1993; Anita Chan 2001, 2003; Pun 2005a).

Hence, contradictions exist within the dormitory labor system. Workers and employers both rely on networks that frequently work at cross purposes. There are forms of intensive intimacy and solidarity that, by building bonds among workers, interfere with management's control over workers' lives on the shop floor and in the dormitories. Workers also participate in localized dormitory networks that generate intensive information exchanges about external job opportunities and thereby create and strengthen workers' mobility power (Smith and Pun 2006).

Operating from their dormitories, workers who find themselves in the midst of a crisis or a strike easily transform these soft supports – the kinship networks, the ethnic enclaves, the spirit of sisterhood, and the personal relationships – into resources for industrial struggle. In a number of cases, I recorded the presence of petition letters that circulated from dorm to dorm, easily collecting many signatures. The relative ease with which workers could use the dorm setting to organize their common cause against management derives in large measure from the limited space that dormitories offer the opponents of collective action. Workers efficiently and spontaneously organize themselves to strike, receiving little or no formal organizational help from trade unions or labor organizations. The integration of workspace and living space that, in the dormitory labor system, is necessary for accumulation, in turn works in favor of collective worker organization by accelerating consensus building and strategy development. One strike I observed in 2003 was against the potential relocation of the factory. The strike was first led by six hundred workers, who were laid off on very short notice, but then gained support from most of the remaining workers, who worried that further removal of production lines would affect them.[11] All of the meetings were convened at the open area of the dormitory buildings. The one-week strike in March 2003 resulted in partial success, with most of the laid-off workers receiving overtime payments that were owed by the company, though still at a rate lower than stipulated by Chinese labor law. However, the labor leaders were all forced to quit their jobs, and none of them struggled to stay for further protests. Though it facilitates workers' mobilization and class consciousness, the dormitory space provides little protection for the leaders to continue their struggles. Nonetheless, spontaneous strikes of migrant workers in China have been mounted since the late 1990s, which is a topic that is very much under-researched. These spontaneous protests could prove a powerful means for bringing about improvements in working conditions.

CONCLUSION

In China, the dormitory labor system is embedded in an increasingly globalized context, reinforcing a new international division of labor that coincides with China's accession to the WTO. This labor system, by the very nature of its existence, helps articulate a challenge to the claim that by entering the WTO, China would ensure its working class a better life. Globalization has created more jobs and more opportunities for rural migrant workers, whose lives have been adversely affected by competition in the global market for agricultural products, and some rural women feel that factory work is the only way to generate cash income and contribute economically to their families. Quite predictably, these workers have entered the urban manufacturing world, encompassed by the dormitory labor system. As a consequence, they are subject to an exploitative employment system that is attached to the jobs.

In this article, I discussed how the employers' use of dormitory labor, linking labor migration and labor reproduction, serves global production. The costs of daily labor reproduction of the individual workers are largely undertaken by the dormitory system that subsidizes the living cost of labor in terms of wages, accommodation, and consumption, and makes cheap workers available for production for the global market. The dormitory labor system contributes to maximizing production and profits through the efficient control of mostly female migrant labor while generating hidden costs for the reproduction of the labor force, physical strain of long hours without sick days, incidences of abuse, and psychological pressures relating to relocation and isolation borne by the migrant women workers. The situation has deteriorated further now that local governments within China compete for foreign investment and thus openly neglect the labor regulations and the social provisions of China's local, provincial, and national governments (Pun 2005b).

The routine provision of dormitories for internal migrant labor facilitates the continuous access to fresh labor reserves from the countryside. The dormitory labor system concentrates labor, nurturing workers' consciousness in the face of acute exploitation by capital; but through the high turnover of a transitory semi-proletarianized class's labor power, it also inhibits the workers' ability to remain long enough to form a stable working-class community. No doubt the dormitory labor system, in concentrating and yet circulating labor, provides the basis for nurturing class consciousness and facilitating class actions in the future.

This new working class has to struggle for improved conditions on two fronts: At the State level, the migrant workers struggle to gain rights to urban citizenship in order to settle in the industrial cities and towns and create their own working-class community. Against employers, the workers need to look for alternate ways of organizing since traditional trade union struggle is not effective in the dormitory labor system in China. Dormitory-based organizing along gender lines that generates sisterhood solidarity among workers may well be one of the alternatives.

Pun Ngai, Hong Kong University of Science and Technology,
Division of Social Science, Rm 3364, Academic Building,
Clear Water Bay, Hong Kong, China
e-mail: sonpun@ust.hk

ACKNOWLEDGMENTS

I would like to acknowledge that the fieldwork studies for this paper were supported by the Hong Kong Research Grant Council for the project, "Living with Global Capitalism: Labor Control and Resistance through the Dormitory Labor System in China" (2003–5). I would also like to thank Chan Wai-ling, an Executive Board member of the Chinese Working Women Network for providing research assistance.

NOTES

1 The *hukou* system requires every Chinese citizen to be recorded with the registration authority at birth, and have his or her residential categorization (either urban or rural) fixed. The mother's *hukou* rather than birthplace decides the location, so a mother with a rural *hukou* can only give her children a rural *hukou*, even if the children were born in the city and their father is an urban resident. Citizenship benefits are tied to one's *hukou*, which can only be changed through government authorization (Dorothy J. Solinger 1999). The system is designed to prevent unplanned urbanization and overcrowding, which is typical of developing countries that lack statutory internal "passport" or "citizenship" controls. Its downside is that rural residents are cut off from benefits of urban residency, creating an urban class of noncitizens. Pressure to change the system is growing and there have already been experiments with eliminating the *hukou* system (Ye Zhang 2002: 32).

2 Floaters refer to migrant workers who move from one location to another either on a short-term or long-term basis, having departed from their registered place of residence without a corresponding transfer of *hukou*.

3 The variation is explained by the different definitions of migrant workers used by researchers and the difficulty of counting people who are transient and may work only part of the year in the city.

4 The Chinese media commonly uses the term *dagongzai* for male migrant workers, which indicates that they do dirty and dangerous work and implies lower status.

5 Workers and their families were provided with life-long accommodation, properly housed in an apartment unit, and hence the urban working class was considered the most privileged class in China. Irrespective of gender or marital status, both male and female employees were provided with apartment units of various sizes. Usually the accommodation buildings were adjacent to production buildings, circled by an architecture of factory and housing estate.

6 *Shenzhen jingji tequ laowugong tiaoli* (Regulations on Labor Conditions in the Shenzhen Special Economic Zone) (1993) defines *laowugong* (temporary hired labor) as those who work in Shenzhen without local permanent residential household status (Article 2). Residents of Hong Kong SAR, Macau SAR, and Taiwan, Province of China, as well as foreign nationals working in the Shenzhen SEZ, are not covered by the regulations on labor conditions (Article 53).

7 This case study is part of a larger field study I conducted in Pearl River Delta from 2003–5 for the project, "Living with Global Capitalism: Labor Control and Resistance through the Dormitory Labor System in China."

8 Thus, instead of being remunerated at RMB 4.9 on the evenings and RMB 6.6 on Saturdays, workers were paid at RMB 4.2 for overtime.

9 A report of ten small-to-medium sized garment factories, by Jenny Chan and Karin Mak (2005), released by the Chinese Working Women Network, a local labor NGO, shows that women workers' wages were below the legal minimum wage and deferral

of wage payments was frequently observed. The workforce of these factories ranges from fifty to 200 people, over 70 percent of which are female workers, primarily young girls in their late teens and middle-aged married women. The smaller factories mainly owned by small subcontractors, who are mainland Chinese from Guangdong and neighboring coastal provinces, have particularly poor working conditions.

10 Contrary to the clothing industry and despite a strong computer campaign organized internationally by NGOs to enforce it, corporate codes of conduct at the workplace are still not a common practice for the electronics industry. The adoption of an international monitoring system in China became a trend for TNCs such as Levi Strauss, Nike, Reebok, The Gap, and others in the late 1990s. The introduction of corporate codes became part of these companies' strategic policies in securing the sale of their goods and services on the global market. Internal monitoring of subcontractors or suppliers by the companies' representatives on a regular basis is the usual case, although sometimes independent monitoring involving invited academics, auditors, and/or NGOs is used to enhance credibility. Corporate codes of conduct have yet to be fully implemented in major economic zones of the Pearl River and Yangtze River deltas in Southeast China. Corruption, false statements and records, and cover-ups are quite common.

11 In March 2003, the factory started to lay off workers when their contracts expired. The 600 workers were laid off immediately after the Chinese New Year holiday, when workers had returned from their hometowns. Without any advance notice or preparation, the 600 workers were asked to leave the factory and the dormitory compound immediately and were provided with only one month's salary in compensation.

REFERENCES

Chan, Anita. 2001. *China's Workers Under Assault: The Exploitation of Labor in a Globalizing Economy.* New York: M. E. Sharpe.

——. 2003. "A 'Race to the Bottom': Globalization and China's Labor Standards." *China Perspectives* 46: 41–9.

Chan, Jenny and Karin Mak. 2005. "Overview of China's Garment Industry." http://cwwn.org/eng/eng_main.html (accessed March 2007).

Chen, Junjie and Gale Summerfield. 2007. "Gender and Rural Reforms in China: A Case Study of Population Control and Land Rights Policies in Northern Liaoning." *Feminist Economics* 13(3/4): 63–92.

China Daily. 2007. "Guangdong Notches Up $520b FDI," March 2. http://www.china daily.com.cn/china/2007-03/02/content_817482.htm (accessed April 2007).

Deyo, Frederic. 1989. *Beneath the Miracle: Labor Subordination in the New Asian Industrialism.* Berkeley: University of California Press.

Elson, Diane and Ruth Pearson. 1981. "The Subordination of Women and the Internationalization of Factory Production," in Kate Young, Carol Wolkowitz, and Roslyn McCullagh, eds. *Of Marriage and the Market*, pp. 18–40. London: Routledge & Kegan Paul.

Foucault, Michel. 1977. *Discipline and Punish: The Birth of the Prison.* New York: Vintage Books.

Gaetano, Arianne M. and Tamara Jacka, eds. 2004. *On the Move: Women in Rural-to-Urban Migration in Contemporary China.* New York: Columbia University Press.

Hare, Denise, Li Yang, and Daniel Englander. "Land Management in Rural China and its Gender Implications." *Feminist Economics* 13(3/4): 35–61.

Harvey, David. 2001. *Spaces of Capital: Towards a Critical Geography.* London: Routledge.

Hershatter, Gail. 1986. *The Workers of Tianjin, 1900–1949.* Palo Alto, CA: Stanford University Press.

Honig, Emily. 1986. *Sisters and Strangers: Women in the Shanghai Cotton Mills, 1919–1949.* Palo Alto, CA: Stanford University Press.

Kondo, Dorinne. 1990. *Crafting Selves: Power, Gender and Discourses of Identity in a Japanese Workplace.* Chicago: University of Chicago Press.

Lavely, William. 2001. "First Impressions of the 2000 Census of China." *Population and Development Review* 27(4): 755–69.

Lee, Ching Kwan. 1998. *Gender and the South China Miracle: Two Worlds of Factory Women.* Berkeley: University of California Press.

——, ed. 2007. *Working in China: Ethnographies of Labor and Workplace Transformations.* London: Routledge.

Liang, Zai and Ma Zhongdong. 2004. "China's Floating Population: New Evidence from the 2000 Census." *Population and Development Review* 30(3): 467–88.

Liu, Jieyu. 2007. "Gender Dynamics and Redundancy in Urban China." *Feminist Economics* 13(3/4): 125–58.

Nash, June and Maria P. Fernández-Kelly, eds. 1983. *Women, Men, and the International Division of Labor.* Albany: State University of New York Press.

Ong, Aihwa. 1987. *Spirits of Resistance and Capitalist Discipline: Factory Women in Malaysia.* Albany: State University of New York Press.

Perry, Elizabeth. 1993. *Shanghai on Strike: The Politics of Chinese Labor.* Palo Alto, CA: Stanford University Press.

——, ed. 1996. *Putting Class in Its Place: Worker Identities in East Asia.* Berkeley: Institute of East Asia Studies, University of California.

Pun Ngai. 1999. "Becoming *Dagongmei*: The Politics of Identity and Difference in Reform China." *The China Journal* 42: 1–19.

——. 2005a. *Made in China: Women Factory Workers in a Global Workplace.* Durham, NC and Hong Kong: Duke University Press and Hong Kong University Press.

——. 2005b. "Global Production, Company Codes of Conduct, and Labor Conditions in China: A Case Study of Two Factories." *The China Journal* 54: 101–13.

Sassen, Saskia. 1988. *The Mobility of Labor and Capital: A Study in International Investment and Labor Flow.* London: Cambridge University Press.

Sklair, Leslie. 2001. *The Transnational Capitalist Class.* Oxford: Blackwell.

Smith, Chris. 2003. "Living at Work: Management Control and the Dormitory Labour System in China." *Asia Pacific Journal of Management* 20(3): 333–58.

Smith, Chris and Pun Ngai. 2006. "The Dormitory Labor Regime in China as a Site for Control and Resistance." *International Journal of Human Resource Management* 17(8): 1456–70.

Solinger, Dorothy J. 1999. *Contesting Citizenship in Urban China.* Berkeley: University of California Press.

Walder, Andrew. 1986. *Communist Neo-Traditionalism: Work and Authority in Chinese Industry.* Berkeley: University of California Press.

Zhang, Ye. 2002. "Hope for China's Migrant Women Workers." *China Business Review* 29(3): 30–6.

Zhongguo laodong he shehuibaozhang nianjian [China Labor and Social Security Yearbook]. 1994–2004.

Chinese Women after the Accession to the World Trade Organization: A Legal Perspective on Women's Labor Rights

Julien Burda

INTRODUCTION

The creation of the World Trade Organization (WTO) in 1995 was one of the most important events in the international arena since the founding of the United Nations (UN) in 1945. Free trade has grown in dominance over the last sixty years, resulting in the expansion of global trade, the increase in foreign capital flows, and the elimination of many domestic economic and regulatory barriers to trade. These trends have been supported by the creation of a new international organization dedicated to international trade in 1995: the WTO. The purpose of the WTO and its core foundations, the WTO Agreements, is to provide legal ground rules for the liberalization of international trade flows of goods, services, and intellectual property rights. The WTO is an international forum where trading states come to negotiate mutually agreed upon concessions. The WTO is also the place where member states settle trade and commercial disputes arising among them. The Dispute Settlement Mechanism offers an efficient tool to settle disputes through a neutral procedure based on a specific agreement, thereby reducing barriers to international trade.

However, the WTO is often seen as the incarnation of uncontrolled globalization that has particularly adverse effects on men and women in developing countries. Although trade is presumed to be gender-neutral, the liberalization process affects men and women differently. Indeed, trade liberalization does not occur without adjustment costs. The obligation to remove tariffs and quotas exposes previously protected sectors to international competition and opens new areas up to exchange. Such trade policies are likely to produce major changes in employment, price, income, and consumption patterns. They are also likely to have gender-differentiated effects, because women and men have different access to resources and have different roles in both the market economy and the household (Lori Pennay 2000).

China provides a very good example for examining the impact of changes in trade policies on women's labor rights. Indeed, the country's accession to the WTO marked an important event in China's current development. After a long period of negotiations, China acceded to the WTO in 2001 (Sylvia Rodhes and John H. Jackson 1999; Yang Guohua and Cheng Jin 2001; Karen Halverson 2004). The extent of its commitments is unprecedented. China agreed, for instance, to lower tariffs from 24.6 percent in 1997 to 9.4 percent by 2005 and to abolish all quotas and discriminatory taxes in industrial sectors (Nicholas R. Lardy 2002). The openness of the Chinese market to foreign products exposed its industry to international competition and has had some consequences for social and labor conditions. The rapid growth of export-oriented industrial production and the massive rural–urban migration have led to working conditions, especially in the industrial sector, that are in many instances characterized by a lack of respect for China's labor laws and international commitments. Even when properly followed, China's national laws and international commitments do not protect workers against forced labor and do not provide independent union rights. While export-oriented production in foreign-invested firms often offers better employment conditions than smaller, domestic private firms, working conditions can be problematic and unsafe. Thus, the objective of this contribution is to underline the negative consequences of China's accession to the WTO on women and to address the question of what can be done in the post-WTO world.

There are, of course, various views on what could be done. Some scholars, for instance, call for a reevaluation of world politics in order to consider the situation and particular interests of women (Ann Tickner 2001). At the same time, feminist legal scholars have drawn attention to the masculine approach in both international law and international economic law (Liane Jarvis 2000). They take the position that norms, institutions, and concepts in the international legal framework should be analyzed from a gendered perspective in order to highlight the male assumptions embedded in the international legal framework (Shelley Wright 1995; Anne Orford 1998; Christine Chinkin and Hillary Charlesworth 2000; Celestine Nyamu 2000; Sundhya Pahuja 2000; Barbara Stark 2000; Mary Childs 2002; Ratna Kapur 2002; Eugenia McGill 2004). At the international level, a variety of international and regional bodies such as the Fourth World Conference on Women held in Beijing, China in 1995; the United Nations Conference on Trade and Development; the United Nations Human Rights bodies; the Asia-Pacific Economic Cooperation; and civil society groups have called for gender and social assessments of trade agreements.

This contribution aims to assess the different solutions that could be used in order to improve Chinese women's working conditions.[1] This paper does not highlight the positive or negative aspects of trade liberalization on Chinese women, as Pun Ngai (2007) and other articles in this volume precisely address these effects. Instead, it begins by underlining the fact that Chinese national and international social obligations are not sufficiently applied in a way that would substantially improve the situation of Chinese women. This paper then goes on to explore the legal mechanisms for improvements within the framework of WTO law. Presently, there is no social clause included within the WTO agreements that would allow a WTO member not to apply WTO provisions when labor rights are violated by another member. Thus, when considering the legal mechanisms, one must first assess both the possibility of and the opportunities for imposing trade sanctions to put pressure on Chinese government so it will implement its legal commitments on labor standards. In order to be justified under WTO law, trade sanctions would have to fulfill some stringent conditions, and even so, sanctions may not be the right approach. For that reason, this paper focuses on another approach that consists of offering trade incentives to those states that respect fundamental principles and rights at work. This broader approach would rely on both vertical and horizontal cooperation among states, international organizations, private companies, and civil society.

CHINESE LAW AND THE IMPACT OF TRADE LIBERALIZATION ON WOMEN'S RIGHTS

The implications of WTO accession on Chinese women's lives

Since the late 1970's, China's economy has seen a remarkable transformation. This transformation has also had an impact on the world economy, as China's transition has been accentuated by a very high and rapidly increasing degree of openness to trade due to the accession to the WTO. As Nicholas R. Lardy states:

China is the best example of the positive connection between openness and economic growth. Reforms in China transformed it from a highly protected market to perhaps the most open emerging market economy by the time it came into the World Trade Organization at the end of 2001. (2003: 13)

There is now no doubt that the accession to the WTO has had social consequences for China, especially for working women. The number of Chinese working women is currently more than 330 million, accounting for 46.7 percent of the total working population in the country, most of whom are working in the agricultural or industrial sectors, especially the garment industry (Mark Williams, Kong Yuk-Choi, and Yan Shen 2002). In its report on the challenge of China's WTO entry for Chinese women in the agricultural and industrial sector, The UN Development Programme (UNDP 2003) underlined the impact of accession on their working conditions.

In the industrial sector, Chinese women have had to face new working conditions since accession to the WTO. Women tend to work in the most labor-intensive sectors. According to the 2003 UNDP report, they accounted for 40 percent of the industrial workforce in 1996 and were highly concentrated in garments and textiles industries: 75.8 percent of garment workers and 67 percent of textile workers were women. Women also tend to be concentrated in activities characterized by high turnover, while men are more likely to be working in low-turnover areas. Recent studies have focused on the city of Shenzhen, where most of the garment and electronics industries are concentrated. In this city, over 90 percent of the total labor force is female and under 25 years of age (Pun Ngai 2004). In 1980, Shenzhen was a small city with 310,000 residents and less than 30,000 workers. At the end of 2000, the total population had increased to 4.33 million and its labor force was 3.09 million. The majority of workers were migrant laborers from rural areas who are not recognized as citizens of Shenzhen because of the China's Household Registration System, *hukou*. As Pun notes:

The economic 'take-off' of Shenzhen and the advancement of its position in the global economy is particularly dependent on the extraction of female labor from the rural areas. The process of "globalizing" Shenzhen depends on female labor, which is the cheapest and most compliant labor, in the development of export-processing industries. (2004: 3)

Because of the *hukou* system, working women are not citizens of the city of Shenzhen and most of them are thus accommodated in the workers' dormitories provided by their employers, within or close to the factories. This dormitory labor system provides employers with absolute control over women's labor time and living spaces, leading to a new form of exploitative labor regime where basic labor rights are not respected (Chris Smith 2003). The dormitory labor system serves as "a highly paternalistic, coercive, and intensive production system, in which workers' lives are dominated by employers, and working time is more closely under the control of employers than in systems where working life and home life are separated" (Chris Smith and Pun Ngai 2006: 1456). These authors cite the example of Shenzhen's China Wonder Electronics. At this company, women between the ages of 22 and 26 represent 70 percent of working women. Women are expected to work twelve hours per day, seven days a week – much more than the Chinese legal rate of forty hours per week. The thirty hours of overtime work is, in general, not well paid (about 4.2 RMB per hour), considering the rate for normal work (3.3 RMB per hour).[2] Unfortunately, women have no choice but to accept these poor working conditions. In light of this evidence, it could be said that this form of labor matches the definition of forced labor given by the International Labour Organization (ILO) Convention (n. 29) on forced labor, which covers "all work or service which is exacted from any person under the menace of any penalty and for which the said person has not offered himself voluntary." Convention (n. 105) also prohibits the use of forced labor as a method of mobilizing and using labor for the purpose of economic development or as a means of labor discipline. In the dormitories, women also face delicate or risky working conditions, like in Shenzhen where some 42.7 percent of the 9,585 industrial enterprises (involving at least 116,000 workers) are situated in a toxic or dangerous working environment (Pun 2004: 13).

Though there is some diversity in labor conditions in the industrial sector – in which foreign-invested firms are generally doing better than national and smaller firms – the dormitory labor system is one example of the possible negative impact that trade liberalization has on Chinese women's lives. Additional negative impacts have been brought to light in other studies that have shown that working conditions of some Chinese women threaten their life or health. Many Chinese women over-work at the expense of their health, suffering from malnutrition and poor eyesight, especially those who work in electronics plants (Jane Dwasi 1999: 386). Occupational accidents and exposure to toxins also cause the injury or death of Chinese women at work. For example, the lack of adequate safety workplace supervision has resulted in factory fires in which women were the majority of the victims (Jude Howell 1997: 239). But aside from the resulting physical and health disabilities, Chinese women workers suffer spiritual damage from being forced to separate from their families, having few support groups in the cities, or enduring sexual harassment (Ulric Killion 2004).

Because of the opening of the economy, companies in China now face greater international competition. Labor costs play a major role, so Chinese companies may be tempted to enter into a kind of "race to the bottom" and not to apply labor rights (like wage and hour legislation or health and safety protection) in order to remain competitive (Michael J. Trebilcock and Robert Howse 1999: 454). In developing or emerging economies, core labor standards are often viewed as costly for export-oriented industries, which may thus be tempted to voluntarily degrade working conditions in order to increase their exports. National governments may also be tempted to deny core labor standards both to expand exports and to attract foreign direct investment (Robert J. Flanagan 2006). In that sense, trade liberalization and accession to the WTO have contradictory effects on women's lives and labor standards. One should recognize that trade liberalization may create new opportunities for women, even in developing or emerging countries (Hildegunn Nordas 2003). But even if export-manufacturing jobs offer a chance for a better life than that in rural China, the increasing world competition leads to the denial of labor rights in some export-oriented industries.

The improvement of Chinese women's working conditions relies firstly upon the implementation of national and international social standards. The liberalization of international trade should be deeply linked with the strict application of labor rights, in order to achieve the "social dimension of globalization."[3] As Bernhard G. Gunter and Rolph van der Hoeven have underlined it, social dimension of globalization refers to "the impact of globalization on the life and work of people, on their families and their societies." They write:

> Concern is often raised about the impact of globalization on employment, working conditions, income and social protection. Beyond the world of work, the social dimension includes security, culture and identity, inclusion or exclusion from society and the cohesiveness of families and communities. (2004: 8)

Chinese Legislation on Women's Rights

In recent years, China has made some visible efforts to answer the critics of its numerous human rights violations, but recent efforts to improve the situation of women by increasing economic and social reforms have had mixed results (Christine Bulger 2000: 345).

From a legislative point of view, China attaches great importance to the protection of women. Article 48 of the Constitution of the People's Republic of China prohibits gender-based offenses. It underlines the fact that Chinese women enjoy equal rights with men in all spheres of life – political, economic, cultural, social, and familial. Article 48 also underlines that the state protects the rights and interests of women, applies the principle of equal pay for equal work for men and women alike, and trains and selects cadres from among women.[4] The principles established by the Constitution of the People's Republic of China have led to the promulgation of more than ten fundamental laws, encompassing electoral, marriage, civil, and criminal law. The most important one, from a legal-feminist perspective, appears to be the *Law of People's Republic on China on the Protection of Rights and Interests of Women* of 1992.[5] Article 1 of this law aims at safeguarding women's legitimate rights and interests and at promoting gender equality. Article 2, like Article 48 of the People's Constitution, specifies that women shall enjoy the same rights as men in all spheres of life. Thus, all kinds of discrimination against women appear to be prohibited.

The protection of women in the workplace is also reaffirmed in this law. Articles 21 and 22 of the 1992 *Law on the Protection of Rights and Interests of Women* insist on equality by decreeing that men and women enjoy the same right to work and that no unit should refuse to hire women or set a higher threshold for hiring women on the sheer basis of sex. This equality also includes the right to be employed and to work, to get equal income for equal work, and to equal treatment concerning housing assignments, material benefits, and remuneration. Under Article 24, there must be no discrimination against women when it comes to promotions or skills assessments. Article 25 intends to protect women's safety and health at work and includes a specific provision saying women should not be assigned any work or labor that is unsuitable for them.[6] Finally, Article 27 states that the state should develop social insurance for old, sick, and disabled women. Other Chinese legislation, like the Women Workers and Employees' Labor Protection Regulations (Labor Protection Regulations)[7] or the *Labor Law*,[8] provides the legal basis for challenging the gendered discriminatory behaviors of employers (women and men shall enjoy equal rights with respect to employment; women may not be refused employment because of their sex; and furthermore, equal pay shall be given for equal work). According to these provisions, Chinese working women seem to be legally protected in the workplace.

At the international level, the ILO is often seen as the international organization dedicated to the protection of social rights. Since its creation after World War I, the ILO adopted a large number of conventions and recommendations in order to ensure an effective protection and promotion of worker's rights. In 1998, the ILO adopted an important Declaration on Fundamental Principles and Rights at Work to reaffirm the basic obligations of every Member State: all ILO member states – regardless of political regime, economic development, and cultural values – have to respect, promote, and realize four fundamental principles and rights at work. These fundamental labor rights are the freedom of association and effective recognition of the right to collective bargaining, the elimination of all forms of forced labor, the effective abolition of child labor, and the elimination of discrimination in respect to employment and occupation. Of the 187 ILO Conventions, eight embody these fundamental rights and principles emphasized in the Declaration and comprise the ILO's core labor standards.[9] However, to date China has only ratified four of the eight fundamental conventions, neglecting four that address forced labor (C. 29 and C. 105) and freedom of association (C. 87 and C. 97).[10]

Though China is now linked by twenty-four ILO conventions,[11] without these additional four fundamental conventions, China's commitment regarding the fundamental principles and rights at work remain incomplete. Like the other ILO members that have not ratified all the fundamental conventions, however, China has an obligation arising from its membership in the ILO to respect, promote, and realize, in good faith and in accordance with its own Constitution, the principles concerning the fundamental rights that are the subject of those Conventions. By virtue of its membership, China must take action to promote the freedom of association and the effective abolition of forced labor.

With respect to women's social rights, China ratified the Convention on the Elimination of All Forms of Discrimination against Women (CEDAW) in 1980, but is still not linked by some other important ILO conventions, like the Convention on Labor Inspection (1947: n. 81). This convention aims to secure the enforcement of the legal provisions relating to conditions of work. If China had ratified this convention, it would have been obligated to enact national measures related to hours, wages, safety, and health and would have had to maintain a system of labor inspection in industrial workplaces. According to this convention, labor inspectors are empowered to freely enter any workplace, without previous notice and at any hour of the day or night, to carry out any examination, test, or inquiry they may consider necessary in order to verify that the legal provisions related to conditions of work are strictly observed.

Even if China has made some steps during the last decades toward the adoption or implementation of labor rights – for instance, China ratified the Convention n. 111 on Discrimination (Employment and Occupation – 1958) in 2006 – its international and national commitments remain unable to ensure the effective protection of Chinese women. This is mainly due to the lack of efficient enforcement mechanisms at both national and international levels (Robert Howse and Brian Langille, with Julien Burda 2006: 160), but also to a lack of real political will to do so (Bulger 2000: 345). As with many areas of law in China, there is a huge and sometimes widening gap between the theory and the implementation of the law. China does possess comprehensive laws and regulations for the protection and the promotion of women's rights at work, but few details are given on what the legal requirements actually are and how to implement those requirements, which is in direct contrast to the relatively clear clauses on forbidden work.[12]

Considering the consequences of accession to the WTO, it now seems essential to enforce these basic human and labor rights in China. Therefore, the purpose of this contribution is to assess whether it is possible to use the WTO itself to pressure the Chinese government to implement all of the fundamental labor rights for women. Such a question invites us to examine whether human and labor rights may find a place within the scope of the WTO and may be improved through the globalization process.

WTO, CORE LABOR STANDARDS, AND TRADE SANCTIONS: IS THERE A RIGHT APPROACH?

WTO and the social clause: The missing link

The question of the interaction between international trade and labor rights – and more generally speaking, between trade and human rights – recurs throughout the literature (Steve Charnovitz 1987: 568). In the field, social dumping – meaning offering less regulation and lower social protection in order to encourage inflows of capital – and the introduction of a social clause appears to be a constant issue. It is often asked whether a social clause in the WTO agreements would be an effective tool for improving working conditions. Most of the support for a social clause relies on positions adopted by northern governments or northern trade unions (Nilüfer Çağatay 1996). Proponents consider the social clause to be a "win–win" solution for workers both in the North and the South. They argue that the application of labor rights would lead to the improvement of working conditions in the South. They believe that the application of the core labor standards would also lead to an increase in the costs of labor and the price of exports from developing countries, thereby reducing their attractiveness to Northern companies. But other studies have challenged this traditional view about the merits of social clauses. Some have argued that a social clause would lead to loss of jobs in developing countries (Naila Kabeer 2004). Moreover, they argue that paid employment in export industries is often hidden in homes or small workshops, at the end of a subcontracting chain. As working women are generally more likely to be employed on a temporary or part-time basis, and in workplaces hidden from those monitoring working conditions, opponents assert that a social clause would therefore not be useful (Chakravarthi Raghavan 1996). Others have underlined the fact that a social clause would only target exporting countries and impose new restrictions on international trade (Gijsbert Van Liemt 1989).

From a WTO point of view, the question of the integration of a social clause seems to have reached a conclusion. The debate about this clause was first introduced in 1945 during the negotiation of the Havana Charter that created the stillborn International Trade Organization (UN 1947, 1948). One of the most significant elements of this charter was Article 7 on "Fair Labor Standards," which was a real social clause (Elissa Alben 2001: 1431) that sets up a link between trade and labor standards in order to ensure "fair" liberalization; however, the Havana Charter was not ratified. Only its residual, the GATT – the General Agreement on Tariffs and Trade of 1947 – came into effect, but no social clause was integrated into that text. Some propositions were subsequently put forward by the US and the European Union between 1947 and 1995 (Howse and Langille with Burda 2006: 177).[13] But considering the opposition by developing countries – which feared loss of their comparative advantage and argued that a social clause was a kind of disguised protectionism – no agreement could be reached. As a result, there is still no social clause within the WTO. The final point in the debate about a possible social clause was reached during the December 1996 WTO Ministerial meeting held in Singapore (Virginia Leary 1997). The WTO members rejected the idea of a social clause within the WTO agreements, but decided to renew their commitment to the observance of the internationally recognized core labor standards, which must be set by the ILO, the international competent body. WTO members objected to the use of the labor standards for protectionist purposes, pointing out that the comparative advantage of countries, particularly low-wage developing countries, must not be threatened. The Singapore Declaration constitutes the WTO's first official text that makes an explicit mention of the core labor standards, even though it states that the WTO is not the proper institution to deal with them. From the WTO's perspective, the ILO remains the competent body, thus there is no more discussion about such a clause at the WTO.

The absence of a social clause has an important consequence: member states are not entitled to suspend the application of their WTO obligations by imposing trade sanctions because of the violation of labor rights. In other words, trade sanctions imposed by the WTO in order to put pressure on another member that does not respect these rights, are prima facie illegal, unless they are justified by one of the exceptions. The question, then, is whether it would be possible to use some of the exceptions provided by the GATT in order to justify such trade sanctions imposed for the improvement of labor rights.

Trade sanctions and their possible justification under GATT's general exceptions

The prohibition of the use of force is nowadays the cornerstone of contemporary international law. But this prohibition increases the importance of trade sanctions, which are currently viewed as the most effective tool to fight, in a peaceful way, against violations of international law in general, and human or labor rights in particular. But since 1994 and the creation of the WTO, trade sanctions have been prohibited in order to strengthen the multilateral trading system. This prompts the question: would it be possible to impose trade sanctions against another WTO member that does not respect women's social rights? Considering the purpose of this article, would it be possible to impose trade sanctions against China in order to improve the working conditions of Chinese women? The question would therefore be to know whether such sanctions could be justified under the exceptions provided by the WTO agreements (invoking the violation of non-WTO law like ILO obligations).

It seems that several provisions of the GATT (for instance, the principles of non-discrimination, dumping, safeguard, and subsidies) may not be successfully invoked in order to justify such unilateral actions (Federico Lenzerini 2001: 298). Therefore, if a member would like to impose trade sanctions against China because it does not apply the core labor standards, it would have to invoke one of the general exceptions of the GATT (Article XX). This measure could, for instance, restrict or ban the importation of Chinese goods because they are made under unfair social conditions or, more generally, because China does not apply the core labor standards.

Article XX of the GATT contains a limited number of provisions that may be invoked in order to justify some limitations or restrictions to international trade. However, one should first underline the fact that Article XX contains no specific provisions for women but concerns the protection of public morals (XX a); the protection of human, animal, or plant life or health (XX b); and the products of prison labor (XX e). But these exceptions could be interpreted in a manner that takes women's interests into consideration. In this paper, I propose to assess whether it would be possible to justify trade sanctions against a WTO member by using one of these specific exceptions.

Some scholars have argued that Article XX (a) might be invoked to justify trade sanctions against products that involve the use of child labor and to address the lack of women's fundamental rights and more generally the denial of core labor standards (Steve Charnovitz 1998; Christopher Fedderson 1998; Jarvis 2000). Until recently, the expression of public morals had not been considered in dispute settlement and its scope was not clear. But in a recent gambling case (US – *Measures Affecting the Cross-Border Supply of Gambling and Betting Services, Antigua and Barbuda vs. United States of America*), a WTO panel has interpreted the term "public morals" for the first time. In 2000, a US Court sentenced Jay Cohen, a US national, for selling gambling services to US citizens from the island of Antigua, in violation of the 1961 Wire Communications Act. Antigua brought the case to the WTO, arguing that the US violated its commitments under the General Agreement on Trade in Services (GATS), as the US agreed not to impose restrictions on the importation of recreational services, which includes the free flow of cross-border gambling services. Thus, the WTO Panel found a violation of Article XIV of the GATS. But the US invoked the escape clause for trade restrictions necessary to protect public morals of GATS Article XIV (a) and explained that gambling may be linked to money laundering and organized crime. The panel defined the phrase "public morals" as standards of right and wrong conduct maintained by or on behalf of a community or nation and ruled in favor of the US (WTO 2004c). Therefore, we assume that the core labor standards – and of course the protection of women at work – possess the element of generality or universality inherent to the notion of public morals.

In addition to the protection of public morals, some labor-rights-related trade sanctions might also be justified under Article XX (b), which refers to measures "necessary" to protect human life and health. And there is no doubt that some Chinese women are facing working conditions that threaten their life or health. Thus, in my view, public morals and health and life exceptions may be invoked in order to defend restrictions to imports of products made by Chinese women. But to be justified under Article XX (a) or (b), social-related measures must pass two tests. The first is the necessity test: the contested measure must be shown to be necessary for the purposes in question. The second is a test of good faith established by the "chapeau" (preamble) of Article XX.

Considering the necessity test, the WTO Korea Beef case (Korea – *Measures Affecting Imports of Fresh, Chilled and Frozen Beef, United States of America and Australia vs. Korea*) stated in 2000 that a measure is considered necessary either if it is "indispensable" for achieving an objective or if it bears a close relation to the objective (even if not indispensable) and its impact on trade is not disproportional (WTO 2000: § 161).[14] The Appellate Body thus created the so-called "necessity test" according to which three conditions must be met. First, the relative importance of the common interests or values that the law or regulation to be enforced is intended to protect must be taken into account: "the more vital or important those common interests or values are, the easier it would be to accept as 'necessary' a measure designed as an enforcement instrument" (WTO 2000: § 162). I would argue that the protection or improvement of women's rights in China and elsewhere constitutes a common interest or value. Second, the contested measure should contribute to the realization of the end pursued. And finally, the restrictive impact of the measure on trade must be assessed (WTO 2000: § 163). The determination of whether a measure is necessary under Article XX (b) involves a process of "weighing and balancing a series of factors" in every case, such as the contribution made by the compliance measure to the enforcement of the law, the importance of the values protected by that law, and the accompanying impact of the law on imports or exports (WTO 2000: § 164). According to this standard, one may argue that less trade-restrictive alternatives to trade sanctions are available. For example, the ILO could take direct action, or a process of social labeling could provide viable alternatives to sanctions. The trade sanction measure would then not be compatible with the provision of the GATT. However, even if these alternatives are available, the real issue is whether they are effective and feasible of these alternatives.

Consider now the second test – the test of good faith – the Appellate Body ruled in the Shrimp-Turtles Case that the contested measure must not constitute a disguised restriction on international trade or a means of arbitrary or unjustifiable discrimination between countries where the same conditions prevail.[15] This means that the contested measures should not be imposed for protectionist purposes. In conclusion, from a legalistic point of view, I would argue that social-related trade sanctions could be imposed on China and justified under Article XX (a) and (b) even if such a case has not yet come up before the WTO Appellate Body.

The last provision that could be invoked is Article XX (e), which provides an exception for the products of prison labor. This article deals with the conditions under which some products are manufactured. There are two opposing views about the scope of the provision. On the one hand, some authors adopt a very narrow interpretation of prison labor, in order to limit its invocation (Eric Robert 1996: 160). On the other hand, some scholars plead for an extension of the scope of Article XX (e) in order to include all kinds of involuntary labor and to protect human and labor rights (Patricia Stirling 1996: 38; Lenzerini 2001: 301). I would say that some of the situations faced by Chinese women are close to forced labor or slavery, like in the Chinese dorms. One should not forget that, these days, the prohibition of slavery constitutes a customary rule of international law, linking all the states of the world, even if they are not WTO members. These international customary rules might also be taken into account for the interpretation of the scope of Article XX (e).[16] But for the moment, the

Appellate Body has never addressed this question, as Article XX (e) has never been invoked by a WTO member in order to justify trade restrictions for reasons of social considerations.

Based on the above legal discussion, social-related trade sanctions against China remain possible if imposed without protectionist objectives. The remaining question is whether such an approach is desirable to improve women's labor rights in China. On the one hand, China is now one of the most powerful trading countries in the world. Considering the gains resulting from the Chinese accession to the WTO for all members, one should – unfortunately – assume that they might feel reluctant to impose trade sanctions just because of the current situation of human and labor rights there. Even if such sanctions are possible in legal terms, they would be difficult to impose in practical and political terms.

On the other hand, there is the issue of the effectiveness of trade sanctions for improving labor rights. Some scholars, like Kimberly Ann Elliott and Richard B. Freeman, have shown that trade sanctions imposed for foreign policy reasons have mixed results. Their study of empirical data underlines the fact that trade sanctions "succeed in some situations not in others" (Elliott and Freeman 2003: 80). Trade sanctions may discourage developing countries from engaging in a constructive dialogue on trade and labor rights. Some authors argue that trade sanctions often do not work (Robert Pape 1997, 1998). Rather than improving social conditions in the targeted country, they may have adverse social consequences for those who lose their export-related jobs (Philip Von Schöppenthau 2001). Trade sanctions may also block social progress instead of promoting it. Considering the situation of women in China, trade sanctions could have a negative effect on working women, especially those employed in export-related jobs in dormitory factories.

One should therefore argue that trade sanctions, even if possible, are perhaps not the right approach. In my view, the improvement of labor rights in China may need to rely on an incentive approach.

The Generalized System of Preferences and labor rights: The incentive approach

Implementation of basic human and labor rights is not a condition for accession to the WTO. However, members could be tempted to use Article XIII of the agreement establishing the WTO in order to pursue social objectives. Article XIII provides an "opt-out" provision, which allows a member to decide – without any justification – not to apply the agreements vis-à-vis a new member. This article has been invoked several times by the US against Moldavia, Kyrgyzstan, Georgia, and Mongolia because of their political regimes (Zdenek Drabek and Mark Bacchetta 2004: 1994). This provision appears to be a kind of mix between a repressive and an incentive approach. It could be seen as a trade sanction because the new member will not benefit from the advantages offered by the member state that invoked Article XIII. But it could also be viewed as a way to put pressure on a member seeking WTO membership during the accession negotiation to adopt another policy. The opt-out provision could therefore be used against a member that does not respect fundamental rights (Janell M. Diller and David A. Levy 1997: 686).

However, the effectiveness of this suspension depends on the number and economic power of members that decide to suspend the application of the agreements. Thus, some scholars have argued the Chinese accession to the WTO was a good opportunity for the US to invoke this "opt-out" provision mostly because of Section 402 of the Trade Act of 1974 (the so-called Jackson–Vanik Amendment), which establishes a scheme to determine whether the US may grant nondiscriminatory treatment to communist countries (Rodhes and Jackson 1999: 502). The threat of using Article XIII during China's negotiations for WTO accession could have focused on the state of human and labor rights in the country. However, no Member state invoked Article XIII against China, most likely because of the economic gains expected from China's accession.

Another possibility would be the use of a more traditional incentive approach by developed countries in their trade with developing countries. Countries such as the US and the EU have adopted the Generalized System of Preferences (GSP), which consists of extending extra market access privileges for developing countries. The European GSP unilateral scheme established in 1971 granted tariff preferences without counterpart to developing countries. Accordingly, in specific products, the scheme provided a complete suspension or reduction of the tariff rate. In 2001, the EU decided to develop a new GSP scheme.[17] The scheme created two arrangements. The first one was general; it was granted to all developing countries. According to the second arrangement, specific preferences – additional tariff reductions – were then granted on the basis of the implementation of specific non-commercial policies, such as the implementation of human and labor rights, the protection of the environment, or the fight against drug production and trafficking. The GSP program was thus established to pressure developing countries into implementing specific policies in order to obtain more economic advantages.

In 2002, India decided to challenge this scheme, as it was not one of the beneficiaries of the specific arrangement. In the recent GSP Case (EC – *Conditions for the Granting of Tariff Preferences to Developing Countries, India vs. EC*), the WTO Appellate Body had to decide whether developed countries are allowed to treat developing countries respecting core labor standards differently than those that do not respect the standards (WTO 2004a). India argued that the use of the GSP to discriminate among WTO members based on non-commercial conditions – the respect of the core labor standards – was inconsistent with GATT's Article I. This article contains the famous "most favored nation clause," which requires a member state to extend one specific advantage to all WTO members.

In its report, the Appellate Body ruled that the European Communities are entitled to establish a regime based on the implementation of labor rights (WTO 2004a: §§ 181–2), but they then have the obligation of treating all the countries that are effectively respecting labor rights in a similar way. Indeed, the non-discrimination principle entails treating developing countries alike. If distinctions between developing countries may be established, identical treatment must be accorded to all that are "similarly situated." And the Appellate Body added that the similarity of the situation must be established on the basis of "objective criteria," which refers, for instance, to the ratification or implementation of an international agreement (WTO 2004a: § 183). Such objective criteria could rely on ILO reports assessing the implementation of labor rights in a specific country. The GSP case is one of the WTO's most important decisions. It ruled that the GSP scheme, based on an incentive approach, is in conformity with WTO law if it relies upon objective criteria. This case opens the door for the improvement of basic labor rights on the basis of trade incentives.

The other question is whether China would be entitled to benefit from the GSP regime. Is it possible to consider China a developing country? Presently, there is no definition of a developing country at the WTO, and every member state remains entitled to consider itself one. If China were considered a developing country, it could benefit from a GSP scheme and be pressured to implement labor rights in order to gain economic advantages. Whether China needs further incentives, when it is the dominant exporter in most labor-intensive products is an open question. The GSP scheme could be an effective tool in improving labor standards in poor, small exporters, rather than China.

One should not forget that this approach relies on the sovereign will of developed countries, which remain free to create such a regime. The US and the EU are the only WTO members that have created such GSP schemes. The unilateral character of this approach constitutes its major limit. Another critic, Sandra Polaski, points out a disadvantage of this incentive scheme: developing countries often face difficulties in the improvement of their basic social obligations, and trade privileges can be withdrawn for such failures (2006: 922). Other approaches, such as bilateral agreements could therefore be used.

The former US–Cambodia Textile Agreement reached in January 1999 and extended through 2004, was a very good example of this alternative solution. Based on a positive, incentive approach, it allowed Cambodia to earn an extra quota each year if it demonstrated that it was making progress in the improvement of working conditions and the support of workers'

270

rights in the garment industry. Part of the US–Cambodia Textile Agreement included factory monitoring by the ILO through the Better Factories Cambodia project. The ILO, the Cambodian government, and Cambodian garment manufacturers launched this monitoring initiative in 2000. Over 200 Cambodian garment factories agreed to register with the Better Factories Cambodia project. According to the Memorandum of Understanding signed jointly by the ILO and the participating factories, each registered manufacturer agreed to provide ILO monitors with full access to the factory. ILO monitors were to interact freely with shop stewards, union representatives, and factory workers, both inside and outside of the factory premises (Kevin Kolben 2004). Because Cambodia demonstrated that working conditions and labor rights in the garment industry were largely in compliance with internationally recognized labor standards, it received an additional 12 percent bonus between 2002 and 2003 (Sandra Polaski 2003: 21) and a 14 percent quota bonus in 2004. Such initiatives are of utmost importance because the January 2005 expiration of the Multi-Fiber Arrangement that protected markets for small textiles and clothing exporter countries through preferences and quotas could have hurt Cambodia's exports. Instead, 30,000 new jobs were created in the Cambodian garment industry between 2005 and 2006, most likely because of Cambodia's reputation for compliance with ILO's core labor standards (Better Factories Cambodia 2006). As Robert Zoellick, the former US Trade Representative, noted, this agreement was "an excellent example of the way trade agreements lead to economic growth and promote a great respect for workers rights" (2001).

Nonetheless, this example of cooperation among the state, an international organization, and industry suggests that unilateral actions solely taken by developed countries are a slow route to improving labor rights. In my view, the improvement of labor rights should rely upon a more global approach, including both the threat of trade sanctions and incentive initiatives like the GSP, and establishing links among international organizations, states, and the civil society (i.e., nongovernmental organizations [NGOs]).

THE NEED FOR HORIZONTAL AND VERTICAL COOPERATION: ESTABLISHING A NEW LINK?

The improvement of labor rights requires strong cooperation among international organizations in order to ensure the social dimension to globalization. In 1996, the members of the WTO declared, "the WTO and ILO Secretariats will continue their existing collaboration" (WTO 1996b: point 4). But more than ten years after the Singapore Declaration, this collaboration remains weak. Existing collaboration between the two organizations is limited to participation by the WTO in meetings of ILO bodies and the exchange of documentation and informal cooperation between the secretariats.

In my view, the collaboration should be deeper and could be based, for instance, on a formal agreement. Some scholars have proposed the creation of a joint "ILO – GATT panel" in order to address the question of collective trade sanctions when core labor standards are repeatedly violated (Daniel Ehrenberg 1996a, 1996b). Accordingly, the ILO would establish the existence of the violation, and the WTO, using its Dispute Settlement Mechanism, would impose sanctions. Unfortunately, states are still not ready to create such a joint-mechanism between the two organizations (Ehrenberg 1996a). But this proposition could be seen as the basis for a more general reflection on the role that the international organizations could play in order to improve labor rights. In my view, the cooperation should integrate not only the ILO and the WTO, but also other international organizations dealing with human rights and economic development, such as the UN Commission on Human Rights (UNCHR), UNICEF, the UN Conference on Trade and Development (UNCTAD), the UNDP, the International Monetary Fund (IMF), and the World Bank (Dukgeun Ahn 2000).[18] The UNDP already plays a major role in China. Since 1979, "UNDP has completed over 900 projects, assisting in a diverse set of fields ranging from agriculture to industry to energy to public health to poverty alleviation to economic restructuring, and many more in-between" (Sustainable Forest Management in China n.d.). The UNDP works closely with international organizations located in China, like the ILO or the International Monetary Fund. Similarly, the ILO launched a series of research programs in cooperation with several other international organizations. One program, entitled "Combating Trafficking in Children and Women" pursuing the end of the trafficking and labor exploitation of children and women and the elimination of child labor, is based on a close collaboration between the ILO, the UN Inter-Agency Project (UNIAP) on Human Trafficking in the Greater Mekong Sub-region, and the International Organization of Migration. Such initiatives show that horizontal collaboration among international organizations is critical for the improvement of women's labor rights in China. But this partnership will not be effective without vertical collaboration, including the participation of civil society and private actors.

NGOs play an important role at the national level, where they can provide several types of assistance (financial, technical, and educational). One of the most important women's organizations in China, the All-China Women's Federation (ACWF), established in April 1949, is a "quasi-official" organization with a broad reach. It works to unite and educate women, to safeguard their rights and interests, and to promote gender equality in China. It has also cooperated with other international organizations like UNICEF, the UNDP, and other NGOs in various projects for poverty reduction, health, women's interests and rights, and other related areas. As the ACWF states:

> To date, over 1000 projects have been completed mainly scattered in ethnic group areas and poor mountainous regions throughout China's 31 provinces, municipalities and autonomous regions. Around one million people are directly involved in these projects and indirect beneficiaries exceed ten million. (ACWF 2000)

In developed countries, NGOs can broaden the public's awareness of the poor conditions faced by women industrial workers in China and could initiate the creation of a social label so as to convince consumers to boycott Chinese products made by women under unfair social conditions. This would also pressure the Chinese government to apply fundamental labor rights. For example, the Women Working Worldwide, a small voluntary organization based in the UK, is working with a global network of women worker organizations to support women's rights. Since the mid-1990s Women Working Worldwide has been helping to coordinate a campaign called Labor Behind the Label, the UK platform of the Clean Clothes Campaign. The purpose of this campaign is to support workers in the globalized garment industry and to pressure foreign companies to stop exploiting women. Other initiatives have been taken by NGOs like the Fair Labor Association, which is monitoring labor standards in clothing factories for major buyers and putting pressure on companies to implement labor laws in the countries of operation.

While such initiatives seem useful, it is quite difficult to assess the extent to which they are working. One of the main problems of NGO-driven initiatives is their fragmented character. In my view, their activities should be accompanied by actions at the international level, where NGOs can play a role in pressuring governments during the decision-making process. At the WTO, however, NGOs have little power, even though the General Council clarified the framework for relations with NGOs by adopting a set of guidelines in July 1996. NGOs are now allowed to attend the plenary sessions of the ministerial conferences every two years if they demonstrate that their activities are concerned with matters related to those of the WTO. More than 150 NGOs attended the first Ministerial Conference held in Singapore in 1996. At the 2005 Hong Kong Ministerial Conference, more than 600 NGOs were invited to attend the discussions. But, this participation remains quite limited. NGOs are not involved in the decision-making process and do not participate in negotiations. Even though they are invited to submit papers, which are posted on the WTO website, NGO representatives cannot have a real influence during the negotiation. According to Howse and Langille "rather than recognizing the role NGOs could play within the WTO, the guidelines merely recognize the role NGOs can play to increase the awareness of the public in respect of

WTO activities" (2006: 227). For the moment, WTO Members seem very reluctant to increase their influence in this organization: "It must continue to be recognized that the primary responsibility for engaging civil society in trade policy matters rests with the Members themselves" (WTO 2004b: 47).

In the view of some scholars, the role of the NGOs should be strengthened (Ernesto Hernández-López 2001). The NGOs acting for the promotion of women's rights should play a greater role at the WTO. They could not only present information on the impact of the trade liberalization on women's lives but also introduce propositions on women's labor rights for the WTOs. A dialog among international organizations and civil society must be established because NGOs now constitute an unavoidable interlocutor at the international level.

CONCLUSION AND PERSPECTIVES

In contrast to much of the writing on core labor standards, this contribution is based upon legal analyses in an attempt to bring to light some elements of what is possible, practical, and desirable in terms of WTO law. In my view, the liberalization of international trade creates new economic opportunities. But, as the UN Millennium Declaration stated, "the central challenge we face today is to ensure that globalization becomes a positive force for all the world's people. For while globalization offers great opportunities, at present its benefits are very unevenly shared, while its costs are unevenly distributed" (UN 2000). More than ten years after the creation of the WTO, it is now time to strive for adding a social dimension to globalization.

In my view, the WTO is not the best forum to discuss the social implications of globalization. The women's rights problem in China or elsewhere cannot be solved exclusively within the WTO, as it was created to liberalize international trade. But WTO, is an international organization that submits to international law and therefore should become more deferential to international human and labor rights law. The ILO appears to be the competent body for dealing with labor standards, as it was created for the protection of labor rights and promotion of social justice. Trade sanctions, even if they fulfilled the stringent conditions to be justified under the WTO law, do not appear to be the best strategy for improving labor rights. The incentive approach, based not only on the GSP scheme but also on bilateral agreements, seems to be, by contrast, a better solution. In my view, the improvement of women's labor rights in China will largely depend upon a global and multilateral approach, including better vertical and horizontal cooperation among other international organizations (i.e., the ILO, the IMF, the World Bank, and the UN and its agencies) and the civil society, where NGOs will have a major role to play in the coming years. Any use of the GSP scheme or bilateral trade agreements must be situated in such a broad framework of cooperation.

Because gender equality is central to the full implementation of social and basic human rights, it is also a condition for international peace based on social justice. The situation of working women in China provides a good example of the problems the international community will have to face during the twenty-first century. Accession to the WTO has accelerated the "occidentalization" of China, leading to a great transformation of its economic system, and maybe of its political regime. This new "Great March of China" to economic, political, and social liberalization and reforms should be viewed as a true chance for the implementation of women's labor rights.

Julien Burda, Graduate Institute of International Studies (IUHEI),
International Law Section, 132 rue de Lausanne, Geneva 1211, Switzerland,
e-mail: burda2@hei.unige.ch

ACKNOWLEDGMENTS

The author would like to thank the guest editors and all the participants at the workshop held at Rice University (March 2006) for their useful comments.

NOTES

1. Even if the proposed solutions could benefit men as well, the example of Chinese women is very relevant when assessing the impact of globalization in China. As trade policies are likely to produce major changes in employment, price, income, and consumption patterns, they are also likely to have gender-differentiated effects in China. Chinese women and men have different access to resources. They have different roles in both the market economy and the household as well.

2. In Chinese, "Renminbi" (RMB) means "People's Currency." The current exchange rate with the US Dollar: US$1 equals about 8 yuan (RMB).

3. In 2002, the ILO created the World Commission on the Social Dimension of Globalization. This commission was initiated to respond to the needs of people as they cope with the unprecedented changes that globalization has brought to their lives, their families, and the societies in which they live. See the World Commission web site: http://www.ilo.org/public/english/fairglobalization/origin/index.htm (accessed January 2007).

4. The Constitution of the People's Republic of China (*Zhonghua renmin gongheguo xianfa*) was adopted at the Fifth Session of the Fifth National People's Congress and Promulgated for Implementation by the Proclamation of the National People's Congress on December 4, 1982. The Constitution was amended at the First Session of the Seventh National People's Congress on April 12, 1988 and again at the First Session of the Seventh National People's Congress on March 29, 1993.

5. The *Law of the People's Republic of China for the Protection of Rights and Interests of Women* (*Funu quanyi baozhangfa*) was adopted at the Fifth Session of the Seventh National People's Congress on April 3, 1992, promulgated by Order N. 58 of the President of

the People's Republic of China on April 3, 1992, and became effective on October 1, 1992.

6 Under Chinese labor law, some work is considered unsuitable for women. It is, for instance, forbidden to arrange poisonous or harmful underground work for women workers at mines; to engage women workers in work high above the ground, under low temperatures, or in cold water during their menstrual periods; and to engage women in physically demanding work during pregnancy or while breastfeeding babies less than a year old (See Articles 59 – 62 of the *Labor Law of the People's Republic of China* of 1994).

7 *Regulations Governing Labor Protection for Women Staff Members and Workers* (*Nuzigong laodong baohu guiding*), September 1, 1988.

8 The *Labor Law of the People's Republic of China* of 1994 was adopted at the Eighth Meeting of the Standing Committee of the Eighth National People's Congress on July 5, 1994 and became effective on January 1, 1995.

9 C.87 on Freedom of Association and Protection of the Right to Organize, 1948; C.98 on the Right to Orgzanize and Collective Bargaining, 1949; C. 29 on Forced Labour, 1930; C.105 on the Abolition of Forced Labour, 1957; C.111 on Discrimination (Employment and Occupation), 1958; C.100 on Equal Remuneration, 1951; C.138 on Minimum Age, 1973; and C.182 on Worst Forms of Child Labour Convention, 1999.

10 See the ILOLEX webpage as the source for ratification of ILO conventions: www.ilo.org/public/english/standards/index.htm (accessed January 2007).

11 C.7 Minimum Age (Sea), 1920; C.11 Right of Association (Agriculture), 1921; C.14 Weekly Rest (Industry), 1921; C.15 Minimum Age (Trimmers and Stokers), 1921; C.16 Medical Examination of Young Persons (Sea), 1921; C.19 Equality of Treatment (Accident Compensation), 1925; C.22 Seamen's Articles of Agreement, 1926; C.23 Repatriation of Seamen, 1926; C.26 Minimum Wage-Fixing Machinery, 1928; C. 27 Marking of Weight (Packages Transported by Vessels), 1929; C.32 Protection against Accidents (Dockers) (Revised), 1932; C.45 Underground Work (Women), 1935; C.59 Minimum Age (Industry) (Revised), 1937; C.80 Final Articles Revision, 1946; C.100 Equal Remuneration, 1951; C.111 on Discrimination (Employment and Occupation), 1958; C.144 Tripartite Consultation (International Labor Standards), 1976; C.159 Vocational Rehabilitation and Employment (Disabled Persons), 1983; C.170 Chemicals, 1990; C.122 Employment Policy, 1964; C.138 Minimum Age, 1973; C.150 Labor Administration, 1978; C.167 Safety and Health in Construction; C.182 Worst Forms of Child Labor, 1999.

12 As underlined before, forbidden works are those unsuitable for women under Chinese Labor Law. See note 6.

13 See, for instance, the US attempt to integrate such a clause within the GATT, *US Commission on Foreign Economic Policy*, Staff Papers 437 – 38 (1954). See also the 1983 and 1986 propositions of the European Parliament: *Resolution on the Delineation and Further Development of GATT and of the Free Trade Principle Underlying the GATT System and Possible Consequences for the EEC and GATT* (OJ C 322, 28/11/1983, p. 281) and the *Resolution on the New Round of Multilateral Trade Negotiations within GATT* (OJ C 255, 13/10/1986, p. 69).

14 In February 1999, the US and Australia requested consultations with Korea regarding a Korean regulatory scheme that discriminates against imported beef by confining sales of imported beef to specialized stores, limiting the manner of its display, and constraining the opportunities for the sale of imported beef. The US contended that these restrictions apply to only imported beef, denying national treatment to beef imports, and that the support to the domestic industry amounts to domestic subsidies that contravene the Agreement on Agriculture. Korea invoked among others article XX b) of the GATT in order to justify the imposed restrictions.

[15] In the *Import Prohibition of Certain Shrimp and Turtle Products, India, Malaysia, Pakistan, and Thailand vs. the United States of America*, India, Malaysia, Pakistan, and Thailand contested a US ban on importation of shrimp and turtle products from these countries. The US 1989 Endangered Species Act requires the US government to certify that all shrimp imported to the country are caught with methods that protect sea turtles from incidental drowning in shrimp trawling nets. The US invoked the protection of the animal's life in order to justify this ban.

[16] See, for instance, Article 31 (3)(c) of the Vienna Convention on the Law of Treaties, which states that one should take into account, "together with the context, any relevant rules of international law applicable in the relations between the parties" in order to interpret a treaty.

[17] Council Regulation (EC) n. 2501/2001 of December 10, 2001, Official Journal L 346 of 31.12.2001.

[18] The WTO is already linked by an agreement with the International Monetary Fund and the World Bank (WTO 1996a).

REFERENCES

Ahn, Dukgeun. 2000. "Linkages between International Financial and Trade Institutions – IMF, World Bank, and WTO." *Journal of World Trade* 34(4): 1–35.

Alben, Elissa. 2001. "GATT and the Fair Wage: A Historical Perspective on the Labor-Trade Link." *Columbia Law Review* 101(6): 1410–47.

All-China Women's Federation. 2000. "Project Cooperation." http://www.women.org.cn/english/english/major/projctex.htm (accessed April 2007).

Better Factories Cambodia. 2006. "Cambodian Garments Industry: One Year Later." http://www.betterfactories.org/ (accessed January 2007).

Bulger, Christine. 2000. "Fighting Gender Discrimination in the Chinese Workplace." *Boston College Third World Law Journal* 20(2): 345–92.

Çağatay, Nilüfer. 1996. "Gender and International Labor Standards." *Review of Radical Political Economics* 28(3): 92–101.

Charnovitz, Steve. 1987. "The Influence of International Labor Standards on the World Trading Regime: A Historical Overview." *International Labor Review* 126(5): 565–82.

———. 1998. "The Moral Exception in GATT." *Virginia Journal of International Law* 38(2): 689–713.

Childs, Mary. 2002. "Feminist Perspectives on International Economic Law," in Asif Qureshi, ed. *Perspectives in International Economic Law*, pp. 163–75. London: Kluwer Law International.

Chinkin, Christine and Hillary Charlesworth. 2000. *The Boundaries of International Law: A Feminist Analysis*. Manchester: Manchester University Press.

Constitution of the People's Republic of China [*Zhonghua renmin gongheguo xianfa*]. 1982/1988/1993. http://english.people.com.cn/constitution/constitution.html (accessed April 2006).

Diller, Janell M. and David A. Levy. 1997. "Child Labor, Trade and Investment Toward the Harmonization of International Law." *American Journal of International Law* 91(4): 663–96.

Drabek, Zdenek and Mark Bacchetta. 2004. "Tracing the Effects of WTO Accession on Policy-Making in Sovereign States: Preliminary Lessons from the Recent Experience of Transition Countries." *The World Economy* 24(7): 1083–125.

Dwasi, Jane. 1999. "Kenya: A Study in International Labor Standards and Their Effect on Working Women in Developing Countries: The Case for Integration of Enforcement Issues in the World Bank's Policies." *Wisconsin International Law Journal* 17(2): 347–462.

Ehrenberg, Daniel. 1996a. "From Intervention to Action: An ILO–GATT/WTO Enforcement Regime for International Labor Rights," in Lance Compa and Stephen Diamonds, eds. *Human Rights, Labor Rights and International Trade*, pp. 163–80. Philadelphia: University of Pennsylvania Press.

———. 1996b. "The Labor Link: Applying the International Trading System to Enforce Violations of Forced and Child Labor." *Yale Journal of International Law* 20(2): 380–90.

Elliott, Kimberly Ann and Richard B. Freeman. 2003. *Can Labor Standards Improve Under Globalization?* Washington, DC: Institute for International Economics.

Fedderson, Christopher. 1998. "Focusing on Substantive Law in International Economic Relations: The Public Morals of GATT's Article XX(a) and 'Conventional' Rules of Interpretation." *Minnesota Journal of Global Trade* 7(1): 76–104.

Flanagan, Robert J. 2006. *Globalization and Labor Conditions*. New York: Oxford University Press.

Guohua, Yang and Cheng Jin. 2001. "The Process of China's Accession to the WTO." *Journal of International Economic Law* 4(2): 297–328.

Gunter, Bernhard G. and Rolph van der Hoeven. 2004. "The Social Dimension of Globalization: A Review of the Literature." *International Labour Review* 143(1/2): 7–43.

Halverson, Karen. 2004. "China's WTO Accession: Economic, Legal and Political Implications." *Boston College International and Comparative Law Review* 27(2): 319–70.

Hernández-López, Ernesto. 2001. "Recent Trends and Perspectives for Non-State Actor Participation in World Trade Organization Disputes." *Journal of World Trade* 35(3): 469–98.

Howell, Jude. 1997. "Post Beijing Reflections: Creating Ripples, But Not Waves in China." *Women's Studies International Forum* 20(2): 235–52.

Howse, Robert and Brian Langille, with Julien Burda. 2006. "The World Trade Organization and Labour Rights: Man Bites Dog," in Virginia Leary and Daniel Warner, eds. *Social Issues, Globalisation and International Institutions*, pp. 157–231. Leiden, the Netherlands: M. Nijhoff Publishers.

International Labour Organization (ILO). 1998. "ILO Declaration on Fundamental Principles and Rights at Work." http://www.ilo.org/dyn/declaris/DECLARATION WEB.INDEXPAGE (accessed May 2006).

Jarvis, Liane. 2000. "The Public Morals Exception of GATT Article 20." *Michigan Journal of International Law* 22(1): 219–38.

Kabeer, Naila. 2004. "Globalization, Labor Standards, and Women's Rights: Dilemmas of Collective (In)Action in an Interdependent World." *Feminist Economics* 10(1): 3–35.

Kapur, Ratna. 2002. "The Tragedy of Victimization Rhetoric: Resurrecting the 'Native' Subject in International/Post-Colonial Feminist Legal Politics." *Harvard Human Rights Journal* 15: 1–39.

Killion, Ulric. 2004. "Post-WTO China: Quest for Human Rights Safeguards in Sexual Harassment Against Working Women." *Tulane Journal of International and Comparative Law* 12(1): 201–35.

Kolben, Kevin. 2004. "Trade, Monitoring and the ILO: Working to Improve Conditions in Cambodia's Garment Factories." *Yale Human Rights & Development Law Journal* 7: 79–120.

Lardy, Nicholas R. 2002. *Integrating China into the Global Economy*. Washington, DC: Brookings Institution Press.

———. 2003. Trade Liberalization and Its Role in Chinese Economic Growth. Paper presented at an International Monetary Fund and National Council of Applied Economic Research Conference, entitled "A Tale of Two Giants: India's and China's Experience with Reform and Growth," New Delhi, November 14–6. http://www.imf.org/external/np/apd/seminars/2003/newdelhi/lardy.pdf (accessed June 2006).

Law of the People's Republic of China for the Protection of Rights and Interests of Women [*Funu quanyi baozhangfa*]. 1992. http://www.women.org.cn/english/english/laws/02.htm (accessed April 2005).

Leary, Virginia. 1997. "The WTO and the Social Clause: Post-Singapore." *European Journal of International Law* 8(1): 118–22.

Lenzerini, Federico. 2001. "International Trade and Child Labour Standards," in Fracesco Francioni, ed. *Environment, Human Rights and International Trade*, pp. 298–99. Oxford: Hart Publishing.

Liemt, Gijsbert Van. 1989. "Minimum Labour Standards and International Law: Would a Social Clause Work?" *International Labour Review* 128(4): 435–44.

McGill, Eugenia. 2004. "Poverty and Social Analysis of Trade Agreements: A More Coherent Approach?" *Boston College International and Comparative Law Review* 27(2): 371–428.

Nordas, Hildegunn. 2003. "The Impact of Trade Liberalization on Women's Job Opportunities and Earnings in Developing Countries." *World Trade Review* 2(2): 221–31.

Nyamu, Celestine. 2000. "How Should Human Rights and Development Respond to Cultural Legitimization of Gender Hierarchy in Developing Countries?" *Harvard International Law Journal* 41(2): 381–418.

Orford, Anne. 1998. "Contesting Globalization: A Feminist Perspective on the Future of Human Rights." *Transnational Law and Contemporary Problems* 8(2): 171–98.

Pahuja, Sundhya. 2000. "Trading Spaces: Locating Sites for Challenge Within International Trade Law." *Australian Feminist Law Journal* 14: 38–54.

Pape, Robert. 1997. "Why Economic Sanctions Do Not Work." *International Security* 22(2): 90–136.

———. 1998. "Why Economic Sanctions Still Do Not Work." *International Security* 23(1): 66–77.

Pennay, Lori. 2000. "The Disproportionate Effect of the Asian Economic Crisis on Women: The Filipina Experience." *University of Pennsylvania Journal of International Economic Law* 21(2): 427–80.

Polaski, Sandra. 2003. "Protecting Labor Rights Through Trade Agreements: An Analytical Guide." *UC Davis Journal of International Law and Policy* 10(1): 13–25.

———. 2006. "Combining Global and Local Forces: The Case of Labor Rights in Cambodia." *World Development* 34(5): 919–32.

Pun Ngai. 2004. A New Practice of Labor Organizing: Community-Based Organization of Migrant Women Workers in South China. Paper prepared for the International Conference on Membership Based Organizations of the Poor: Theory, Experience and Poverty, hosted by Harvard University's Women in Informal Employment Globalizing and Organizing (WIEGO) Program, Cornell University Department of Economics, and the Self-Employed Women's Association of India. http://www.eldis.org/static/DOC18698.htm (accessed January 2006).

———. 2007. "Gendering the Dormitory Labor System: Production, Reproduction, and Migrant Labor in South China." *Feminist Economics* 13(3/4): 239–58.

Raghavan, Chakravarthi. 1996. "Barking Up the Wrong Tree: Trade and Social Clause Links," *Third World Economics* 129: 11–15. http://www.twnside.org.sg/title/tree-ch.htm (accessed December 2006).

Robert, Eric. 1996. "Enjeux et ambiguïtés du concept de clause sociale ou les rapports entre les normes de travail et le commerce international." *Revue belge de droit international* 29(1): 145–90.

Rodhes, Sylvia and John H. Jackson. 1999. "United States Law and China's Accession Process." *Journal of International Economic Law* 2(3): 497–510.

Smith, Chris. 2003. "Living at Work: Management Control and the Dormitory Labour System in China." *Asia Pacific Journal of Management* 20(3): 333–58.

Smith, Chris and Pun Ngai. 2006. "The Dormitory Labour Regime in China as a Site for Control and Resistance." *International Journal of Human Resource Management* 17(8): 1456–70.

Stark, Barbara. 2000. "Women and Globalization: The Failure and Postmodern Possibilities of International Law." *Vanderbilt Journal of Transnational Law* 33(3): 503–71.

Stirling, Patricia. 1996. "The Use of Trade Sanctions as an Enforcement Mechanism for Basic Human Rights: A Proposal for Addition to the World Trade Organization." *American University Journal of International Law and Policy* 11(1): 26–46.

Sustainable Forest Management in China. n.d. "UNDP." http://sfmchina.cn/english/ UNDP-content01.asp (accessed June 2007).

Tickner, Ann. 2001. *Gendering World Politics, Issues and Approaches in the Post-Cold War Era.* New York: Columbia University Press.

Trebilcock, Michael J. and Robert Howse. 1999. *The Regulation of International Trade.* London: Routledge.

United Nations (UN). 1947. *Reports of the Commissions*, United Nations Conference on Trade and Employment held at Havana, Cuba from November 21, 1947, to March 24, 1948, Final Act and Related Documents, New York.

——. 1948. The Final Act of the United Nations Conference on Trade and Employment, Havana Charter for an International Trade Organization, *UN Doc. E/CONF/2/78.*

——. 2000. *United Nations Millennium Declaration*, adopted by the General Assembly of the United Nations, A.G Resol. A/RES/55/2, September 8.

United Nations Development Programme (UNDP). 2003. "China's Accession to WTO: Challenges of WTO Entry on Chinese Women in the Agricultural and Industrial Sector." http://www.undp.org.cn/ (accessed November 2006).

Von Schöppenthau, Philip. 2001. "Trade and Labour Standards: Harnessing Globalization?" in Klaus Deutsch and Bernhard Speyer, eds. *World Trade Organization Millennium Round, The Freer Trade in the Twenty First Century*, pp. 224–36. New York: Routledge.

Williams, Mark, Kong Yuk-Choi, and Yan Shen. 2002. "Bonanza or Mirage? Textiles and China's Accession to the WTO." *Journal of World Trade* 36(3): 577–91.

World Trade Organization. 1996a. *Guidelines for Arrangements on Relations with Non-Governmental Organizations.* Decision adopted by the General Council on July 18, WT/L/162.

——. 1996b. "The Singapore Ministerial Declaration." WTO doc. WT/MIN(96)/DEC. The engagements taken at Singapore were renewed during the second Ministerial Conference held in Geneva in May 1998, WTO doc. WT/MIN(98)/DEC/1, May 25, 1998.

——. 1998. *Import Prohibition of Certain Shrimp and Shrimp Products* (US). Report of the Appellate Body, WT/DS58/AB/R, October 12. § 161–76.

——. 2000. *Measures Affecting Imports of Fresh, Chilled, and Frozen Beef* (Korea). Report of the Appellate Body, WT/DS161/AB/R, WT/DS169/AB/R, December 11.

——. 2004a. *Conditions for the Granting of Tariff Preferences to Developing Countries* (EC). Report of the Appellate Body, WT/DS246/AB/R, April 7.

——. 2004b. "The Future of the WTO: Addressing Institutional Challenges in the New Millennium." Report by the Consultative Board to the Director-General Supachai Panitchpakdi. http://www.wto.org/english/thewto_e/10anniv_e/10anniv _e.htm#future (accessed December 2006).

————. 2004c. *Measures Affecting the Cross-Border Supply of Gambling and Betting Services* (US). Report of the Panel, WT/DS285/R, November 10. § 6.465.

Wright, Shelley. 1995. "Interdisciplinary Approaches to International Economic Law: Women and the Global Economic Order – A Feminist Perspective." *American University Journal of International Law and Policy* 10(2): 861–93.

Zoellick, Robert. 2001. "U.S.-Cambodian Textile Agreement Links Increasing Trade with Improving Workers' Rights." http://www.ustr.gov/releases/2002/01/02-03.htm (accessed January 2007).

WESTERN COSMETICS IN THE GENDERED DEVELOPMENT OF CONSUMER CULTURE IN CHINA

Barbara E. Hopkins

INTRODUCTION

Changes in the public display of gender are clear to anyone visiting China's major cities. Propaganda images of women "holding up half the sky" have given way to images of business women dressed for success, Western models, and "Westernized" Chinese women displaying standards of beauty that are generally unattainable for most Chinese women.[1] Fashion magazines are everywhere – in kiosks and small convenience stores – and cosmetics advertising dominates the faces of department stores and pharmacies. These are visible manifestations of a fundamental shift in the Chinese gender regime from an ideal of androgyny, under which the communists de-emphasized gender differences, to a new ideal that emphasizes gender differences and associates beauty with femininity.[2]

The gender regime is more than a set of traditional norms that determine women's behavior: it is both the set of formal rules that govern legal access to assets and opportunities – such as land, jobs, and voting rights – and the set of informal rules that govern expectations of appropriate behaviors for men and women and the interpretation of behaviors as masculine or feminine. My focus is on the informal rules, with a particular interest in changes in consumption, especially the consumption of fashion and cosmetics. Changes in the consumption of fashion and cosmetics are reflections of changes in the gender regime and perceptions of femininity.

While changes in the gender regime and consumer behavior are the result of many causal factors, this paper centers on the influence of economic changes, such as those negotiated as part of China's commitments to the World Trade Organization (WTO). Using a theoretical framework for analyzing gendered consumption of cosmetics, this paper illustrates how globalization, as exemplified by China's accession to the WTO, impacts the gender regime in urban China through the development of a consumer culture among professional, administrative, and service workers. I review the changes in gender regime during the reform period, particularly the increasing association of femininity with beauty and consumption of beauty products that accelerated in the period leading up to and after China's accession to the WTO. In order to interpret these changes, I build a theoretical framework that explains changes in China's gender regime and pays attention to women's agency in this process. This framework extends institutionalist theories of consumption and advertising to incorporate gender differences. Because institutionalist theories recognize a symbolic purpose for consumption that could be viewed as a performance of one's status, they are compatible with the sociological theory of "doing gender" that characterizes gender not as a rigid set of norms, but as a never-ending performance of behaviors that signal femininity or masculinity. Theories of advertising then add a mechanism for explaining change in the social interpretation of gender performance: it is primarily through advertising and marketing that the formal rules of China's commitments to the WTO affect the informal rules of the gender regime, as reflected in cosmetic consumption changes. Thus, my argument is that the new gender regime does not necessarily represent what women want but is the result of women making choices within a new social structure in which the meanings of goods like cosmetics are transformed through advertising and global media. This framework could be used in future research investigating changes in gendered consumption patterns in China and elsewhere.

THE GENDERED TRANSFORMATION OF CONSUMPTION IN POST-REFORM CHINA

The gradual transformation of Chinese society during economic reform included fundamental changes in attitudes towards consumption and gender. These changes were facilitated by both a change in the ideology expressed by the Communist Party and in the breakdown of the Party's monopoly on persuasive power caused by the development of private advertising and private media. Globalization and the WTO introduced foreign advertising and media, contributing to the development of private advertising and media. The resulting ideological shift included a revaluing of "bourgeois" consumption and femininity that can be observed in women's increased consumption of goods that display femininity, such as cosmetics.

In the pre-reform period, especially during the Cultural Revolution, communist ideology elevated peasant ways of living and discouraged consumption of goods identified with a bourgeois lifestyle. In her autobiography, Jung Chang explains: "beauty was so despised that [her] family was sent to [a] lovely house as a punishment" (1991: 374). Citizens displayed political commitment by limiting consumption. Chang also describes an acquaintance who "took to rolling up his sleeves and trouser legs and wearing a pair of straw sandals like a peasant, in the spirit of a model youth in the propaganda posters" to conform to Communist Party expectations (1991: 394). Similarly, Nien Cheng (1988) recounts how long before the Cultural Revolution a local Communist Party official often criticized her by saying that her tailored shirt represented her bourgeois values. Any good that could signal adherence to a correct political position was useful for one's survival. Clothing that symbolized political commitment served as protection against Red Guards who might use appearance as a reason to persecute someone in the name of protecting the Communist Revolution.

Not only did the ideology of Mao's China shape the nature of consumption, it also rejected displays of difference of any kind, including gender. Rejecting the rigid gender and class hierarchies of the pre-communist era, numerous slogans emphasized an equal role for women in communist society. Propaganda presented model women as exemplifying lifestyles to emulate because they did the same jobs as men and rejected domestic duties (Elisabeth J. Croll 1995), but the propaganda did not reflect women's actual experience. Mao's ideology did not resolve the conflict between women's household responsibilities and work responsibilities common to all societies. While state-owned enterprises provided childcare facilities and dining halls that reduced the burden for some urban women, these were unable to replace all the housework for all women. Although women were required to participate in political activities that taught citizens to support the policies of the regime, they were unable to express their own concerns if contrary to government policies. And because the experience of difference could not be expressed, femininity had to be hidden. Use of cosmetics visible to others was unacceptable, and only the most basic soaps were produced by the state factories.[3] Chang recalls: "The women in books and films who made themselves up ... were invariably wicked characters, like concubines" (1991: 265). Dress was androgynous with most pieces of clothing looking like parts of an army uniform. After 1964, Chang adhered to a form of dress "more suited to the atmosphere of class struggle. [She] put patches on [her] trousers to try to look 'proletarian' and wore [her] hair in the uniform style of two plaits with no colors" (Chang 1991: 289). Later, when long hair was also condemned, she cut her hair. Militant red guards would stop passersby and cut long hair or skirts and break semi-high-heeled shoes, all symbols of bourgeois femininity.

With the death of Mao and the rise of Deng Xiaoping, the government's attitude towards consumption and difference changed. Deng's practical approach to economic development sought to reward productivity by rehabilitating the value of consumption. With slogans like "to get rich is glorious," he signaled the return to a social hierarchy with wealthy lifestyles on top. Conspicuous "bourgeois" consumption became the new ideal. By the time reform was in full gear in the early 1980s, fashionable clothing and cosmetics, especially foreign brands, had come to signal status (Russell W. Belk and Nan Zhou 1987). In the early stages of conspicuous foreign consumption, before expensive brands became easily recognizable, foreign-made sunglasses were often worn with the tag still on, and men wore suits with the labels still on the cuffs to call attention to the brand (Belk and Zhou 1987). In addition to consumption itself, Chinese reform rehabili-tated femininity, and beauty became a marketable characteristic of women. Local Communist Party officials used women as window dressing for the opening of new shopping centers and for trade shows, and hotels used beautiful women to greet guests. And, as Gary Xu and Susan Feiner (2007) describe in this collection, the state began to sponsor beauty pageants.

The changing attitudes towards consumption and femininity were not just driven by changes in the party line but by the growth of private media and advertising. Croll commented that in 1995 "popular magazines... devoted to fashion, beauty and lifestyle...and billboard images...of women retailers or customers in the company of [a] washing machine, cooking pot, watch, television and toothpaste or cosmetics" were on every street corner (1995: 109). Even the image of imperial concubines has been partially rehabilitated in the name of commerce; little girls visiting the Forbidden Palace in Beijing get souvenir headdresses modeled on those worn by concubines before the 1911 Revolution.

Growth in consumption of products that display gender such as cosmetics reflects these changes in attitudes. For example, sales of cosmetics grew from less than 500 million yuan per year before 1980 to 4 billion yuan in 1990 (Hong Kong Trade Development Council 2000), and they continued to grow in the 1990s and early 2000s. Household expenditures on cosmetics have increased as a share of total household spending from an average of 1.28 percent in 1999 to 2.86 percent in 2003.[4] The urban centers most open to Western investment, Beijing, Shanghai, and Guangzhou, have seen the most growth. Consumers in these cities spent an average of 150 to 180 yuan per year in 2000 compared to an average of 25 yuan per year nationally (Business Victoria 2006).

This resurgence of femininity has multiple meanings. Often, displays of feminine dress in post-communist societies signal a break from the communist past. Expressions of femininity and masculinity through clothing and other fashion accessories provide the most basic opportunity to assert self in opposition to the homogenizing identity asserted by communist regimes. Throughout Eastern Europe, displays of femininity through short skirts and high heels were political acts of rejection of communism and reclamation of personal identity (Jacqui True 1999). Similarly, Chinese women are expressing a post-communist femininity through clothing, jewelry, and cosmetics (Croll 1995). Consumption is also an expression of Asian nationalism, and marketers in China have identified what they label "J-sense" or the emulation of Japanese consumer habits (Paul French 2005), as can be observed in the popularity of Japanese cosmetics brands such as Sofina.

Yet there are also those who see the new expression of femininity as a return to the subordination of women. In 2001 the ubiquitous images of women in more traditional domestic roles prompted women activists and social workers to call for the Shanghai Women's Federation to denounce this type of advertising. Zhou Meizhan, a teacher at the Shanghai Women's Cadre Training School that trains women party officials, sent a report to the Federation stating that beauty and a woman's role as housewife are the two major themes in the ads (Eastday 2001). She argued that advertisers are reinforcing traditional gender roles, in which a woman's identity is derived exclusively from her attachment to a man and a family. In what is a typical exchange between advertisers and their critics worldwide, advertisers responded by arguing that advertising reflects reality. They reasoned that models for advertisements are based on the ad's target audience; if a product is targeting women who care about their appearance, the ad is going to feature beautiful models (Eastday 2001). It is also clear that advertisers are targeting well-paid women with careers in the new business sector or, perhaps, men who want to display their status through a wife embodying this revamped image of beauty and femininity; comrade Zhou's worldview and the lifestyle choices of a teacher in the Women's Cadre Training School are not likely to be reflected in advertising.

Consumption of goods that display femininity may also reflect the desire to earn more because these goods developed practical value during the reform period; competition in China's job markets has created an incentive to follow a set of standards for feminine dress because inappropriate dress may keep a woman from getting a lucrative job. The role of employers in enforcing conformity is often overlooked in the economics literature despite standard business school fare of "dress for success" ideas.

The point is simple: in increasingly competitive labor markets, those who closely follow the dress codes desired by employers will get the job. Global norms influence this enforcement mechanism because employers are also subject to the power of customers and other business associates whose decision to trade depends partly on having their expectations for acceptable appearance of workers met. This then reinforces the association between those standards of acceptable appearance and the social status that comes from more lucrative jobs in the export sector and office jobs. Similarly, through appropriate appearance, women might be striving to achieve a successful marriage or acceptance from a desirable social group.

Plastic surgery, like the consumption of clothing, cosmetics, and jewelry, defines one's social status, which shapes one's economic opportunities. In an article by *Washington Post* reporter Peter S. Goodman, a Chinese woman explains: "We think this surgery is a good investment for our daughter. If you're better-looking, you get preferential treatment" (2004). Goodman also quotes Cao Yilin, the head of the plastic surgery clinic at Shanghai's Ninth People's Hospital, on plastic surgery that makes eyes look more Western and breast enlargement: "Young people today accept Western culture... They think the breast is a symbol of the woman, so a woman without a breast is not really a woman" (2004).

But most Chinese cannot afford plastic surgery, and although less expensive, unlicensed, and more dangerous options exist, many would not consider them.[5] Cosmetics are affordable in some form to most urban residents, and similar considerations influence women's decisions to "invest" in cosmetics. Not surprisingly, the "premium products are favored by affluent women, most of whom are 'office ladies' working in multi-national companies" (Cosmetics Design 2004). Daniel S. Hamermesh, Xin Meng, and Junsen Zhang (2002) find that there is indeed a payoff in terms of higher wages for women who improve their appearance with cosmetics.

These changes in women's dress and the use of cosmetics reflect a tension between using one's appearance as self-expression and new social structures that offer a new set of prescriptions for acceptable appearance. Chinese feminist Xiaoping Li summarizes this point:

> Fashion in post-Mao China... has ambiguous effects. It undercuts the politicized codes of masculinity and femininity prevalent in Maoist socialism, but at the same time subjects the body, especially the female body, to another set of bodily inscriptions and prescriptions. Moreover, fashion and the re-fashioned female roles have created the illusion of an affluent modern China and women's emancipation. The political content of change in dress codes is consequently undermined. (1998: 87)

Cosmetics, like the broader category of fashion, offer women the opportunity to challenge the androgeneity of the pre-reform era, but the image of affluence, modernity, and freedom for women is only an illusion if the new styles are simply new prescriptions for acceptability.

THE WTO AND COSMETICS

Economic reform and increasing global integration had already caused a shift in the gender regime in China before accession to the WTO, but I argue that the changes in laws governing advertising and retail trade that were required as a condition for WTO membership have likely intensified this shift. China justified its membership with the standard economic arguments about the mutual benefits of trade for consumers and producers on both sides of a border, but the focus was on the benefits for Chinese producers derived from access to foreign markets. China could have unilaterally opened its market to foreign goods and achieved the resulting lower prices for its consumers, but following standard practice in trade negotiations, it held out on access to its markets in exchange for increased access to the markets of the US and the EU. Thus, opening up China's cosmetics and fashion markets to foreign influence was treated as a small part of the sacrifice necessary to achieve export-driven economic growth and increased standards of living even though the Chinese were actively anticipating the benefits of lower tariffs and greater access to foreign products.

The cosmetics industry in China at the time of accession had grown out of the few cosmetics firms that survived the 1970s producing soap and shampoo: before 1980, China had about fifty cosmetics firms (Hong Kong Trade Development Council 2000). The Japanese firm Shiseido was the first foreign firm to enter the Chinese market in 1981, but it was not until economic reform progressed enough to dramatically increase discretionary income that the market for skin care products and color cosmetics, such as lipsticks and eye shadows, took off. In 1990, US-based Avon entered the Chinese market with a direct sales strategy that offered cosmetics training on how to apply it, and entrepreneurial opportunities to the *yafang xiaojie*, as the Avon ladies are called. Avon was promptly followed in 1992 by Mininurse, a private Chinese company, and Yuxi (Yue-Sai) Cosmetics, started by a Chinese-American television celebrity in China. US and Japanese brands were often produced in China to avoid import restrictions and high tariffs. The US firm Mary Kay Cosmetics opened a factory in Hangzhou in 1995 to facilitate that company's access to the Chinese market. Small manufacturing firms developed to produce cosmetics and intermediate products for larger brands, and by the end of 1999, China had 3,514 licensed cosmetics manufacturers, including 703 foreign-invested companies (Hong Kong Trade Development Council 2000).

China's cosmetics industry grew up in the shadow of China's lengthy (fifteen year) negotiations to enter the world trading system. In order to join the WTO, China agreed to gradually lower tariff barriers on cosmetics, along with many other products. Import tariffs on cosmetics had been lowered in the years before joining the WTO, from over 55 percent before 1997 to between 20 and 28.7 percent at the time of accession in 2001, depending on the product (Shuquan Li 2003; Trade Information Center of the US Government 2005). China lowered import tariffs on most cosmetics to 22.5 percent in 2002, 18.3 percent in 2003, 14.2 percent in 2004, and 10 percent in 2005 (Trade Information Center of the US Government 2005). Before joining the WTO, only a small number of Chinese firms were granted import licenses, creating a monopoly for those few firms. In order to join the WTO, China promised to streamline the process of getting import licenses and no longer requires proof of sufficient demand for the good (China WTO 2001).

Beyond lowering tariff barriers, accession to the WTO also required developing regulatory institutions that would treat foreign and Chinese firms equally. In the context of transition from a centrally planned economy, developing regulatory institutions meant shifting from an environment where managers of state-owned enterprises needed to satisfy whatever rules their bosses imposed to an environment where managers need to satisfy new regulations and licensing procedures. Since the cosmetics industry developed in the private sector and was not a top priority for government regulators, domestic producers enjoyed benign neglect in the 1990s, while foreign firms were required to obtain permission from government officials to operate without any clear guidelines, resulting in licensing restrictions for all foreign firms in China (Hong Kong Trade Development Council 2000). Under the rules of the WTO, licensing regulations cannot create preferential treatment for domestic producers; so new regulations were applied to all firms leading to an increase in regulation for domestic firms.

For foreign exporters, new regulations requiring product testing and labeling function as non-tariff barriers that replace tariffs and quotas but are still within WTO rules (Hong Kong Trade Development Council 2000). China already invoked these rules in the spring of 2002 when fear of mad cow disease led China to ban European cosmetics containing animal byproducts (Ruoqian Yang 2002). China began easing the ban in December 2003, and most European imports have resumed (China Internet Information Center 2003). A similar conflict arose when US cosmetics imports were suspended for four months after an incidence of mad cow disease in Washington State (HealthDay 2004). Nevertheless, the long period of negotiations before accession to the WTO established communication channels that facilitated the resolution of these crises, and China has made an effort to include the US and the EU in discussions before new regulations were finalized and implemented to avoid the formal dispute structure of the WTO.

Theoretically, lower tariffs, ceteris paribus, should make foreign investment in production facilities in China less attractive as the cost of importing falls. However, since most foreign cosmetics brands have production facilities in China, the initial costs of establishing factories in China have already been paid, and avoiding trade barriers is not the only rationale for foreign investment. Production costs in China are likely to be lower than in the US, Japan, or France, and accession to the WTO makes it more profitable for multinational corporations to expand production in China, even if they export products back to where the brand originated. Also, multinational companies interested in sales in China want a local presence; Chinese subsidiaries of multinational firms are in a better position to understand the new regulations, get necessary approvals, and develop local marketing strategies for marketing to Chinese customers.

These changes in regulations had an impact on the cosmetics market in China. Before accession to the WTO, regulations neither encouraged nor discouraged foreign investment in cosmetics, but foreign firms experienced the general restrictions on foreign investment. With accession, China agreed to remove restrictions on the importation of raw materials for foreign-invested companies,[6] and these companies were no longer required to export more than they imported or to prove that imported raw materials could not be purchased in China (Trade Information Center of US Government 2005).[7] While WTO rules require that the new regulations apply to local and foreign cosmetics companies equally, foreign companies complain that the registration process still takes longer than for domestic firms and that regulations on cosmetics are particularly cumbersome because they need to satisfy the regulations of two different agencies, the Ministry of Health and the Ministry of Commerce, in order to be licensed (European Union Chamber of Commerce in China 2004). Nevertheless, the regulatory environment for foreign firms has improved after the accession and channels to resolve complaints have been established. Through these channels, China has made a commitment to the EU Chamber of Commerce to reduce the delays in licensing. Reducing restrictions on foreign firms as part of the WTO agreement has encouraged an increase in competition and consolidation of the growing cosmetics market. In 2004, L'Oreal purchased Yuxi (Yue-Sai) cosmetics and Mininurse, both popular mid-level local brands,[8] to round out its product base (Peter Morris 2004).

For the purposes of this article, the changes in rules about marketing cosmetics had perhaps the most important impact on consumer's interest in these goods. As a condition for entering the WTO, China agreed to lift restrictions in 2004 on wholesale and retail distribution by foreign companies, and although these measures were delayed, they were implemented by 2006 (US Trade Representative 2006). Foreign cosmetics companies can now own retail stores without a Chinese partner or special permissions and can set up shop outside of China's major cities (US Trade Representative 2002). Foreign cosmetics companies had previously concentrated on markets in the largest cities (American Marketing Association 2005), but increased access to retail expanded marketing to smaller cities, requiring development of lower-priced brands aimed at mass market consumers (Li 2003).

Foreign brands can also sell their cosmetics using direct marketing strategies that are part of the traditions of US sellers Avon and Mary Kay and the Japanese cosmetics line Sofina. The new regulations will allow enterprises that meet minimum size requirements, have premises in China, and agree to only sell goods from their own production facilities to have direct sales operators, such as the *yafang xiaojie*. While direct marketing began in the late 1980s, China actually banned direct sales in April of 1998 amid fears that direct sales organizations would turn out like the pyramid investment schemes that led to rioting and 2,000 deaths in Albania when they collapsed (Morris 2004).[9] The Chinese government considers direct sales organizations cults, raising concern about their noneconomic influence. According to an editorial in the *Washington Times*, Mary Kay changed its slogan from "God first, family second, and career third" to "faith first, family second, and career third" in an effort to satisfy Chinese authorities and forced all of its sales consultants to sign a statement promising never to practice or advocate for Falun Gong (Xiaoxia Gong 2003).[10] Avon, the largest foreign seller, started building boutiques when direct sales were banned in 1998 and by 2004 had established 5,500 boutiques with a commission sales force of 700,000 Avon ladies while still meeting the rules of the direct sales ban (*China Daily* 2004a).

The lifting of the ban against direct sales allows cosmetics sellers a greater opportunity to persuade consumers of the value of their image of femininity. Direct marketers provide education on how to use cosmetics, which according to market analyses, is a key element in the growth of the cosmetics market, especially for color cosmetics, the use of which is less intuitive than skin creams (Li 2003). The one-on-one interaction also allows for more aggressive persuasion. Avon's first training sessions in 1993 included consumer psychology, which taught the *yafang xiaojie* to distinguish between different consumers and target the message accordingly: "the 'pragmatic' client (worried about the price) [would] be persuaded with reference to her 'entry' into the international (American) society of consumption" (Maria Jaschok 1995: 117).

China also opened up its advertising industry to foreign investors in order to join the WTO. Majority-owned foreign firms were permitted in 2003 and wholly owned foreign advertising and marketing firms were allowed in 2005, ahead of schedule (US Trade Representative 2006). Foreign firms are gaining a larger share of the growing advertising market, but one would expect the foreign influence on the industry to be mixed. Although foreign advertising firms bring more sophisticated marketing techniques, they often lack appropriate local cultural knowledge to fully utilize those techniques. Joint ventures, permitted even before 2005, provided an opportunity for both local and foreign firms to combine their respective expertise. The combination has been successful: in Shanghai, only sixty of the 2,100 advertising companies were joint ventures, but they represented one-third of the market (Hong Kong Trade and Development Council 2004).

The advertising industry has continued to grow since China's accession to the WTO. Advertising expenditures have increased from 9.6 billion US dollars in 2001 to 15.3 billion US dollars in 2004 (China Media Monitor 2005). In 2004, cosmetics products ranked fourth in spending on advertising among the top ten product categories (China Media Monitor 2005). Among foreign-invested firms, cosmetics firms spend more on advertising than any other industry (*China Daily* 2004c). Oil of Olay was the most advertised brand, with expenditures of US$698 million in 2004, up from US$566 million in 2003, a 23 percent increase (*China Daily* 2005; Lia Braaten Hager and Liz Grubow 2005). Aggressive advertising has been responsible for the success of the joint ventures in cosmetics (Li 2003). Increasing competition in the industry is only likely to further increase its demand for advertising services. An ethnographic study of the advertising industry in Trinidad found that the major reason for investing in advertising was fear of the competition (Daniel Miller 1997).

Finally, the decision by China's leaders to join the WTO implies an endorsement of what they deem to be "modern" lifestyles.[11] Membership in the WTO is not only a means to increase trade but also has symbolic value. WTO membership represents acceptance of China by the world's economic powers. In return for membership, China agreed to emulate, at least partially, the economic policies of powerful capitalist nations. Once a member, the WTO gave China not only access to North American and European markets but also the recognition of being part of the global trading system.

All of these changes have led to increasing consumption of cosmetics, especially foreign brands. Cosmetics sales in China increased from 13.2 billion yuan in 2000 to 20.6 billion yuan in 2003 (National Bureau of Statistics [NBS] China 2002, 2004). After accession to the WTO, foreign cosmetics have progressively dominated the market. According to official statistics, imports of cosmetics grew faster than cosmetics consumption overall, growing from US$161 million in 2000 to US$201 million in 2002. After the ban on cosmetics from the EU during the mad cow scare was lifted, imports of cosmetics grew much faster (by 39 percent) to US$281 million in 2003.[12] Among the 3,000 cosmetics firms in China in 2003, 32 percent were foreign-invested companies that, together with imports, had 68 percent of the market share (Chen Wen 2004). Foreign brands are most important in the premium market: they are responsible for half of the sales volume but 80 percent of value (Li 2003).

A FRAMEWORK FOR UNDERSTANDING GENDER AND CONSUMPTION IN CHINA

In order to explain how accession to the WTO has influenced the gender regime in China as observed through changes in consumption behavior, I extend economic theories of consumption to incorporate gender. The dominant economic paradigm, neoclassical economics, does not have much to offer for this project. The neoclassical theory of revealed preference assumes that observed consumption is a reflection of preferences. It reduces all changes in consumption – such as those in beauty products and services described above – to exogenous changes, whether they be liberation from obstacles to the free expression of preferences or emergence of new preferences. Gender, as a socially constructed set of informal rules, constantly shaping and being shaped by consumption, is beyond the scope of this model.

By contrast, institutional economists provide a theory of consumer behavior that incorporates the social nature of consumption. While neoclassical theory considers only the instrumental (or practical) purpose of consumption – a good's ability to provide some service to the consumer, institutionalist theory also considers the symbolic purpose – a good's ability to symbolize one's social position (Thorstein Veblen 1899/1931). Veblen's (1894/1964) analysis of women's dress is a specific application of this theory; a woman's dress represents her husband's high class status when it is so constrictive that the wearer must be a woman of leisure. Each class then emulates the consumption patterns of the class above in a futile effort to obtain higher social status. Some recent institutionalist theories of contemporary consumption patterns argue that social class no longer shapes consumption as much as group identities that cross class lines (Andrew B. Trigg 2001). In this lifestyle model, consumers identify with a particular group and then emulate those consumption patterns (Roger Mason 2000). Richard McIntyre (1992) argues that consumers no longer display identity as much as they consume it. Trigg (2001) reconciles the lifestyle model with Veblen's class model using the concept of cultural capital. Building on Pierre Bourdieu's work, he argues that one has the choice to adopt different lifestyles only if one has the necessary cultural capital, which is the knowledge of what consumption is appropriate to different social situations or different lifestyles. He argues that lifestyles reflect various combinations of economic capital and cultural capital that continue to position people within a social hierarchy (Trigg 2001).

Institutionalist theory also offers several explanations for the transmission of a good's symbolic value from one group of consumers to another, including some specifically addressing the process of globalization. Applying the concept of emulation to globalization, consumers in developing countries may be viewed as emulating the consumption patterns of developed nations because on a global scale, those goods symbolize status (Frank Ackerman 1997; Paulette Olson 1998). Foreign products display status because they are likely to be harder to get and more expensive but also because they are recognizable global brands. Because the media is important in the spread of symbolic meaning, institutionalists emphasize advertising in the creation of consumer tastes (John K. Galbraith 1958).

While the institutionalist literature does not specifically address gender as an example of identity,[13] economic models of consumption that focus on its symbolic value are consistent with feminist theories of "doing gender." The "doing gender" approach argues that gendered behavior is not a rigid set of rules but rather a performance of behaviors that signal to others femininity or masculinity (Candice West and Don H. Zimmerman 2002). Since commodities, such as cosmetics and clothing, often embody gender stereotypes, consumption represents a performance of the consumer's gender identity (Susan Willis 1997). Gendered objects are consumed to display pride and success at fulfilling gender roles (Janeen Arnold Costa 2000). However, the argument that objects acquire gender based on established social roles and the gender division of labor (Costa 2000) only explains how consumption reinforces existing traditional gender roles. Consumption can also reflect an improvement in women's status (Alladi Venkatesh 1994). Women will make more decisions about consumption if they control a larger share of income because of better labor market opportunities or improvements in family structure. However, like neoclassical economics, Venkatesh's focus on women as decision makers with growing authority takes women's preferences as given and can only explain the emphasis on beauty in post-Mao China as a new opportunity for women to buy what they want. To explain the new gender regime, one needs to consider that the commodities women want change in response to changing symbolic meanings.

Commodities take on new symbolic meanings, including gender and other identities, through the process of globalization. Carla Freeman's (2000) study of women office workers in multinational corporations in the Caribbean provides a case study in which employer-dictated dress codes symbolize both gender and class in the culture at large. The rules of the multinational corporations could be characterized as a gender regime imposed by the multinational corporations – a direct result of globalization. Yet Freeman also found that the attire required of office workers was an important part of the production of class identity as professional women. Freeman's interviews indicated that women used dress as an important site for the expression of their identity and often followed the dress codes even when not going to work, though this style of dress was more costly, and they did not earn higher wages than women in manufacturing jobs. Freeman's analysis shows that consumption choices can simultaneously display conformity to social expectations and self-expression.

Freeman's research also provides an important insight that I believe is the key to understanding change in gender regimes: the display of gender is intertwined with other aspects of identity such as class. This is consistent with other studies of gender acquisition in which children assert a gendered identity as part of the adoption of some other desirable characteristic such as maturity (West and Zimmerman 2002).[14] If women display a particular gendered identity, such as feminine beauty, because they wish to assert another aspect of identity, such as class status or perhaps worldly sophistication, then one cannot assume that women buy cosmetics because they simply like the way they look wearing it or that they accept the new associations between femininity and beauty. One can recognize women's agency in the sense that dress constitutes self-expression but may still misinterpret which aspect of self is being expressed.

I interpret consumption as a performance of the consumer's identity or lifestyle choices, which are constrained by class and gender. This framework is an extension of Trigg's model that integrates the horizontal elements of lifestyle choices and the vertical elements of class position. In order to include gender, I add another dimension: each lifestyle choice contains a division between masculine and feminine reflections of that lifestyle. Thus, for each particular act of consumption, a woman faces a choice to display a lifestyle, but the possibilities are limited by her stock of economic capital (wealth), her stock of cultural capital (knowledge of consumption patterns associated with different lifestyles), and by her identity as a woman. Men's choices are similarly constrained. Gender, like class position in Veblen's analysis, constrains the set of possibilities. Consuming goods appropriate for one's gender identity is necessary to gain social acceptance. The identity that each individual displays to the world is the sum total of all of her or his choices including both consumption and other behaviors. Because identity represents a series of behaviors, individuals "develop their strategies over time" (Trigg 2001: 109). Subsequent opportunities are shaped by past decisions. Indeed each individual's stock of both economic and cultural capital is partly a result of circumstance and partly a result of their previous choices. Decisions are not made with full information: it will not necessarily be obvious to individuals how each choice that they make leads them towards a particular set of opportunities.

In general, the opportunities to accumulate economic or cultural capital associated with different lifestyles will vary. Some lifestyles will grant access to better jobs or to social contacts that in turn can create access to better jobs, business opportunities, or opportunities to acquire valuable knowledge. The fact that not all lifestyle choices are available to both men and women means that men and women face different opportunities to accumulate economic and cultural capital. Even when a masculine and feminine version of a lifestyle choice exists, the difference between the consumption patterns of the two versions is likely to generate different economic costs. Women may have to pay more or take more time to display the same lifestyle as men.

Advertising is an important instrument for associating a particular good with a lifestyle and for promoting lifestyles. Branding – producing advertising that defines the "brand" as a set of intangible characteristics associated with a particular set of lifestyles – is a critical strategy in advertising as competition becomes more intense and marketing surveys begin to differentiate target audiences (Sheila Byfield and Linda Caller 1997). Another strategy involves promoting a lifestyle already associated with a product; in the case of Western cosmetics, this generates a powerful economic incentive to produce media that positively depicts the lifestyles of glamorous Western women. Like media images in the West, these images need not be accurate depictions of the lifestyles of Western women. Persuading consumers to purchase cosmetics must start by placing a high value on beauty and physical attractiveness to the opposite sex. Thus, marketing fashion and cosmetics to women promotes lifestyles that sharply differentiate masculinity and femininity, emphasizing beauty as an important aspect of femininity. However, if these lifestyles encourage people to consume more, they have to resonate with something that consumers already embrace. Thus, the depicted lifestyles are not simply the creations of advertisers or transplants from the home country but develop out of an effort to marry the characteristics of their goods to existing identities discovered by market research. Nevertheless, some existing identities more clearly lend themselves to promoting consumption and, as such, are more likely to find themselves depicted in media. This explains why the androgynous identity of the Cultural Revolution is not likely to be depicted in media driven by advertising money from multinational cosmetics firms, even if it is still an identity that some older Chinese women embrace.

When we understand consumption as the performance of lifestyles and consider the importance of advertising in shaping those lifestyles, it is easy to see how joining the WTO and opening up the Chinese market to Western cosmetics could intensify the shift towards a new gender regime in China. The growth of the cosmetics market in China and the femininity it reflects are not the result of a collective effort by Chinese women to redefine femininity but instead are unintended consequences of the interaction between a new structure of lifestyle choices and each woman's pursuit of identity. China's entry into the global economy increases the status associated with lifestyles that emulate foreign consumption patterns (Olson 1998). Industrialized economies are perceived as "modern"; thus, the consumption patterns of the middle class in industrialized countries are associated with lifestyles that are "modern." The value of the modern worldly lifestyle is reflected in magazines like *Xiandaifunu* (Modern Woman) and *Nuxingdashijie* (World of Women), which advertise the consumption goods, including cosmetics, that define the style of the modern, worldly woman. Foreign brands benefit from a symbolic meaning of modernity and prestige associated with foreign lifestyles (Lianxi Zhou and Michael K. Hui 2003). Thus, when a woman uses Avon or L'Oreal eye shadow, it may not necessarily be because she likes it but because she wants to look modern and worldly.

The appeal of foreign consumption patterns does not simply reflect a value placed on things foreign, but the association of foreign consumption patterns with some other ideal, such as wealth or modernity. As a counter-example to cross-national emulation, Chinese women prefer skin creams that lighten the skin, while the US market is dominated by foundations and tanning products that darken the skin. While it might be possible to interpret Chinese preferences and the advertisements that encourage them as a longing for a "white" racial identity, the meaning is contextual; in China, dark skin symbolizes that the bearer works under the sun in low status, back-breaking work, while in the US darkened skin implies leisure to tan. Cosmetics producers do not care whether the ideal is lighter or darker skin as long as they can promote an ideal that requires the use of some product, and they can convince consumers that the product is a necessity.

CONCLUSION

The framework I have presented provides an explanation of how China's accession to the WTO could reinforce the cultural processes that shift the gender regime to emphasize beauty as an important characteristic of femininity. The WTO has increased competition in the Chinese cosmetics market and allowed for increased consolidation by multinational firms like L'Oreal. This increased competition created the impetus for aggressive marketing techniques at the same time that changes in regulations over direct marketing and foreign advertising firms increased their supply. Aggressive marketing, both in the form of advertising and in the form of the pitch used by direct sellers, has influenced which lifestyle each good symbolizes.

Although women make decisions about what to buy and how to dress, they do not control the symbolic value of the goods they buy. The symbolic language that assigns a gender and lifestyle to each good is the constraint that could generate gender inequality in consumer markets. Thus, the decision to consume more cosmetics is not necessarily a reflection of women's preferences for cosmetics; rather, the consumer of cosmetics may be choosing a modern, urban professional lifestyle that is constructed by informal rules that associate a beauty-based femininity with modernity. Thus, the new gender regime, as reflected in the increased consumption of cosmetics, is not necessarily the result of free choice but may be constrained by the new structures of meanings attached to commodities in which women make choices about what to consume.

This framework, in which consumption is viewed as a performance of lifestyles, is consistent with Xiaoping Li's (1998) characterization of fashion described above. The marketing literature that describes both the need to define the brand (Byfield and Caller 1997) and the identity associated with the purchase of foreign cosmetics (Cosmetics Design 2004) provides some evidence that consumption is tied to lifestyles. However, more direct evidence of women's consumption behavior is needed to confirm the validity of this framework. Ethnographic research similar to the study conducted by Freeman (2000) in the Caribbean could provide this kind of evidence.

Barbara E. Hopkins, Department of Economics, Wright State University,
3640 Colonel Glenn Hwy, Dayton, Ohio 45435, USA
e-mail: barbara.hopkins@wright.edu

ACKNOWLEDGMENTS

The preliminary research for this project was completed on a sabbatical funded by Wright State University and the Raj Soin College of Business. This paper has benefited from comments by S. Charusheela, Paulette Olson, and Nancy Folbre. The editors for this volume and the other participants of the seminar organized at Rice University also provided valuable comments. In particular, Günseli Berik provided immeasurable advice on how to organize the paper. All remaining errors are, of course, mine.

NOTES

[1] These comments reflect my own impressions from visits to Shanghai and Beijing in 1993, 1995, and 2005. My impressions were supported by discussions with friends and acquaintances who were also exchange students at Fudan University in the early 1990s and who visited China after 2000.

[2] Woman is used to denote biological categories and feminine is used to denote socially constructed gender categories.

[3] At the time, cosmetics as a category of manufactured goods included soaps and face creams.

[4] These figures are calculated from data available in the *Zhongguo jiaoji nianjian* [China Statistical Yearbook] (NBS China 2001, 2005).

[5] According to a survey of residents in Beijing, Shanghai, and Guangzhou cited in the *China Daily*, 36 percent would never have surgery and fewer than half think plastic surgery will become popular across China (2004b).

[6] "Foreign-invested firms" refers to firms owned jointly by Chinese and foreign investors or firms owned entirely by citizens of foreign countries.

[7] Though China placed foreign exchange requirements on foreign investment before accession, Chinese exports of cosmetics were large enough that these requirements did not hinder the growth of foreign investment during the 1990s.

[8] Yuxi is foreign owned but is considered a Chinese brand because it was developed in China for Asian skin types.

[9] For more on the financial crisis in Albania, see Christopher Jarvis (2000).

[10] The Chinese government banned Falun Gong, claiming that the spiritual group is a cult.

[11] Modern has taken on different meanings in China during the twentieth century, but is always associated with an idea of economic development. Detailing the complexity of current representations of modernity is beyond the scope of this paper. Nevertheless, it is important to recognize that modernity at this point in Chinese history incorporates both the importance of crossing borders and learning from the West and also asserting a specifically Chinese identity. Membership in the WTO represents both of these aspects because it reflects acceptance by the world's economic powers and an opportunity for China to assert her rightly deserved power by having a seat at the table. Readers should recognize that modern, global, or cosmopolitan are fluid concepts with an ever-changing set of fashion accessories.

[12] These numbers are calculated from data in the *Zhongguo Tongji Nianjian* [China Statistical Yearbook] (NBS China various years).

[13] Veblen (1899/1931) does address gender in the sense that women's dress, enjoyment of leisure, and jewelry are used by their husbands to display his status. Yet, institutionalist theory does not address the use of consumption to display gendered identity.

[14] Children in the study would insist on a label of boy or girl, rejecting the label baby (West and Zimmerman 2002).

REFERENCES

Ackerman, Frank. 1997. "Consumed in Theory: Alternative Perspectives on the Economics of Consumption." *Journal of Economic Issues* 31(3): 651–65.

American Marketing Association. 2005. *Marketing to China's Consumers.* http://www.marketingpower.com/content21165C211.php (accessed October 2005).

Belk, Russell W. and Nan Zhou. 1987. "Learning to Want Things." *Journal of Consumer Research* 14: 478–81.

Business Victoria. 2006. "Cosmetic Market in China and Hong Kong." http://www.business.vic.gov.au/BUSVIC/STANDARD/1001/PC_61606.html (accessed May 2006).

Byfield, Sheila and Linda Caller. 1997. "Horses for Courses: Stewarding Brands Across Borders in Times of Rapid Change." *Journal of the Market Research Society* 39(4): 589–602.

Chang, Jung. 1991. *Wild Swans: Three Daughters of China.* New York: Simon and Schuster.

Cheng, Nien. 1988. *Life and Death in Shanghai.* New York: Penguin Books.

China Daily. 2004a. "Avon to Become Solely Foreign Funded in China." March 22. http://english.people.com.cn/200403/22/eng20040322_138140.shtml (accessed May 2006).

———. 2004b. "Beauty Comes at a Price – and Risk." February 9. http://www.chinadaily.com.cn/english/doc/200403/22/eng20040322_138140.shtml (accessed May 2006).

———. 2004c. "Introduction to Foreign Investment in the Advertising Industry." December 7. http://bizchina.chinadaily.com.cn/guide/industry/industry16-02.htm (accessed October 2005).

———. 2005. "P&G Working to Consolidate Market Position." March 29. http://english.people.com.cn/200503/29/eng20050329_178542.html (accessed October 2006).

China Internet Information Center. 2003. "China Easing Ban on EU Cosmetics Imports." http://www.china.org.cn/english/BAT/75682.htm (accessed November 2005).

China Media Monitor. 2005. "China Media Facts." http://www.cmmintelligence.com/site_en/pop-fact.htm (accessed October 2005).

China WTO. 2000. "Summary of U.S.–China Bilateral WTO Agreement February 2, 2000." http://www.chinawto.com/wto/index-e.asp?sel=info&info=summary (accessed November 2005).

Cosmetics Design. 2004. "Chinese Men Contribute to Vigorous Growth of Cosmetics, Toiletries Market." http://cosmeticsdesign.com/news/ng.asp?id=53288&n=wh28&ec=%23emailcode (accessed October 2005).

Costa, Janeen Arnold. 2000. "Gender and Consumption in a Cultural Context," in Miriam Catterall, Lorna Stevens, and Pauline Maclaran, eds. *Marketing and Feminism: Current Issues and Research*, pp. 255–75. New York: Routledge.

Croll, Elisabeth J. 1995. *Changing Identities of Chinese Women: Rhetoric, Experience and Self-Perception in Twentieth-Century China.* London: Zed Books.

Eastday. 2001. "'Sex-Discrimination' Ads Come Under Attack." http://service.china.org.cn/link/wcm/Show_Text?info_id=15646 (accessed October 2005).

European Union Chamber of Commerce in China. 2004. "Cosmetics Working Group Position Paper 2004." http://www.europeanchamber.com.cn/groups/presentations.php?id=13 (accessed October 2005).

Freeman, Carla. 2000. *High Tech and High Heels in the Global Economy: Women, Work, and Pink-Collar Identities in the Caribbean.* Durham, NC: Duke University Press.

French, Paul. 2005. "The Business of Beauty: A Booming Market Does Not Mean Everyone's Happy." *Eurobiz*, February. http://www.sinomedia.net/eurobiz/v200402/story0402.html (accessed October 2005).

Galbraith, John K. 1958. *The Affluent Society.* Boston: Houghton Mifflin.

Gong, Xiaoxia. 2003. "Mary Kay in China." *The Washington Times*, December 3.

Goodman, Peter S. 2004. "In China, Socialism With a Lifted Face." *Washington Post*, March 28.

Hager, Lia Braaten and Liz Grubow. 2005. "Olay Gets Local in China." *Global Cosmetic Industry* 173(8): 34.

Hamermesh, Daniel S., Xin Meng, and Junsen Zhang. 2002. "Dress for Success – Does Primping Pay?" *Labour Economics* 9(3): 361–73.

HealthDay. 2004. "U.S., China Resolve Trade Dispute Over Mad Cow." http://www.hon.ch/News/HSN/518541.html/ (accessed April 2004).

Hong Kong Trade Development Council. 2000. "Opportunities in Ten Major Industries: Cosmetics: Foreign Brands Emerge as the Winner." *Business Alert – China* 11. http://www.tdctrade.com/alert/chwto0011ac.htm (accessed November 2000).

———. 2004. "New Rules for Foreign Participation in Advertising." *Business Alert – China* 6. http://www.tdctrade.com/alert/cba-e0406e.htm (accessed November 2005).

Jarvis, Christopher. 2000. "The Rise and Fall of Albania's Pyramid Schemes." *Finance and Development* 37(1): 46–9.

Jaschok, Maria. 1995. "On the Construction of Desire and Anxiety: Contestations Over Female Nature and Identity in China's Modern Market Society," in Barbara Einhorn and Eileen Janes Yeo, eds. *Women and Market Societies: Crisis and Opportunity*, pp. 179–92. Aldershot, UK: Edward Elgar.

Li, Shuquan. 2003. "China Cosmetic Market–STAT-USA Market Research Reports." http://strategis.ic.gc.ca/epic/internet/inimr-ri.nsf/en/gr109991e.html (accessed October 2005).

Li, Xiaoping. 1998. "Fashioning the Body in Post-Mao China," in Anne Brydon and Sandra Niessen, eds. *Consuming Fashion: Adorning the Transnational Body*, pp. 71–89. New York: Berg.

Mason, Roger. 2000. "The Social Significance of Consumption: James Duesenberry's Contribution to Consumer Theory." *Journal of Economic Issues* 34(3): 553–73.

McIntyre, Richard. 1992. "Consumption in Contemporary Capitalism: Beyond Marx and Veblen." *Review of Social Economy* 50(1): 40–60.

Miller, Daniel. 1997. *Capitalism: An Ethnographic Approach.* New York: Berg.

Morris, Peter. 2004. "Watch Out China, the Avon Lady May Come Calling." *Asia Times,* February 20.

National Bureau of Statistics (NBS) China. Various years. *Zhongguo tongji nianjian* [China Statistical Yearbook]. Beijing: China Statistics Press.

Olson, Paulette. 1998. "My Dam is Bigger than Yours: Emulation in Global Capitalism," in Doug Brown, ed. *Thorstein Veblen in the Twenty-First Century: A Commemoration of the Theory of the Leisure Class (1899–1999)*, pp. 189–207. Cheltenham, UK: Edward Elgar.

Trade Information Center of the US Government. 2005. *Market Access and Compliance Tariff Schedule.* http://www.mac.doc.gov/China/Docs/searchableothertariffs.pdf (accessed October 2005).

Trigg, Andrew B. 2001. "Veblen, Bourdieu, and Conspicuous Consumption." *Journal of Economic Issues* 35(1): 99–115.

True, Jacqui. 1999. "Expanding Markets and Marketing Gender: The Integration of the Post-Socialist Czech Republic." *Review of International Political Economy* 6(3): 360–89.

US Trade Representative. 2002. *2002 Report to Congress on China's WTO Compliance.* http://www.cecc.gov/pages/virtualAcad/commercial/USTR.china.2002.pdf (accessed April 2006).

US Trade Representative. 2006. *2006 Report to Congress on China's WTO Compliance.* http://www.ustr.gov/assets/Document_Library/Reports_Publications/2006/asset _upload_file688_10223.pdf (accessed April 2006).

Veblen, Thorstein. 1894/1964. "The Economic Theory of Women's Dress." Reprinted from *Popular Science Monthly* in Ardzroon, Leon, ed. *Essays in Our Changing Order,* pp. 65–77. New York: Sentry Press.

——. 1899/1931. *The Theory of the Leisure Class.* New York: The Modern Library.

Venkatesh, Alladi. 1994. "Gender Identity in the Indian Context: A Sociocultural Construction of the Female Consumer," in Janeen Arnold Costa, ed. *Gender Issues and Consumer Behavior,* pp. 42–62. Thousand Oaks: Sage.

Wen, Chen. 2004. "Who is the Fairest of All?" *Beijing Review* 47(8): 38–9.

West, Candace and Don H. Zimmerman. 2002. "Doing Gender," in Sarah Fenstermaker, Candace West, and Dorothy E. Smith, eds. *Doing Gender, Doing Difference: Inequality, Power, and Institutional Change,* pp. 3–23. London: Routledge.

Willis, Susan. 1997. "Gender as a Commodity," in Neva R. Goodwin, Frank Ackerman, and David Kiron, eds. *The Consumer Society,* pp. 92–5. Washington, DC: Island Press.

Xu, Gary and Susan Feiner. 2007. "*Meinu Jingji*/China's 'Beauty Economy': Westernization, Fetishism, and Global Neoliberalism." *Feminist Economics* 13(3/4): 307–23.

Yang, Ruoqian. 2002. "China Bans Cosmetics from Countries Suffering from 'Mad-Cow' Disease." March 8. http://english.people.com.cn/200203/08/eng20020308_91718 .shtml (accessed November 2005).

Zhou, Lianxi and Michael K. Hui. 2003. "Symbolic Value of Foreign Products in the People's Republic of China." *Journal of International Marketing* 11(2): 36–58.

MEINÜ JINGJI/
CHINA'S BEAUTY ECONOMY:
BUYING LOOKS, SHIFTING VALUE,
AND CHANGING PLACE

Gary Xu and Susan Feiner

INTRODUCTION

One is not born, rather one becomes a woman.
    —*Simone de Beauvoir, 1948*

Along with the new products, modes of behavior, and economic relations that followed China's access to the World Trade Organization (WTO) in 2001, came the introduction of new words in everyday language. The new vocabulary, which is largely comprised of compound terms imported from new-found economic realities, television, and videogames, can be understood as expressing the impact of economic change on the culture. Indeed, few of these new terms would have meaning without the cultural changes following China's entry into the global economy: Ru-shi, for example, means "to enter the world or join the WTO." Another new word, PK, meaning "to kill each other off or compete," is borrowed from an online video game. And chaonü, or Supergirl, is lifted from a talent show that mimics "American Idol." Without China's integration into the global economy, words such as these would lack context and purpose.

As these terms suggest, China's connection to the global economy has had far-reaching effects. These words, especially the increasingly ubiquitous *meinü jingji* (beauty economy), link economy, culture, and gender in ways that change both individual consciousness and shared ideologies to make them amenable to the goals of neoliberal economics. This paper discusses several aspects of *meinü jingji* to show how neoliberal economic change impacts gender relations in China. In particular, we explore the connection between women's accentuated roles as objects of male approval and gratification (the male gaze) and China's entry into the WTO to help us understand the role of the beauty economy in creating the consumer mentality so necessary for neoliberal economic policies.

New vocabularies have historically grown out of the proliferation of commodities associated with economic growth.[1] Economic growth in China is no exception, and the term *meinü*, meaning beautiful women, is an example of this process. A popular prefix, it is used to form many new compounds regularly used in casual conversation, state-sponsored media, the press, and the Internet. The Chinese language now includes dozens of words with the prefix *meinü*, such as *meinü zuojia* (beautiful woman writer),[2] *meinü qishou* (beautiful woman chess player), *meinü yundongyuan* (beautiful woman athlete), *meinü jingcha* (beautiful woman police officer), *meinü jiaoshou* (beautiful woman professor), and so on. Although *meinü jingji* is the most frequently used of these terms, all of them express the acceptance of the male gaze. In China, as in other patriarchal cultures, the male gaze reinforces the social construction of woman as "other," as the "object" of history and culture, rather than as the agent of her own subjectivity (de Beauvoir 1948).

Broadly defined, *meinü jingji* refers to activities like beauty pageants that are typically commercialized and localized festivities that put beautiful women on parade, as well as the accompanying range of advertisements for TV shows and movies, cosmetics, plastic surgery centers, weight loss products, fitness programs, and the ubiquitous beauty parlors. Narrowly defined, *meinü jingji* refers exclusively to the beauty pageants and model competitions that are wildly popular in China. Desire for these activities is not restricted to the masses; the Chinese bureaucracy is heavily invested in the promotion of the beauty economy as a source of employment, growth, and glory for China.

Chen Jie claims: "The two most successful and most productive economic sectors in today's China are real estate and *meinü jingji*" (2004: 1). The *People's Daily* reports that the beauty industry "employs more than 16 million of the country's labor force" (2005). According to Zhang Xiaomei, a member of the tenth National Committee of the Chinese People's Political Consultative Conference and President of China's Beauty and Fashion Daily, "China has nearly 1.6 million beauty parlors, employing 9.4 million people and reporting business incomes of 176.2 billion yuan ($21.3 billion USD)" (quoted by Wen Chen 2005).

These beauty salons offer the usual range of services: hair coloring and styling; make-up applications, training, and sales; manicures and pedicures; hair removal; and skin whitening. Statistics offered by Pan Xiaoming, president assistant of the China Beauty and Cosmetics Chamber, claim that each urban resident currently spends an average of 30 yuan (roughly US$3.70) on cosmetics every month (*People's Daily* 2004). Some even brag that they spend "half of my income every month on skincare and cosmetics." This huge beauty market plays a significant role in the transformation of women's social position.

Women's equality was a major part of the Chinese Communist Party's platform. After the Communist victory in 1949, women were pushed into the workplace, foot binding and prostitution were outlawed, and women were celebrated as equal comrades. "In the films, songs, and plays of the 1950s and '60s, the brave female worker was a celebrated trope, encouraging women to focus on their contribution to society rather than on their looks and families" (Lisa Movius 2004). But with the liberalization of trade and huge growth in the media, advertisements touting women's importance as beauty objects are eroding women's status as equals in production. Women are increasingly viewed in terms of what they look like rather than what they can do.

THE EXCHANGE OF EQUALS

Commodity. The pudendum muliebre: coll.; late C.16–19. Shakespeare, in King John, "Tickling commodity; commodity – the bias of the world."
2. Occ., but only in context, a whore: late C.16.

—*Francis Grose 1811/1971*

Commodity. A woman's commodity; the private parts of a modest woman, and the public parts of a prostitute.

—*Eric Partridge 1990*

The state's praise for and investment in *meinü jingji* accentuates and legitimizes a new set of gender asymmetries in China. Women of all ages consume beauty products, while young women (ages 18–24) dominate the beauty economy's labor force. Focusing on beauty as a significant source of individual economic success and China's economic growth reduces women's economic agency to their achievement of "beauty," or more accurately, to their ability to appeal to the male gaze. Symbolically, each woman's contribution to the national economy is grounded not in her productive activities, but rather in her ability to meet Western norms of beauty and sexuality. The attempts of Chinese women to refashion themselves in terms of Western beauty standards represents a transformation of the communist ideal of woman as producer into the neoliberal image of woman as consumer that epitomizes Western affluent society. Consumers buy items that give one a sense of self, but as each woman buys the beauty accoutrements that she believes will make her look her best, she makes herself over into an idealized image of womanhood. As each woman aspires to this ideal, she is assimilated into the realm of commodities.

This stands in stark contrast to the persistent communist practice of referring to all Chinese as "comrade," which elides gender differentiation and so marks women qua workers, as equal contributors to the nation's pool of productive labor. Although women – every bit as much as men – form an indispensable portion of society's labor supply, woman qua woman is increasingly expected to meet physical standards almost wholly derived from Anglo-European (Western) bourgeois culture. As Anglo-European standards of beauty permeate the culture, Chinese women become interchangeable with international beauties (all fashioned after a Western prototype), signifying the global nature of beauty standards and accentuating the continuity of global commodity exchange.

Women's bodies represent commodification in myriad ways. In Marxist political economy, commodification is understood as a process of abstraction and objectification. Capitalist production is, among other things, the production of commodities (exchange values) for the purpose of generating and appropriating surplus value in the form of monetary profits. Workers produce exchange values to be realized by capitalist enterprises when commodities are sold. The official rhetoric of the Chinese Communist Party places the production and consumption of "female beauty" at the center of the Chinese economy. The Chinese state, personifying masculinity, stresses that China has a supply of beautiful women who look as glamorous as all other women, thereby allowing Chinese bodies and goods to enter the flow of commodities connecting China to the global economy.

Woman as commodity can, in principle, be traded for any other commodity. In China, women can literally be purchased; even official statistics show that prostitution and sex slavery run rampant.[3] In the Chinese sex industry, as in Thailand, Cambodia, and Amsterdam, international currencies are favored for sexual transactions. A similar, though subtler exchange enrolls women as "public relation specialists," or catalysts for business transactions in the male-dominated *guanxi* network.[4]

Maverick Chinese filmmaker Jia Zhangke illustrates the commodification of women in the celebrated film *Unknown Pleasures* (2002). While holding a US dollar bill, the central male character casually remarks: "Wow, an American bill. Do you know what it is? It's the pussy of the Americans!" This is a pun on the Chinese word for currency: *Bi*, as in *renminbi* (the Chinese currency), is a homophone for the colloquial slang for vagina. This dialogue makes the point that in contemporary China the dramatic imagination equates money, women, and commodities.

The shared pun suggests some commonalities between England at the end of the sixteenth century and China at the dawn of the twenty-first century. When England was on the verge of empire, exotic goods acquired during the travels of Britain's sea merchants began to appear in the lives of the emerging bourgeoisie. Replace British sails with cargo containers and one parallel becomes clear. Another commonality concerns the transformation of public, or common, property. In late sixteenth-century England, the enclosure movement was in full swing. Whole villages were thrown off their ancestral lands, leaving peasants with nothing to sell but their labor power. How different is this really from the economic reforms that close hundreds of Chinese factories – a form of common property – leaving millions without work?

Despite the centuries and the technologies separating England and China, desperate poverty appears alongside magnificent fortunes. In both places, this economic polarity is at least partially stabilized by an explosion of market exchange, an arena coded as masculine: in markets, men exchange goods for money and money for goods. And today in China, the vernacular equates women's sex, money, and commodity in a way that highlights how each woman is exchangeable for any other. In this global circulation of Chinese goods exchanged against money, a beautiful woman can serve as a symbol of the universal equivalent.

The pun on the linguistic connection (woman – money – commodity) accentuates the dramatic tension in the subplot of *Unknown Pleasures*, an affair between a young man (whose character stands in for the unemployed millions of China's *lumpenproletariat*) and a beautiful young woman (who personifies the desires of millions of Chinese to join the global *consumerati*). The woman moves in counterpoint to a commentary on economic decline; she is an aspiring business student working as a "performance artist," dancing at wine promotions, and flirting with local officials and the nouveau riche. The young woman, lacking access to capital or land, cannot sell her labor power because the (male) economy is mired in urban unemployment and rural stagnation. Her body is therefore all she has to offer. This affair is both a protest against the way women must devote their bodies to male pleasure to survive, and an unconscious repetition of that use since the boy's desire represents his wish to participate in China's new wealth even as he recognizes that this is totally beyond his reach.

CHINESE BEAUTY AND THE BARBARIAN BEAST

Women are given in marriage, taken in battle, exchanged for favors, sent as tribute, traded, bought and sold. Far from being confined to the "primitive" world, these practices seem only to become more pronounced and commercialized in more "civilized" societies.

—*Gayle Rubin (1975: 175)*

Meinü jingji did not spring fully formed from the head of *Chuang-Mu*, the mythical Chinese goddess of the bedchamber. Rather, the social conventions of beauty in China have a long history. Since the onslaught of Western imperialism in the nineteenth century, Chinese beauty practices have mimicked those of the Anglo-European world. Today, the mélange of performances constituting *meinü jingji* is an amalgam of indigenous (pre-nineteenth century) and Western practices. The beauty pageant and the "beauty economy" have roots deep in Chinese history.

In pre-modern China, beautiful women were ranked through public activities enjoyed by both the educated elite and the peasantry. Oral traditions passed on the stories of "The Four Great Beauties" (Xishi, fifth century BCE; Wang Zhaojun, first century BCE; Diaochan, second century CE; and Yang Guifei, seventh century CE). Countless poems and stories were written about these beauties, all of whom were involved in struggles for court power and duplicity in military conquests. Beautiful women were seen as the "origin of all disasters" (*hongyan huoshui*). The "Four Great Courtesans" or the "Ten Great Courtesans" were often blamed for specific tragedies. In popular history, courtesan Chen Yuanyuan is, for example, widely held responsible for the fall of the Ming Dynasty in 1644. Similarly, a famous Chinese novel, *Dream of the Red Chamber* (*Honglou meng*, eighteenth century), tells the tale of the "Twelve Beauties of Nanjing." Romantic stories about beautiful but dangerous women are widely enjoyed by Chinese readers in all walks of life.

The enjoyment of feminine beauty plays a key role in the formation of Chinese national identity, which derives from the historical differentiation between the Han ethnicity and the "barbarians" and between the "cultivated" aesthetics of the Chinese and the "primitive" sensibilities of outsiders (Lydia Liu 2006). When Western "barbarians" invaded China in the middle of the nineteenth century, traditional notions of Chinese national identity were undermined by the barbarians' greater power and technological superiority. At the same time, "their women" (white women now visible, but taboo) began to displace traditional Chinese beauties as objects of desire.

This shift can be seen most clearly in Colonial Shanghai, China's cultural capital in the first half of the twentieth century. Here, emigré Russian cabaret dancers and prostitutes were more popular (and expensive) than Chinese women (Andrew Field 1999). During this period, Chinese pictorials attracted readers with photos of Western beauties. And even while Chinese prostitutes continued to receive rankings and appraisals from their customers in local tabloids (Han Bangqing 1894/1930; Gail Hershatter 1999), Western-style beauty pageants gradually came into vogue. By 1946, the Miss Shanghai competition was a full-blown imitation of the Western form:

> He'nan Province was devastated by flood. Throughout China people made generous donations to help those who suffered. Shanghai was no exception. But even for philanthropy, Shanghai had to do it with a romantic and splendid twist. The Miss Shanghai beauty pageant was immediately staged as a fundraising event with all the proceeds going to the flood victims.... "Shanghai" was synonymous with "modern," and "Miss Shanghai" was even more representative of "modern." In Shanghai, what could be more modern than the "Miss" title? (Wang Anyi 1996: 62)

The People's Republic of China, founded in 1949, put an end to these Western practices. Mao's revolutionary rhetoric made beauty pageants a spectacle of the corrupt and bourgeois past. In the early post-Revolutionary period, notions of female beauty, especially Western ones, were condemned as bourgeois. Beauty pageants and fashion shows were unthinkable. Even colorful clothes and make-up were deemed counterrevolutionary. A Soviet-influenced notion of "sublime" beauty – de-sexed, militarized, and masculine – became the only acceptable form of beauty (see Ban Wang [1997] and Barbara E. Hopkins's contribution to this issue [2007]).

Against the somber, monochromatic background of the Cultural Revolution, the beauty and modeling competitions that reappeared in 1976 were initially seen as liberating. Many Chinese fondly remember the excitement of the post-Cultural Revolution Beijing fashion show staged by Pierre Cardin in 1979. While first held in secret on college campuses, in only a few years, beauty pageants were both publicly staged and officially endorsed.

The year 2003 was the turning point for *meinü jingji*. Previously, beauty pageants were only found in a few major cities, where they served as a means for selecting fashion models. As the state lessened its restrictions on individual expression, these displays of female bodies spread. In 2003, after two decades of Deng Xiaoping's liberalizations, the Chinese government officially endorsed Wu Wei, the first ever "Miss China," and the first representative of China to ever appear at a Miss Universe pageant.[5] The pageant was beamed live to 1.3 billion Chinese, making the audience for the 2003 Miss Universe broadcast the largest in history, so the potential for commercial exploitation could not have been more obvious.

This commercial exploitation of beauty pageants worked synergistically with the reform process. After China embarked on reforms with the household responsibility system in rural areas, private economic organization slowly displaced collective agriculture and then displaced centrally planned industrial production from its previous dominance. In the wake of these reforms, China directed less attention to repressing expressions of individual beauty. At first, many Chinese embraced Deng Xiaoping's reforms. They welcomed de-collectivization in the countryside, industrialization in small towns, "special economic zones," and public works projects on a world-historic scale, like the many infrastructure development projects in Shanghai's Pudong district. The Chinese government promoted these reforms as a means to bring about prosperity and, later, to stem the rising tide of unemployment and rural stagnation. But, rural–urban migration and urbanization accelerated.

China's entry into the WTO spurred both economic and personal changes, including urbanization and privatization. But the WTO-prompted loosening of state restrictions on individual consumption was not the beginning of a movement toward greater political liberalization; instead, this move undermined the urban unrest associated with unemployment by promoting preoccupation with the personal over the political. In this climate, after more than four decades of sexual repression and moral rigidity, beauty pageants could be portrayed by the official state media as symbols of women's liberation and modernization, rather than as the tools of sexual repression and women's oppression, as per the initial views of the Chinese Communist Party.

Due to what they saw as enormous potential for economic and political gain associated with these pageants, Chinese officials decided that the country would host the next Miss World contest. Officials from many cities needed little urging from the central State to compete for the right to host major pageants; the economic reforms of the 1990s had produced fierce competition between China's fast growing urban areas. To boost its image as representative of the "new China," Sanya, the capital city of the tropical island Hainan, reached deep into the public purse to entice the organizers of the Miss World competition. The city made no charges for the use of the competition facilities; instead, a US$4.8 million "permission fee" was offered to the Miss World organization. Sanya also allowed the organization to pocket the broadcasting fees paid by TV networks outside China. Sanya's officials were determined to land this prize.

The deal was so lucrative that the pageant organizers could not turn it down. But sponsors were still nervous since the previous year's contest in Nigeria had been disrupted by protests.[6] Sanya's government officials promised the Miss World organizers that they were in a unique position to provide a setting of peace and stability. In contrast to the politicization of the contest that occurred in Nigeria, China was committed to showing that political oppression and moral rigidity had been banished from the cultural landscape. When Miss China (Guan Qi) was selected as the runner-up to Miss World 2003, all of China joined Sanya in celebrating this symbol of successful global competition.

Following this highly profitable competition in 2003, the Miss World organizers decided to keep the competition in China and raised the hosting fee to US$6 million. Other Chinese cities, including Dalian, Shenzhen, Xiamen, and Qingdao, were invited to bid for the event. Despite the continuation of urban economic competition associated with liberalization, none of the cities, including Sanya, were willing to pay US$6 million. The Miss World organizers were eventually forced to waive the fee and the pageant stayed in Sanya. By then, billions of Chinese were fascinated by the drama of beauty competitions. The 2004 Miss World event was widely viewed across China, and disappointment was keen when Miss China did not make it into the 2004 finals.[7]

In 2004, China hosted more than six major international beauty competitions, including Miss World, Miss Universe, Miss Asia, Miss Tourism World, Miss Tourism International (Hangzhou), and Miss Intercontinental (Huhehaote). These contests created a hugely profitable chain of economic transactions: contest franchises in every major city and in all the provinces enter contestants in the pageants, all the contests have both live and TV audiences, and relevant government authorities promote the contests. The largest factories and retail establishments get in on the act as well: beauty consultants come in during lunch breaks to offer advice on hairstyles and hawk the latest cosmetics.

China also established numerous regional and urban beauty pageants, making China home to thousands of beauty contests, with millions of contestants, tens of millions of participants, and spectators numbering in the hundreds of millions. This dynamic chain linking representations of feminine beauty along with producing, buying, and selling the accoutrements of physical display raise *meinü jingji* to its incredible prominence in the Chinese economy. As every city and region in China competes to increase its standing vis-à-vis its contribution to China's GDP, the emphasis on profitability and the importance of the beauty economy rises. Simultaneously, however, each contest represents and reinforces the standardization of beauty features based on Anglo-European norms.

THE GLOBAL BARBIE

Usually there are other objects circulating as well as women. Women move in one direction, cattle, shells, or mats in the other.

—Rubin (1975: 191)

During China's application for membership in the WTO, the slogan, "Let's connect the track seamlessly with the world outside China" (*yu guoji jiegui*) was endlessly repeated. In giant posters displayed everywhere, this slogan dominated the foreground while China's pre-WTO backwardness was represented in the background with narrow train tracks epitomizing the absence of centralized, consistent economic regulations based on the rules of the market, few workers with foreign language proficiencies, and a confusing maze of local protectionist rules. The poster's not-so-hidden message was that when China enters the WTO and embraces international standards, the Chinese economic engine will face no barriers as it speeds around the world.

The same slogan is used to promote China's participation and hosting of international beauty pageants. The same logic is at work: all pageants must conform to international standards; all must include swimsuit, nightgown, and talent competitions; and all must end with a final interview. To domesticate the pageants, organizers add "Chinese characteristics" by substituting a *cheongsam* competition for the nightgown competition.[8]

While the not-quite-hidden imaginary of "the Western lifestyle" stimulates consumerism in indirect ways, the strict physical demands of beauty pageants produce direct and immediately damaging effects on Chinese women's bodies. Beauty pageants have a minimal height requirement of 5 feet 9 to 10 inches, which is significantly taller than typical Chinese women who are approximately 5 feet 2 inches tall (Ching-ching Ni 2005). The Chinese are among the fastest growing people in the world; with improved nutrition and living standards, they are now about 0.8 inches taller than they were a decade ago. Despite the increase in average heights, the press is full of painful stories of Chinese women going through excruciating leg surgeries – literarily having their legs broken – for which they pay US$6,000, to increase their height 3 inches or more. Ni (2005) argues that the flood of images of glamorous, tall Chinese supermodels on catwalks and at beauty pageants is to blame.

The routinization of beauty pageants is also changing traditional Chinese notions of feminine beauty and, by extension, the historic Chinese aesthetic. The most desirable physiognomy in early twenty-first century China mimics the Western ideal. The features of superstars like Nicole Kidman and Angelina Jolie (lean face; small cheekbones; straight, high nose; thin, large mouth; thick lips; and white teeth) have displaced traditionally defined Chinese beauty (round faces like melon-seeds, chubby cheeks like almonds, and noses small and round like green onions). From the edible Chinese courtesans of the distant Ming past, to today's transcultural beauty, shifting power relations have created this cultural traffic between West and East.

One may argue that changes in the concepts of beauty are natural, normal, and not culturally specific, and that the changes we are describing in China are merely reflections of the recurring vicissitudes of fashion. While it is one thing to change one's make-up, weight, and clothing to fit current trends, it is something else entirely to pursue an appearance antithetical to one's own ethnicity. To enhance their "Western look" Chinese women by the thousands flock to Korea – Asia's Mecca of cosmetic surgery – to have their high cheekbones sawed flat, their noses raised high, and their lips injected with filler. The natural faces of Asian women are now rarely seen in either China's beauty pageants or mass media.

These changes in the Chinese concept of beauty have far-reaching consequences, including the admiration and imitation of whiteness, contempt for one's own cultural and ethnic heritage, and discrimination against those who look "native." A reserved, calm, and indigenous aesthetic has been devalued in favor of a foreign, outgoing, aggressive, athletic aesthetic. One result of the internalization of Western norms of beauty is their pursuit through cosmetic surgery, skin bleaching, hair coloring, and other beauty practices. Together these celebrations of Anglo-European aesthetics (i.e., Occidentalism: "the West is better than the rest") further promote the internalization of the logic of imitation.[9]

In what seems like a paradox, the Western fantasy of Chinese beauty is very much at odds with the norms of Anglo-European beauty. The success story of Lü Yan provides a fine example. Born to a poor mining family in Jiangxi, Lü Yan was always teased as a child for being tall and ugly. She is still 5 feet 11, but now she's beautiful. What changed? In 1999, she attended a Beijing modeling school to correct her posture. She met two French talent agents who, amazed by her "quintessential Oriental face," brought her to France to train for modeling competitions. Four months later, she gained instant fame by becoming the first runner-up at an important modeling competition in Paris. When the news was reported in China and Lü Yan's photos appeared in the Chinese media, people were stunned by her "ugliness." They were surprised that a top model could have slanted, narrow, wide-set eyes that tilted toward her pointed cheekbones.

Today, Lü Yan earns US$2,600 per shoot, making her the highest paid Chinese model in the world. Oddly enough, no one seems to have consciously noticed that Lü Yan, Lucy Liu (the Hollywood star), and Mulan (the Disney cartoon princess-in-drag) share such similar facial features that they could be triplets. These are quintessential Oriental faces associated with the "Chinatown hostess" or "Madame Butterfly" stereotype. Each is a menacing seducer, inscrutable, and mysterious – personalities that are squarely in the tradition of China's "Great Beauties," though none of these traditional beauties look remotely like Lü Yan. Among Chinese intellectuals, the public, or the press we find no trace of debate about or recognition of the orientalist logic of Lü Yan's popularity. Absent a critical response to the sociocultural values represented by Lü Yan and the beauty economy that produced her, billions of Chinese are drawn to Western fantasies of imagined Asian beauty. Lü Yan is a project of the Western male gaze creating an exotic, orientalist vision of Oriental beauty. To the Chinese, however, she is not nearly "Western" enough to represent a beauty ideal. Striving to meet Anglo-European beauty standards requires a complete rejection of the indigenous Chinese aesthetic.

An example of the Occidentalism at the heart of *meinü jingji* can be found in a Chinese bestseller, *Meili liandan zhang dami* [Beautiful Faces Grow Rice] by Lu Junqing (2004). Labeling itself as "the groundbreaking work for China's *meinü jingji*" on the book's back cover, this massively popular book celebrates women's beauty as the means to all that is important. Beautiful women will have the best jobs, the most glamorous lives, and the richest husbands. The author, head of one of China's largest PR agencies, *Tianjiu chuanmei* [Heavenly Media], franchises beauty pageants and trains contestants. Not surprisingly, the first Miss Universe China, Wu Wei, is one of the agency's most successful clients.

This book offers a post-socialist twist on the famed cliché of US journalist Horace Greeley, "go west, young man."[10] In Greeley's fables, young men seeking fame and fortune set off to the American West. Inevitably, the hero rescues the beautiful daughter of a very wealthy entrepreneur. To express his gratitude, the entrepreneurial father bestows a fortune on the young man. In Lu's version, the message is: "This is what happened in the West, now it can happen to you." To show how Western women benefit from *meinü jingji*, Lu fills his book with fanciful statements masquerading as facts. One of the most outrageous is that "the top ten models of the world earn an annual income from as low as 20 million dollars to as high as 68 million dollars" (Lu 2004: 1). Lu's "estimate" of a beauty multiplier is equally as ludicrous: "every dollar spent on beauty pageants generates four additional dollars of income" (2004: 28).

Lu invents a "typical" American company, "Yamaxun" (loosely translated as Amazon), in which female employees are divided into ten levels based on their looks:

> The top tier beauty earns a basic monthly salary of $5,000 and is guaranteed a 20 percent commission for the cell phones, digital cameras, and camcorders she sells. The second tier beauty's basic salary is $400 lower and receives a smaller percentage of commission.

The lowest tier thus only gets a monthly salary of $1,400. (Lu 2004: 17)

He goes on to present a list of "the top ten cities of beauty" in the world (allegedly selected by Internet users).[11] According to Lu, tourism in Rio de Janeiro, Caracas, Milan, Copenhagen, Prague, Los Angeles, Miami, Stockholm, Montreal, Tel Aviv, and Hong Kong "relies on flaunting beautiful women on the street" (2004: 12–3). Another assertion is that Western nations rely increasingly on the beauty economy, which he also calls the "GDP economy," because beauty is alleged to account for an increasing percentage of each nation's GDP. According to Lu, the 2003 Miss World competition brought Sanya into the ranks of the world's elite cities of beauty while delivering US$3.6 billion to the urban economy (2004: 42).

This book is a bestseller at least, in part, because it makes the attainment of Western beauty the key to a woman's economic success. Most Chinese readers, however, do not know that women in the US workplace earn less than men, on average, and many factors other than looks play roles in career advancement. Moreover, the firm cannot legally pursue a policy of rewarding female personnel for their looks. Nor do US companies advertise the beauty and sex appeal of their female employees, as such behavior can be challenged in the courts. Rather, companies seek to avoid the litigation, fines, and adverse publicity associated with charges of sex discrimination and/or sexual harassment. In Lu's imagined US, beauty queens and sovereign consumers represent the glory of liberal democracy.

CONCLUSION

The cosmos have the greatest of beauty that cannot be described in words.
—*Zhuang Zi, fourth century BCE*

The interpretation of the film title *Unknown Pleasures* reveals a startling disjuncture between the traditional Chinese past and the global present: in Chinese, the title *Ren xiaoyao* is not a direct translation for "unknown pleasures"; the literal translation is "as free as you can be." Zhuang Zi, one of the two founders of Taoism, coined the term *xiaoyao* to refer to freedom from material anxieties, from this-worldly concerns, from desire, and from imbalance in the relations between people and their natural environment. *Xiaoyao* is only possible when communities are in harmony with nature, and when a peaceful worldview allows nature to take its own course.

By contrast, today *xiaoyao* has lost its Taoist meaning and refers instead to the "free and unfettered" individual, a freedom centered on material existence, concerned with freedom from poverty, state supervision, or scarcity. In early twenty-first century China, the most popular compound with *xiaoyao* is *xiaoyao zizai*, which means "carefree with a great amount of leisure and wealth." The Chinese media associate such activities as surfing, sunbathing, traveling, and, no less significantly, preening and modeling with *xiaoyao zizai*. The WTO, as emphasized in the Chinese media, is the ultimate means to achieving *xiaoyao zizai* since it promises unimpeded market freedom and unlimited economic prosperity. Most ironically, the original Taoist notion of *xiaoyao* is the opposite of the form of universal freedom promised by the neoliberalism of the WTO. By evoking the duality of meaning, Jia Zhangke, the film's director, is bringing up the sharp contrast between the two meanings and how far Chinese culture has moved away from the Taoist practice.

As far as Taoism is concerned, the ideal social structure is not a vast and homogenized mega-world of consumers and commodities. It is rather, in the words of the other founder of Taoism, Lao Zi, "*xiaoguo guamin*," which means small countries and small populations, each with their own traditions and unique human relationships. No less ironically, "to join the WTO" is often shortened in Chinese as *ru-shi* (to enter the world), which is exactly the same word used by traditional Chinese intellectuals to describe their Confucian worldly ambitions – to be engaged in politics and government affairs. The opposite of *ru-shi* is the Taoist *chu-shi*, to exit this world – to yield to the constant call of simple living and renounce the mundane.

To go back to small countries and small populations is both utopian and impossible. But is it possible to imagine "*chu-shi*" and "*xiaoyao*" while China is becoming a full member of the WTO? While we are not advocating Chinese withdrawal from the WTO, we are calling for a serious scrutiny of the notions of universal, free market economic policies that equate development with Western consumerism.

This analysis of *meinü jingji* highlights the ways in which the commodification of beauty has facilitated the economic reforms that enable China's entry into the WTO. *Meinü jingji* performs an indispensable function as it allows China to overcome its ambivalence toward the neoliberal economic policies of the West by associating Westernization with women's mimicry of Anglo-European aesthetics. Tacit and explicit encouragement of the consumption of beauty products as well as the objectification of women as things of beauty soften China's traditional hostility to the West, and enable the enthusiastic embrace of neoliberal economic policies that favor consumerism over socialism.

The contradiction is stunning: even as the State continues to denounce pre-revolutionary forms of beauty performance like prostitution and traffic in women, government officials regularly praise participation in *meinü jingji* as essential to the growth of the economy. Beauty performance is neither a simple tool for the oppression of women, nor is it the natural expression of women's desire to appeal to men. Instead, it is both of these and more. *Meinü jingji* is the sine qua non of neoliberalism with Chinese characteristics: the freedom to assume any appearance at all coexists with the freedom to fade into oblivion through starvation.

Gary Xu, University of Illinois-Urbana Champaign,
East Asian Languages and Cultures,
707 South Mathews #2090, Urbana, IL 61801, USA
e-mail: garyxu@uiuc.edu

Susan Feiner, University of Southern Maine, Women and Gender Studies Program,
94 Bedford Street, Portland, ME 04104, USA
e-mail: sffein@usm.maine.edu

NOTES

[1] For example, with the emergence of the Roman Empire, "farmer," or one who pays rent, entered the lexicon. With economic expansion new words enter cultures to name previously unknown items, such as coffee, bagel, turkey, and rice.

[2] One of the popular contemporary writers, Wei Hui, advertises herself as a "beauty writer" and fills her books and websites with her narcissistic photo portraits. Wei Hui's most notorious book, *Shanghai Baby* (*Shanghai baobei*), is available in English (2002). Another writer, Peng Jiuyang, became an overnight sensation after she posted her nude pictures on the Internet. See her personal webpage at http://www.pengjiuyang.com.cn.

[3] For example, a 2004 government-sponsored survey in Guangdong Province shows that, among 724 randomly chosen beauty salon employees, 74.2 percent engaged in prostitution either out of their own choice or because they were forced (see You Man'ni and Chen Yongfeng 2004).

[4] *Guanxi* is the Chinese term for social connections that are crucial for business and personal advancement. See Andrew B. Kipnis (1997), Y. H. Wong and Thomas K. P. Leung (2001), and Thomas Gold, Doug Guthrie, and David Wank (2002) for insightful analyses of *guanxi*, and Jieyu Liu in this issue (2007) for the importance of *guanxi* in job searches by former women workers of state-owned enterprises.

[5] Is it not the height of irony that the term *wuwei* is one of the central teachings of Taoism? *Wuwei* refers to behavior that arises from a sense of oneself as connected to others and to one's environment. It is spontaneous and effortless action but is not to be considered inertia, laziness, or mere passivity. Our contemporary expression, "going with the flow," is a direct expression of this fundamental Taoist principle, which in its most basic form refers to behavior occurring in response to the flow of the Tao.

[6] The controversy began when a Nigerian court upheld the death by stoning sentence of a woman convicted of adultery. After some Miss World contestants protested and threatened to withdraw from the competition, the Nigerian government intervened and overturned the sentence. Then, a riot ensued after the northern Muslim state of Zamfara issued a fatwa to kill a female journalist who wrote that the Prophet Mohammed might have approved of the contest. More than 200 people died in Kaduma, Zamfara's capital. (James Astill 2002). The Miss World pageant was forced to change the competition site from Nigeria to London on December 7, 2002 (Astill 2002).

[7] Most of the information was gathered through Gary Xu's field investigation in the summers of 2003 and 2004. Various websites, including the Miss World and Miss Universe homepages also proved helpful. The most informative is a Chinese-language website, see Zhong Zhiyuan (2004).

[8] The *cheongsam* is a traditional dress worn by Chinese women, typified by a high collar, long length (mid-calf usually), and button or frog closures near the shoulder. This fitted dress is often made of shimmering silk, embroidered satin, or other sensual fabric. Best on athletic or slim figures, the *cheongsam* is an acceptable alternative to a little black dress for special occasions (About.com n.d.).

[9] It will be helpful to clarify the connection between Occidentalism and Orientalism. Edward Said, the originator of these terms, defined Orientalism as:

A style of thought based upon ontological and epistemological distinctions made between 'the Orient' and 'the Occident.' Many writers, including poets, novelists, philosophers, political theorists, economists, and imperial administrators, take this basic East/West dualism as a starting point for their elaboration of the so-called 'Orient,' its people, customs, mind, destiny, and so on. (1978: 3)

Orientalism constructs the world and its cultures that lie outside the Anglo-European West as "other," as inferior. Orientalism was crucial to the ideological underpinnings of the development of capitalism in Anglo-European as it emphasized the superiority of Western values.

Today, Occidentalism works in much the same way to provide ideological supports for China's economic reforms. This often occurs through the production of consumer desire. Consumerism works hand in hand with the emergence of individuals who see their individuality in terms of the goods they own and the personal look they project (John Kenneth Galbraith 1958). In China, as in the US, the emphasis on the consuming individual tends to displace concern for the social and so mutes the political discontent. But in China, where Mao's "mass consciousness" was the foundation for the revolutionary unity of peasants, workers, and state bureaucrats, the rise of consumerist ideology is a necessary, though not sufficient, condition for the acceptance of neoliberal forms of economic organization.

[10] This phrase was originally coined by John Soule in 1851, although Greeley is often cited as the originator because he used the phrase so effectively.

[11] The authors could find no trace of any such poll.

REFERENCES

About.com. n.d. "Definition of a Cheongsam." http://fashion.about.com/cs/glossary/g/bldefcheongsam.htm (accessed March 2007).

Astill, James. 2002. "Miss World's Nigerian Odyssey Abandoned After Three Days of Rioting Leave 100 Dead." *Guardian*, November 23. http://www.guardian.co.uk/international/story/0,3604,845956,00.html (accessed May 2007).

de Beauvoir, Simone. 1948/1989. *The Second Sex*. New York: Vintage Books.

Chen Jie. 2004. "The Value of the Beauty." *Renmin huabao* [China Pictorial] 3. German version available at: http://www.rmhb.com.cn/chpic/htdocs/rmhb/german/200403/2-1.htm (accessed April 2007).

Chen, Wen. 2005. "Beauty Lies in the Hands of the Spender." *Beijing Review* 48(24). http://www.bjreview.cn/EN/En-2005/05-24-e/china1.htm (accessed February 2007).

Field, Andrew. 1999. "Selling Souls in Sin City: Shanghai Singing and Dancing Hostesses in Print, Film, and Politics, 1920–49," in Yingjin Zhang, ed. *Cinema and Urban Culture in Shanghai, 1922–1943*, pp. 99–127. Palo Alto, CA: Stanford University Press.

Galbraith, John Kenneth. 1958. *The Affluent Society*. Boston: Houghton Mifflin.

Gold, Thomas, Doug Guthrie, and David Wank, eds. 2002. *Social Connections in China: Institutions, Culture, and the Changing Nature of Guanxi*. New York: Cambridge University Press.

Grose, Francis. 1811/1971. *Dictionary of the Vulgar Tongue: A Dictionary of Buckish Slang, University Wit, and Pickpocket Eloquence*. Northfield, IL: Digest Books.

Han Bangqing. 1894/1930. *Haishang hua liezhuan* [Flowers of Shanghai]. Shanghai: Dadong shuju. Originally serialized in *Haishang qishu* (Shanghai: 1892–4).

Hershatter, Gail. 1999. *Dangerous Pleasures: Prostitution and Modernity in Twentieth-Century Shanghai*. Berkeley: University of California Press.

Hopkins, Barbara E. 2007. "Western Cosmetics in the Gendered Development of Consumer Culture in China." *Feminist Economics* 13(3/4): 287–306.

Kipnis, Andrew B. 1997. *Producing Guanxi: Sentiment, Self, and Subculture in a North China Village*. Durham, NC: Duke University Press.

Liu, Jieyu. 2007. "Gender Dynamics and Redundancy in Urban China." *Feminist Economics* 13(3/4): 125–58.

Liu, Lydia. 2006. *The Clash of Empires: The Invention of China in Modern World Making*. Cambridge, MA: Harvard University Press.

Lu Junqing. 2004. *Meili liandan zhang dami* [Beautiful Faces Grow Rice]. Shanghai: Dandai shijie chubanshe.

Movius, Lisa. 2004. "Cultural Devolution." *The New Republic*. http://www.tnr.com/doc.mhtml?i=dispatch&s=movius030104 (accessed April 2007).

Ni, Ching-ching. 2005. "Stature of Limitations in China." *Los Angeles Times*, March 31.

Partridge, Eric. 1990. *A Dictionary of Slang and Unconventional English: Colloquialisms and Catch-Phrases, Solecisms and Catachreses, Nicknames and Vulgarisms*, 8th ed. New York: Macmillian Publishing Company.

People's Daily. 2004. "Regulation to Guide Beauty Industry." March 30. http://english.people.com.cn/200403/30/eng20040330_138874.shtml (accessed April 2007).

———. 2005. "Number of China's Beauty Parlors Grow by 6 Percent Annually." March 29. http://english.people.com.cn/200503/29/eng20050329_178632.html (accessed April 2007).

Rubin, Gayle. 1975. "The Traffic in Women: Notes on the 'Political Economy' of Sex," in Rayna R. Reiter, ed. *Toward an Anthropology of Women*, pp. 157–210. New York: Monthly Review Press.

Said, Edward. 1978. *Orientalism*. New York: Pantheon Books.

Wang Anyi. 1996. *Changhen ge* [The Song of Everlasting Sorrow]. Taipei: Maitian.

Wang, Ban. 1997. *The Sublime Figure of History: Aesthetics and Politics in Twentieth-Century China*. Palo Alto, CA: Stanford University Press.

Wei Hui. 2002. *Shanghai Baby*. Translated by Bruce Humes. New York: Simon and Schuster. Originally published as *Shanghai baobei* (Shenyang: Chufeng wenyi chubanshen, 1999).

Wong, Y. H. and Thomas K. P. Leung. 2001. *Guanxi: Relationship Marketing in a Chinese Context*. New York: Haworth Press.

You Man'ni and Chen Yongfeng. 2004. "Guangdong dui anmonü jieguo xianshi: Qicheng anmounü ceng maiying" [Guangdong Province's Survey of Massage Girls Shows: 70% of Massage Girls Have Engaged in Prostitution]. *Xinxi shibao* [The Information Times], December 21. http://news.21cn.com/social/shixiang/2004/12/21/1907724.shtml (accessed April 2007).

Zhong Zhiyuan. 2004. "Meinü jingji fengqiyunyong, jiaore zhongguo" [Beauty Economy is in Vogue Stirring China]. *Jingji* [Journal of Economics], June 21. http://business.sohu.com/2004/06/21/88/article220638886.shtml (accessed April 2007).

INDEX

Page numbers in *Italics* represent tables.